VAUDEVILLE HUMOR

VAUDEVILLE HUMOR

THE COLLECTED JOKES ROUTINES AND SKITS OF ED LOWRY

Edited and with an
Introduction by
PAUL M. LEVITT

Southern Illinois University Press
Carbondale and
Edwardsville

Printed in the United States of America
09 08 07 06   4 3 2 1
Publication partially funded by a subvention grant
from the University of Colorado Foundation.

Library of Congress Cataloging-in-Publication Data
Lowry, Ed, 1896–1983.
Vaudeville humor : the collected jokes, routines, and skits of Ed Lowry / edited and
with an introduction by Paul M. Levitt.
p. cm.
Includes bibliographical references and index.
1. American wit and humor. 2. Lowry, Ed, 1896–1983. I. Levitt, Paul M. II. Title.

PN6165 .L68 2002
818'.602—dc21

2002024044

ISBN 0-8093-2453-9 (cloth : alk. paper)
ISBN-13: 978-0-8093-2720-1 (pbk. : alk. paper)
ISBN-10: 0-8093-2720-1 (pbk. : alk. paper)

Printed on recycled paper. ♻
The paper used in this publication meets the minimum requirements of
American National Standard for Information Sciences—Permanence of Paper for
Printed Library Materials, ANSI Z39.48-1992. ♾

CONTENTS

ACKNOWLEDGMENTS

"All art," wrote J. M. Synge, "is a collaboration." So too is scholarship. Without the aid of others, this book could not have been written. Those others include all the unknown authors who wrote the jokes that compose this collection, as well as the people who enabled me to assemble it.

Ed Lowry collected the material. His is the greatest contribution of all. Florrie Lowry, Ed's widow, gave me all but one of the books in her possession and, by so doing, launched *Vaudeville Humor*. Her gift is invaluable. Joy King spent months helping me catalogue the material. Her work not only saved me time but also solved innumerable problems. She has a place in the pantheon of heroines. Nancy Mann, surely one of the country's best editors, assisted with the cataloguing, the typing, and the introduction. Sandra Levitt, my sister and dear friend, contributed to the glossary of names and, more important, gave me one of the scrapbooks, which Florrie had given to her. Elissa Guralnick functioned as a treasured arbiter, deciding, when others could not, how to catalogue difficult jokes and consoling me when I thought the project would never end.

INTRODUCTION

If stealing jokes had been a crime, most vaudevillians would have ended up in jail. So great was the traffic in stolen jokes that the trade itself became a source of humor. At the conclusion of their acts, comedians would dash off to other vaude houses to hear competitors' routines. Shamelessly taking what they liked, sometimes altering the material, sometimes not, they rarely if ever acknowledged the source of their humor. When radio comedians became popular, the stage performers also stole from them—and vice versa. The traffic became so blatant that one wag quipped, "I was listening to the radio in order to steal some gags. Some of them came so fast, I almost dropped my pencil." But piracy had begun long before the advent of radio and was nothing new, as some doggerel from the early 1920s makes clear.

> Good old King Tut, a waggish nut,
>   Made all his people happy;
> He made up jokes to please the folks,
>   And some of them were snappy.
> His ancient puns are famous ones,
>   We never can forget them,
> Howe'er we try; they cannot die—
>   Ed Wynn will never let them!

> Tut little dreamed, as people screamed
>   And doubled up in laughter,
> That other wags would use his gags
>   Three thousand long years after.
> He didn't know the radio
>   Would ever be perfected—
> And that his wit would bolster it
>   He never once suspected.

> But every night his nifties bright,
>   Revived by Pearl or Bernie,
> Have got us awed when sent abroad
>   On their ethereal journey.
> His merry quips, when on the lips
>   Of Jolson, are so funny
> That sponsors rush and crowd and push
>   To pay Al heavy money.

> We do not know the debt we owe
>   To this long mummied punster,
> Nor how his stuff has smoothed the rough
>   For many a modern funster.

1

> The gags he sprung when he was young,
>   In jocund barroom banter,
> Convulse the land and get a hand
>   When cracked by Eddie Cantor.

> Yes, old King Tut should get a cut
>   In what these lads are making;
> If he can see the things that be,
>   I bet his sides are shaking;
> But when those gags invade his rags
>   And in his ear go seeping,
> If we'd unwrap his mummied map
>   I bet we'd find him weeping!

From the Renaissance to the present, poets and playwrights have pillaged the ancients. Comedy has especially been fair game because jokes satirize or make light of universal subjects and therefore never go stale.

In the plagiarizing fraternity, Ed Lowry (1896–1983) had a reputation for theft on a grand scale. From the entries in his scrapbooks, I know that he stole jokes from an array of sources: other comedians (Joe Frisco, Harry Lauder, Bert Wheeler), the radio, newspapers, literary weeklies, college humor magazines. On occasion, he even bought jokes, noting in one scrapbook that he'd purchased the material from Al Boasberg, a talented gag writer.

Theft often serves the public good, as the treasures in the British Museum attest. Had Ed Lowry not pilfered so widely, many in this collection of jokes, skits, and routines—which we are at liberty to steal from—would not be available to us now. Although some of the jokes can undoubtedly be found in other places, I know of no source as rich as this one for the twenties and thirties, a period so abundant in humor that for years afterward it fueled radio, cinema, and television. An inveterate collector, Ed Lowry left behind at his death three full scrapbooks of comic material. At one time there may have been more. His widow, Florrie, told me that during Ed's performing heyday, she remembered seeing four or five. (For a detailed explanation of how I acquired this material, see my introduction to *Joe Frisco: Comic, Jazz Dancer, and Railbird.*)

Ed's glory years were those he spent in St. Louis. In the late 1920s, as vaudeville waned, he set his sights on a new form of show business, stage band policy. Said to have started in San Francisco, it combined cinema and variety acts. Big motion picture theatres, with large orchestras, used movies as "teasers" before the extravagant stage shows. Actually recycled vaudeville skits, the shows ran about an hour and revolved entirely around the bandleader, who, as master of ceremonies, not only introduced the different acts and specialties but also participated in them. Never off the stage, the

MC was always in the spotlight. Unlike other variety-film houses, which sought big-name guest stars, the Skouras brothers' St. Louis moving-picture palace, the Ambassador, featured newcomers, many of whom became famous only later: Ray Bolger, Jane Froman, Betty Grable, Joe Penner, Martha Raye, and Ginger Rogers, among others. The absence of celebrities enabled the Skouras brothers to offer Ed top billing. A self-confessed ham, he accepted, and so successful was Ed's tenure at the Ambassador that he stayed for almost five years and presided over more than four thousand performances.

It was doubtless the stringent conditions imposed by this new form of entertainment that led Ed to save the acts and jokes found in his scrapbooks. "The show," Ed says in his unpublished autobiography, "had to be completed in fifty-eight minutes. We were constantly warned to conform to our schedule, which was adhered to just as strictly as a railroad timetable. The slogan was 'get 'em in and get 'em out'—four shows a day, five on Saturday and Sunday." Ad-libbing and improvising were verboten. Every joke and dance was timed; every acrobatic turn finished on the beat. Moreover, each week, a new and lavish variety show introduced new (and old) skits, songs, stories, band numbers, dances, jokes, and acrobatics. Small wonder, then, that Ed carefully archived his daily bread.

Ed Lowry's scrapbooks include well over a thousand neatly glued bits of paper. Most of the entries have been typed, but those that he snipped from newspapers and magazines remain in their original printed form. The large number of typed entries and Ed's abbreviated education explain the numerous errors in grammar, spelling, punctuation, and style. Ed often repeats a joke or changes an ending without omitting the original punch line. He transposes words. He digresses and deflates the effect of a joke. I have edited the collection with an eye—and ear—to keeping the original flavor while rendering the jokes in a form that approximates standard English usage and yet lends itself to performance.

But the real editorial problem was organization. Lowry's collection includes what I would call jokes, skits, and routines, as well as MC "biz," a form of comic patter. Jokes run from one line to several and involve one, two, or more people. Skits are lengthier and treat one subject. Routines, the lengthiest of all, usually involve two people and normally introduce an act. Ed's many years as a master of ceremonies, first in the theatre and later in the USO camp shows, taught him how to introduce a show by means of a routine. A cursory look shows that he constructed the routines from the jokes. All his routines proceed by way of association: one subject suggests another. Marriage, for example, gravitates toward sex, which in turn leads to children, money, and cars. In general, the routines read like a pastiche, but as we all know, the difference between the page and the stage depends on the artistry of the performers.

Understandably, Ed himself organized much of the material under headings useful to an MC, for example, "Band Biz," "Blackouts," "Intros," "Single Girl and Double Girl," "One-Line Gags." I have chosen to classify the short jokes by subject matter but to group together the material that clearly belongs under "Master of Ceremonies." Even so, the task has been daunting. Many jokes touch upon several subjects, making precise classification impossible. Take, for example, the following black humor. "A Russian was being led off to execution by a squad of Bolshevik soldiers on a rainy morning. 'What brutes you Bolsheviks are,' grumbled the doomed man, 'to march me through the rain like this.' 'How about us?' retorted one of the squad. 'We have to march back.'" Should the gag be categorized as execution, police, political, or Russia? Or consider this one. "The teacher told me to stay after school. / Did you do wrong? / I didn't stay." Does it belong under the category children, sex, or school? Cross-referencing helps; but the art of classifying jokes is by no means foolproof. Trying to give this collection a discernible shape has taxed not only my organizing skills but also those of Joy King, my emerita colleague from Classics, whose assistance with this material has proved invaluable.

The work of classification is made all the more difficult by the issue of genre or type of humor. Why not, Joy asked, group the jokes under such headings as anomaly, burlesque, contradiction, dialect, hyperbole, irony, mistaken identity, paradox, and wordplay, all of which are found in this collection? My answer was that organization by genre does not allow for as many distinctions as subject matter does (hundreds of jokes are ironic, many depend on puns). The more distinctions there are, the easier for readers to find what they want. But organization by subject matter does not solve every problem. Some jokes really have no subject matter; and those, in fact, I have catalogued by genre, for example, dialects and wordplay.

In the end, trying to preserve some of the flavor of Ed's scrapbooks and yet provide finer distinctions, I organized the collection into three parts: (1) jokes, organized by subject matter; (2) MC material, organized into "biz," jokes germane to the job of MC, routines, and skits; and (3) an appendix, *Ed Lowry Laffter*, which reproduces a privately published collection that is now a rare collector's item. In parts one and two, the material under a single subject heading has been organized by similarity—jokes that take the same tack —and by length. One-line jokes come before longer jokes. The routines and skits, too, have been organized by similarity and length. To assist the reader, I have in some cases divided subject matter into subcategories. Crime, for example, has three: gangsters, murder, and robbers and robbery. I have also cross-referenced related categories. Finally, I have added a glossary of names because some of the jokes are topical and the people mentioned in them are no longer familiar.

"This world," said Horace Walpole, "is a comedy to those that think, a tragedy to those that feel." Most literary historians would probably agree that comedy provides an insight into the thinking of a time and place. Vaudeville humor certainly does; as John DiMeglio observes, "[it] was a mirror of its times" (40). The jokes reflect the attitudes of a country learning how to live with its immigrant millions, periodic hard times, Prohibition, women's voting rights, and liberalized divorce laws. That many of those attitudes seem to be at odds with our own might lead one to assume that we have gained in compassion and understanding for the underdog. But in light of homophobic and racial crimes, wife and child abuse, political tawdriness, and needless poverty, I would be loath to draw such a conclusion. Vaudevillians, like us, cracked ethnic jokes, laughed at women, moaned about marriage, teased about sex, found children amusing, loved puns, and snickered, though not as much as one might suppose, about nances (short for Nancys, that is, homosexual men). What distances the humor of the twenties and thirties from contemporary comedy is not just its dated slang (a "swell" for a fashionable person, "all wet" for mistaken, "grip" for suitcase) and some of its dated topical references (the Depression, Prohibition, Peggy Joyce's numerous marriages, Walter Winchell's appetite for gossip) but its nature—not sentimental or romantic but satiric. Moreover, we're uncomfortable with its choice of targets. We would never publicly countenance vaudeville's racial stereotyping (African Americans associated with watermelons) and its laughing at groups now regarded as off-limits—midgets, stutterers, old maids, the insane, the obese, suicides, drunks, beggars, hoboes, unattractive people, and women. Of all the satirized groups, women receive the harshest treatment. In skits with guns, they are frequently shot; in other skits, often slugged. Time and again, gags ridicule them for garrulousness, gold digging, prodigality, and coldness. The ideal woman was ostensibly compliant; if she agreed (though not too eagerly) to be kissed and caressed, she escaped the wrath of comedy.

The treatment of women and the frequency of guns suggest that the society was violent. Guns loom large. The twenties and thirties were, after all, known for their gangs, which proliferated during Prohibition. Many of the one-liners suggest that men were expected to talk tough, out of the side of the mouth. It is not surprising that Chicago, the principal turf of Al Capone and other mobsters, receives comic treatment. America as seen through these jokes is still partly a rural country, divided between city slickers and hayseeds. It is also divided between natives and immigrants—of whom more will be said shortly—and, of course, between dominant men and restive women. Indeed, I would hazard that all these conflicts underlie a large body of jokes that reflect men and women trying to define the grounds of a healthy, modern "American" courtship and marriage. But apparently failures, if not divorces, were as frequent then as now. Divorce was difficult to obtain and, even when granted, considered a social stigma. Judging from the number of skits and jokes bearing on "love triangles," I would have to conclude that men and women relieved their frustrations through adultery.

The explanation for all the hanky-panky in Ed's routines, however, may simply lie in the fact that courtship and marriage, like drama, presuppose conflict and thus offer the comedian a wealth of material. In Ed Lowry's world, men have seduction on their minds, women marriage. The bachelor wants his freedom and fun, the woman a family and furs. The young woman's parents see in the suitor a ravisher, or a sugar daddy, or a deadbeat. "Has the young man who's been calling on you given you any encouragement? / Oh, yes, father. Last night he asked me if you and mother were pleasant to live with." The daughter (never a son) represents a salable product, marketable only so long as she keeps her virtue intact. The parents have to protect her from becoming damaged goods; the suitor wants to sample the goods without buying. This is all grist for the comic mill. Once the courting ends and the marriage begins, the battle of the sexes commences. In this collection, the state of marriage itself is a principal source of humor—"Marriage is like a three-ring circus: engagement ring, wedding ring, and suffer-ing" —but specific complaints also find voice: absence from home, bad cooking, bossiness, drunkenness, frigidity, garrulity, having the last word, infidelity, in-laws, and on and on through the alphabet.

Children add to the conflict. Their frankness discloses information the husband or wife would prefer to keep quiet, father kissing the maid or mother embracing the milkman; their paternity may be an issue (no pun intended); their expenses chafe; their misbehavior divides; and of course their replies are often crushing retorts. "Do you realize that when Lincoln was your age, he was chopping wood and helping his parents? / Yeah, and when he was your age he was president." School-age children extend the comic boundaries and give the comedian a treasure trove of material: teachers, lessons, grammar, syntax—and teenagers in heat.

Families have always been the taproot of laughter and tears. When those families are foreign, with different customs and values, they become especially attractive to satirists. In the twenties and thirties, immigration was greatly reduced and xenophobia was rampant. Foreigners were viewed as dangerous radicals, unfair competitors who threatened "American" jobs and wages, cultural aliens who would contaminate "American" values. Especially after the Russian Revolution, immigrants of all political persuasions were looked at askance. Boardinghouses frequently displayed signs prohibiting room rentals to foreigners, people of color, Jews, and Catholics. Lynchings in the south were matched by race riots in the north. The aptly named "Protestant Crusade" looked unkindly on foreigners, many of whom were Catholics and Jews. Worsening economic conditions, leading to the Depression, led some groups to insist that the few available jobs should be reserved for American *men*. (In hard times, women, too, became outsiders.) Given all this turmoil, one would expect the vaudeville jokes to reflect the interethnic bitterness of the period. They do and they don't—and for good reason. Immigrants flocked to vaude houses. Insulting the customer, even when done with tongue in cheek, is risky. While foreign cultures, customs, and accents receive a great deal of ragging, the tone lacks the viciousness found in the political and religious rhetoric of the day. Paradoxically, the nationality most panned, judging from Ed Lowry's collection, was the Scottish, even though they settled a large part of the country. The Scots receive unrelenting ridicule for their presumed stinginess, which one scholar of humor attributes to a neo-Calvinism that placed "great emphasis on the duty to labour in one's calling and to lead a frugal and systemically moral life" (Davies 45). Any reader of this collection would certainly infer that the Scottish were either hard bargainers or zealously thrifty. A typical joke finds a Scotsman cutting corners or acting irrationally just to save money. "A Scotsman's wife was running a fever of 105, so he had her moved into the basement and used her to heat the house."

The absorption of millions of immigrants into American culture remains one of the great social achievements of the twentieth century. Given Constance Rourke's observation that American humor's "objective—the unconscious objective of a disunited people —has seemed to be that of creating fresh bonds, a new unity, the semblance of a society and the rounded completion of an American type" (232), I would hazard that to some degree immigrants became acculturated by seeing themselves satirized in cartoons, stories, and vaudeville. Hearing their culture or group laughed at, they must surely have striven to rid themselves of those traits Americans found comic. Before the immigrants of the twenties and thirties die out, I would like to see some scholar of American culture test my hypothesis that vaudeville to some degree teased out of them the old ways and helped introduce the new.

We know that many immigrants spoke no English or spoke it poorly, yet they flocked to the vaude houses that "proliferated in immigrant and working-class neighborhoods" (Snyder 84). Although vaudeville offered more than just comic acts—for example, singers, dancers, acrobats, impersonators, magicians, trained animals, and playlets—"the monarchs of the vaudeville stage," in DiMeglio's words, "were the funny men" (34). If DiMeglio is right, and I have no reason to doubt him, I wonder how foreign speakers in the audience understood the jokes, which were delivered rapidly and often rested on puns. In reading these jokes today, I find that many of them take a few seconds to comprehend. An ear not attuned to English would, it seems to me, be deaf to the humor, especially the double entendres. It's no marvel that Yiddish speakers laughed in Yiddish vaude houses (there were two in New York City), but ethnic vaude houses were few and far between. Why immigrants laughed at puns in English—and we know that they did—mystifies. Perhaps the newcomers felt the need to blend in with the audience or be polite; perhaps they had seen the same show several times; or perhaps the comedian's expression and body language were enough to elicit a laugh. But still the question remains: did they actually comprehend the wordplay and, if so, how?

In particular, how did they understand sexual double entendres, which relied on subtleties not taught at the settlement houses and for which many of them were culturally unprepared? What did they make of vaudeville's pervasive blue humor? For make no mistake, blue humor existed—and thrived. Though vaudeville had for years been selling itself as suitable for families, and though some contemporary observers, like Marian Spitzer, found it "so pure that it needs no Christian supervision" (35), Robert Snyder argues that this is a myth promulgated by vaudeville entrepreneurs. A perusal of Ed Lowry's collection supports Snyder's contention.

It is true that from the 1880s until the First World War, the major figures behind vaudeville—Tony Pastor, Benjamin Franklin Keith, and Edward Franklin Albee—had tried repeatedly to ban blue humor. Keith had, according to Marian Spitzer, two kinds of rules: "no avowedly immoral character may be presented on the stage" and "the words hell and damn are absolutely and irrevocably barred from the vaudevillian's vocabulary" (36). But war brought an end to innocence and a rush to laugh about the raw and the rude. Although Joe Laurie Jr. in *Vaudeville* dates the introduction of off-color jokes to the late twenties, such jokes had in fact been around since the war. His claim that smut "was one of the poisons that helped kill vaudeville!" (286) does not ring true. By the end of World War I, much of the comic material had become distinctly ribald.

The Roaring Twenties did not acquire their moniker by accident. Ankle-length dresses with numerous petticoats gave way to flapper flimsies well above the knee. Dance, enlivened by the hot jazz blaring from Harlem, lit up New York. So too did lightbulbs, making Broadway the Great White Way. Speakeasies flourished; scams abounded; slang proliferated; and sex became something to laugh at openly. It is not surprising that vaudeville jokes and skits also roared. By 1925, when Marshall Beuick outlined the state of the drama, there were

certain standard subjects that are used almost every
night on vaudeville stages through the country. An audience, composed of many persons mentally fatigued after
a day's work, learns . . . such precepts as: marriage is an
unfortunate institution to which the majority of us resign ourselves; women are fashion-crazy, spend money
heedlessly and believe that their husbands are fools; politics is all bunk; Prohibition should be prohibited; mothers are the finest persons in the world . . . next to grand-
mothers; fathers are unfortunate persons upon whom
fall most of life's woes; marital infidelity is widespread;
clandestine affairs . . . are comical; and finally "nothing
in life really matters. The main thing to do is get all the
money you can and keep your mother-in-law as far off as
possible." (92)

Imagine the shock of these "precepts" on socially conservative
immigrants, especially those who came from villages and shtetls,
where the priest or rabbi dominated the community, where arranged marriages were not uncommon, and where many husbands
never saw their wives undressed. Whether such humor contributed
to immigrant acculturation is not known, but I would guess that it
did. Once marriage and adultery became risible, then no subject
was beyond the pale, not chastity, not the clergy, not father's role
in the family, not even mother's purity—all Victorian sacred cows.
Yet immigrants attended vaudeville houses in outstanding numbers, until radio and the Depression put out the lights.

What continued to glow were the lessons that vaudevillian humor taught immigrant audiences: that in America one was free to
laugh at people and institutions, free to poke fun at religious and
patriotic groups, free to snicker in public about sex. The comedians
taught them that what evokes laughter comes from the earth, not
the heavens, and that all creatures, including ourselves, are subjects for mirth. As comic writers from Aristophanes to Woody Allen have known, if you can't laugh about sex, politics, and religion,
what is there to laugh about? Having come to America to escape
hardships and hierarchies, to replace lamentation with laughter,
the immigrants learned that humor, although sometimes painful,
liberates, because it is iconoclastic. Authority can survive polemics
and screeds but not satire. Tyrants can apprehend and imprison
our persons, but a joke, like the air that we breathe, cannot be arrested. And yet, for all its immateriality, humor puts us in stitches,
weakens the knees, moves us to tears, splits our sides, gladdens our
hearts, rollicks our bellies, and tickles our lungs.

Humor is a drug that we willingly abuse for its subversive and
hurly-burly high. Under its influence, we disenthrall ourselves from
others and even from our selves, often the cruelest tyrants of all.

With pain and with glee, we laugh at fools and foes, at gilded but-
terflies, at leisure, at lovers' perjuries, at quaint opinions, and even
at our own cenotaphs. Our warrant for laughter comes from on
high—because, as Homer says, laughter first arose among the gods.

BIBLIOGRAPHY

Beuick, Marshall D. "The Vaudeville Philosopher." *Drama* 16.3
   (Dec. 1925): 92–93, 116. Rpt. in *American Vaudeville as Seen by
   Its Contemporaries.* Ed. Charles W. Stein. New York: Knopf,
   1984. 329–30. Also rpt. in Snyder 153.
Davies, Christie. *Jokes and Their Relation to Society.* Humor Re-
   search. 4. Ed. Victor Raskin and Willibald Ruch. New York:
   Mouton de Gruyter, 1998.
DiMeglio, John E. *Vaudeville U.S.A.* Bowling Green, OH: Bowling
   Green U Popular P, 1973.
Laurie, Joe, Jr. *Vaudeville: From the Honky-Tonks to the Palace.* New
   York: Holt, 1953.
Rourke, Constance. *American Humor: A Study of the National Char-
   acter.* New York: Harcourt, 1931.
Snyder, Robert W. *The Voice of the City.* New York: Oxford UP,
   1989.
Spitzer, Marian. "Morals in the Two-A-Day." *American Mercury* 3
   (Sept. 1924): 35–39.

PART ONE

Jokes

ACCIDENTS

I went to see my girl. She was in the bathroom. I told her to slip on something and she did. She slipped on a bar of soap.

ACTING AND ACTORS

As an actor he was quite well off, better off than on.

An actress was late for the show because she went over to a big piano store for a sitting.

Actor: What are your terms for actors?
Clerk: I don't use that kind of language.

Father: What's your ambition, son?
Son: I've got none. I wanna be an actor.

I know a movie actor who claims that he is an actor of the first water. And I think he's right, because he's all wet!

Actor: A famous restaurant has named a sandwich after me.
Dancer: What kind of sandwich is it, ham?

Director: Just go in and say, "Ham."
Actor: Who's that for?
Director: No one, just an admission.

Director: I want you to appear in a picture. Have you had any experience acting without an audience?
Actor: Mister, that's why I'm here!

Stage Manager (discussing chorus girl who has just auditioned): Well, what do you think of her?
Producer: A peach, but no melba.

I know an actor who was injured in a fall from a horse. He tried to collect insurance, but the company defaulted with the excuse that the horse must have known the actor and thrown him on purpose!

An instrument has been perfected that will throw the voice of a speaker (or: actor) a mile. Now for one that will throw the speaker that far.

Executive: So you're having trouble correcting the new French star's accent?
Voice Teacher: Listen, I've been working with it for six weeks now, and you can still tell she comes from Brooklyn.

My friend was reading a paper and said, "This is remarkable. It says, 'Lightning strikes actor when he was grumbling about his billing.'" "Nothing remarkable in that," I replied. "It would be surprising if it said, "Lightning strikes actor when he isn't grumbling about his billing."

Director: In this scene, my dear, the young man rushes into the room, grabs you, binds you with rope from head to foot and then smothers you with hugs and kisses.
Actress: Is the young man tall, dark, and handsome?
Director: Yes, why?
Actress: Then he won't need any rope.

Comedians

—If you're a comedian, I'm an Admiral.
—Hya, Admiral!

—If you're a comedian, I'm a monkey.
—Well, I'm a comedian, so start climbing.

ADVERTISEMENTS AND ADVERTISING

—Bones, I understand that Jones is going to have his name stamped on fifty million toothpicks.
—Yes. He wants his name in everybody's mouth.

Mr. Cohen joined a swanky golf club and was in the clubhouse buying a few balls before teeing off for his first round. The Caddie Master showed him the balls and asked him, "Wouldn't you like to have your name printed on them, Dr. Cohen?" Cohen said, "Sure." The Caddie master put the balls in a printing machine and started to inscribe Cohen's initials when Cohen said, "If it's all the same to you, put Doctor Cohen. Dentist." The other man said, "Okay," but just as he was getting set to print, Cohen had another thought. "If you don't mind," he said, "after Dr. Cohen, Dentist, put office hours, one to six."

(Variation)
A Jewish doctor, born in Scotland, joined a country club and on the first day he was told that if he had his name inked on the golf ball, it would be returned if lost and found. "So all right," he said, "put down on mine ball Ginzburg, plizz." The man in the golf supply shop wrote his name on it. "Hmm," he hmm'd, "dot's dendy. Would you ulso plizz put don M.D. efter mine name? I'm a ductor!" "Be glad to," said the fellow as he added M.D. to Mr. G.'s tag. As Mr. Ginzburg inspected the finished product he cooed: "Would you mind doong me one murr favor, plizz?" "Of course," said the man. "What?" "Put don hours 10 to 3."

Commercial Products

I've kept that schoolgirl complexion, [Palmolive]
I've walked a mile for a smoke, [Camels]
I've asked the man who owns one, [Packard]

And he tells me it keeps him broke,
I know that a child can play it
To guard the danger line I try,
I know when it's time to retire, [Fisk tires]
And I've heard that they satisfy, [Chesterfields]
But there's one thing that baffles me,
Even for a life time I strive,
I'd love to know just whether or not,
I'm one of the Four Out of Five. [Pyorrhea]

Sandwich Boards

I saw a fellow with a blank sandwich board. I asked him what's the idea. He said: I'm not working during lunch hours.

Two fellows were carrying sandwich boards, one had advertising and the other was blank. The one with the blank said he was waiting for a sponsor.

AFRICA AND AFRICANS

—I was in the middle of the African jungle when suddenly I saw a tribe of savages charging down on me.
—Good heavens! And what did you do?
—I stared at them until I was black in the face, and they took me for one of their own tribe.

AFRICAN AMERICANS

He's so black that lightning bugs follow him around in the daytime.

Doctor: Why, man, you are color blind.
Patient: Heavens, Doc, I got married last week, too.

—Rastus, I'll give you a pint of Scotch if you'll hurry over to my house and get my grip. Hurry now . . . what! Haven't you gone yet?
—Gone? Boss, I's back!

—Say, Mose, whafor youall name youah baby "Electricity"?
—Well mah wife's name's Dinah and mine's Mose and by golly, if Dinahmose don't make "Electricity," ah don't know what does.

A Negro preacher discovered two men playing cards on Sunday and for money. "Rastus," said the preacher, "don't you know it's wrong to play cards on de Sabbath?" "Yes, pahson," answered Rastus ruefully, "but believe me, ah's payin' foh ma sins."

A Negro parson held forth one Sunday with a fine sermon, which was sympathetically received by the entire congregation. He was about to close. "Brudders and sistern, Ah want to warn yo' against the heinous crime of stealin' watermelons." At this point

an old Negro rose, snapped his fingers, and sat down again.
"Wharfo', brudder, does yo' rise up an' snap yo' fingers when Ah
speaks of watermelion stealin'?"

"Yo' jes' reminds me, pahson, whah ah done lef' mah knife."

—Whuffo you rubberin' at me lak 'at foah, black boy?
—Ah's jus' a lookin' you over foah a grand slam, pardner.
—Well, jus' don't try any of you' tricks, bub, 'cause I'll club you
down, trump all ovah yo' daid body, spade you under, an' bury
you wid simple honors.

Two colored men were standing on the corner discussing family
trees.
—Yes suh, man, I can trace my relations back to a family tree.
—Chase 'em back to a family tree?
—Naw man, trace 'em, trace 'em, get me?
—Well, they ain't but two kind of things dat live in trees. Birds
and monkeys and you sho' ain't got no feathers on you.

The other day in a courtroom, Judge White was reproving a colored man for deserting his wife, and dwelt at great length on the
injustice he was doing. "Wife desertion is something, Rastus, that
I just deal with severely. I'm afraid I feel very strongly on the subject." "But Judge," said Rastus, "you don't know that woman. I
ain't no deserter, I'se a refugee."

A man stopped a small colored boy on the street and asked him
his name. The little boy answered, "Abraham Lincoln Jackson
Smith." The man said, "What a wonderful thing to be named
after such important people," and asked the boy, "Do you know
who Abraham Lincoln is?" The little boy said that he didn't. The
man was surprised and said, "Do you know who George Washington is?" The colored kid's face brightened and said, "Sure!
That's my brother."

Rufus: What's matter with yo' head, man?
Rastus: Arithmetical bugs.
Rufus: What?
Rastus: Cooties.
Rufus: Why arithmetical bugs?
Rastus: Well, dey add to my misery, subtract from my pleasure,
divide my attention, and multiply like the dickens.

Two white men and a Negro were discussing a recent suicide
in their midst, all agreeing that the tragedy was a sad one and
placed a heavy loss upon the community. After various opinions
were aired between the three, one of the men addressed the old
darky. "It seems queer, Uncle Henry, but I've never heard of a
colored man who committed suicide. How do you account for
that?" "No, sah," mused Uncle Henry, "I spec's yo-all nevah did.

Hits this way, I reckon. When a man gwine commit suicide he sho'ly do stop 'n think, and when a cul'ud man stops to think he falls asleep."

Fright

Andy: Amos, Ah bet you wuz relieved when you found out there wuz no spook followin' you.
Amos: Say, ah wuz so relieved, ah done slowed right down to a gallop.

Colored Gent: Ah's almost out ob wind. A ghost started after me when ah left mah house dis ebenin', and it's been chasin' me fo' de past hour!
Colored Villager: Hmm! Isn't yo' a stranger in dese parts, suh?
Colored Gent: Lawdy, yes. Ah lives sixty miles from heah.

An old black man who had spent many years in a wheelchair wanted to go on one last coon hunt before he died. So he and his grandchildren, accompanied by several dogs, started out. Hardly had they penetrated the swamps when they met a bear. All turned tail and ran, leaving poor Grandpap to his fate. As they came panting into the yard they called, "Oh, Mammy, Mammy, Grandpap done got et up by a b'ar." "Foolishment what yo' speaks, children. Yo' Grandpap done come in ten minutes ago wid de dogs!"

AGE AND AGING

May I call you "girlie"—or am I too late?

She is so old, she knew Father Time when he was a baby.

I'd rather have two at sixteen than one at thirty-two.

A woman is as old as she looks; a man is old when he stops looking.

She: Do you think a girl should love before twenty?
He: No, that's too large an audience.

First Man: So your new stenographer is young and willing.
Second Man: Well, she ain't so young.

The girl of today is more popular than the girl of twenty years ago—providing it's not the same girl.

She: How old do you think I am?
He: You don't look it.

Claire: What! Jim and Mae engaged? Does he know how old she is?
Irene: Well, partly.

—Peggy's age surprised me. She doesn't look twenty-three, does she?
—No, but I suppose she did once.

He: I'll love only you, even if I live to be a thousand years old.
She: Yeah, then I suppose you'll start chasing around.

—None of your impudence. I knew you when you wore short pants.
—Yeah, and I knew you when you wore three-cornered ones.

—Do you think I look twenty-five?
—No! But you used to.

—Boy, you're getting old.
—Yeah. It's been five years since you could see a telephone number.

When a man gets too old to set a bad example, he usually decides it's time to give good advice.

Joe says that when his wife gets to be forty, he's gonna trade her in for two twenties.

She: I wonder what the modern girl will be twenty years from now.
He: About three years older.

—What's the difference between a girl of twenty and one of forty-five?
—Twenty-five years.

—It must be terribly lonesome for a young woman to marry an old man.
—Oh, I don't know; you can sit at home in the evenings and listen to his arteries harden.

—This fellow looks so young, you wouldn't think he was the father of four, would you?
—He isn't.

—Gwen, your face is dirty.
—Oh, Mr. Lowry, your face is dirtier than mine.
—Well, Gwen, I'm older than you are.
—Ha, how alluring! You remind me of lavender and old lace . . . like an old cameo.
—Yeah, well you're not so hot either.

He: I like that dress you're wearing.
She: I'm glad you like it. My dad bought it for my eighteenth birthday.
He: Yes, it wears well.

First Chorine: This is my twenty-first birthday.
Second Chorine: Which one?
First Chorine: My twenty-first.

Second Chorine: No, I mean which one of your twenty-first birth-days is it?

He: How old are you?
She: Sixteen.
He: How old?
She: Sixteen, I said twice, sixteen.
He: Oh, twice sixteen, that's better.

He: Have you been reducing? You seem smaller than you used to be.
She: I haven't grown since I was ten years old, six years ago.
He: What! You're sixteen?
She: Yes, and I was asking _____ how old he was today, and he's eighteen. How old are you?
He: I'll be three next Tuesday.

He: How old are you?
She: Sixteen.
He: How old?
She: Sixteen, I say, sixteen.
He: How old!
She: I said three times, sixteen.
He: You're too old for me.

—Guess how old I am.
—Twenty-one?
—No.
—Twenty-four?
—No.
—Twenty-three?
—No . . . try twenty-two.
—Twenty-two?
—No.

AIR-CONDITIONING AND HEATING

The owner turned down the air conditioning when he saw two enterprising fellows selling fur coats in the lobby this morning.

The owners of this theatre had to raise the temperature 'cause they found lots of folks bringing butter and meat and hanging 'em up here.

AIRPLANES

Shortly after taking off, an airplane pilot decided to take a side spin. After it was over, he called through to the passengers, "Say, I'll bet fifty percent of the people on the ground thought we were taking a nose dive." One of the passengers shouted, "Yeah, and fifty percent of the people up here thought the same."

The aviator's wife was taking her first trip with her husband in his airship. "Wait a moment, George," she said, "I'm afraid we will have to go down again." "What's wrong?" asked the husband. "I believe I have dropped one of the buttons off my jacket. I think I can see it glistening on the ground." "Keep your seat, my dear," said the aviator. "That's a lake."

AMERICANS

—Where were you Americans born?
—Windsor, Ontario, Canada.
—Then you're naturalized Americans.
—Naturalized nothin'. We're petrified.

ANCIENT ROME

I feel like Nero. You just fiddle around while I burn up.

We remember hearing somewhere or other that they had to discontinue the Roman holidays because of the overhead. The lions were eating up the prophets.

ANIMALS, INSECTS, AND WILDLIFE

Ants

A tiny ant gazed longingly but helplessly at the body of a dead horse. Just then a bootlegger's truck rattled by and a case of stuff fell over the endgate and crashed to the ground. A puddle formed and the ant took one sip. Then he seized the dead horse by the tail and shouted: "Come on, big boy, we're going home."

Birds

—I just bought a bird and it won't sing. It just sits on the perch all day.
—It must be one of those stool pigeons.

Boll Weevils

The little lady weevil was undecided about a date with a little weevil and a big strong weevil. So she asked her mom. Her mom said, "Always choose the lesser of the two weevils."

Camels

—Orville, my lad, do you know a camel goes eight days without drinking?
—Gee, Paternoster, I wonder how long it will go if it does drink?

Cats

An Octopus is an eight-sided cat.

A black cat is in a hell of a mess when another black cat crosses its path.

First Cat: I'm going to a tennis match.
Second Cat: What's the idea?
First Cat: My father's in that racket.

He: Don't be catty or you'll never go to heaven.
She: How do you know there are cats in heaven?
He: Well, if there're no cats in heaven, where do they get the strings for their harps?

Kreisler: Lady, your cat has kept me awake now for a week with its serenade.
Tenant: What should I do, shoot it?
Kreisler: No, have it tuned.

A few summers ago I was in the suburbs of London and noticed a remarkable number of tailless cats—Manx cats. They were from the Manx Island where cats are born minus tails. One day while waiting at the station for the 5:15 train to London, a cat having no tail scampered across the platform of the station. I turned to the station agent and asked, "Manx?" "No," he replied, "5:15." [The train cut off the tail of the cat.]

A friend of mine has a cat. The other night, I went round to his house and half a block away a cat skipped by me. When I got a little nearer, the same cat skipped out of an alley and ran like mad. Just as I got to my friend's house, the cat ran around from behind the house and dashed across the road. I recognized it as my friend's cat. So when my friend came to the door, I asked him why his cat was dashing around like that. He said, "We're going away tomorrow and the cat is out cancelling his appointments."

Chickens and Roosters

First Hen: That big rooster has been making love to me.
Second Hen: Did you give him any encouragement?
First Hen: Just egged him on a bit.

In Chicago, the bricklayers get fifteen bucks a day. We'd better not let the hens know about that, or we'll be getting bricks instead of eggs.

Big Hen (boastfully): I get thirty cents a dozen for my eggs. How much do you get for yours?
Small Hen: I get twenty-five cents a dozen.
Big Hen (scornfully): Why don't you lay big eggs and get thirty cents a dozen, too?
Small Hen: Huh! I should exert myself for a nickel!

My uncle has a farm, with a prize rooster he values very highly. It was strutting around one day when suddenly a football came flying into the yard. The rooster walked around the football, looked it over carefully, and then called all the hens together. He said, "Ladies, I don't want you to think I'm grumbling, but I want you to see the kind of work that's being done by others."

Cows

Our cow wouldn't give any milk so we sold HIM.

Proverb: You can't get milk from a cow named Jake.

My cow has hiccups and churns her own butter.

A judge says that a cow has a legal right to use the road. Motorists say this only confirms what the cow seems to have known all along.

How to milk a cow: Take her to the barn, give her a drink of water, then go to the back, and drain her crankcase.

City Man: Milking the cow?
Hiram: Naw, just feeling her pulse.

We've got a black cow . . . eats green grass . . . gives white milk and makes yellow butter.

Dogs

One man's mutt is another man's poison.

I saw a dog sitting on a nail. It was too lazy to move.

That dog of mine is very smart. He took a post-graduate course.

That dog is a setter pointer. He sets in the kitchen and points at the icebox.

—Will your dog eat candy?
—He's crazy about old shoes, so he should love candy.

Customer: Your dog seems very fond of watching you cut hair.
Barber: It ain't that; sometimes I snip off a bit of the customer's ear.

—Say, mister, are you the man who gave my brother a dog last week?
—Yes.
—Well, Ma says to come and take THEM back.

—He's sure got hair on his chest.
—Who?
—Rin Tin Tin.

The dogs in New York are very friendly. I've seen one dog follow another for blocks. When I was there, one followed me for nearly a mile.

I went into a pet shop to buy a dog muzzle. A fellow showed me one, but I said, "I'm afraid it won't fit." He replied, "I just sold one like this to an old lady." I answered, "I want mine for a dog."

She (*girl crying*): I lost a little dog.
He: Why don't you advertise for it?
She: That's no use; he can't read.

My dog is so intelligent that when I talk about him I have to say B.A.D. The other day I was saying what a fine looking dog he is, and he immediately jumped up and looked himself over in the mirror.

—Telling my dog to lay down doesn't do any good. You have to tell him to lie down.
—Why's that?
—Because he's a Boston terrier.

—This dog cost us virtually nothing. He was a real bargain.
—Oh, that's nice. Because a bargain dog never bites.

—Why did you run from that dog?
—It wasn't dead.

—That's some pup. He's the most hospitable dog in the country.
—What do you mean "hospitable"?
—Why, he'd give you a bite any old time.

—I tell you we're going to get rid of that poodle. It just bit me in the ankle.
—That's too bad.
—Darn right it's too bad.
—Yes, we should have gotten a St. Bernard.

—My little Dachshund caught a tramp in the yard and sat on him till I got there. Now he's awfully sick.
—How was it that he sat on a tramp?
—His stomach was on the bum.

—What kind of a dog is that?
—That's an Einstein dog.
—Meaning what?
—We're not sure of its relativity.

—I call my dog Outboard Motor.
—Outboard Motor? Why do you call her that?
—Well, ever since I've had her, it's been nothin' but pup, pup, pup.

A friend of mine has a dog and every time he takes it outside, it starts chasing after automobiles. I asked him, "Does the dog always do that?" He said, "I can't break him of it. Every time a car comes whizzing by, he's after it like a flash." I asked him, "Why does he do that?" He said, "I dunno. But I don't worry about why he does it so much as what he's going to do with an auto when he gets it."

—My sister has a dog that sings.
—That must be something.
—But she always sings off key.
—What kind of a dog is she?
—She's a setter.
—Maybe she's a falsetter.

A "doggy" lady met a friend who propounded this riddle. "What do you see when you look down a dog's throat?" The lady could not guess, and was amused by the answer, which is "the seat of his pants." So on her return home she asked her husband. "What do you see when you look down a dog's throat?" Her husband confessed bafflement. "Why," said the lady between gusts of laughter, "the seat of his trousers, you silly."

Dogcatchers

Do you know the Dog Catchers' Union theme song? "Here we go gathering mutts in May."

Elephants

No matter how tired an elephant might be, he cannot sit on his trunk.

—Git away from that thar elephant.
—Aw, I ain't hurtin' him.

A news item claims that over two thousand elephants were used to make ivory billiard balls last year. Damn clever, those elephants!

A flea and an elephant walked side by side over a little bridge. After they had crossed it, the flea said to the elephant: "Boy, we sure did shake that thing!"

—Tell me why you fed the elephant a box of moth balls yesterday?
—The boss says that we're going to store him for the winter, and I don't want him to get any moths in his trunk.

Fish

The reason that catfish don't have kittens is that tomcats haven't yet learned to swim.

Fish have no method of communication. That's why they don't respond when we drop them a line.

Do fish ever sleep? Well, they ought to with all the free river, lake, and ocean beds.

In Hackensack, they use a hammer and a watch to catch fish with. The fish come up to see what time it is and they hit 'em on the head with the hammer.

Fleas

—Have you got anything for fleas?
—No, get a dog.

Hogs and Pigs

They just sleep around
And grow fat and big.
Don't you wish you were a pig?

Walking through a wood, I noticed a herd of hogs running one way and then turning and running the other way. They dashed this way and that. In fact, it was a relief to get out of the wood. A farmer was sitting on a log, so I asked him, "Say, what's wrong with those hogs; are they wild?" The farmer said in a whisper, "No, they're not wild." I replied, "What makes them run around as they do?" "Well," he said, "it's this way. I useter call them, but lost my voice. So then I got them so's they come running when I tapped this log. Well, it's spring, and they're having a hell of a time with these woodpeckers." (*Or:* these woodpeckers have got 'em crazy.)

Horses

My horse got so thin we had to put a knot on his tail to keep him from slipping out of his collar.

—I thought you told me that horse you sold me was gaited.
—That's right . . . he is . . . variegated.

—Why did you transfer from the cavalry to the air force?
—Well, when you fall off a plane, at least the darn things don't bite you.

—What is it that lives in a stall, eats oats, and can see equally well at both ends?
—Beats me.
—A blind horse.

A country cabby, on coming to a hill, got down and violently banged the door, to the consternation of his fare inside, who asked why he did it. "Why, sir, it's to make the horse believe you got out," whispered the driver.

He: Say, young lady, what were you feeding that horse doughnuts for? You've given him a whole bag full.
She: I was just seeing how many he would eat before he asked for a cup of coffee.

—You know what the difference is between you and a horse? A horse wears shoes.
—But I wear shoes.
—Then there's no difference.

(Variation)
—What's the difference between you and a horse?
—I give up.
—A horse wears a collar.
—But I wear a collar.
—Then there's no difference.

A man bought a horse and was warned not to pass a corn field because of the horse's fondness for corn. The man went out riding and the horse sat right down in the middle of a pond. Taking the horse back to the store, the man asked what gives. The seller said, "I forgot to tell you, he likes goldfish too."

A fellow bought a horse for his wagon. After he hitched it up, the horse kicked the wagon to bits, dashed down the alley, ran its head into a brick wall, and killed itself. The man returned to the place where he'd bought the animal and told the dealer, "Say, you know, that horse you sold me, it was blind." The dealer said, "That horse was okay when you took him away from here." The man explained how the horse ran away and then ran his head into a brick wall. The dealer replied, "Why, that horse wasn't blind, he just didn't give a damn."

Lions

—Did a lion bite you?
—Yes, but it got well again.

Two lions met in the jungle and ferociously fought, until all that was left were their two tails [tales].

—I'm off to Africa.
—Drop me a lion once in a while.

—I hunted lions (*or:* tigers) in Africa.
—But I heard there are no more lions in Africa.
—That's right, I shot them all.

Mice

Animals may not be superstitious, but we have yet to hear of a mouse crossing the path of a black cat.

A mouse in a stocking-shop window said, "There's something wrong. I've been here two minutes, and not a move or a murmur."

Monkeys

I played the organ for years, but the monkey died.

—Did you give the penny to the monkey, dear?
—Yes, mama.

—And what did the monkey do with it?

—He gave it to his father, who played the organ.

Mosquitoes

All day long mosquitoes bothered him. At night he saw some fireflies, and he said, "Good heavens, now they're coming after us with lanterns."

Moths

A terrible thing is happening among the moths. There's an awful case of anaemia among them—a lack of red flannel.

Mules

—You're limping.

—I was kicked by a mule.

—Where?

—On the highway.

—I mean on what part of your anatomy?

—Well, sir, if my back were an automobile, that pesky animal would have smashed my license plate.

Parrots

I have an underworld parrot, he won't talk.

A fellow had to deliver fifty chickens, but when he counted, he found he had only forty-nine. Not wanting to disappoint a good customer, he decided to put a parrot in with the bunch. Driving toward town on a lonely country road, he heard a noise at the back of his wagon. He looked round, and there was the parrot perched on top of the wagon and all the chickens out on the road. The parrot was saying, "Well, if any of you girls change your minds, you can jump in and ride."

Rats

—Gimme a quarter's worth of rat poison.

—Do you wanna take it with you?

—Naw. I'll send the rats in after it.

Sheep

—Where does virgin wool come from?

—From the sheep that can run the fastest.

—I hear you have a sheep ranch.

—Yes, and a monkey wrench. But I like sheep raising.

—Do you raise a lot of wool?

—No, I leave that to the sheep.

Skunks

Lecturer: I speak the language of wild animals. Voice in rear: Next time you meet a skunk, ask him what's the big stink.

Storks

The stork refused to carry a baby named Paul because it didn't want to be a Paul Bearer.

Whales

—Did you ever see a whale blubber?
—It must be very sad to see such a big animal cry.

Other Wild Animals

Reporter: Were you well-liked in the jungle?
Explorer: Oh, yes; everyone was wild about me.

—I love hunting tigers, lions, and wild animals.
—Did you ever hunt bear?
—No, I always wear clothes.

ANTICIPATION

He promised to be here at four and it's only one. I wonder where he can be? While I'm waiting, I think I'll go home.

APPEARANCE

That's not a lavaliere; that's her lower lip.

Her face was her fortune, but she had it lifted.

She wanted her face lifted, so he gave her an uppercut.

She had the face of a saint—a Saint Bernard.

She looked like a bad photograph: overexposed and under-developed.

She's two-faced. One face when she gets up, and one when she goes out.

If we could only see ourselves as others see us, we'd never speak to ourselves.

When a girl's face is her fortune, it usually runs into an attractive figure.

—My maiden aunt is afraid of her own shadow.
—Well, I don't blame her, with that profile of hers.

—Every time I look at you I get spots before the eyes.
—They're freckles.

She: Do you really think I'm beautiful?
He: Baby, when I'm in this mood anybody is beautiful.

—Don't you think I looked like a million last night?
—What? Dollars or years?

She: The man I marry must be tall, upright, and grand.
He: You don't want a man, you want a piano.

—Why, Ed, I'm surprised. Don't you know that beauty is only skin deep?
—All right, that's deep enough for me.

A woman rushed into a police station with a photograph in her hand. "My husband has disappeared," she sobbed. "Here is his photograph. I want you to find him." The sergeant looked at the photograph. "Why?" he asked.

—Elaine, what's your new boyfriend like?
—Well, can you picture a man with the looks of Romeo, the physique of Hercules, the gentleness of a saint, the manners of Sir Walter Raleigh?
—Yes?
—That's not him.

Beards and Mustaches

A mustache is a bang in the mouth.

—It's a pity some people don't see what's right under their nose.
—If they did, they'd be shaving off a lot of mustaches.

He: My razor doesn't cut at all.
She: You don't mean to tell me your beard is tougher than oil-cloth.

She: Your small mustache saddens me.
He: How so, dear?
She: Well, when you kiss me I feel a little down in the mouth.

Man with a Beard: I want a haircut, singe, and shampoo. I want my mustache clipped, and beard trimmed, and . . . er . . . where can I put this cigar?
Barber: Would you mind keeping it in your mouth, sir? It'll be sort of a landmark.

—And you are sure that the preparation you told me of will positively remove my whiskers?
—Will it? Why, the other day the boss spilled some on the rug, and the next morning we came in and found a linoleum.

A fellow left home leaving his five brothers behind. After he'd been away twenty years, he returned. His brothers were at the station to meet him. When he got off the train he found them all with beards down to their waists. He asked, "How come you all have such long beards?" One of them replied, "You went away with the razor."

Bowlegs

I know a man who is so bowlegged that he has to have his shoes soled on the side.

I just saw the funniest thing—a bowlegged woman telling her knock-kneed husband to go straight home.

Talk about bowlegged, I knew a girl who used to model for a barrel factory. She walked like a duck. In fact, she was so bowlegged, she had to get out of bed to turn over.

Cosmetics

A smart girl is one who can make her complexion taste as good as it looks.

—I use this lipstick to keep the chap off my lips.
—What's his name? [See Fast Women under Women.]

Gym Teacher: Lots of girls use dumbbells to get color in their cheeks.
Girl: And lots of girls use color on their cheeks to get dumbbells.

Cross-eyes

He wasn't exactly cross-eyed, but one eye ignored the other.

She has witching eyes. You can't tell which way they're looking.

Did you ever drink with a cross-eyed man and have him say, "Here's looking at you?"

A cross-eyed judge was trying three men. He asked the first one, "What's your name?" The second one replied, "Smith." The judge said, "I wasn't talking to you." The third said, "I didn't say anything."

She's got eyes like pins: headed in one direction and pointed in the other.

Dandruff

—What are those white flakes on your shoulder?
—Just a little dandruff trying to get ahead.

Ears

Her ears were so big, she had to use chandeliers for earrings.

Her ears are so big that when she goes out on a windy day she has to pin them back to keep them from flapping her brains out.

Nature is a wonderful thing! A million years ago she didn't know we were going to wear spectacles, yet look at the way she placed our ears.

Eyes

She's got lovely almond eyes; they drive me nuts.

A ring is better on the fingers than under the eyes.

—He doesn't have to look at the world through rose-colored glasses.
—Why?
—He's bloodshot.

—That man you introduced me to last night has sparrow eyes.
—You mean they are brown?
—No, they flit from limb to limb.

—I can't see a thing without my glasses. Gotta have my glasses.
—Aw, that's a crazy idea. Take off your glasses, I'll prove it to you.
—There, now, how many men in the control booth (*or:* box)?
—Seventeen.
—Ach!
—I told you I can't see a thing without my glasses.
—Put 'em on again. Now, how many people in that booth?
—What booth?

Feet

—What would you do if you were in my shoes?
—I'd get a shine!

—My feet are burning something awful.
—Why not get some mustard for them.
—Mustard?
—Sure. Mustard is good for hot dogs.

Figure

She had an arm like a leg of mutton.

She: So you think I've got the nicest figure in town?
He: Yeah. I knows a good thing when I seize it.

—Your figure reminds me of a roller coaster.
—What do you mean?
—Your curves take my breath away.

—One thing I admire about you is your figure. How do you keep such a beautiful form?
—Oh, just calories and vitamins.
—You mean Gab Callories and Paul Vitamins. [Cab Calloway and Paul Whiteman, band leaders]

Hair

—I saw you out with a Harvard blue blood last night. Swell boy?
—Swell? He's so highbrow he's baldheaded!

He has imported hair. He's bald on one side and has to bring his hair over from the other side.

—Our hair restorer will grow hair on a billiard ball.
—Yeah, but who wants a billiard ball with hair?

—Are you losing your hair?
—No, I don't lose it. It falls out and I throw it away.

—I thought your girlfriend was a brunette.
—She was. I'm going to sue her for bleach-of-promise.

—Do you mind, dearest, if I dye my hair henna color?
—Dye it henna color at all. I don't care.

—Dear heart, will you love me when my hair turns gray?
—Why not? I've already loved you from black through henna to platinum.

—What have you got there?
—A bottle of carbolic acid and a curling iron.
—What do you want with that?
—I'm going to curl up and dye.

Old Gentleman (indignantly): Look at that girl wearing knickers, and at her hair cut just like a man's. Why, it's a disgrace!
—Sir, that's my daughter!
—Oh, I beg your pardon; I didn't realize you were her father.
—Father! Say, I'm her mother.

Haircuts

—Did you just have your hair cut?
—No, I just moved my ears down an inch.

—Do I need a haircut?
—Oh, that's it. I thought you had a fur cap on.

Rubinoff went to a barbershop and asked the barber, "Are you the guy who cut my hair before?" The guy said, "Naw, I been here only two years."

—A report from a hairdressers' convention says that women face the danger of being bald.
—Yeah, soon the women will be going for a whole roof instead of just a shingle.

After little Joey's grandma had her hair bobbed, he remarked:
—You don't look like an old lady any more.
—Don't I, darling?
—No, you look more like an old man.

A youth was having a haircut. At the end of that operation the barber inquired:
Barber: Anything else, sir?
Young Man: Well, I'd like my mustache trimmed. I'm afraid it isn't very much of a mustache so far, is it?

Barber: Well, as a matter of fact, I have an aunt in Chicago who has a better one.

Height

I know a guy who is so small, he could be a pro on a miniature golf course.

—The man I marry must be tall and handsome.
—Gimme a chance, I'm still growing.

Noses

If they ever cut off his nose he'd fall backwards.

He had his nose lifted to enable him to drink out of a glass.

What a nose that guy had. The baby used to grab hold of it for a rattle.

Her nose is turned up so much that every time she sneezes she blows her hat off.

—Pardon me. You have something on the end of your nose.
—Well, brush it off. You're closer to it than I am.

—Don't you think I have a beautiful nose!
—Oh, it's pretty good, as noses run.

He: Dear, your eyes are like deep pools of sparkling water; your lips are like two little red rosebuds wet with dew; your teeth are like the finest pearls nature ever made; but you have the damn'dest looking nose I ever saw on anything except an African anteater.

Obesity

Not all flat tires are on automobiles.

He's so fat he sits on his own lap.

He lives off the fat of the land. He makes girdles.

He's so fat, he used to model for a barrel factory.

She's so fat, when she wears red earrings she looks like the rear end of a bus.

She's so fat that when she goes out walking, most of her body goes on ahead.

Stout people may be easygoing, but it is often difficult to get around them.

He's so fat that when he gets a shoeshine, he has to take the bootblack's word for it.

Fat lady: I want you to measure me for a new dress.
Tailor: You need a surveyor.

—The vest of his suit looked like a venetian blind.
—Covering a bay window, wasn't it?

He: Are you on a diet?
She: I should say not, I'm not fat.
He: Well, if you're not fat, you're certainly well-upholstered.

The overweight woman was being watched by two boys as she stepped on the scales. The machine registered seventy-five pounds. "Gosh, Bill, she's hollow!"

—What's your best exercise for reducing?
—Just move the head slowly from right to left when offered a second helping.

Sex Appeal

She was only a hat manufacturer's daughter, but she was no slouch.

She was only a miner's daughter but, oh! what natural resources.

Teeth

He has teeth like stars. They come out every night.

She has western teeth: full of wide open spaces.

There is something bird-like about her. She has no teeth.

She's got buck teeth. They cost ten bucks for the set.

If you see my husband out there, tell him to look in the icebox when he gets home. His teeth just came from Gimbels.

Try our new dental cream. Try a good paste in the mouth. Watch your teeth. Don't neglect to look at your teeth. Watch 'em. Take 'em out and have a good look at 'em.

—Look at that picture of me when I was six years old.
—Ha, ha, what happened to your front teeth?
—I changed gears on a lollipop.

Ugliness

He's so ugly that when he buys a mirror, the saleslady looks at him and says, "For a friend, I hope."

—Does he have a face that grows on one?
—Yes, there's one like it growing on an ape in the zoo.

She's got one of those faces . . . well, if she refused you a kiss, you would think all the more of her for it.

Weight

You're so skinny, if you closed one eye, you'd pass for a needle.

He: You're thinner.
She: Yes, I've lost so much weight you can count my ribs.
He: Gee, thanks!

ARABS

—What language does that toothless old sheik use?
—Gum Arabic, I guess.

ARGUMENTS

—Say, who do you think you're pushing?
—How many guesses do I get?

ARMY

My hard-boiled first sergeant wasn't born, he was quarried.

Once there was a mean army officer. He was rotten to the corps.

A major in the army called the officers and men out on parade. He made a long speech about a seven-pound baby boy. When he concluded, he said, "I thank you, gentlemen, I thank you for your sincere congratulations on the birth of my son."

A soldier went to his colonel and asked for leave to go home to help his wife with the spring house cleaning. "I don't like to refuse you," said the colonel, "but I've just received a letter from your wife saying that you are no use around the house." The soldier saluted and turned to go. At the door he stopped. "Colonel, there are two persons in this regiment who handle the truth loosely, and I'm one of them. I'm not married."

An army major was drilling the boys. On every command he would say, "Form fours—you, too—right face—you, too—stand at ease—you, too." His superior officer was passing and heard him. Thinking it very funny, he asked him the reason for saying "you, too" after each command. The major told him, "Well, sir, when I first came into the army, I was an ambitious boy. First I got to be a corporal, then a sergeant, then a lieutenant. When I first began to give commands, the boys would say under their breath, "Go to hell," so I would say 'You, too—you, too.'"

ASSURANCE

Hysterical assurance: Don't worry, kid, it's in the baggage.

—No matter what happens, there are always several things I can count on.

—What are they?
—My fingers.

ASTROLOGICAL SIGNS

Man: Some people were born under the sign of Taurus and some people were born under the sign of Capricorn. Now, Tim, where were you born?
Tim: In a hospital.
Man: I know. But under what sign?
Tim: Visiting hours from two to four.

AUTOMOBILES

A nut sundae is taking the car out on the crowded roads.

Nothing is more dangerous than a loose nut at a steering wheel.

Drive carefully and make *(name local town)* a one hearse town.

Automobile suggestion: open cars for tobacco chewers.

It's one of those foreign cars—four in front and four in back.

A used automobile is one that father would like to use.

It's just my luck, now I've got a used car that makes mountains out of molehills.

—You'd never think this car was a second-hand one, would you?
—No, it looks as if you had made it yourself.

Burro: Well, and what might you be?
Second-Hand Car: An automobile. And you?
Burro: A horse.

Learn to drive: ten dollars
How to fold a road map: ten dollars extra.

—I've had a car for years and never had a wreck.
—I've had a wreck for years and never had a car.

Never leave your car parked on a lonely road without locking the doors; someone may swipe your other seat.

One advantage of an auto over an airplane is that when the engine stops so does the auto.

My car is just like a big baby. It won't go any place without a rattle.

(Variation)
Our baby is always crying out for the auto. It rattles so much.

—Hey, the bill on that car has been running now for six months.
—Good, it's the only thing about the car that runs.

—Is that a Jersey cow?
—I didn't see its license.

The driver of a big car pulled alongside a driver in a midget auto, leaned out, and shouted, "Where's your other roller skate?"

—Have you seen my Uncle Ben's new toupee?
—What make car is it?

All the world loves a lover, except when he is driving a car in crowded traffic.

The new cars are going to have welded bodies, but that doesn't mean they will have fewer nuts in them.

Girl: What shall we get Dad for Christmas?
Boy: I hear he's buying us a car; let's get him a chauffeur's outfit!

A devoted son is one who permits his father to drive his own car once in a while.

—How did your father know we used his car yesterday?
—Remember when we came out of the driveway?
—Yes.
—And we felt an awful bump.
—Yes.
—Then we ran over something.
—Yes.
—That was Father.

—What kind of a car have you?
—Oh, a runabout. You know—run about a mile, then stop.

Lady: Give me one gallon of gasoline.
Garage Man: S'matter, madam, got her on a diet?

—I found an oyster in my exhaust this morning.
—How come?
—Been using Shell gasoline.

—Hey, your headlights are out.
—Yes, I put wood alcohol in the radiator and the gosh darn things went blind.

Salesman: Yes, sir. Of all our cars, this is the one we feel confident and justified in pushing.
Customer: That's no good to me. I want one I can ride in.

Customer: The horn on this car is broken.
Salesman: No, it's not; it's just indifferent.
Customer: What do you mean?
Salesman: It just doesn't give a hoot.

The rather boring old professor of history was talking to the bright young thing at a dinner party. "Do you know, my dear," he said, "that Columbus traveled over two thousand five hundred miles on a galleon?" "Go on!" scoffed the young lady. "You don't believe all those stories you hear about cars, do you?"

(Variation)
Columbus was the only man to get three thousand miles out of two galleons.

> Listen my children and you shall hear,
> Of the midnight ride of Paul Revere.
> He jumped in his flivver and turned on the gas.
> The bottom fell out and he broke his arm.

A rich man lying on his deathbed called his chauffeur and said, "Sykes, I am going on a long journey, rugged and worse than you ever drove me."

"Well, sir," consoled the chauffeur, "there's one consolation; it's all downhill."

The genteel motorist had just pulled into the gasoline station for the inevitable gasoline. That being over, the attendant was going through his little ritual,
—Check the oil, sir?
—Naw, it's o.k.
—Got enough water in the radiator?
—Yep, filled up.
—Anything else, sir?
—Yes, would you please stick out your tongue so I can seal this letter?

She's got personality. That's what I like about her. She's beautiful, too. She's blessedly quiet but nevertheless she's got enough pep to suit me. I admire her because she doesn't smoke, but in other ways you could hardly call her old-fashioned. In fact, she's a darned good sport—ready to go any crazy place you think of the day or night. She has charm, grace, chic. She's up to date in every way and yet possesses the solid virtues of her predecessors in popularity. But above all, she's got personality. That's what I like about her. Others seem to like it, too. I was told today that I couldn't get a delivery on her for more than two months.

Accidents

My wife's a magician. She turned a Buick into a lamppost.

She: So your wife likes the Mardyke roadster you won for her?
He: Yes, she'll back it against any car on the highway.

A certain motorist who, when asked if his wife ever talked him into anything, replied: "Yes, only yesterday she talked me into a telephone pole."

Woman: I had a slight accident and bent fender. Can you fix this fender so that my husband won't know it was bent?

Garage Man: No, but I can fix it so that in a coupla days you can ask him how he bent it.

Pleasant company shortens the miles, but one-handed drivers shorten the years.

—What happened to your new car?
—Well, I'll make it short for you: car, caress, careless, carless.

The four wheel brake is a wonderful invention. Now the automobile can stop on top of the pedestrian rather than run over him.

—Are you a careful driver?
—I certainly am. Every accident I've ever had has been the other fellow's fault.

—I hear your car was ruined, Mr. Wilson?
—Smashed to pieces, but I was unharmed.
—What a pity!

After a smash up.
—Hey, what are you doing?
—I'm going to England next week and want to practice driving on the wrong side of the street.

Mae Murray, stage and film star, sojourning in New York, was asked by a friend how long it took her to learn to drive an auto.
Mae: Just ten lessons. All in a week.
Friend: Ten lessons—was that all?
Mae: And three cars.

Buying on Time

They have very polite thieves around here. Someone stole my auto last June and brought it back yesterday with the July and August payments made.

What, I should buy a new car, when I'm still paying installments on the car I traded in on the car I sold in part payment of the car I've got now!?

—Do you have a car?
—Let me see: June, July, August. Yes, I've got a car. It's mine now.

Cost

In an airplane it's the upkeep; but in an automobile it's the turnover.

Friend: I wish I could afford a car like this!
Owner: So do I.

Salesman: This is the kind of a car that actually pays for itself.
Buyer: Well, as soon as that's done, deliver it to me.

If all the bills I've paid for repairs to this car were laid end to end, they would reach from my house to the poorhouse.

It is now estimated that it costs about six cents a mile to run the average U.S. car. To run it some places, such as beyond a red light, the rate is slightly higher.

—Say, how much did you pay for that old car?
—I got it for free from my brother-in-law.
—You were robbed.

I saved fifty percent with a new fitting on the spark plugs, fifty percent with a new carburetor fitting, and another fifty percent using the new ethyl gas. I saved so much that when I went for a ride the other day, I travelled forty miles and the tank ran over.

Hit-and-Run Drivers

If all the hit-and-run drivers in the country were laid end to end it would be a darn good idea if they stayed that way.

Hitchhiking

Her hat was on one side, her clothes rumpled, and her shoes were in shreds. Sympathetic Bystander: Were you knocked down by a motorist? Young Woman: No, picked up.

Parking

I hear they're going to equip all autos in New York with a bike—so you can ride to where you have to park.

—How much does it cost to run your new car?
—Can't say yet, but it cost me twenty-five dollars to leave it standing still today.

Rumble Seats

—Who was driving the car?
—No one. We were all in the rumble seat.

—Her lips quivered, her frame trembled, her body shook, his chin vibrated and he shuddered. Boy, what a love scene!
—Love scene, hell, they were talking in a rumble seat.

Speeding

Farmer: I see you've reduced the fine for speeding from ten to five dollars.
Country Judge: Yes, the motorists were beginning to slow up.

Streamlined Cars

I jumped into what I thought was a rumble—and burned myself on the engine.

(Variation)
Poor father, he can't figure out these new streamlined cars. He got burned when he tried to climb in the rumble seat and it turned out to be the motor.

These streamlined cars make it difficult for the average pedestrian to know whether he's been run over or backed into.

(Variation)
The average guy can't tell whether a streamlined car is coming or going.

Types

An Austin is a kiddie car with mumps.

He throws chewing gum in the streets for Austins to get stuck on.

There's many an Austin mind riding around in a Rolls Royce.

A man is sitting in his Austin and it's jerking. A cop asks him if something is wrong. He says no, "I've just got the hiccups."

I hear they're putting whiskers on the new Fords to make 'em look like Lincolns.

—My father was killed in a feud. [Ford]
—I never would ride in one of those cheap cars.

I see that they're painting the new Chevrolets green. That's so they can hide in the grass while the Fords go by.

—I've named my car "hen."
—Is that so? Chevrolet any eggs?

—Every time I go out in my car, it turns over.
—How is that?
—It's a Paige. [A car no longer manufactured.]

—Jim, you should see what I just picked up. What a body! Lovely lines, fast, damn near shifts for herself and cheap.
—What's her name?
—Her name? Hell, it's a Dodge.

> I sit in my last year's flivver,
> With the mien and air of a lord,
> Though my vertebrae's aquiver,
> I sing like a king in my Ford.
> Though other cars have passed me,
> I turn up my nose and I ride,
> Scorning a vibrating liver
> And other things paining inside.
> Do you think that I'd swap my old flivver
> For a Packard sedan if I could?

Why the thought of it makes me shiver—
You bet your sweet life I would.

(Variation)
I sit in my new little Austin
With the mien and air of a king,
Though three of my ribs are forced in
And my left arm is now in a sling.
Though other cars have passed me,
I turn up my nose as I ride,
Scorning a vibrating liver,
And other things paining inside.
Do you think I'd trade in this baby
For a Packard sedan if I could?
You say you think I would maybe?
You bet your sweet life that I would.

Women Drivers

After she hit me and knocked me down, I said, "What's the matter, can't you blow your horn?" She said, "Yes, but I can't drive."

A woman motorist was driving along a country road when she noticed a couple of repair men climbing telephone poles. "Fools!" she exclaimed to her companion, "they must think I never drove a car before."

An old lady from the country was driving in the city. She went through a traffic light and a cop hollered at her, "Don't you know what those lights are for?" The lady said, "I thought they were street decorations left over from Christmas."

Following an auto accident, in which a woman ran into a man, the man said, "I'll have to take your number." She replied, "That won't do you any good. My husband always answers the phone and he's jealous. Can't we just sit down here and talk a while?"

Women Backseat Drivers

She and her husband have a very nice car. He steers it and she drives it.

One American in five knows how to drive a car—and she prefers the back seat.

A terrible accident happened just outside the theatre. A fellow drove right into the corner store. But it wasn't his fault. His wife fell asleep in the back seat.

BANKS AND BANKERS

A banker is a man who charges you for the use of other people's money and then feels that he has done you a favor.

—I spent hundreds on busts. I bought one of Columbus, one of Lord Nelson, and one of George Washington.
—I had a bust of Chase Bank. It cost me a million.

An Italian bought a bust of Columbus for a hundred dollars, an Irishman bought one of St. Patrick for two hundred dollars, and an Englishman bought one of Shakespeare for three hundred dollars. They were all proudly talking about the worth of their busts. Finally, an American told them about the bust of the U.S. bank that cost him ten grand.

Two friends, one a bank manager and the other a businessman, were sitting in the banker's office. The banker was refusing to give his friend a loan. The businessman went into a long harangue about old times, friendship, the closeness of their children, the days they spent together at school, etc. The banker, who by the end of the spiel was crying, rang a bell. A man entered and the banker told him, "Throw this guy into the alley. He's broken my heart."

BEDS

—The Sultan of Turkey sleeps in a bed eight feet wide and fifteen feet long.
—That's a lot of bunk.

—What is a quadruped?
—Anything with four legs.
—Then I sleep in a quadruped.
—How can a bed be a quadruped; a quadruped is alive.
—Ha, you don't know my bed.

BEGGING

—Boss, will you give me a dime for a sandwich?
—Let's see the sandwich.

—Will you give me a nickel for a cup of coffee?
—Is it hot?

—Gimme a dime, mister, for car fare home.
—Sorry, I've only got a dollar.
—Okay, I'll take a taxi.

—Excuse me, sir, but would you let me have a quarter, so I can join my family?
—I'm always ready to help those in distress. Here's a quarter.
—Oh, thank you, sir, thank you.
—By the way, where is your family?
—In a picture theatre.

A weary and hungry tramp decided to beg a meal at the next farmhouse he came to. A short ways down the road, he came to a little farm that was well-kept and painted. He felt sure that he would get a good meal there. Knocking on the front door, and putting on a woebegone appearance when the lady of the house appeared, he said, "Madam, I haven't had a thing to eat for three days. I would appreciate it if you could give me something to eat." "I'm awfully sorry," she replied, "I just put away the dinner things, and there isn't a thing in the house." As the disappointed tramp turned to leave, he decided to make an attempt to excite the lady's sympathy, so he got down on his hands and knees in the front yard and started to eat the grass. When the lady of the house saw him eating the grass, she said, "Oh, my poor man, don't do that. Come around to the back of the house. The grass is much taller there."

BIBLICAL REFERENCES

Eve was made for Adams Express Company.

How do you call a cop? Say Moses, and the bull rushes.

—I've just heard that one about Moses getting sick on a mountain.
—Sick? You're ridiculous.
—I am not. Doesn't the Bible say the Lord gave Moses two tablets?

—Adam married Eve the moment he saw her.
—Well, why not? He saw what he was getting.

—If you're so smart, could you tell me how Adam got his wife?
—Easy! He bit an apple twice and got a beautiful wife for two bits.

She: A man stopped me in the alley just now.
He: A man you didn't know?
She: Didn't know him from Adam.
He: Surely he had more clothes on.

—Let's play Adam and Eve.
—How do you play it?
—With an apple. Haven't you ever been tempted?
—Not with an apple.

Mother (to precocious daughter): Mary, did you give William half of your apple?
Mary: No, ma'am, I didn't. Eve has been criticized for that little performance ever since it occurred.

He: I'm going in the farming business.
She: Why?
He: It's profitable, and you never know where a garden may lead to. You know, Mother Eve married a gardener.
She: Yeah, but it cost him his job.

BLACKMAIL

—Do you keep all your old love letters?
—Sure, some day I expect them to keep me.

BORROWING AND LENDING

The spring song: I owe everybody I owe.

I always make it a point to borrow money from pessimists. They don't expect to get it back anyway.

—Do the people next door borrow much from you?
—Borrow! Why, I feel more at home in their house than in my own.

—What a lot of friends we lose through their borrowing money from us.
—Yes, it is touch and go with most of them.

—I'm looking for someone to lend me ten dollars.
—Well, it's a nice day, you should make it.

—When are you going to pay me that five you owe me? I've asked you for it four times now.
—Well, I had to ask you ten times before you lent it to me.

—Could I borrow your tux?
—Yes, if you'll return it to Joe Smith and tell him to be sure and give it back to Bill Doakes.

—Hey, what is this? Why are you wearing my overcoat?
—Well, I figured you weren't using it, and I didn't want to get your new suit wet.

—Lend me fifty dollars.
—Sorry, I have only forty.
—Well, then let me have the forty and you can owe me ten.

A fellow was always borrowing. He'd get fifty from Abe, and then get fifty from Jake to pay Abe, and vice versa, until one day he met both of them on the street. "Say, Jake," he said, "will you give Abe the fifty bucks, and in the future leave me out of it."

Someone was calling long distance.
—Jake? Yes, this is Jake. It's probably the connection. I'm Jake. Oh, it's Abe. What's on your mind? *(Pause)* Am I right, this is Abe, talking from Los Angeles, and you want to borrow a hundred dollars? A hundred did you say? Well, you want Jake. Just a minute, I'll try to get him.

(Variation)
—Hello, is that you, Abie?
—Yes, this is Abie.
—You sure this is Abie?

—Yes, this is Abie.
—It does not sound like Abie.
—Yes, I told you, this is Abie.
—Well, Abie, will you please send me the five dollars you
owe me?
—All right, I'll tell Abie when he comes home.

Two men were in a boat that capsized. The one who could swim
held up the one who could not until he thought he could do it no
longer and said:
—Can you float alone, Bill?
—What's the good of talking business at a time like this!

Abe Kabibble was talking to his father-in-law.
—The banker says that if you will write your name across the
back of my note he will give me the five thousand dollars.
—Abe, I'll do better than that. Go back and tell the banker to
write HIS name across the back of your note, and I will give you
the five thousand dollars myself.

Cohen was dying and called for a lawyer. Cohen's wife was in
the room when the lawyer arrived. He told Cohen to conserve
his breath and just state his affairs briefly. Cohen said, "Rosen-
bloom owes me five hundred dollars." His wife said, "Isn't that
wonderful—sensible to the last!" Cohen went on. "Let me see:
Goldstein owes me three hundred dollars." Mrs. Cohen said
again, "Ain't that wonderful—sensible to the last!" Just then
Cohen said, "Oh yes, and to Morris Angel I owe six hundred
dollars." His wife threw up her hands and said, "My God, he's
raving again!"

BROADWAY

The only man who ever got his money out of Broadway is
Thomas Edison.

Did you ever hear of the Broadwayite who was in his four flush
of success?

A Broadway girl doesn't mind living in a fool's paradise, so long
as the fool pays the rent.

A friend is one who shares everything he has with you. A Broadway pal shares everything you have with you.

BUSES

And now the interstate buses seem to be competing successfully
with the railroads every place but at grade crossings.

BUSINESS

He's in the rubber business. He drives a sightseeing bus.

He heard the country was going to the dogs so he started making dog biscuits.

Someone ought to set up a beauty parlor at the race track to lift fallen faces.

Her old man is a hardware dealer, which explains why she is just a bit screwy.

I'd like to go into business making vanishing cream—for bank presidents.

Her people are in the iron and steal business. Her mother irons and her dad steals.

—Gentlemen, I think that we glue manufacturers must stick together.
—The feeling is mucilage.

They put him in jail for competition. He made the same kind of dollar bills as the government did.

This may be a boom period, but then again it may be just the sound of a lot of people being fired.

—Where are the contracts?
—They're down in the blacksmith shop being forged.

The fellow who makes his money by giving calisthenics to stout people is living off the fat of the land.

That guy must be going into the harem business. Outside his garage I saw a sign that read: "Eight gals for a dollar."

The reason some women don't have the same success in business as men is that they can't prop their feet up on the desk.

I'm going into the fur business. I plan to cross raccoons with kangaroos. Then I can have fur coats with pockets.

For years they've been trying to get talking animal crackers and now it looks as if they'll soon have them. A merger is going through between National Biscuit Co. and Warner Brothers.

Boss: Are you the boss of this office?
Clerk: N-n-n-no s-sir.
Boss: Then don't act like a driveling idiot.

—My fortune is made.
—How so?
—I've succeeded in crossing a homing pigeon with a collar button.

(Variation)
Why the deuce doesn't someone cross collar studs with homing pigeons?

—Would you advise a young man to go into any business where he saw a good opening?
—Yes, if he were sure the opening wouldn't get him into a hole.

He's an efficiency expert, one of those guys smart enough to tell you how to run your business but not smart enough to have a business of his own.

He: He made a fortune in crooked dough.
She: Counterfeiter?
He: No, pretzel manufacturer.

—The boss offered me an interest in the business today.
—He did!
—Yes, he said that if I didn't take an interest pretty soon he'd fire me.

—Is it true, dear, that you've turned down the presidency of the General Motors Corporation? Why?
—Yes, I just couldn't take a job where there wouldn't be any chance for advancement.

Two men were talking over their respective shoe businesses.
—I don't see how you can sell those shoes for a dollar. I steal the leather and I steal the laces, and still I can't sell them for a buck.
—Ah, that's it. I steal mine already made.

A certain firm had the following legend printed on its salary receipt forms: "Your salary is your personal business and should not be disclosed to anyone." The new employee, in signing the receipt, added: "I won't mention it to anybody. I'm just as much ashamed of it as you are."

Traveling Salesman: Can I show you some fine articles I have here?
Potential Customer: No, thanks, I'm not interested.
T.S. (opening suitcase): You should at least take a look at what I have here.
P.C.: No . . . definitely no! Close your suitcase.
T.S.: Well, do you mind if I look at them myself?

—Say, what are you anyhow?
—I'm a yachtsman. Most of the time you'll find me in the Atlantic and Pacific.
—In the Atlantic and Pacific?
—Yes, in the Atlantic and Pacific.
—You're not a yachtsman—you're a grocery clerk. [Atlantic and Pacific was once a grocery chain.]

CALIFORNIA

I own a small home in Beverly Hills, one room and five garages.

I own a small home in Beverly Hills, one room and five swimming pools.

All's fair in love, war, and the California weather reports.

California is the only state with two active volcanoes: Mount Lassen and Hiram Johnson.

She is a California girl, one of those orange girls: orange you going to buy me this and orange you going to buy me that?

A scientist says there is no such thing as a perfect climate. Californians say there is no such thing as a perfect scientist.

Bragging about living on the west coast.
—I went back there for a visit and even the tires rode better as soon as I filled them with that good old California air.

In that earthquake, when the first tremor happened, I was on my front porch in Beverly Hills. When the second one happened, I was in the train depot downtown.

An easterner visiting on the west coast heard nothing but praise for the wonderful climate. By the time he reached California he felt he knew what heaven must be like. One day he stopped to admire some huge apples in an orchard. "What makes these apples grow so large?" "Oh, the climate, the climate," said his guide. Continuing his walk he saw some large redwood trees. He asked why they grew so large. "The climate, the wonderful climate," his guide remarked. "Well," remarked the easterner, "they aren't so wonderful after all. We have buildings back east thirty stories high, and not a single elevator in them." "But how do you reach the top?" asked his guide. "Oh climate, climate," said the easterner walking away.

(Variation)
—California, that's a wonderful place. Out there we raise the biggest oranges in the world and have the finest vineyards in the world. Do you know what does that?
—No, what is it?
—Climate, climate. And the apples we grow there—best apples in the world. Climate, that's climate.
—Well, we have a hotel on Broadway, ten stories high and there're no steps or elevators.
—Now, that's silly. How do people get to their rooms?
—Climate, climate.

CENSORS

—What's a censor?
—A censor is a man who sees three meanings in a joke that has only two.

CHARITY

I wrote a check for charity, but since I wanted it to be anonymous, I didn't sign it.

Mary: I got bighearted this morning and gave a bum five dollars.
Carol: What did your husband say?
Mary: Thanks.

A bum sat down in a restaurant, ordered a meal, ate it, and couldn't pay for the bill. The manager got tough with him and threatened to wring his neck. A drunk sitting nearby called the manager over and told him that he'd pay the other's bill. As the drunk reached for his wallet, the bum got up to leave. The drunk, upon discovering that he didn't have enough to pay for both bills, called out to the manager, "Hey, throw out that bum and give me fifty cents change."

—If you had two hundred dollars and I was broke, would you give me a hundred?
—Soitanly!
—And if you had two shirts and I none, you'd give me one?
—Naw!
—No?
—Naw. I got two shoits.

CHICAGO

The guy from Chicago said, "Have a shot on me."

A Chicagoan's home is any place where he hangs his gat.

In Chicago they are laying down their arms, but they still put up their hands.

Perhaps Mexico would entertain a proposal to swap Lower California for Chicago.

Law enforcement will receive its greatest boost when murder in Chicago is treated as seriously as parking alongside a fire hydrant.

Another gangster has been arrested in Chicago. Probably for parking his machine gun in front of a fireplug.

She was very stylish and dressed with taste. She reminded me of Chicago: well-dressed beef.

I heard that a sculptor is dissatisfied with the statues in Chicago. They would certainly appear more realistic with their hands in the air.

A Chicago bandit held up a man on his way to the dentist, so that he was unable to keep his appointment. Some of those bandits are not bad at heart.

CHILDREN

One trouble with the rising generation is that it doesn't rise early enough.

—My, my, that fellow has been married for only ten years and he has ten children.
—Yes, he's gone stork mad.

Babies

Never slap a baby's face, nature provided a better place.

We just had a baby boy at our house. Given the fuss my wife is making, you'd think it came from Paris.

Then there's the guy who became father of such an ugly son that he went down to the zoo and tossed rocks at the stork.

—I change my clothes twice a day.
—I have a sis who changes ten times a day . . . age six months.

My mother wrote me that my baby brother has three legs. Her letter says he grew an extra foot since I left!

—Does little Johnny look like his father?
—Oh, no. My husband would be furious.

Fat Man (fondling baby): What do you think of my son, Jim?
Jim (surveying father): Well, I'd say that he was a stave off the old barrel.

Friend: Who does your little son look like?
Happy father: His eyes are mine, the nose is my wife's, and his voice, I think, he got from our auto horn.

"I hope your children are acrobats," snarled the villain to the hero. And lo and behold, several months later the doctor announced to our hero that he was the father of a bouncing baby boy.

—My friend Jones has a bouncing baby boy.
—How do you know?
—I dropped it.

—We've had a miracle at our house.
—What is it?
—Mother says a fairy brought a baby.

—The baby swallowed a bottle of ink!
—Incredible!
—No. Indelible!

—And what would you say, Fifi, if I told you that I used to hold you on my lap when you were a baby?
—I would say that you were all wet, monsieur!

—Can you crawl on your hands and knees?
—Sure I can.
—Well, don't. It's babyish.

—What did the boss do when you told him it was triplets?
—He promoted me to the head of my department.
—What department are you in?
—Production.

She: We're going to have a little boy at my sister's house.
He: How do you know it's going to be a boy?
She: Last year, sister was sick and they had a girl, and now my brother-in-law is sick.

Discipline

Pappa, Mamma, and son, Willie, were crossing the ocean. Willie had done something for which his mother thought he needed correction, but not feeling equal to the occasion she turned to her henpecked husband. "John," she said, "can't you speak to Willie?" Pappa replied in a thin, weak voice, "Howdy, Willie."

Fathers and Young Sons

I took my son to the fair and asked him if he'd like to go on the merry-go-round. He said, "I don't mind, Pop, if it will amuse you."

First Kid: So you asked your father a very unusual question?
Second Kid: Yeah, one he could answer.

A little kid (talking to another): Aw, there ain't no devil. It's like Santa Claus. It's your father.

Mother to son: Don't argue with me. I knew you when you were only a wicked gleam in your father's eye.

Boy: Pap, I saved a dime today. I ran all the way home behind the street car.
Pap: Why didn't you run behind a taxi and save a dollar?

Little Archie: Gee! pop, I just swallowed a worm!
Anxious Father: Take a drink of water—quick! quick!—and wash it down.
Little Archie: Aw, no, let him walk.

I saw a little boy crying and asked him what was the matter. He sniffled and told me his mamma had just had a little baby. I said, "Why, that's no reason for you to cry. You should be glad." He said, "Aw, you don't know my dad, he blames me for everything."

Just imagine it: married . . . in a little vine-clad cottage. A little Lowry around the house—a little son and heir—copying all his daddy's little tricks. Imitating his daddy's little mannerisms, absorbing all my little habits. Ha . . . Absorbent Junior.

Little Bobby had a habit of telling fibs, so on Washington's Birthday, as a shining example, his father told him the story of the famous cherry tree. "Well, Bobby," he concluded at the finish, "what would you have said if you had cut down the tree and your daddy had asked you about it?" "I'd have said brother Jack did it" was the quick reply.

"Paddy has been run over and killed," the mother said to her son. He took it very quietly, finished his dinner with appetite and spirits unimpaired. All day it was the same. But five minutes after he had gone up to bed, there echoed through the house a shrill and sudden lamentation. His mother rushed upstairs with solicitude and sympathy. "Nurse says," he sobbed, "that Paddy has been run over and killed." "But, dear, I told you that at dinner, and you didn't seem troubled at all." "No, but I didn't realize you said Paddy. I thought you said Daddy!"

Innocence

Friend: What is your new brother's name?
Little Jane: I don't know yet. We can't understand a word he says.

Mother *(to young son):* You don't seem to like the new governess.
Son: No, Mom, I hate her. I'd like to grab her and bite her on the neck like daddy does.

Man: Well, my boy, what did you get for your birthday?
Three-year-old: Aw, I got a little red chair but it ain't much good. It's got a hole in the bottom of it.

A kid was standing at the stage door begging and crying: "Ma's dead, Pa's dead, all my sisters and brothers are dead—and if I don't bring somethin' home, they'll kick the stuffin' out of me."

A young boy was bathing in the reservoir in the park. I said, "Don't bathe in that water. Don't you know that's the water we drink?" He said, "Gee, mister, I ain't using any soap."

Elsie *(aged five):* I do hope some Dutchman will marry me when I grow up!
Aunt Mary: Why, dear?
Elsie: 'Cause I want to be a duchess!

A little boy, seeing his mother greet a clergyman, asked her, "Mommy, who's that?" The mother answered, "That's the man who married me, Tommy." The kid was silent for a few minutes and then said, "Well, Mommy, then what's Pop doing in our house?"

Boy: Mother, is father in the fruit business?
Mother: No, son. What put that idea into your head?
Boy: Well, when he took me for a walk the other day, he met Uncle Harry, and all they talked about was peaches, pippins, and dates.

I went to the zoo, strolled around, and came to the bird house. A little kid was studiously eyeing a huge bird. She stood there watching and watching. So intent was she that I finally asked her:
—What are you studying this bird for, little girl?
—Well, I just found out there ain't no Santa Claus, and now I'm here to investigate this stork proposition.

A young boy stole a ride in his big brother's rumble seat. His brother picked up a girl and they went for a long ride in the country, where they parked. The next day, the kid was out in his little wagon and saw a playmate, a girl. He asked her to come for a ride with him. She got in and he put his little arm around her. They rode for a little way, then he leaned over and gave her a kiss. A little further and he stopped the wagon, scratched his head, and muttered, "Gee, what do I do next?"

Just as I was leaving the stage door after the last show, a little girl met me. She said, "I know who you are." I said, "Oh, who am I?" She said, "You're Ed Lowry." I said, "You're right." She said, "Tell me, Mr. Lowry, how old are you?" So I told her. She then said, "Tell me, are you married?" I replied, "Yes, I'm married." She then asked me, "Do you go home every night after the show?" I said, "Yeah, I go home every night." Turning around, she called, "Mom, is there anything else you want to know?"

Bobbie, a young lad who hailed from a very large family, was allowed to see his sick father. He was told that he would have to be very quiet. At the hospital, Bobbie sat in silence for a long while and looked at his father. Finally, he spoke.
—Well, Dad, I guess I had better go. Have I bothered you any?
—No, son.
—Are you sure, Dad?
—Yes, son.
—Well, can I come back sometime, Dad?
—Why, sure, son.
—Well, Dad, before I go, won't you let me see the baby?

In School and Sunday School

The teacher, noticing little Timmy moving his jaw, said, "Give me what's in your mouth." The kid said, "I can't. It's a toothache."

Teacher: If Columbus were alive today would he be looked on as a remarkable man?

Billy: Yes, he'd be five hundred years old.

The teacher was a very pretty young thing and Sonny had been misbehaving at school all day. Finally, she said, "Sonny, you stay in after school tonight." Sonny replied, "Okay, Toots, it's a date."

Mother: Well, children, what did you learn at Sunday School today?

Son: Kitty learned to wiggle her ears and I learned to whistle through my teeth.

> Please, sir, may I leave the room?
> The teacher answered, No.
> But the joke was on the teacher
> 'Cause I didn't have to go.

An inspector, examining a class in religious knowledge, asked the following question of a little girl, intending it for a catch: "What was the difference between Noah's Ark and Joan of Arc?" He was not a little surprised when the child, answering, said: "Noah's Ark was made of wood and Joan of Arc was never made."

Mothers

Alice, you've been a very naughty girl. Go to the vibrator this minute and give yourself a good shaking!

Little Girl: Now kin I go out and play?

Mother: Not with that dirty neck.

Little Girl: But maw, she's a nice girl.

Fond Mother: How much do you charge for taking children's photographs?

Photographer: Five dollars a dozen.

Fond Mother: You'll have to give me more time; I have only ten now.

A little girl went to the store for a loaf of bread. Her mother gave her the money. The girl lost the money on her way to the store. *(Repeat several times that she returned home and told her mother that the money was lost.)* Finally, her mother angrily said: "If you lose the money this time, I'll kill you." The child came back and said she had lost the money—and her mother killed her.

When small Margaret entered the first grade, she found herself in a class where the foreign element was in the majority. Most of these children were dirty, and the teacher was, of course, glad to have one clean pupil. Wishing to impress this fact upon the class, she said one day to Margaret: "My! but I am glad to see you looking so nice and clean, Margaret." "Well," observed Margaret seriously, "you'd be clean, too, if you had my mamma to wash you."

Parents

—There's something dove-like about our child.
—Yes, he's pigeon-toed.

He's a very nice boy, but a little funny. Just before he was born, his folks had a terrible row. His mom wanted a little boy and his dad wanted a little girl. But he came, and they're both satisfied.

Man: You look happy.
Child: I feel happy. I just took part in a pie-eating contest and won first prize after swallowing twenty pies.
Man: You say you just swallowed twenty pies?
Child: Yes, sir, but don't tell any one.
Man: Why not?
Child: Because I'm on my way home, and if my folks find out about it, they may not give me any supper.

Child: God gives us our daily bread, doesn't He, Mamma?
Mother: Yes, dear.
Child: And Santa Claus brings the presents?
Mother: Yes, dear.
Child: And the stork brings the babies?
Mother: Yes, dear.
Child: Then, tell me, Mamma, just what is the use of having Papa hang around?

Prayers

A lazy kid typed his prayers and pasted them on his bedroom wall. Every night, he said, "There they are, Lord, read 'em."

A kid was saying his prayers.
—Please God, make Sally stop throwing stones at me. By the way, I've mentioned this before . . . so please note.

Did you ever hear the story about Deacon Miller's little nephew, Jimmy, who was racing to school one Monday morning not long ago? "Oh, Lord," prayed the boy as he almost flew along the ground, "please don't let me be late for school." Thirty seconds later he tried it again. "Please, Lord, don't let me be late to school." A minute later he was at it again. "Oh, Lord," he breathed, "don't let me be late for school." Suddenly Jimmy tripped and fell headlong into a puddle. He arose, brushed himself off and looked up at the sky. "Listen," he muttered angrily, "did I ask You to shove me?"

(Variation)
A small lad hurrying to school one morning began to pray for aid. "Dear God, please don't let me be late; please help me to hurry!" He traveled but a short distance when he stumbled and fell, exclaiming: "Damn it, you didn't have to shove me!"

Precocity

Dad *(to precocious son):* What's wrong?
Son: I've just had a scene with your wife.

—Be careful now and don't hurt those kittens.
—It's all right, Dad, I'm carrying them by their stems.

—When I was your age I'd think nothing of walking ten miles.
—I don't think much of it either.

The doctor showed little Jimmy the new baby and said, "Look what they sent you from heaven." Jimmy said, "They musta kicked him out."

—Has your baby learned to talk yet?
—Sure, now we're trying to keep him quiet.

The father said to his son, "You've got a baby sister down at the hospital." The kid replied, "What's the matter; is she sick already?"

"Billy broke doll," sobbed little Emily. "How did he break it, dear?" asked her mother. "I hit him on the head with it."

Aunt: Come, Sonny, kiss your old auntie and I'll give you a nickel.
Boy: Naw, I get that at home just for taking castor oil.

(Variation)
—Come, Sonny, kiss auntie.
—Haw, why Mom? I ain't done nuthin'.

A man fell overboard and yelled, "Help, I can't swim!" A kid leaned over the rail and said, "Ya picked a hell of a place to learn."

Father: Son, don't you think it's time for little boys to go to bed?
Son: I couldn't say. I have no little boys.

Iceman *(entering kitchen with a cake of ice):* Hello, sonny.
Little Boy: Hey, when you call me that, smile.

Boy: Daddy, if you'll give me ten cents, I'll tell you what the ice-man said to Mamma.
Dad *(all excited):* Okay, son, here's your dime.
Boy: He said, "Do you want any ice today, lady?"

Mother: If you are really good, I'll give you an apple.
Modern Child: How long do I have to be good—and how big is the apple, Mamma?

Proud Mother: Yes, he's a year old now, and he's been walking since he was eight months.
Bored Visitor: Really? He must be awfully tired.

Voice from the Next Room: George, are you teaching that parrot to swear?
George: No, mother, I'm only telling him what not to say.

Father *(to daughter coming in at 3 A.M.):* Good morning, child of Satan.
Daughter *(sweetly):* Good morning, father.

Son: Quick, Dad, there's a black cat in the dining room.
Father: Black cats are lucky, son.
Son: This one is; he's eating your dinner.

A little boy walked away from home for about an hour, felt lonesome, and walked back into the room where his parents, who hadn't even missed him, were sitting. "Well," he said, "I see you've got the same old cat."

Bobby: Mama, my new suit is tighter than my skin.
Mother: Why, Bobby, that can't be. The suit goes over your skin.
Bobby: But, mother, I can sit down without tearing my skin.

(Variation)
He: When I passed your house last night, I heard loud voices.
She: Father was angry because the tailor had sent him a pair of trousers tighter than his skin.
He: That's impossible. How could your father's trousers be tighter than his skin?
She: Because, you silly, father can sit down in his skin but he can't sit down in those trousers.

Father: Do you realize that when Lincoln was your age, he was chopping wood and helping his parents?
Son: Yeah, and when he was your age he was president.

Aunt: What will you do when you grow up to be a big woman like your mother?
Small Daughter: Diet!

—Papa, are you growing taller all the time?
—No, my child. Why do you ask?
—'Cause the top of your head is poking up through your hair.

Stern Father: Johnny, I'd like to go through a whole day without once scolding or punishing you.
Johnny: Well, Dad, you have my consent.

An old lady indignantly said to a little boy, "Stop sniffing like that! Can't you do something with your nose?" He replied, "Yes, ma'am, I can keep it out of other folks' business."

Mother *(to four-year-old daughter):* You go right upstairs and wash your face and neck.
Daughter: Who?

Lady: Little boy, why aren't you in school?
Little Boy: Hell, lady, I ain't but three years old.

Boy *(to his father):* Dad, can you sign your name with your eyes shut?
Father: Certainly.
Boy: Well, shut your eyes and sign this school report card.

A father was teaching his young son arithmetic. The boy couldn't add two and one. So the father asked, "How much does Daddy and Mommy and your baby brother make?" The boy answered, "Two—and one to carry."

Son: Daddy, help me with this sum, will ya, please?
Father: Oh, Sonny, you must do it yourself. If I helped you with it, it wouldn't be right.
Son: Well, maybe it wouldn't but at least you could do your best.

Mother: What took place in class today?
Son: The teacher asked all the children where they were born.
Mother: What did you tell her?
Son: Well, little Joey said he was born at the Women's Hospital. I didn't want her to think I was a sissy, so I told her I was born at Yankee Stadium.

Three boys, aged ten, seven, and five, ransacked the pantry and found a bottle. They each took a taste. The oldest asked, "What is it?" The second one answered, "Scotch" (*or:* whiskey), and the little one said, "Yeah, and it's been cut a couple of times."

A young boy asked his father, "Pop, will I look like you when I grow up?" The father replied, "I hope so, son." The boy studied his father for a minute, heaved a sigh, and said, "Well, I won't have to grow up for a long time, will I, Pop?"

—How old are you?
—I dunno.
—What day were you born on?
—What do you care? You ain't gonna gimme any present.

—Why don't hens have teeth?
—They don't need them; they have bills for their teeth.
—Aunt Kate has a bill for her teeth. Is that why they call her an old hen?

Little Janie: Mother, if baby swallowed the goldfish, would he be able to swim like one?
Mother: Oh, my heavens, no, child. They'd kill him.
Little Janie: But they didn't.

A girl's kid brother was looking on while a young man was wooing his sister. Finally, the man said, "Look, as man to man, here's two bucks, now scram." The kid said, "Listen, sport, as man to man, I want to watch."

A little boy helped an old lady across the street. Reaching the other side, she wanted to give him a dime, but he said, "No, lady, I'm a boy scout and that is my good deed for the day. Scouts don't take pay. But my little brother here, he's not a scout."

A small boy was leaning against a wall and smoking. A woman saw him and asked, "Does your father know that you smoke?" The boy looked up at her nonchalantly and asked, "You're a married woman, aren't you?" She replied, "Yes," and the boy said, "Does your husband know you speak to strange men?"

He was very quiet during the first part of the dinner, and everyone forgot that he was there. As dessert was being served, however, the host told a story. When he had finished and the laughter had ceased, his little son exclaimed delightedly: "Now, father, tell the other one."

"Grandma," said little Willie to his visiting grandmother, "please make a noise like a frog." "Why, what on earth can you mean?" exclaimed the astonished grandmother. "Well," explained Willie, "I heard Papa tell Mama last night that we'll get fifty thousand dollars when you croak!"

The little boy was gazing pensively at a gooseberry bush. "What's the matter, darling?" asked his mother. "Have gooseberries any legs, mother?" asked the little chap. "No, darling, of course they haven't," said his mother. The boy's look became more pensive than ever. "Then I guess I must have swallowed a caterpillar," he said.

Our little girl is at an age now where she wants to know why. Why? Everything is Why? The other day my wife was powdering her face and the kid said, "Mommy, why do you do that?" My wife answered, "I'm powdering my face." "Why?" asked my daughter. "Honey, I put powder on to make me beautiful." The kid said, "Mommy, why doesn't it work?"

About midnight, I heard footsteps in my little boy's room. So I snuck in, and there he was pacing the floor, up and down, with his hands clasped behind his back and the most worried expression on his face. I said, "Sonny, what's wrong?" He replied, "Well, here I am five, going on six, and what the hell have I got to show for it?"

—What's the matter, little girl?
—Two boys were fightin' and I got struck with a stone.
—That's it; the innocent bystander always gets hurt.
—But I don't know as I was an innocent bystander. I was what they was fightin' about!

A mother told her little boy, just as he was going outside, to be careful and not go into anyone's house where there was a sign on the door, because there was an epidemic of smallpox in the neighborhood. When he came back, his mother asked him if he had been playing with Billie Smith. He said, "No, I didn't play with him. There's a sign on his door that says, 'hemstitching.'"

A kid wanted a nickel for peanuts and candy. His father, afraid that he'd make himself sick, told him he couldn't have a nickel. A little later, the father heard him saying to his mother, "Look, Mom, we're going to play elephants at the zoo and we want you to play with us." His mother said, "What can I do?" The boy answered, "You can be the lady who gives the animals peanuts and candy."

A little Canadian boy had never seen a Negro before, so when he saw one he asked his uncle, "Why does this woman black her face?" "She doesn't; that's her natural color" was the reply. "Is she black like that all over?" the boy pursued. "Why, yes," said the uncle. The boy looked up beaming. "Gee, uncle," he exclaimed, "you know everything, don't you?"

A little girl was standing next to her mother, who was talking to a friend about a newborn. The little girl said, "Please, mother, may I see the new baby?" The mother said, "You can't go to see the new baby." The little girl began to insist and her mother said, "Now don't ask me again. I said no, you can't go to see the new baby." The little girl replied, "Why, Mom, is it catching?"

My kid is running around with the lawyer's kid who lives next door. As a result, he keeps learning legal phrases. The other day, the nurse was going to spank him and he dared her. So she said, "I'll wait till your father gets home and then I'll tell him to spank you." "All right," he said, "If you do, I'll get an injunction from my mom, and a stay of execution. And then I'll finally get it annulled by my grandma."

They were standing toe to toe, exchanging verbal blows that would have done credit to a professional heckler. Each lad held an apple in his hand about which the argument seemed to revolve. "You are impolite!" one youth observed heatedly. "Here I offered you the choice of my two apples and you took the biggest. Say, I'll betcha if you had offered 'em to me I'd a taken the littlest one." "Well," was the answer, "If you'd a' done that you'd have the same one you got now, wouldn't you?" "Yes." "Then, for goodness sakes, what are you bellyachin' about?"

A little boy had a ten dollar bill. He went into a store to get it changed and asked for five one dollar bills and one five. Then he counted the money, went into a second store, and asked the man at the counter to give him change for the five dollar bill. Leaving, he again counted the money, entered a third store, and asked the fellow to give him some silver for two dollar bills. On the street, while he was counting, the man from the first store appeared and asked him why he was trying to change money all over the place. The little kid said, "Well, somebody's got to make a mistake."

The other day I met a young lady I used to go to school with. We talked for a while, and then I offered to take her home in my car. We went to her house and sat down on the couch. A few minutes later, I put my arm around her and stole a little kiss. But just as I did, a little girl popped out from under the couch and said, "Aha, I seen ya! I seen ya! I'm gonna snitch." I said, "Look, here, you don't say anything," and I pulled out my wallet. But all I had was a two dollar bill, which I gave to her. She pulled out a little purse and handed me a dollar bill. I said, "What's that for?" She said, "That's a dollar change. All I charge is a dollar—same price for everybody."

The Browns had been trying to break their son of saying naughty words. "I don't know where he picks 'em up," said Mrs. Brown; "he certainly doesn't hear them at home." Lo and behold, their son was invited to a party at the actor Jackie Cooper's home. Every day for two weeks preceding the party, his mother drilled it into him that if he said one naughty word at the party, the nurse would bring him right home, and he'd get a spanking he'd remember for the rest of his life. Saturday finally arrived, and he was all dressed up. Off he went to the party. He hadn't been gone half an hour when the nurse brought him home. His mother didn't say a word. She just dragged him into the bedroom and started to spank him with a brush, first the bristles and then the wood side. *(Action of slapping and turning hand over)* She gave it to him good. When she couldn't spank him any more, she stood him up and shouted, "Now what did you say? What did you say at the party?" He cried, "Leave me alone. The damn party's next Saturday!"

Rambunctious Behavior

He got into more things than a head of lettuce in a sandwich shop.

What a kidder! Only yesterday he put chloroform in his granny's smelling salts.

Friend: How's your little boy?
Mother: 'e's always up to mischief. I expect 'e'll soon be followin' 'is father's fingerprints.

The possibility of a landslide so intimidated the inhabitants of a small village that one couple decided to send their son, aged nine, to an uncle until the danger had passed. Three days later they received a telegram: "Am returning boy. Please send landslide instead."

Two old college chums, Dan and Hal, met for the first time in many years. Dan was married and a family man to boot. He invited Hal, still wearing the smile of a bachelor, out to his house for supper to meet the wife and Junior, his five-year-old offspring. At the house Hal did everything he could to amuse the kid, including giving him his watch to play with. It was while Hal was in one room talking to the missus that Dan came running in from another where he'd been playing with Junior and exclaimed, "Gosh, Junior is going to be an auctioneer when he grows up. Ha! Ha! Ha!" "What makes you think so?" queried Hal. "Why, he just put your watch under the hammer!"

CHRISTMAS

Christmas was a huge success at our house. Somebody left a roller skate on the stoop, and an installment collector stepped on it.

Merry Christmas to you. If you will send me five dollars, Yuletide me over the holidays.

CITY SLICKERS AND COUNTRY HICKS

She's just a simple country girl, more simple than country.

I was out in the country and stopped at a town that was so quiet, it was the first cemetery I ever saw with paved streets.

City Visitor: My, but those are delicious strawberries you have here. Do you use fertilizer for them?
Farmer: Nope, just sugar and cream.

First Hitch Hiker: I sure hate the city. I'm always getting into trouble.

Second Hitch Hiker: How come?
First Hitch Hiker: Oh, I keep forgetting myself and hail taxicabs.

A father bought his son and daughter-in-law a ranch next door, which was an eighty mile ride over the range. Four years later, the father paid his son a visit and asked him about his wife. The son said that the first year she broke her leg and he had to shoot her.

Do you know the story of the city fellow who went into the country and all cut and bleeding came running up to a farmer and said, "My God! One of those big black snakes has been chasing me for half an hour." The farmer replied, "What are you all excited about? Those snakes are not poisonous." The city fellow said, "Hell, after he chases me about ten miles through bushes and up and down trees and I jump a fifty foot embankment and nearly break my neck—is he supposed to poison me?"

A city girl was invited by a country boy to take a look about the farm. After a while they came upon a couple of cows. As cows sometimes will, they were rubbing noses. "I'd like to do that," said the country boy. "Go ahead," said the city girl, "it's your cow."

A city slicker, wanting to outshine a country boy well-known for his strength, got off his horse and said, "Say, I've come for a showdown. I hear you're a very tough fellow." The country boy, without saying a word, picked him up and threw him over a fence and right out of the barnyard. The slicker picked himself up and looked back. The strong man shouted, "Is there anything else you'd like to know?" The other fellow said, "Yes. Would you mind throwing my horse out here?"

I invited my cousin, a hillbilly from Arkansas, to visit me in the big city. The town he comes from doesn't have sidewalks. They just swing from bough to bough. His four brothers had to hold him down while they put shoes on him. He hadn't read a newspaper since the one I sent him announcing the Armistice. The last time I saw that kid, he was tending sheep, sitting for hours reading the label on an old tomato can. When he arrived in New York, I showed him around. We went into a drugstore; he leaned over the glass counter and started staring at something. I looked and he said, "Hey, what are these things?" I said, "Those are toothbrushes. You brush your teeth with them." He said, "Gosh, what will they think of next?"

CLEANLINESS

Say, it looks like Saturday here. Everybody looks so clean.

Hubby: Our water bill is higher than usual.
Wife: Of course! Weren't there five Saturday nights in last month?

Voice Over the Phone: Is this the lady who washes?
Society Snob: Indeed, I should say not!
Phone Voice: Why, you dirty thing!

He: How long does it take you to dress in the morning?
She: 'Bout half an hour.
He *(bragging):* It only takes me ten minutes.
She: Ha . . . but I wash.

CLOCKS, WATCHES, AND TIME

This is a wonder watch. Every time I look at it, I wonder what the time is.

—I woke up last night with the feeling that my watch was gone. So I got up and looked for it.
—Was it gone?
—No, but it was going.

Sound: (CUCKOO-CUCKOO-CUCKOO)
Louie: Hm . . . three o-clock.
Sound: (CUCK—)
Sammy: Hm . . . three-thirty.

CLOTHING

Have you ever heard of clothing sickness? The tongue is coated and your breath comes in short pants.

They're making bathrobes from bananas, just a little thing to slip on when you're in a hurry.

—Pray, why the large handkerchief?
—For crying out loud.

Bathing Suits

Have you seen the new bathing suits? No hooks on 'em, but plenty of eyes.

I know a girl who had a terrible accident in her bathing suit. She went swimming in it.

Summer Girl *(at seashore):* A penny for your thoughts.
Her Escort: I was just thinking that if a moth had only your bathing-suit to eat, it would starve to death.

Cloth

"Give a girl an inch," says June, "and she'll make a dress out of it."

This is a cotton suit. *(Whispers)* It's really wool. I just say cotton to fool the moths.

Cost

Cora says she got her fur coat on time—and what a time it was!

Like this suit? I got it cheap. A dollar down and a sheriff a week.

Tailor *(measuring a new customer):* What about a small deposit, sir?
Customer: Just as you like. Put one in if it's smart.

—Why, this suit cost me a hundred and fifty dollars, custom made.
—You mean costoomuch.

It's uncanny when you think of it that all the silk used in women's dresses comes from a little bit of a worm; and some big worm has to pay for them.

I went into a store to buy a pair of trousers. When I haggled with the salesman, he threw up his arms and cried, "You're robbing me! Just take the trousers for nothing!" I said, "In that case, give me two pairs."

I've been asked to announce that the week after next, for the benefit of the married ladies, we will hold a "Break Your Husband's Heart" Revue. At that time, we will stage a fashion show of two and three thousand dollar fur coats. All the ladies are invited to bring their husbands, and there will be plenty of nurses to carry them out of the theatre.

Dirty Clothes

There's a dress specially recommended. Beer stains won't show.

It doesn't seem right. The coat and pants do all the work, and the vest gets all the gravy.

—What are those spots on your lapel? Gravy?
—No, that's rust. They said this suit would wear like iron.

—Where be my overalls, Mirandy?
—They be a standin' up in the carner, Pappy.

—I like that dress. What color is it?
—This? It's pink. *(Spit.)*
—Say, good thing it isn't purple.

Fashion

—What do you think of the fashions? Do you like tight skirts?
—Naw, I think women oughta leave likker alone.

This is what's known as a cocktail jacket. Of course, if you drink beer, you won't have a bit of use for it.

My idea of the really collegiately dressed fellow is one who has to take two steps before his pants start moving.

You talk about a swell place . . . they even put on riding habits to play horseshoes.

Here's a guy who's a real smart dresser. He likes to be sure of his color schemes. He even threw over his girl 'cause she was a blonde and her hair didn't match his suit.

> In days of old when knights were bold,
> Girls dressed like old Mother Hubbard,
> But nowadays the girls are bold,
> They dress like Old Mother Hubbard's cupboard.

Fit

These shoes are awfully tight, but they'll do in a pinch.

—I had this suit tailored in London.
—Where were you at the time?

Irving, he's a great boy. Look at that suit, how it fits. Say, Irving, why don't you buy it?

Gushing Clerk: That coat fits you like a glove, sir.
Purchaser *(dryly):* So I see. The sleeves cover my hands.

—Where did you get those trousers? They fit you like a glove.
—That's just why I'm kicking about them; they should fit like trousers.

A fellow, accompanied by his wife, went in to buy a suit. *(Ad-lib about store and buying a suit.)* The wife noticed that one shoulder was bigger than the other and called it to the attention of the salesman. He said, "What do you mean?" She said, "Just look! His left shoulder is lower than his right." The salesman replied, "Can I help it if the floor slants?"

Hat Exchanges

I've been eating in this restaurant so long, I've got my own hat back.

He's a fastidious dresser. He gets all his hats at the delicatessen.

(Variation)
He's a fastidious dresser. He gets all his hats at Lindy's restaurant.

—That's a nice looking hat you have on.
—It should be. It's been cleaned twice and changed once at Macy's.

—Why did you give that checkroom girl a dollar tip?
—Look at the hat she gave me!

I like the sign in my favorite restaurant: All you can eat and any hat that fits you for sixty cents.

—That's a good-looking hat, Bill.
—I bought it five years ago, had it cleaned three times, changed it twice in restaurants, and it's still as good as new.

—Gimme a dime, will ya, guv? I wanna go into this classy restaurant.
—Why, you poor fellow, what can you get for a dime in that high-toned place?
—A cup of coffee, some silverware, a linen napkin, and a new hat.

Scant Clothing

The shorter the skirts, the longer they look.

The coeds' clothes seem to be going to their heads.

I'm dying to see what the well-dressed girl will leave off this season.

A doctor says that since clothing has become less confining, girls who dance seldom have a stitch in the side. Nor on the back, either.

He: Say, has that girl lost her dress or am I seeing things?
She: Both!

Joe: Isn't Yvonne's new gown a perfect song?
Hal: Yes, sweet and low.

—They say girls dress merely to please men.
—Well, it certainly takes very little to please me.

The fashion critics say that women are wearing fewer clothes nowadays. If you don't believe it, look at the figures.

Now that some of the women are wearing longer skirts, we miss a great many of the old joints.

The old-fashioned wife used to ask her husband to button up her back. The modern one asks him to powder it.

—How long should a girl of twenty wear her skirts?
—You can generally wear them longer at home than you can if you go out to work.

—Do you think I look all right in my new gown, dear?
—Hm! Yes, but I would suggest that if possible you get in a little further.

He: That's one of those hand-grenade dresses.
She: What do you mean hand-grenade dresses?
He: Pull the pin and it's every man for himself.

He: I'm giving a party tonight, and the girl with the most daring costume will get a prize.
She: Whoopee! I'll be there with bells on.

She: Didn't I see you at a party last week?
He: Did you wear a red dress?
She: No, my dress was checked.
He: No, I wasn't at that party.

(Variation)
Sorority Girl: What kind of a dress did Betty wear to the party last night?
Frat Boy: I don't remember. I think it was checked.
Sorority Girl: That must have been SOME party.

Did you hear the latest? Girls are going to dress according to the city they live in. For instance, a girl from Greensburg will wear a green dress, a girl from Brownsville a brown dress, a girl from Pinkton a pink dress. She'll sure be in a mess if she lives in Bare Mountain.

Men's Clothes

Wear socks that can be put on from either end and save time.

He wears athletic clothes: the colors run and the prices jump.

—Why are you so fidgety?
—I'm wearing athletic underwear.

(Variation)
—What's that?
—Athletic underwear *(fidgeting)*—it keeps me jumping.

A man recently lost his sight, but recovered it an hour later. By that time, the first blinding effect of his new tie had worn off.

I knew a guy who in order to be thrifty took long strides to save his six dollar shoes. As a result, he ripped his eight dollar pants.

Viewing the trousers of my old evening suit convinces me that moths are not averse to taking a back seat.

How come when they had those old fashioned hair sofas no one thought of non-skid pants?

My mother was doing her spring cleaning and she threw out a pair of pop's trousers; but he was still in 'em.

—Do you like smoking jackets?
—Never smoked one.

—Say, why do you have your socks turned inside out?
—My feet got so hot I had to turn the hose on them.

—Nice pants you got there.
—Like 'em? Slacks . . . from Gimbels.
—Like these . . . Saks.

Bill here—he's a wily fellow. Someone bought him some collars for a present, size fifteen. He only wears size fourteen, so he's taking up wrestling to get a big neck.

Girl (to companion): I like a man's suit to match his hair: brown hair, brown suit; black hair, black suit.
Bald Man: And what suit for me?

—Everett had on one of those William Tell ties this weekend.
—What might that be?
—You know, the kind you can pull back on the bow, release, and hit the apple. Ain't you heard of them?

—Your husband has a new suit.
—No, he hasn't.
—Well, something's different.
—It's a new husband.

A man walked reluctantly into a hat store. "I just lost a bet," he said, "and I want to get a soft hat." The salesman, selecting a hat from the shelf behind him, handed it to the prospective purchaser with the remark: "This is the softest that we have." The customer gazed at it speculatively. "What I want," he said wistfully, "is something a little more tender. I've got to eat it."

Nightclothes

He gave his wife a present she could never wear out—a nightgown.

—You know what pajamas are?
—Yeah, isn't that a suit you keep under the pillow in case of fire?

Another advantage of the old-fashioned nightshirt over pajamas was that nobody was ever tempted to wear one out on the street.

I don't like nightgowns. I wouldn't buy one if I saw it a third off. When you go to bed it reaches down to your feet; and when you wake up in the morning it's choking you.

No Clothes

If you think clothes don't mean anything, try walking down the street without any.

> Old Mother Hubbard went to the cupboard
> To get her poor daughter a dress.
> When she got there, the cupboard was bare,
> And so was her daughter, I guess.

Shopping

She: I'm leaving the country for a while. I'm going to Paris for some clothes.
He: Did you just remember where you left them?

In a department store, a fussy lady came up to the floor walker and said, "I bought these undies here yesterday and want to change them." The walker blushed a little and said, "Sorry, Madam, you can't change them here." (*Or:* "Sorry, you'll have to go home to do that.")

She was very well dressed and, as she walked into the fashionable milliner's shop, the manager herself came forward to serve her. "I see by your advertisement," she said, "that you have just received two thousand hats from Paris." "Yes, madam," the respectful manager informed her. "Good," said the girl, removing her hat, "I wish to try them on."

The boxer entered the fur department of a large store and fixed the assistant with an eye that showed he was one who stood no nonsense. "I want a set of furs," he said. "A present for a friend." "Yes, sir," replied the assistant. "Any special kind?" The man of muscle glanced about him. "That dark brown set in the window looks like the sort of thing I want. It mustn't be too expensive, though." The assistant followed his gaze. "Oh," he exclaimed, "you mean skunk!" When the assistant woke up, he found himself in the hospital.

Women and Clothes

He: Did you sew the button on my overcoat?
She: No, I couldn't find the button, so I sewed up the hole.

—Who would sew the buttons on pants if there were no women?
—Oh . . . if there were no women, we wouldn't need them.

He: You look like Helen Brown.
She: I look even worse in white.

If all the animals that gave up their lives so that milady might have a fox, squirrel, raccoon, or wolf coat were to come back to life there would be exactly 8,787 foxes, 89,251 squirrels, 12,800 raccoons, 8,600 wolves, and 8,000,000,321 rabbits.

The girl rushed breathlessly into her sister's room. Her eyes were two blue flashes of excitement, her hair mussed in golden, glorious disarray. She clutched her sister excitedly by the arm and panted, "Oh, sister, just as I came up the steps a man leaving the house grabbed me and kissed me!"

"That's what you get for wearing my dress," replied her sister.

COLLEGE

If I'm studying when you get back, wake me up.

—Why the toothbrush in your coat lapel?
—It's my class pin. I go to Colgate.

The typical college boy: he has ties with dots in them, suits with stripes in them, and letters with checks in them.

The most resourceful farmer we've heard of recently was the one who left his son to run the farm and went away to college.

Dean: So you're back. I thought I expelled you last week.
Student: You did. But don't do it again because my dad was plenty sore last time.

The amount of liquor consumed in a year by the average college sophomore would be enough to last the average college sophomore for ten years.

—Well, how's your football team this year?
—Pretty good.
—Fine, let's hire a couple of professors and start a university!

First Student: What shall we do tonight?
Second: I'll spin a coin. If it's heads we'll go to the dance; if it's tails we'll go to the movies; and if it stands on edge we'll study.

—I heard that young Whiffle had a nervous breakdown.
—Yes; among his high school commencement gifts he received a pair of pink pajamas and a set of military brushes, and it wore him out trying to decide whether to go to Harvard or West Point.

A middle-aged man knocked at the door of a college student. "May I come in? It's the room I had when I went to college in '09," he said. The young man invited him in. "Yes, sir," said the older man, lost in revery, "same old room. Same old windows. Same old furniture. Same old view of the campus. Same old closet." He opened the door. There stood a girl, terrified, half clothed. "This is my sister," said the young man. "Yes, sir. Same old story!"

—What does the chemistry professor get?
—Oh, about three thousand dollars a year.
—And the football coach?
—About twelve thousand dollars a year.
—Quite a discrepancy.
—Well, did you ever hear forty thousand people cheering a recitation in chemistry?

Once upon a time there were three coeds, a great big coed, a medium-sized coed, and a little coed, who went for a walk in the woods. When they came back they were very tired and wished to go to bed. So they went to their rooms. Suddenly: "Someone's been sleeping in my bed," said the great big coed in a great big voice. "Someone's been sleeping in my bed," said the medium-sized coed in the medium-sized voice. "Good night, girls," said the little coed in a little bit of a voice. [See The Three Old Maids *under* Monologues *in part two.*]

Absent-Minded Professors

Did you ever hear about the absent-minded professor who swallowed the powder-puff and then dusted his wife's back with a marshmallow?

Prof (*slightly distracted*): Nice to see you again, George. How's your wife?
George: But I'm not married, professor.
Prof: Ah, no; then of course your wife's still single!

Prof: I forgot my umbrella this morning, dear.
Wife: How'd you remember that you'd forgotten it?
Prof: Well, I missed it when I raised my hand to close it after the rain had stopped.

Have you heard the one about the absent-minded professor and his absent-minded wife? It seems that the professor had just come home from a hard day's work, and after dinner he and his wife settled down in the living room to enjoy the radio. Suddenly there came a sharp knock on the door. "My husband!" the absent-minded wife gasped. "My God!" said the professor and jumped out of the window.

Courses

—Why is an upperclassman like a good old Londoner?
—Always in a fog, sir.

—Your work is quite original?
—Oh, yes, professor. Even the spelling is my own.

A fellow studying geography told the professor not to bother with it. "You ought to wait," he said, "till things are more settled."

—There's a fine fellow in the college crew.
—Yes, he's a gentleman and a sculler.

History Prof: Zilch, for what was Louis XIV chiefly responsible?
Zilch: Louis XV, sir?

During history class the teacher asked: "What happened in 1483?" "Luther was born," answered a student promptly. "Correct! What happened in 1487?" After a long pause: "Luther was four years old."

Prof: Young man, are you the teacher of this class?
Student: No, sir.
Prof: Then don't talk like an idiot.

Prof: You girls made so much noise during my lecture I couldn't hear myself speak.
Student: It's all right; you didn't miss much.

English Prof: Correct this sentence: "Before any damage could be done, the fire was put out by the volunteer fire department."
Student: The fire was put out before any damage could be done by the volunteer fire department.

Prof: Give the principal parts of the word "swim."
Student: Swim, swam, swum.
Prof: Of the word "dim."
Student: Dim, damn—say, are you trying to kid me?

Prof in Ethics: I will lecture today on liars. How many of you have read the twenty-fifth chapter?
(Nearly all raised their hands.)
Prof: That's fine. You're the very group to whom I wish to speak. There is no twenty-fifth chapter.

—I went to college.
—What course did you take there?
—I took pastronomy.
—Pastronomy? You mean delicatessen.
—No, no, I took pastronomy. It's all about the stars in the feenamint.
—Stars in the feenamint. You mean you took physics.

Outcome of Going to College

I went to college. I finished with 103 degrees—fever.

—My brother just left Yale.
—Oh, he got out then.

—Ha! Ha! Ra for pa! So your son got his B.A. and M.A.?
—Yes, indeed, but pa still supports him.

He used to be a mind reader, but he went to work at *(local college)* and starved.

—Think your son will soon forget what he learned at college?
—I hope so. He can't make a living drinking.

—What did your son learn at college?
—Well, sir, he can ask for money in such a way that it seems like an honor to give it to him.

A college education seldom hurts a man if he is willing to learn a little something after he is graduated.

Fewer college girls (*or:* boys) are getting married. I'm glad to see that higher education is improving their judgment.

He used to be a sickly kid. Then he went to the University of Michigan and took medicine. He's feeling much better now.

The only mark I got at school was a vaccination mark, and even that didn't take.

—George comes from a very poor family.
—Why, they sent him to college, didn't they?
—Yes, that's how they got so poor.

—I see Gray graduated from college with very high honors.
—Indeed he did. He has so many letters after his name that his card looks as if he were advertising several broadcasting stations.

—Frosh, you're the greenest I ever saw. Why, look at the hay seed on your coat!
—Them ain't hay seed, wise guy, them's wild oats!

We found out what they mean by college bread. It is a combination of a wad of dough, plenty of crust, and a lot of crumbs bunched together for a good loaf.

Jones is just fifty percent in everything, including his studies. He is a half-wit, halfback on the football team, usually half tight, and he may half to quit school!

One of our tiny students, working in one of the chemistry research labs, accidentally sat down in a mixture he was preparing. The poor fellow, he got a little behind in his work.

Yeah, sezzee, before I came up here to college I was pretty conceited, but now that they've knocked it out of me, I'm one of the best fellows they've got.

—Where is your son?
—In college.
—What's he doing?
—Ageing.

A gentleman was walking along the street of a small town in Alabama. On the other side of the street he noticed an old negro mammy walking very slowly. Every few moments she would turn around and call to a child who was toddling along behind her. "Cum on ther', Diploma. Huhry, cose we got to git home." The gentleman took particular notice of the fact that this woman was calling the child Diploma. Being very curious, he walked up to her and asked why did she call the child Diploma. She replied: "Well, you see ma dotter, she done went off to collij last yeah. And she tol' me dat she was gwine ta bring back a diploma. (*Pointing to the child*) Dat's what she brung back."

Pledging

The life of a sorority pledge is a life of dues and don'ts.

Pledge *(at dinner table):* Must I eat this egg?
Brother: Yer damn right!
Pledge: The beak too?

Professors

A prof had to flunk a pretty coed because of a matter of arithmetic. His wife put two and two together.

"I don't mind," said the professor, "if I see a student fidget toward the end of the hour. I don't mind seeing him take out his watch and look at it. But when he takes out his watch, stares at it, puts it to his ear, and then shakes it, it riles me!"

> Baa, baa, black sheep! Have you any wool?
> Yes sir, yes sir, three bags full,
> One for my master and one for my dame,
> And one for college students to pull over the eyes of
> 34,473,890 professors.

A student rang the bell of a professor's house late at night. The professor stuck his head out the window.
Student: One of your windows is open.
Professor: Which one?
Student: The one you're looking out of!

The freshman passed slowly by, then for want of companionship he flopped into a seat opposite the stranger. The stranger looked up from his newspaper and, after a cursory inspection of the youth, placidly resumed his reading. Minutes passed. Finally, the freshman could no longer contain himself.
—My name's Jones. How are you?
(There was no answer. The freshman was about to repeat his question when the newspaper was thrust aside and a rather distinguished-looking head emerged.)
—Fine, except for a slight touch of leprosy.
—Er—er, traveling for your health?
—No, I've been to see my twin brother. Everybody thinks he's me, but—*(whispering)* they're wrong. Ha! Ha! I'm him.
—You're—that is—are you going to Philadelphia?
—No. To Chicago.
—But this train goes to Philadelphia.
—Oh, that's all right. We'll get to Chicago eventually. Besides, I'm in no hurry. I just want to escape from my keeper.
—K-k-keeper?
—Certainly, I took an elephant from the zoo and the keeper's after him. *(Whispering)* Sh! Sh! I've got him in my suitcase.
—*(Incredulously)* The elephant?

—Ha! Ha! No, my twin brother.
—But what's the keeper after?
—After him. They thought he was me and put him in an asylum. But, ha-ha, the joke's on them. I'm him. Anyway, I'm going back tomorrow.
(Just then the train pulled into the station, and Jones arose rather nervously.)
—Back to the asylum?
(The stranger looked pained.)
—No, back to college. I'm a professor!

Social Life

Coeds should be heard but not sin.

College: the land of midnight sons!

A sailor may have a girl in every port, but a college man has a girl on every davenport.

—Dear, am I the first man you ever loved?
—Yes, Reginald, all the others were fraternity boys.

Some coeds are so fast, they don't wait until April to make fools out of themselves.

Sorority Sue says that John isn't much of a violinist, but he likes to fiddle around!

"Come out in the woods," said the freshman, "I hear a nightingale."
She followed him. It wasn't a nightingale; it was just a lark.

Personally I often wonder whether wrestlers get ideas at college dances or whether the college dancers get ideas at wrestling bouts.

And then there are those college boys who carry this being a gentleman so far that they are perfect ladies, too.

Frosh: I was out with a nurse last night.
Coed: Well, cheer up. Maybe your mother will let you go without one soon.

Polite Salesman: Yes, sir, and what is your pleasure?
College Student: Drinking and necking, sir, but just now I would like to buy a tie.

Frosh *(to fraternity brother)*: Someone wants you on the phone.
Brother: Well, if it's a girl, tell her I'll be there; and if it's a man, tell him I'll take a pint.

Housemother: It's after twelve o'clock; do you think you can stay here all night?
Frat Boy: Oh, I'd have to call home first.

Dad: How do you spend your weekends at college?
Son: In the evenings we usually have dates and go to some lonely spot and neck. That ain't nice, but I like it.
Dad: A whole year in college and you still say ain't.

Sorority Girl: What did Betty wear to the party last night?
Frat Boy: A see-through, I think.
Sorority Girl: If it was a see-through, you didn't have to think.

Fraternity Boy: Well, dear, you lost your bet, and now I want the forfeit.
Sorority Girl: I don't know what you mean, and besides, someone might see us.

Dear Momma: It is sure lonesome here at the Pi Phi house. Love, Bertha.
Dear Bertha: What do you mean "lonesome"? Aren't there a lot of other girls living in the same house with you? More love, Momma.
Dear Momma: Yes, "lonesome"! You know a dog can have fleas and still be lonesome. Still more love, Bertha.

Coed: I think the way college men discuss necking is terrible.
Soph (*very anxious to please*): So do I.
Coed: It's unhygienic.
Soph: It certainly is.
Coed: And vulgar.
Soph: Absolutely.
Coed (*after gazing at him expectantly for a few minutes*): Well, we might as well go in and dance.

COMIC STRIPS

Don't judge the Neanderthals too harshly. What will future archaeologists think of us, if they dig up comic strips?

CONSCIENCE

He's wrestling with his conscience. It's a featherweight match.

CONSOLATION

No matter how sad you are, a blanket is always a comforter.

(*Variation*)
Cheer up, a blanket is still a comforter.

She: Oh, I feel so blue. Nobody loves me—and my hands are cold.
He: Don't say that. God loves you. Your mom and pop love you. And you can always sit on your hands.

COUPONS

—How are you getting on in your new eight-room house?
—Oh fine. We furnished one room out of saving soap coupons.
—Did you furnish the other seven rooms yet?
—We can't. They're full of soap.

COWARDICE AND TOUGHNESS

It's so tough where I come from that the canaries sing bass.

She: I want a big, strong man—one with hair on his chest.
He: Will a little bit of fuzz do?

—You have the form of Venus De Milo.
—Yeah, and I'm just as tough.

—Mister, did you hit that little girl?
—Yeah, what of it?
—Gosh, what a wallop!

—I once shot myself in the back.
—You shot yourself in the back? Why did you do that?
—Can I help it if I'm a coward?

—Boy! Is that girl (or: boy) hard-boiled!
—Well, if you were in hot water as much as she is, you'd be hard-boiled too.

Teacher: Johnny, if you are always very kind and polite to all your playmates, what will they think of you?
Johnny: Some of 'em would think they could lick me.

—I went to the fights last night, and, boy, was that crowd tough!
—Did any one bother you?
—Bother me? One fellow next to me wanted to bet that I wasn't even living, and I was too scared to bet.

—You're a liar.
—You just say that again, and I'll bust yer jaw.
—Consider it said again.
—Consider your jaw busted.

A backwoods woman, the soles of whose feet had been toughened by a lifetime of shoelessness, was standing in front of her cabin fireplace one day when her husband addressed her. "You'd better move your foot a mite, maw, you're standin' on a live coal." Said she, nonchalantly: "Which foot, paw?"

CREDIT

—I'm selling vacuum cleaners, Ma'am. Five dollars down and you don't pay anything for six months.
—Yeah? Who told you about us?

CRIME

First Villain: How did you get rid of those bloodhounds that were trailing us?
Hairbreadth Harry: I threw a penny in the river and they followed the scent.

Gangsters

Gangsters do not believe in sparing the rod.

First Gangster: Did Joe the Turk get those tools concealed in the pie we sent to the prison last week?
Second Gangster: No, he had eaten the pie before I could tip him off.

Murder

—Someone touched my father on the head with a sword and made him a knight.
—That's nothing. Someone touched my dad on the head with an axe and made him an angel.

Robbers and Robbery

He came from Pittsburgh where they manufacture iron and STEAL.

Police say that Christmas shoplifting is being done early this year.

How time flies in that place! I lost my watch before I was there five minutes.

He started at the bottom of the ladder and worked himself up to being a second-story man.

Joan knows a man who thinks silver spoons are medicine—to be taken after every meal.

The average thief is simply out for what he can get—and eventually in for what he has got.

A travelling salesman died and left an estate of five-hundred towels and a hotel key.

—Is that a hooked rug?
—Hell, no, Mom bought it.

—Rockefeller worked for a dollar a week and now look at him. He owns the Standard Oil company and is worth millions.
—Yeah, but in those days they didn't have cash registers.

—He stole ten thousand dollars and a lot of bugs.
—Ten thousand dollars and bugs?
—That's what the paper says. Takes ten thousand dollars and flees.

Boss: Two dollars are missing from my desk drawer, and no one but you and I have a key to it.
Office Boy: Well, let's each put a dollar back and forget it.

—He's a kleptomaniac.
—What's he doing for it?
—Oh, he's taken everything.

—Have you seen a policeman around?
—No.
—Then stick 'em up.

The old belief that if you drop a knife or fork it means company is coming is quite true. What's more, if you miss a knife or fork it means the company has gone.

I always wanted a raccoon coat. Last night, when I saw a beautiful coat in the Colorado Cafe, I dashed inside and took it. When I got out on the sidewalk and went to put the coat on, I found there was a college student inside of it!

—Are there any slick crooks in this city?
—Slick crooks! Man, one evening at a dance they stole my trousers and hung weights on my braces so that I wouldn't miss them until they had gone.

—Some burglars got into the house last night, bound me to a chair, and gagged me.
—Then what did you do?
—Why, I sat around all night and chewed the rag.

One chap ran up to another and said, "My God, I've been robbed. I had my wallet right here in my back pocket and it's gone." The other said, "You darn fool, you keep your money in your back pocket? That's no place to keep a wallet." And he reached into his inside pocket. "Here's the place to keep your wallet. My God, I've been robbed!"

The businessman dashed into the employment agency. "Look here," he said to the clerk, "I'm looking for a cashier." The clerk looked somewhat surprised. "Why, sir," he said, "I thought I furnished you with one last week." "I know," came the irritable reply. "That's the one I'm looking for."

—I just had trouble wid a rubber.
—Were you held up?
—I was held up and beaten up. Den we argue . . .
—You argued with the robber?
—Yeah, but I finally gave him de money.
—Where were you held up by this terrible robber?
—In a Turkish bath. He's the rubber down there.

CRITICS

Criticism is the work of the incompetent; it enables them to be jealous and show it without feeling embarrassed.

The literary critic met a young and aspiring author at his club.
Critic: I've just read a book of yours.
Writer: My last one?
Critic: I certainly hope so.

CUBA

Things are so tough down in Cuba that even silence has gone off the gold(en) standard.

They've just elected a new president in Cuba. He must be a very popular guy. They held him over for a second week.

DANCING

A fan dancer is merely a nudist with a cooling system.

The modern wallflower is the girl who dances all the time.

Every woman would like to be a rhumba dancer. They are all twisters under the skin.

"A strip dancer," says Gypsy, "is just a girl who looks good in anything she takes off."

He: Say, that's a funny step you're doing; what's it called?
She: That's not a step. I'm losing my garter.

—How well he dances with that fat lady!
—So he ought to. He used to drive a bus.

—Pray tell me, sir, are you from the frozen north?
—No, little one, why?
—You dance as if you were wearing snow shoes.

—This is the elevator dance.
—But you're not moving.
—That's it. There're no steps in it.

She: What's the difference between dancing and marching?
He: I don't know.
She: I didn't think you did. Let's sit down.

—Do you care for dancing?
—No.
—What don't you like about it?
—It's only hugging set to music.

> There was an old lady from Wheeling.
> Who once in her garden was kneeling
> When by some strange chance

She got ants in her pants
And invented Virginia Reeling.

DATING AND COURTSHIP

On a sofa, it's often couch as couch can.

I've been stood up so much I've got flat feet.

He sent flowers to his best girl on Mother's Day.

She was the light of my life, but she went out too much.

You're a million miles from nowhere when you're only holding her hand.

Is she bashful? Oh boy! She won't even look up at a mail plane.

A girl got a date with an Italian because she wanted to make Wop-ee.

He is her Don Juan. She Don Juan [don't want] to see him anymore.

I'd rather stay home with Mickey Mouse than go out with you, you rat.

I used to go with a girl with a wooden leg, but I broke it off.

She was the light of his life till he saw her shining up to another guy.

I met this girl in a revolving door, and now we're going around together.

No guy likes to go out riding with a girl who carries a lead pipe for a swagger stick.

He went around with a girl he thought was single, but her husband changed his mind.

—Who was the blonde you were out with Tuesday and Thursday?
—Oh, she was the brunette I was out with Wednesday and Friday.

Sometimes a lonely girl goes for a stroll on a winter's evening and has a chap on her hands the rest of her life.

He's a young blade and goes around with an old battle axe. They just love to cut up together.

He: And why do you call me Pilgrim?
She: Well, every time you call, you make a little progress.

—My boyfriend thinks he's Napoleon. Should I be alarmed?
—Yes, if he thinks you're Josephine.

—Does your girlfriend have her own way?
—Does she? Why she writes her diary a week ahead of time.

—Last night I had an awful pain in my arms.
—Who was she?

—Young man, what do you mean bringing my daughter in at this hour?
—Gosh, I gotta be at work by six.

—My girl said she is going to throw me over.
—Yeah, but you know how a girl throws.

—Was she the kind of a girl you would give your name to?
—Yes, but not your right name.

—Don't worry about the girl who gave you the air. There's others.
—I know, but I can't help but feel sorry for her.

He: Are you going to be busy tonight?
She: I don't know. This is the first time I've been out with him.

She's the kind of a girl who can make you feel she's taking dinner with you instead of from you.

She: Why have you been making googoo eyes at me all night?
He: Honey, when ya gotta goo, ya gotta goo.

Suitor (on phone): Will you please put Mary Jane on the wire?
Father: What'dya think my daughter is, a tightrope walker?

He: Wanna neck?
She: No, thanks. I have one of my own.

—My boy friend stood me up.
—He did.
—Yeah, I was getting heavy on his lap.

He: See that man playing fullback? He'll be our best man in about a week.
She: Oh, this is so sudden.

She: We've been waiting here a long time for that mother of mine.
He: Hours, I should say.
She: Oh, Jack, this is so sudden.

—Is it good form for a girl to give a fellow a pair of socks on his birthday?
—Not if he behaves himself.

—I don't like going out with Charles. He knows too many dirty songs.
—Does he sing them to you?
—No, but he whistles them.

Nancy: But Suzie, is it fair to go to the movies with a boy you don't like?

Suzie: Sure, Nancy, why not? I enjoy the pictures and he enjoys my company.

—I thought you had a date with Helen tonight.
—Well, when I saw her leave her house at five minutes of eight with someone else, I got sore and called it off.

—Before I make a date, I always depend on the weather.
—The weather?
—Yeah, whether she will or whether she won't.

—Sorry I'm late, but I was busy being crushed in the arms of a lovely man.
—Really, anyone you knew?

Mary: Have a good time last night?
Ruth: Yah, but take my advice and never slap a fellow when he's chewing tobacco.

—Had a date with a World's Fair girl last night.
—How's that?
—If I had spent a century, I wouldn't have made any progress.

—My girl is so forgetful.
—I know it. I've had to remind her a dozen times she's engaged to you.

—Now that we're alone, I want to ask you something.
—But you're not alone. I'm with you.
—Well, practically alone.

—I have a date with two girls and I don't know which one to meet.
—Why don't you toss a coin?
—I did, and it didn't come out right.

—Say, are you still going around with that wealthy girl?
—Didn't you hear? She's married now.
—Answer my question.

Pap: Say, Zeke, when you goin' to marry Eliza Jane? You know you been goin' round with her for twenty years.
Zeke: Don't rush me, Pap. I want to make sure she isn't a passing fancy.

—We're going to have a swell time tonight. I've got three seats for the theatre.
—Why do we need three seats?
—They're for your father, mother, and kid brother.

—Courtship is nothing but a game of cards.
—That's the first I've heard of it. Explain yourself.

—Simple enough. A girl has a heart. A man takes it with a diamond and then her hand is his.

—When I knocked last night she came to the door and gave me a kiss.
—Great! I have an idea.
—What is it?
—I'm going to see her tonight and I'll ring the bell.

—I took a blonde out in a canoe, and when she refused to give me a kiss, I made her walk home.
—Are you trying to tell me that she walked on water?
—No! She froze everything around her.

—Who were the two women you and Jack were out with last night?
—A pair of convent girls.
—How so?
—Oh, it was nun o' this and nun o' that.

When the clock struck the midnight hour, father came to the head of the stairs and in a rather bold tone of voice, said: "Young man, is your self-starter out of order tonight?" "What's the difference," retorted the young man, "as long as there's a crank in the house?"

I was bawling out this fellow for making love to my girl. I really gave him a piece of my mind. (Elaborate.) When I finished, I said, "I'll teach you to make love to my girl," . . . and the other fellow said, "I wish you would, 'cause I'm making no headway at all."

She: Say, I'm so hungry I could eat a doorknob.
He: Well, if I had a doorknob you should have it.
She: Honest, wouldn't you like to buy me something to eat?
He: No. Keep 'em hungry and they stick with you. Feed 'em and you'll fatten 'em up for somebody else.

—That red-headed charmer you go with: where did you meet her?
—In a skating rink.
—How is it that a big, grown-up man like you indulges in roller skating?
—Well, you see, the doctor told me to keep off my feet as much as possible.

Chat-Up Lines and Flirting

Many a mash note is the cause of a mashed nose.

Flirtation is attention without intention.

She: If I were you, I wouldn't be so forward.
He: If you were like me, what a time we'd have!

He: Shall we go outside for a little walk?
She: You boys have the funniest way of saying what you mean.

He: If I could change places with Clark Gable right now, I wouldn't.
She: You never do anything to please me.

She: If you were half a man, you'd take me to the circus, tomorrow.
He: Honey, if I were half a man, I'd be in the circus.

She: If I go out with you, will I be good for a new hat?
He: After going out with me, you'll be good for nothing.

—What did your girl say last night when you put your arm around her?
—Well, she said, "Hey, what do you think this is, a world tour?"

He: You're the world to me.
She: Yeah? Well, you're not going to make any Cook's tour tonight.

She: No fooling?
He: Hell, that's up to you.

He: Do you ever take long walks in the country?
She: That depends on whom I go riding with.

She: Go, go, leave me, I never want to see your face again.
He: All right, I'll grow a beard.

He: May I hold your hand?
She: No, it's not heavy.

She: Are you going with any certain girl?
He: Nowadays no girl is certain.

(Variation)
She: Are you going with any particular girl?
He: None of the girls I go with are particular.

He: Are all the girls in this town as pretty as you?
She: I don't know. I only look at the men.

He: You're one in a million.
She: So are your chances.

He: My heart flames like blazing fire.
She: Don't be a fuel.

He: Does that rouge of yours come off very easily?
She: No, indeed, I always put up a struggle.

She: Your girlfriend called up and said she wouldn't be able to meet you today at all.
He: Well, that's a wait off my mind.

He: Do you know the difference between right and wrong?
She: Between right and wrong? No!
He: All right, how about a date?

May: He told me he could live on my kisses.
Fay: Well, are you going to feed him some?
May: Not till I find out what he expects for dessert!

He: Say, will you dine with me tomorrow night?
She: Sure.
He: All right, eight o'clock at your house.

He: Hello, baby!
She: I'll have you know that I'm nobody's baby.
He: Well, wouldn't you feel like hell at a family reunion? (*Or:*
Well, don't you feel out of place at home?)

Father: Has the young man who's been calling on you given you
any encouragement?
Daughter: Oh, yes, father. Last night he asked me if you and
mother were pleasant to live with.

> Mary had a little lamb,
>   And salad and dessert;
> And then she gave the wrong address,
>   The dirty little flirt!

Woman Passenger: Captain, I wish you could arrange it so that
the lights on both sides of the boat were red.
Captain: Young lady, we have to have one red and one green.
That is the law of the sea.
Woman Passenger: Oh, I know, Captain, but you see it was this
way: The first night out I met a young fellow from Dartmouth.
And we sat on the deck and it was dark, and the ocean was beautiful, and the moon was pale, and the air was warm, and—oh,
well, I kept looking up at that red light and it kept saying, "Stop,
stop, stop!" And the next night, Captain, we sat on the other side
of the boat, and the ocean and the moon and the air were all the
same, and I kept looking up at the green light, and it kept saying,
"Go, go, go!" And, oh, Captain, in a case like that I just ain't got
no will power. And Captain, there's four more nights to this trip,
and that light's still green.
Captain: Young lady, for your own good I think you'd better
come up here on the bridge tonight and talk to me. I have a collection of old mariners' lanterns that I'd like to show you.

Dating and Cars

An automobile ride has put many a good girl on her feet.

A girl doesn't have to watch the speedometer to know what her
boy friend is driving at.

Many a fellow has started trouble in his car by failing to release his clutch in time.

Any girl who drives out with my brother doesn't have to walk back. He drives a hearse.

How would you like to go riding with me in my car? I've just had the springs reinforced.

I know a man who's an automotive engineer. He engineers girls into his auto with only one motive.

There are two kinds of girls: those that walk home from automobile rides and those that automobile ride home from walks.

She: I don't like to drive with you, Paul, you're too reckless.
He: Yes, we've had some tight squeezes, haven't we?

—What kind of oil do you use in your car?
—Oh, I usually start by telling how lonely I am.

He (out driving): You look lovelier to me every minute. Do you know what that's a sign of?
She: Sure. You're going to run out of gas any minute.

I took a girl for a ride in a taxicab, which suddenly came to a dead stop. When I asked the driver what the trouble was, he said, "Didn't the lady say stop?" I answered, "Keep driving, she wasn't talking to you."

A fellow met a girl and took her for a long ride in the country. When they got out on a lonely road, the car stalled. Getting out, the fellow looked at the engine, jumped back in the car, and drove home. Girls, there's a moral to this story: never go riding with a mechanic.

She: Last night, Jack took me riding in his new car.
He: How far did he go?
She: It's none of your business.

—He took his dream girl out in his car.
—How did it turn out?
—Did you ever see a dream walking?

He: Do you have yellow fever?
She: No, why do you ask?
He: Every time I take you out, you say, "Let's take a yellow, let's take a yellow." [Yellow Cab]

Sambo: Ah calls mah girl "taxicab!"
Bimbo: Why?
Sambo: She has a checkered past. [The reference is to Checker cabs.]

—I used to date a girl who worked in a nightclub as a torch singer.

—Oh, she sang "blue" songs.
—No, she didn't sing "blue" songs.
—Then why do you say she was a torch singer?
—Because whenever I took her riding in a taxi, she'd say, "Don't torch me."

A fellow riding in an auto with a girl went through a stoplight at about sixty miles an hour. A cop gave chase, caught him, told him to pull over to the curb, and asked him for his license. The fellow didn't have one. The cop said he'd be ticketed for that, as well as driving with his lights out and speeding. The girl, trying to help, leaned over and said to the cop, "Please understand, officer, he's drunk."

Dating and Money

Heaven will protect the working girl, but who will protect the guy she's working?

She: I can never be more than a sister to you.
He: Well, then, sis, lend me two-bits!

He: I have a record of all our good times together.
She: Oh, a diary?
He: No, my checkbook.

He: Since I met you I can't eat, I can't sleep, I can't drink.
She (shyly): Why not?
He: I'm broke.

Mazie: Grace certainly knows how to manage the men.
Daisy: Indeed, she does. They have to handle her with kid gloves and silk stockings.

DEAF AND DUMB

I know a fellow who is deaf and dumb, but he has a speech impediment: his little finger is broken.

Mazie: I'm in love with a deaf and dumb guy. He makes love to me with both hands.
Daisy: Say, he may be deaf but he ain't dumb.

The old lady was stone deaf. "Auntie," the girl screamed, "this is Mr. Specknoodle!" "What did you say?" asked Auntie with a puzzled frown. "I said, this is Mr. Specknoodle!" With an apologetic smile, the dear old soul said, "I'm sorry, but do you know, it sounds just as though you were saying 'Specknoodle.'"

I went to a deaf and dumb dance to entertain. After the entertainment, I stayed to have a dance with one of the pretty girls. I saw one sitting near me and gave her the sign that I wanted to have the next dance. She nodded her head in agreement. As we

danced around the room, another fellow asked her to dance. She
said, "Okay, just as soon as I finish with the dummy."

DEBTS

They like me in St. Louis; they want me to settle there. I had lots
of letters asking me to come back and settle.

Louie's just about even with the world. He owes about as many
people as he doesn't owe.

If all the taxpayers were laid end to end, they would reach about
half-way around the federal deficit.

—You the 'stallment man?
—Yeah.
—Well, Mom sent me to stall you off again.

First Sailor: So you knew a fellow who came to this faraway
island because of respiratory trouble?
Second Sailor: Yes; back in his home town his creditors wouldn't
let him breathe easily. (*Or:* wanted to stop his breathing.)

A fellow met a bloke who owed him a hundred dollars. "Listen,"
he said, "I'm desperate. I'll make concessions; I'll meet you half
way. If you give me fifty, I'll forget half of it." The bloke said,
"Just to show you I'm a sport, I'll meet you half way. I'll forget
the other half. Now we're straight."

—My grandad came over here and he didn't have a dime; but he
wasn't discouraged. He went down to the corner store, asked
them to trust him with a basket, and peddled articles for a nickel
and a dime a throw. And what do you think?
—He made a fortune.
—No, he still owes for the basket.

Client: I lent a chap five hundred pounds and he won't give me a
receipt. What shall I do?
Lawyer: Write and ask for the return of the thousand pounds.
Client: But it was only five hundred.
Lawyer: He will soon write and tell you it was five hundred, and
that shall be your receipt.

A doctor was summoned to treat a sick maid. The lady of the
house was hovering nearby. The doctor opened his bag and
began his examination. The mistress then left the room. After
she exited, the doctor told the maid he couldn't find anything
wrong with her. The maid told him there was nothing wrong
with her. She was staying in bed only because her employers
owed her ten dollars. The doctor grabbed his bag, closed it, and
told her to move over, saying, "They owe me five."

DECEPTION

—What an innocent girl she is.
—Yes, it has taken her years to acquire that innocence.

Crooked? Why that guy is so crooked that the wool he pulls over your eyes is half cotton.

He: Why do you want me to go away?
She: You deceived me. You told me you were a Southern planter and I find you're an undertaker in Birmingham.

I took out fire insurance on my house—a big policy—and asked the agent how much I would get if my house burned down the day after. The guy said about ten years.

Boy: Extra, Extra! Fifty people swindled!
Man: Here boy, give me a paper. Why there's nothing here about fifty people being swindled!
Boy: Extra, Extra! Fifty-one people swindled!

He: What do you intend to do at the ball tonight?
She: I'm going to sell kisses.
He: What do you expect to charge?
She: Well, do you think a dollar would be too much?
He: No, people expect to be cheated at those affairs.

A fond mother, whose daughter had not come home at the usual hour, grew worried at her absence, so she telegraphed five of her daughter's best friends, asking where Mary was. Shortly after the daughter's return, the answers to her telegrams arrived. Each one read, "Don't worry, Mary is staying with me tonight."

—Nice blind on the window.
—Yes.
—Who paid for it?
—The customers.
—How is that?
—I put a little box on the counter "for the blind" and they paid for it.

A lady stopped at the ticket office and requested change for a quarter. The man gave her five nickels. She then went through the gate to the train. The ticket man said to the next person in line, "Gee, there she goes and she didn't pay her fare. She thought I took it, but I didn't." The person in line said, "What are you going to do about it?" The ticket man said, "I'm going to do nothing. Just wait till she tries to change that lead nickel."

A fellow went into a clothing store to buy a suit. He picked one out, and when he felt in his pocket for the money—fifty dollars—

he discovered he had only ten. He asked the owner to trust him, and he'd bring in the other forty. The owner said, "I don't know you. I couldn't do that." The buyer said, "Well, Pinkus across the street knows me." So the owner said, "Go across there and let Pinkus give you the forty." The fellow went across the street to Pinkus's bakery and asked for a hundred and forty doughnuts. Pinkus said, "I don't have that many here right now, but I'll have them made for you and deliver, if you like." The fellow said, "No, don't bother." He then left the bakery, crossed the street to the tailor shop, and, before entering, yelled: "Pinkus, send forty here and the rest send home."

DIRECTIONS

I can't seem to get my bearings in this town. I went for a walk, got confused, and asked a kid: "Where's Sixth Street?" The kid replied, "I dunno." "Well, where's the local hotel?" "I dunno." So I said, "Well, where is the local theatre?" The kid said, "I dunno." I said, "Hrrumph, you don't know much, do you?" The kid said, "Hmm, I'm not lost."

DISMISSIVE REMARKS

Don't hurry, here's your hat.

—Would you put yourself out for me?
—Certainly.
—Well, do so now. I want to be alone.

Gal: Get hot!
Guy: Get hot? Oh, boy.
Gal: Yes, get hot from my house.

Business Man: Say, young fellow, do you believe in building and loan?
Salesman: Er, yes.
Business Man: Well, get out of this building and let me alone.

—You're limping. I'll wager I know what the trouble is. Gout!
—What did you say?
—Gout.
—Why should I go out when I just came in?
—No, no, you don't understand. Gout is an inflammation of the joints. Perhaps you've been living too high.
—No, sir; my room is on the ground floor.
—Maybe you're limping on account of rheumatism.
—No, on account of love. I proposed to a young lady at the top of the stairs.
—But why should that make you limp?
—She threw me down.

DOUBLE MEANINGS

If your palm itches, you'll get something. If your head itches, you've got it.

—How would you go about seeing the night life in New York?
—Take a taxi!

Two cannibal chiefs caught a missionary on a raid and split the prophet among themselves.

—What does X at the end of a letter mean?
—Usually, that's where a body lies.

—I spring from a line of peers.
—I jumped off a dock once myself.

—What do you think of relativity?
—One thing, don't have them live with you.

—See that drum? My great grandfather used it in the revolution.
—Yes, and I suppose he beat it when he saw the enemy.

—Could I see the captain of the ship?
—He's forward, miss.
—I'm not afraid. I'm used to men.

(Variation)
—I'd like to see the captain, sir.
—He's forward, miss.
—I don't care. This is a vacation.

—I just finished reading *Ivanhoe*. Have you ever tried anything of Scott's?
—Oh yes, I'm very fond of his emulsion. [Scott's was a laxative.]

—I wonder what time it is. I'm invited to dinner at six-thirty, and my watch isn't going.
—Why, isn't your watch invited?

—You say that milk keeps you awake? Why, milk can't keep anybody awake.
—The heck it can't. You never heard 'em deliver it around my neighborhood.

DREAMS AND DREAMING

I like to dream. You meet a better class of people.

I dreamed I was pitching pennies, and I tossed all night.

(Variation)
I didn't sleep well. I dreamt I was pitching horseshoes and I tossed all night.

I dreamt it was raining twenty dollar gold pieces and I had boxing gloves on!

A terrible thing happened last night. I had to stay downtown and paid four bucks for a room. I went to bed and dreamt all night I was sleeping on a park bench.

(Variation)
I had a terrible night's sleep last night. I dreamed I was sleeping on a park bench after paying ten bucks for a room.

—I just dreamed I met the most beautiful girl in the world and she loved me at first sight.
—Go back to sleep and see if she's got a friend.

—Whatcha so sad about?
—Last night, I dreamt that I was in a harem and the keeper asked me if I'd like to have a femme. I said, "Yes," so he was just about to go out and get me one when a brunette passed. But I said I wanted a blonde. Then he sent the brunette upstairs to get a blonde for me. While we were standin' around waiting, I woke up, and I've been kickin' myself all day long for not havin' taken the brunette.

DRINKS, DRINKING, DRUNKS, AND DRUNKENNESS
Drinks and Drinking

Youth must be served—and then carried out.

Champagne makes you see double and feel single.

His breath was strong enough to start a windmill.

He's a "bigamy" drinker. You know, he takes one too many.

The best way to open a conversation is with a corkscrew.

A speakeasy is where you go in like a lion and pass out like a lamp.

He's in his second childhood. He's gone back to the bottle.

He drinks liquor like water; it's the only kind he can afford.

Drink? Hell, no, he doesn't drink. He freezes it and eats it.

Rockefeller says that he was born a teetotaler. Well, weren't we all?

He gets so lit up his wife has to wear dark glasses to get to sleep nights.

Two joy riders, two girls, two quarts, two A.M., two funerals, too bad.

The only time the drinks were on him was when he was run over by a brewery wagon.

I know a chap who got a green nose from drinking too much creme de menthe.

You can win a woman with "applesauce," but it takes "applejack" to win a man.

I have a friend who has been feeding his heifers liquor in an effort to raise potted beef.

She's very broadminded. She doesn't care so much about your English if your Scotch is good.

—He drinks something awful.
—Yeah, I know. He gave me some. It was rotten.

—My grandfather lived to be nearly ninety and never used glasses.
—Well, lots of people prefer to drink from a bottle.

—I drank six cocktails last night. Did I do wrong?
—Don't you remember?

—What do you call those people who put you in contact with the spirit world?
—Bartenders.

—For the picnic, I'll bring some whiskey in case of snake bite.
—Okay, I'll bring a snake.

Baby: I want my bottle.
Mother: Shut up, you sound like your father.

—How did you get that red nose?
—I just passed my bar examination.

—How was the party last night?
—Good, as long as I lasted.

—You'll ruin your stomach drinking that stuff.
—Thash all right. It won't show with my coat on.

—You say beer makes you lean?
—Yes, against buildings, poles, and lampposts.

He: How many beers does it take to make you dizzy?
She: Oh, four or five, but don't call me Dizzy.

—I had to quit dancing last night.
—Corn?
—No, rye.

—I had great fun at the club last night. They had a beer-drinking contest.
—You don't say. Who won second prize?

—Phwat are ye lookin' fer?
—Nothin'.
—Thin ye'll find it in the jug where the whiskey was.

Wife: Every time you get a few drinks, do you always have to recite poetry?
Hubby: Sure. Don't you know that two pints make one quote?

—I fell down the stairs yesterday with two pints of whiskey.
—Did you spill any of it?
—No, I kept my mouth shut.

—Twenty saloons in this block, and I haven't been seen in one of them.
—Which one was that?

—This liquor is terrible.
—Then I guess I won't ask you to have another drink.
—Oh, it isn't that bad.

—What's wrong, Louie?
—Wrong! I lost a blooming bet and had to buy the drinks. I got a bad four-bit piece in my change, and darned if I didn't knock over my beer!

—I used to be a tightrope walker.
—Could you teach me tightrope walking?
—I could teach you how to get tight, but rope walking you'll have to learn yourself.

Teacher: How do you spell straight?
Boy: S-T-R-A-I-G-H-T.
Teacher: Correct, what does straight mean?
Boy: Without ginger ale.

On the train, I saw a fellow I knew. He took a bottle out of his pocket and invited me to have a drink. I did, and about two seconds later everything went black. I yelled, "I've gone blind! I can't see!" and he said, "Pipe down, we're in a tunnel."

> This little pig went to market
> This little pig stayed home
> This little pig had Blue Ribbon
> And went wee, wee, wee
> All the way home. [Pabst Blue Ribbon beer]

She: I don't think I should finish my drink.
He: No? Why not?
She: It might make me drunk.
He: Do you mean to tell me that one little drink like that would make you drunk?
She: Sure, if it's the tenth or eleventh.

You know what the definition is:
Of a high-school cocktail? One drink and you're in a class by yourself.
Of a block and tackle cocktail? You walk a block and you'll tackle anything.
Of an elephant cocktail? One drink and you throw your trunk out the window.

> The horse and mule live thirty years,
> They never taste light wine and beers,
> Sheep and goats are dead at twenty,
> They drink no liquor . . . water plenty.
> At fifteen dogs are mostly dead,
> They look not on the wine when red;
> At ten the cat's lost all nine lives.
> No beast on milk or water thrives,
> At five, most birds have passed away,
> Far, Far from alcohol they stay.
> Bugs speed but few days on this earth,
> They never know the cocktail's worth,
> But evil, wicked, rum-soaked men,
> Live on to three score years and ten.

A Barfly's Dictionary

Absinthe—Non-appearance in classes.
Aged—Chemical symbol for hydrogen, as in Aged 2 O.
Ale—A word that goes with hearty.
Bar—Animal that's in them thar hills.
Bottle—A combat, a frightful brawl.
Bourbon—Extended regurgitation.
Champagne—Faked illness; his headache was only a champagne.
Cognac—"Cognac, all is forgiven."
Decanter—Goggle-eyed comedian.
Drunk—Part of a tree.
Fizz—Hats that Turks and Shriners wear.
Gin—Physical education.
Gin Rickey—Oriental medium of transportation used at World's Fair.
Goblet—A small sailor.
Hangover—A town in New Hampshire where Dartmouth College is located.

Hennessey—State in which Memphis is located.
Hiccup—Part of popular title "Hic-cup the British."
Ice—Located immediately behind spectacles.
Kummel—Ship of the desert.
Lapel—Where pledge buttons are placed on the coat.
Malt—What happens to birds when they lose their feathers.
Mix—Collective term for Irishmen.
Rum—Things into which houses are divided; also, what Babe Ruth hits home.
Sherry—What grew on the tree that George Washington chopped down.
Stein—What results when wine is spilled on the tablecloth.
Swizzle—Chair used by professors.
Tokay—All right; as, "Tokay with me, keed."
Vermouth—A command to remove oneself from the vicinity.
Wine—Used to start questions; such as "Wine hell were you late?"

Drunks and Drunkenness

He was a man of regular habits—always drunk.

He drinks so much he ripples. In fact, when he falls down, he splashes.

When he's sober there's not another man who will work harder—for a second drink.

Hint to drunks: Left-handed beer mugs can be made into right-handed ones by walking around the counter.

A drunk, standing up against the door of a saloon, finally fell over. A kid ran in and shouted, "Hey, mister, your sign's fallen down."

(Variation)
I saw a drunk outside a speakeasy and watched him for a while. He reeled and finally fell. Another drunk went to the door and said, "Hey, your sign just fell down."

—He plays the part of a drunk.
—He should be good. He's been rehearsing for years.

—Remember, girls, I know just how drunk I am.
—Yes, a man is as oiled as he feels.

—They say bread contains alcohol.
—Is that so? Let's drink a little toast.

A fellow, having drunk too much, was thrown out of a saloon. He turned and said, "All right, throw me out my blonde and I'll go home."

—Was it very crowded at the cabaret last night?
—Not under my table.

She: You seem infatuated.
He: What do you mean? I haven't had a drink all day.

He came home to the wrong auto trailer after a night of celebrating and woke up the next morning in Kansas City.

—Shay, y'know that wooden Indian down in front of Jack's shigarstore?
—Yeah, sure I do.
—Well, he dunno you.

Drunk: Believe it or not, offisher, I'm huntin' fur a parkin' plashe!
Officer: But you haven't got an automobile.
Drunk: Oh, yaesh I have. Itsh in the parkin' plashe I'm huntin' fur!

—Why did you fire your cook?
—I came home one night, found my wine all gone, and the cook in the kitchen trying to knit a sweater with spaghetti.

The drunk halted in front of an enormous stuffed tarpon in a glass case. He stared at it for a minute or two in silence. Then he said: "The fella who caught—hic—that fish is a—hic—liar!"

A drunk, staggering along the streets, bumped into a telegraph pole. He felt his way around it several times, then muttered, "S'no use. I'm walled in."

Drunk: Shay, offisher, where does Tom Maloney live?
Officer: Why, you're Tom, old boy.
Drunk: Shure, but where does he live?

Two students were uncertainly flivvering their way home. "Bill," said Henry, "I wancha be very careful. Firs' thing ya know you'll have us ina ditch." Bill, astonished and badly shaken up, replied: "Me? Why, I thought you was driving."

(Variation)
First Drunk: I want you to be very careful. First thing you know, you'll have us both in a ditch.
Second Drunk: Me? I thought you were driving.

—It's a good thing our wives didn't find out where we were last night.
—Darn right. Where were we?
—Darned if I know.

A policeman, making his rounds in the early morning, found an inebriated individual standing in a horse trough and waving his handkerchief over his head. "Hey, what are you doing there?"

asked the cop. "Save the women and children first . . . I can swim!"

At two in the morning, a drunk was sitting on the curb. Parked in front of him was a large moving van. "Hello," said the cop, "waiting for something?" "No," said the drunk, "I'm just wondering who in hell put the house on top of my car!"

Two drunks were walking along the street arguing who was the drunker. One said, "I'll walk in front and you tell me if I'm walking straight." He did and the other fellow said, "Sure you walk straight, but who's the other fellow with you?"

A drunk was staggering down the street when suddenly fire engines came whizzing by, with whistles shrieking. The drunk started to run after them, but after a few blocks he stopped, exhausted, and said, "Oh, the hell with you and your old peanuts!"

> They had to carry Carrie to the ferry,
>   The ferry carried Carrie to the shore;
> The reason that they had to carry Carrie,
>   Was that Carrie couldn't carry any more.

Drunk: Shay, call me a taxi, will ya'?
Bystander: My good man, I was married tonight and haven't time. I'm a groom.
Drunk: Awright, call me a horse; I gotta get home.

(Variation)
Drunk *(to splendidly uniformed bystander):* Shay, call me a cab, will ya?
Splendidly Uniformed Bystander: My good man, I am not the doorman, I am a naval officer.
Drunk: Awright, then call me a boat. I gotta get home.

Two drunks, holding up a third, walked to their car, a small sports roadster with a rumble. They were going to put him in the rumble, but one of them said, "Hey, shupposh he should fall out of the rumble?" The other said, "Thash right . . . how can we work this out?" The other said, "I know, we'll both get in the rumble and let him drive."

First Barfly: How did you get that black eye?
Second Barfly: Oh, that's the remains of a royal time I had last night.
First Barfly: What do you mean, royal time?
Second Barfly: Why, at a party I attended, the guests began getting rough. Everybody put up their dukes and I took the count.

The drunk was noisily trying to unlock the door to his flat late one night, when a window opened upstairs and an angry voice yelled.

—Haven't you got your key?
—Sure, I got lotsha keys, but shay, would you jushashoon throw me down a coupla o' keyholes?

First drunk: I found (*hic*) a half dollar.
Second drunk: It'sh mine, it'sh got my name on it.
First: Whatsh your name?
Second: E Pluribus Unum.
First: Yeah, it'sh yoursh.

A drunk, visiting a friend in San Francisco, staggered into the house. When he reached the sitting room, an earthquake started. After it was over, he lay on the floor and noticed that everything around him was broken. He said, "Okay now, don't worry, I'll pay for any damage I've caused."

The officer had laid violent hands on the drunk who stood on the corner. Finally the drunk got angry.
—Shay, I've a good notion to punch you again.
—Again? Why, you haven't done it the first time.
—Well, I had the shame notion before.

—Delighted to have met you. Come over one evening soon and bring your husband.
—Thank you so much, but we never go anywhere. You see, my husband is paralyzed.
—Don't mind that, dear, my husband's that way half the time himself.

A drunken fellow was staggering home and stopped to watch some men digging a hole. He watched them for a long time and then asked what they were digging. The foreman told him they were making a subway. He stood around a while longer and at last said, "I don't think I'll wait. I had better take a streetcar."

A fellow was staggering down the street, carrying a tall clock (*or:* a grandfather clock) that was ticking and showing the right time. A little ways down the street, he stopped and put it down to mop his brow. He repeated this routine several times, walking and stopping to rest. A drunk, who had been watching him, went over and said, "Hey there, why don't you buy a wristwatch?"

Judge: Are you positive that the defendant was drunk?
Officer: No doubt.
Judge: Why are you so certain?
Officer: Well, I saw him put a penny in the patrol box on Fourth Street, then look up at the clock on the Presbyterian Church and shout: "Gawd, I've lost fourteen pounds!"

After fumbling with the key, the drunk found the keyhole and stamped into the house, where he stumbled around looking for the lights.

Wife: That you, Henry?
(No answer. A big crash of glass.)
Wife: Henry! What in this world are you doing?
Henry: Teaching your goldfish not to bark at me.

As a drunk stumbled onto a train, the girl sitting across from him pulled her skirts tightly around her legs. The drunk waved his hand at her and said, "S'all right, lady, beers are my hobby." A parson, who boarded the train right behind the drunk, started to bawl the fellow out for drinking. The drunk said, "What are you talking about? Why, you're drunk right now. Look, you've got your collar on the wrong way."

The waitress in the Greasy Spoon restaurant pulled a good one on Gus one night last week when he went in for something to eat. Gus had been imbibing too freely in panther fizz and, after eating, fell asleep. "I've already wakened him twice," said one waitress, "and I'm going to waken him a third time." "But why not have him taken out?" suggested another waitress. "Not on your life," whispered the first. "Every time I wake him up he pays his bill."

I was over visiting some friends of mine at the *(local)* hotel. They have a large life-sized picture of me in the lobby advertising the theatre. It was one o'clock in the morning, and the scrub women were cleaning the lobby. They had shoved this big picture of me over against the wall, and alongside of it there were about a dozen of those big brass cuspidors. As I walked out, a drunk staggered in and looked at my picture. Then he looked at the cuspidors and said, "S-S-shay, what did this guy do to get all those loving cups?"

Joe was telling his pal about the trouble he gets into when he comes home drunk late at night. The pal advised him to take his clothes off before going upstairs. Then, he said, "if the wife catches you, tell her you've been in for hours—reading." Joe promised to try it. The next day, seeing his pal, he told him how the experiment worked. "I came to the stairs and took off my shoes, my shirt and pants, and then my underwear. When I reached the top of the stairs, I found myself standing on the platform of an elevated railroad."

A drunk staggered into a hotel with a girl and went up to his room. For weeks the hotel had been trying to find an excuse to throw him out. So the manager, hot under the collar, went to the drunk's room to throw him out. Puffing himself up, the manager knocked loudly on the door, which opened just a little. The manager started, "Sir, you have violated the most rigid rule of this hotel!" The drunk shushed him. With his finger to his lips, he said, "Not so loud! I gotta dame in here now. Come back later."

There's the wonderful love of a true maid,
And the love of a staunch, true man,
And the love of a baby that's unafraid—
All have existed since time began,
But the most wonderful love, the love of loves—
Even greater than that of a Mother,
Is the tenderest, infinite, passionate love
Of one dead drunk for another.

A drunk staggered into a hotel late one night and asked the clerk for the key to his room. "What's your name and what room do you occupy?" asked the clerk. "Bill Brown's me name and I'm in 908." After verifying the statement, the clerk handed him his key and the drunk went to his room. In about fifteen minutes a drunken individual again appeared at the desk, his face bleeding, his clothes dirty, and his hat smashed in. "Give me the key to 908," he said. "Why I just gave a drunk the key to that room," replied the clerk angrily. "Oh, thash all right, I'm the same son-of-a-gun; I just fell out the window."

I decided to get a good night's sleep, so I turned in at eleven o'clock. About twelve, someone knocks on the door. I got up, pushed aside the bureau and three chairs, and opened the door. There stood a drunk. He staggered into my room and looked me over. Then he said: "Sorry, srong room," and staggered down the hall. I went back to bed and was just dozing off when knock, knock again. It was the same drunk and again he said: "Sorry, sorry, srong room." This happened four times. Finally, at three o'clock I was awakened again. When I opened the door, he looked at me amazed and said, "My goodness, have you got every room in the house?"

It was in the cold grey dawn. The man was plastered to the gills. A cop was following him. And he knew it. Too scared to think clearly, yet with a single idea in his mind—to avoid being arrested for disorderly conduct—he ducked into a kitchenette apartment. The cop followed. Now, thoroughly rattled, the drunk took out his keys and made a pretense of opening the door to one of the apartments. To his surprise the key fit and there was nothing else for him to do but enter. But the cop—one of those persistent birds—came in directly behind him.
Drunk (*whispering*): Sh-h-h-h, wife's asleep.
Cop: This your apartment?
Drunk: 'Course it is. Don't I know this furniture? Don't I know this hallway? Don't I know them goldfishes?
(*The officer, however, was still dubious. When the drunk walked into the bedroom, he followed. There were twin beds.*)
Drunk (*whispering*): See the lady sleeping there? That's my wife.

Cop: Well, how about the man sleeping in the other bed?
Drunk *(grunting):* Huh, that's me!

(Variation)
A well-dressed drunk was having difficulty opening the door of
his house. A cop strolled by and questioned him. The drunk said
he could prove this was his house. He could show him receipts
for everything that was in it: Oriental rugs, Tiffany lamps, Water-
ford glass, etc. The man, accompanied by the cop, finally opened
the door and went in. The drunk produced the receipts and
showed the cop through the house. Finally, the drunk said, "I'll
even show you my bedroom. This is it. See that big bed there;
see that woman? Well, that's my wife. And see the fellow in bed
with her? That's me!"

Women Drinkers

I call her my little prune. She's always stewed.

She was positively radiant . . . always lit up.

(Variation)
There's something radiant about her. She's always lit up.

Cavemen used to knock girls senseless and carry them off. That
isn't necessary these days.

The old-fashioned girl who stepped out as fit as a fiddle now has
a girl who comes home tight as a drum.

The old-fashioned girl who spent her evenings at home making
rugs now has a daughter who weaves all over town.

A Pacific Coast bootleggerette was nabbed by the coppers, who
found six pint flasks in her bloomers. How's that for a kick in the
pants?

I went to a party last night and the girl I was with drank a gallon
of gasoline. It took three of us to back her into a garage.

An intoxicated young woman was sitting at a table in a restaurant. A waiter with a gimpy leg talked the girl into ordering
tomato juice. As he slowly limped away from the table, she said,
"If you have to go downstairs for it, to hell with it."

DUST

Dust is mud with the juice squeezed out of it.

EAVESDROPPING

Chauffeur: I'll bet you were startled when you heard that the
master and his wife were going to separate.
Maid: Was I! I nearly broke my head on the doorknob!

EDUCATION

She might not be so good at mathematics, but boy, what a figure.

She would have been a very brilliant girl, but she left school because of pneumonia. She couldn't spell it.

—When I was a kid, not even six, I could spell my name backwards.
—What's your name?
—Otto.

—I wrote my people I was coming home. I wanted to surprise them.
—If you wrote them about it, how could you surprise them?
—They didn't know I could write.

Schools

—Yeah, I remember how you were at the bottom of the class.
—Yeah, but they taught the same at both ends.

Teacher: Give me an example of non-sense.
Johnny: An elephant hanging over a cliff with his tail tied to a daisy.

Teacher: Why do you keep looking at that blotter?
Johnny: Oh, it's so absorbing.

—The teacher told me to stay after school.
—Did you do wrong?
—I didn't stay.

A teacher wrote home to a boy's parents: "Your boy is the worst boy in the class." The mother wrote back: "Do what you want. I'm having enough trouble with the old man."

Teacher: Subtract five from five and what is the answer, Micky?
Micky (carefree): I'll be damned if it makes any difference to me.
Teacher: That's right, Micky, sit down.

(Variation)
Teacher: Now, if I subtract 25 from 37, what's the difference?
Little Willie: Yeah! That's what I say. Who cares?

A school teacher was speaking to her class. "Now Children," she said, "the lesson for today will be on the stork." Little Millie leaned over to the girl sitting next to her and said, "Say, this gal will be telling us next there's a Santa Claus."

Father: What's this I hear about your little brother being punished by his teacher just because his nose itched?
Daughter: Yes, but daddy, he didn't tell you he was scratching it with his thumb.

Teacher: Johnny, what could be worse than a man with fleas?
Johnny: I know.
Teacher: What?
Johnny: Supposin' they chirped?

After a lesson on snow.
Teacher: As we walk along the road on a cold winter's day and look around us, what do we see on every hand?
Student: Gloves.

Teacher: Francis, how do you spell stovepipe?
Student: S-t-o-v-e, stove, pig-e-dy, wig-e-dy, ipe, pipe, stovepipe.
Teacher: What's the pig-e-dy wig-e-dy, ipe, pipe for?
Student: Oh, that's for the wrinkles in the elbow.

A small boy was watching a glorious red glow in the sky in the direction of the village with an expression of delighted awe. "Ah, my boy," said an old man, "I see that you, too, admire the beauties of nature. That is a wonderful sunset, isn't it?" "That's not a sunset," said the boy. "That's our school on fire!"

As soon as the bell sounded, the teacher stood up and addressed the class, saying: "Now children, as you all know, America is a great continent, bounded on one side by the Atlantic and on the other side by the Pacific Ocean. On the north, we have the Great Lakes. In Florida it's warm in the winter; the Mormons live in Salt Lake City; Edison invented the phonograph, so how old am I?" One kid jumped up and said, "I know, teacher. You're thirty-four." The teacher said, "That's amazing. How ever did you know that?" The kid said, "Well, teacher, I have a brother who's seventeen and he's just half nuts."

Schoolteachers

An absent-minded school marm was driving down the street. A cop held his arm up and she said, "Yes, dear, you may leave the room."

(Variation)
Traffic cop: Don't you know what I mean when I hold up my hand?
She: I ought to, I've been a school teacher for twenty-five years.

EGOTISM

An egotist is one who, reading a book and not understanding something in it, decides it is a misprint.

—I'm all wrapped up in myself.
—You make a hell of a looking bundle.

Has he got a big head! After the last radio program, he sent himself ten wires of congratulations.

Visitor: I spent last evening in the company of the one I love best in all the world.
Bored Host: And weren't you tired of being all on your own?

A husband, having offended, came home the evening of the quarrel with a parcel under his arm. "Darling," he said to his wife. "Look here. I've got something here for the person I love best in all the world." She came forward with a shrug. "Humph! What is it?" she said, "a box of stogies?"

—I come from a great family. They're all outstanding people. My mother wrote a book. My father competed in the Olympics. My sister went to law school.
—Oh that's nothing. My pop did some wonderful things too.
—What did your father ever do?
—Look me over, kid, look me over!

ELECTRIC CHAIR

—Do you realize you are facing the electric chair?
—I don't mind facing it. It's sitting in it that has me worried.

We had a great Christmas at home. We had an electrical Christmas. Everybody got electrical presents. My kid sister got an electric curling iron, my brother got electric trains, my mom got an electric washing machine . . . and pop got the electric chair.

Doctor: Sambo, I can think of but one thing that will cure you, and that is an electric bath.
Sambo: Now, suh, doctah, yo' ain't talking to dis here nigger. I had a frien' what took one of them things down in Sing Sing and it drowned him.

ELECTRICITY

Two people. One asks the other: "What's more important, a safety pin or electricity?" The first person extols the virtues of electricity. The second person says: "If you lost all the buttons off your pants, electricity couldn't keep them up." (*Or:* "electricity would have a heck of a time keeping them up.")

EMPIRE STATE BUILDING

I went to the top of the Empire State building. My stomach followed me ten floors later.

—A fellow jumped from the top of the Empire State Building.
—Did he get killed?
—I don't know. He lands tomorrow noon.

ENEMIES

—Do you think Joan has any enemies?
—No, but her friends hate her.

ENGAGEMENTS, WEDDINGS, AND HONEYMOONS

Engagements

Flo: How do you know he's engaged to Mary?
Dot: 'Cause she's got a ring and he's always broke.

She: We're going to give the bride a shower tonight.
He: Okay, count on me; I'll bring the soap.

Weddings

Our wedding was a swell affair. Even the rice was puffed.

We had a runaway marriage. I ran away and she ran after me.

The wedding went over with a bang—the bang of father's shotgun.

Many a struggling clerk marries because he is tired of struggling.

My friends had their wedding ceremony performed in the back-yard so that the chickens could pick up the rice.

No one threw any old shoes at the wedding. At the time, the old shoes were all occupied by feet.

A couple was married aboard ship in mid-Atlantic. The Pacific is said to be equally treacherous.

She's a nice girl. She thinks she's married. She doesn't know it was an illegal wedding. Her father didn't have a license to carry a gun.

Maw and Paw had an awful time getting married. Maw wouldn't marry Paw when he was drunk, and Paw wouldn't marry Maw when he was sober.

—You're always late. Why, you were even late on our wedding day.
—Yes, but not late enough.

Bob: If your father catches us eloping tonight I wonder what he'll say to your mother?
Betty: He'll probably say, "Sh-h-h-!"

—One of the Jones girls is going to be married this morning.
—How do you know?
—Her old man borrowed our shotgun today.

A girl went into a shop and asked for a pound of rice. The store-keeper asked, "Should I wrap it up?" She said, "No, throw it at me. I just got married."

Jerry: You used to boast that your love for pretty girls was just a passing fancy. And yet you got married.
Jim: Yes, I lingered too long in passing the last one.

Most people think that a mother cries at a wedding because she is losing a daughter. Actually, she is crying for the poor mug who's getting her.

It hasn't been proven that a cannon shot will cause enough vibration in the air to make it rain, but a shotgun has brought on many a shower.

—Y' love this jane?
—Yep, your honor.
—This your bimbo, girlie?
—You said a mouthful, judgie.
—S'nuff. He's your'n. You're his'n. Ten bucks and take the air on the right. Next.

The train came to a sudden stop with a tremendous grinding of brakes. A much worried young man emerged from one of the cars to see what was the matter. "An accident?" he inquired. "No. Someone pulled the communication cord, and the driver applied the brakes too suddenly, and one of the cars got off the track. We'll be held up for about an hour." "Great Scot! I'm to be married this afternoon." Instantly the conductor turned on the young man and bellowed, "Say, you ain't the guy what pulled this cord, are you?"

Honeymoons

Bride: Oh, what a lovely suite! And such a delicious supper . . . the champagne . . . the marvelous music. What does it make you think of, darling?
Groom: The check!

He: Where shall we go on our honeymoon?
She: I'd love St. Moritz and its soft snows; or Florida and those tropical nights; or California, sunny California; or Venice, Italy, where we can glide along in a gondola; or the Nile, those lovely moonlit nights on the Nile. I'll go anywhere with you, sweetheart. I could be happy with you even on Coney Island.
He: All right, we'll go to Coney Island.

ENGLAND AND THE ENGLISH

When English lassies with permanent waves go bathing they start singing that old favorite, "God Save the Kink!"

An Englishman walked up to a soda fountain and ordered a cocktail. He was given a feather duster.

An Englishman was seeing some "collegiate" dancing for the first time. He seemed greatly impressed, and after a lengthy pause inquired of his guide, "I say, my dear chappie, they do marry afterwards, don't they?"

The difference between an Englishman and an American is that an Englishman walks into a restaurant as if he owns the place. An American walks in as if he doesn't give a damn who owns the place.

I went into a little music shop in London and said, "I want an 'E' string for my fiddle." The fellow handed me a box and said, "Would you mind picking it out yourself? I 'ardly can tell the 'E's' from the she's."

—They don't show comedies in the English movies on Saturday nights any more.
—Whyzzat?
—They don't want any more laughing in church on Sundays.

A Bostonian was showing a visiting Briton around. "This is Bunker Hill Monument . . . where Warren fell, you know." The visitor surveyed the lofty shaft thoughtfully, and then said: "Nasty fall! Killed him, of course?"

The American was telling his English friend about a new sign his company was erecting. "It will have twenty thousand white lights, seventeen thousand green lights, fifteen thousand red lights, and in the middle a glorious sunburst with twelve thousand purple and orange lights," he boasted. "It will be some sign!" "Very interesting," conceded the Englishman. "But don't you think it will be just a bit conspicuous?"

This is the story of a man who went to London and took a walk one Sunday. He asked a bobby (a cop) to recommend a good place to hear some music over dinner in a good restaurant. "Simpsons," the bobby said. "Simpsons is just down the Strand on the right. But it's closed. This is Sunday." He then asked the bobby to direct him to the Criterion Bar, which he had heard was a good place to get a drink. After giving him directions, the bobby said, "But this is Sunday. It's closed." Just then a pretty girl came along and the man picked her up. They were just about to leave when the bobby said, "Not allowed." The man said, "I know. It's Sunday."

An Englishman ran across the street with packages under his arm. A traffic cop asked him, "What's that you've got under your coat?" The Englishman said, "Sugar for my tea." Then the cop pointed to the other package and said, "Well, what's that?" The Limey said, "That's sugar for my coffee." The cop thought he was trying to kid him, so he socked him with a billy club and said, "Here's one for your cocoa." The Englishman landed in a hospital. When a friend came to visit, he told him what happened. At the end of the story, the friend laughed and said, "Well, if it's any consolation, the cop was wrong. You wouldn't use lump sugar in cocoa."

ESKIMOS

An Eskimo wife was telling her friend about her husband coming home late one night. He didn't get in till half past January.

EUROPE

We're going to furnish our apartment on the European plan. You don't have to pay.

A visitor from Europe had just arrived in this country when he saw a diver coming out of the sea. "If I had a suit like that," he said, "I'd have walked here."

EVOLUTION

We call him cuff button; he reminds us of the missing link.

Have you heard about the evolution highball? One drink and you make a monkey out of yourself.

—Man is descended from vegetable.
—Why do you say that?
—Man descended from monkey, and monkey descended from trees.

EXAGGERATION AND HYPERBOLE

His feet are so big he has to put his pants on over his head.

I played violin for years. At one time I was making a thousand dollars a night. Of course, I used to pick up a couple of bucks in the daytime.

Her feet were so big that when she dangled them over the side of the boat, disembarking passengers mistook them for the gangplank and drowned.

The quack was selling an elixir which he declared would make men live to a great age. "Look at me," he shouted. "Hale and hearty, and I'm over three hundred years old." "Is he really as old as that?" asked a listener of the youthful assistant. "I can't say," replied the assistant, "I've only worked for him one hundred years!"

The season's first tall story about grasshoppers has just come in from New England. It seems that a farmer drove his team of horses into Colebrook, N.H., and parked them outside the general store while he did a little shopping. Half an hour later, when the farmer returned, the horses had disappeared and the grasshoppers were pitching horseshoes for the wagon.

One Farmer: Out where I come from, the squashes grow so big we have to haul them in with a team of horses.

Another One: That's nothing. Out where I live, the corn grows so fast that we have to keep two men at the base of each stalk to chop the ears off as they go by. One day, a fellow missed the ear and it caught under his belt. By heck, you won't believe it, but it carried him up so far that we had to shoot dog biscuits up to him with a shotgun to keep him from starving.

Sitting around the Beta house they were swapping lies. "When I was up in Montana," said one of them, "I saw a mountain lion come right up to the camp one day. It was a fierce beast, but I, with great presence of mind, threw a bucket of water in its face and it slunk away." "Boys," said a man sitting in the corner, "I can vouch for the truth of that story. A few minutes after that happened I was coming down the side of the hill. I met this lion and, as is my habit, stopped to stroke its whiskers. Boys, those whiskers were wet."

EXCLUSIVITY

I know a club that's so exclusive, they couldn't get a fourth for bridge.

FADS

—How did you like those Chinese back-scratchers I brought you?
—Is that what they were? Chinese back-scratchers! My wife's been making me eat salad with them.

FAMILY

Of all my wife's relations, I like myself the best.

Where there's a will there's relations.

It's easy to be affectionate to our distant relatives.

Pop is the idol of the family. He's been idle all his life.

My dad never struck any of his children, except in self-defence.

Remember what Mom always said: Your kin kin do no wrong.

My relatives have their shortcomings, but hers have their long stayings.

She's from a very good family. Her mom and dad stop at the Plaza Hotel. Her brothers stop at the Waldorf. And she stops at nothing.

—I've got a half sister in Canada.
—Where's the other half?

Father: Tell that man to take his arm from around your waist.
Daughter: Tell him yourself. He is a perfect stranger to me.

Visitor: That boy of yours seems to have a rare thirst for knowledge.
Mother: Yes, he gets his thirst from his father, and his knowledge from me.

I have three brothers. One lives on a farm and is itching to get to the big city; one is in the city just itching to get to the farm; and my other brother is a bum. He's just itching.

—See that man? He's my grandfather.
—On your mother's or father's side?
—Oh, he sticks up for both of them.

Son: If I'm a good boy will you give me a dime?
Mother: Why do you have to be good for a dime? Be like your father and be good for nothing.

—Sorry, dear, I couldn't cash you a check. It's a rule with me, I wouldn't even cash a check for my own brother.
—Well, you know your family better than I do.

—I have eight sisters and five brothers.
—Eight sisters and five brothers. Gee . . .
—The stork visits us often.
—Visits you! He must live with you.

I know a very old Boston family, so old that the family history is recorded in about ten volumes. In one volume—about the fourth—there's a note in the margin: "About this time, the world was created."

—How are your children getting along?
—Oh, fine. Tony wants to be a racketeer, and Molly wants to be a chorus girl.
—But what happened to Al?
—Oh, we had to kill him. He wanted to go to college.

—I'm from a big family, you know.
—You are? How many of you are there?
—There are ten boys, and each of them has a sister.
—What! Twenty of you?
—Oh, no, only eleven.

—I come from a very old family. My great-great-grandfather had a bed that was two hundred years old.
—Two hundred years old? That must have been one of the beds George Washington slept in.
—Probably, but we could never get great grandma to admit it.

—My sister got married.

—Who did she marry?

—A man.

—I know that, nitwit. Did you ever hear of anyone marrying a woman?

—Yes, my brother.

—Isn't it funny, Edna? Here I am right in my own hometown, and I've no desire to go home.

—Why, Ethel, I can't understand that. What seems to be the trouble?

—Oh, I don't know. My folks don't get along. They're always fighting. The last time I went home, my dad knocked my mother down, just punched her. It was terrible! *(She sobs.)*

—Why, who is your father?

—That's what the argument's about. (Bert Wheeler gag)

(Variation)

—Isn't it strange. My parents live right near here, and I've been home two days and haven't even been home to see them.

—You mean to say you haven't been home to see your Pa and Ma?

—No, I know it sounds funny, but I dread seeing them. They fight so. Would you believe it, the last time I went home, my father punched my mother and knocked her down.

—My God, who is your father?

—That's what they're fighting about.

The Most Related Man

I am the most related man that walks the earth today;
And when I tell you who I am, you'll almost faint away.
So listen what I tell you, what I say you'll find is true;
I am my own grandfather, and I'll prove it now to you.
I won the handsome widow White, one winter we were wed;
She had a daughter whom my father unto the altar led.
Just see what strange relationship we bear to one another:
My father is my son, and my daughter is my mother.
My father had a baby boy, I also had another,
And both were lovely little lads,
They looked just like each other.
My boy is my uncle, for he's my mother's brother;
My wife is now my grandma, for she's my mother's mother.
When Daddy did my daughter wed, of course you all agree,

That I became his father just as plain as ABC.
If I'm my father's father, 'tis fact without a flaw,
I am my own grandfather then, according to the law.
And I have no hesitation, when I make this declaration,
Not a nation in creation can produce another man
In this trying situation of relation complication.
I invite investigation; introduce him if you can.

Family Life

—Do your daughters live at home?
—No, they're not married yet.

(Variation)
—I have three sisters.
—All live at home?
—No, they're not married yet.

—Daughter, you shouldn't go through Bob's pants like that. Just suppose you caught him going through your—
—Why, Mother!

Father *(at three A.M., to restless son):* Now what are you crying about?
Infant: Wanta drink.
Father: So do I. Go to sleep.

Fathers and Older Sons

—Did you learn right from wrong at your mother's knee?
—No, across my father's.

Many a son not only successfully fills his father's shoes, but his shirts and suits and hats, as well.

—Did you have the car out last night?
—Yes, Dad; I took some of the boys for a run round.
—Well, tell them I've found two of their lipsticks!

A letter from a son to his father.
"Dear Dad, I don't want you to be strange with me. If you see me on the street, just say, 'Hello, Dan, why don't you come on up to the house for dinner?' Hoping this finds you the same, I am your loving son, Stanley."

—What did her father say when you asked him for her hand?
—He wanted to know if I could support him in the same style that she did.

—Where's your father?
—He's home.
—How do you know he's home?
—I've got his shoes on.

A father is addressing his son.

—The trouble with you is that you're living in my past, present, and future. You're wearing my last year's suit, driving my this year's car, and living on my next year's income!

Father: Now, son, start saving your pennies and put them in this yellow box, and when you get five pennies give them to me and I'll give you a nickel and you can put that in this blue box; then, when you get five nickels, give them to me and I'll give you a quarter and you can put it in this red box. Seventeen years later the boy discovered that the red box was the gas meter.

FAMOUS PEOPLE

Poor Tarzan, he certainly leads a dog's life. From tree to tree.

If Cleopatra made Mark Antony the mark he was, if Julius Caesar made Brutus the brute he was, who made Lydia Pinkham the pill she is?

Barnum and Bailey

—When those two guys get together, there's always a circus.
—Which two?
—Barnum and Bailey.

Burbank, Luther

"Here's one Luther Burbank didn't try," said the girl as she crossed her legs.

Caruso, Enrico

This young man studied under Caruso. Caruso lived upstairs.

Chevalier, Maurice

—I speak English in little bits . . . all cracked up . . . in pieces.
—You mean you speak broken English.
—That's it . . . rotten English.
—I must try to get Chevalier to teach you English.

Einstein, Albert

He studied under Einstein. He lived on the fourth floor, Einstein on the fifth.

There's one thing about Einstein: no one has ever accused him of plagiarism.

Einstein can't decide whether the universe is static or dynamic. We can—we own a radio.

Einstein has a plan to end war. I hope it is something more than twelve people can understand.

Fairbanks, Douglas

She: You kiss like Douglas Fairbanks.
He: Oh, so you've been cheating on me.

Ford, Henry

—I hear Ford made quite a speech at the meeting the other day.
—What was he talking about?
—He didn't say.

Lady: Billy Sunday is marvelous. He has already converted thousands since he started preaching.
Gent: He isn't in the same league with Henry Ford. He shakes the hell out of millions every day.

Gable, Clark

—Peggy, did you get my check worth a thousand kisses?
—Yes, I want to thank you very much. I had Clark Gable cash it.

Gandhi, Mohandas "Mahatma"

Anyhow, Gandhi is one statesman who has nothing up his sleeve.

Sometimes etiquette means a lot. What if Gandhi thoughtlessly tucked his napkin under his chin?

Henie, Sonja

—I had some Sonja Henie dessert.
—Sonja Henie dessert?
—Yes, you know, a "Peach on Ice."

Hoover, President Herbert

Another year or so of Hoover and nude colonies will be no novelty.

—Where's the ladies' restroom, please?
—It's just around the corner.
—Don't give me that Hoover stuff; I've really got to go!

An old lady was walking back and forth outside a bank. She had lost her money and was blaming it in a loud voice on President Hoover. "He should drop dead," she kept repeating. A cop came along and said, "You must stop saying those things about the president." She said, "All right, can I talk about Mrs. Hoover?" The cop says, "Yes, Mrs. Hoover is just another citizen." The old lady says, "Oh, Mrs. Hoover, you should wake up in the morning a widow."

Joyce, Peggy

A Scotsman liked rice pudding, so he moved next door to Peggy Joyce.
[Peggy Joyce was frequently married.]

This is her last week on the stage, she has a permanent job. She is going to be bridesmaid for Peggy Joyce.

—Did you hear Peggy Joyce is going to be married again?
—Well, that's her business.

—Henry Ford has made many millionaires.
—Yeah, so has Peggy Joyce.

"I don't believe," says Miss Peggy Joyce, "I shall ever marry again." If she doesn't, it will be the first time.

Peggy Joyce gets married so often, the wedding bells must sound to her like an alarm clock.

—Hello, is this Miss Joyce's fifth husband?
—No, I'm her fourth. You have the wrong number.

Now that Peggy Joyce is going to promise to love, honor, and obey for the fifth time, she ought to know whether four out of every five have it.

Long, Huey

Originally there were just seven jokes, but that was before Huey Long went to the Senate.

Moore, Grace

He's such a good-looking guy. If he were a woman, he'd be Grace Moore.

Novarro, Ramon

—Hello, sweetie, what would I have to give you for a swell hug and a kiss?
—Ramon Novarro!

Smith, Albert

Al went to see a friend and asked him why he hadn't been elected president. Al asked all kinds of questions: "Do you think they didn't like my cigar? Was it my derby? Maybe it was because of my religion (Catholic)? Did I sound like a boob on the radio? I know my accent don't make me sound so good." Finally, his friend reluctantly said, "I'll tell you, Al, since you insist. The people think you're illiterate." Al replied, "Well, can you beat that! And my mom and dad were married two years before I was born."

Walker, Jimmy

A news item says, "Looks like Jimmy Walker will return to New York." The terrible thing will be if they return New York to Jimmy Walker.

Two city guys were out walking in the country. They saw a horse and started making bets on whether the horse was a mare or a stallion. After making their bets, they asked a farmer. The first city fellow said, "I say this horse is a stallion and my friend says it's a mare. We want you to settle it for us." The farmer lifted up the tail of the horse and said, "Did you ever see anything like that on a mare?" The second city fellow said, "Yeah, Mayor Walker."

West, Mae

I call my girl Mae West, and not because of her eyes, either.

Winchell, Walter

Little Red Riding Hood: What big eyes you have, Granny.
Granny: The better to work for Winchell, kiddo.

A couple of pigeons were flying over Hollywood, when one looked down and said, "Why, there's Walter Winchell!" "So it is," said the other pigeon. "Well, what are we waiting for?"

FOOD

A pretzel is a donut with cramps.

I make money on crooked dough. I bake pretzels.

A fresh-air fiend invented the donut.

Proverb: You can't bounce a meatball.

No food for seven days makes one weak.

An oyster is a fish dressed up like a nut.

If rye bread is a dime, how much is pumpernickel?

A pretzel is a donut that died trying to do the Carioca.

When the roll is called up yonder, what will we dunk in our coffee?

—Do you have animal crackers?
—Here, boy, show this gentleman the dog biscuits.

Lady: Are these eggs fresh?
Grocer: Fresh? Why, lady, even the chickens haven't missed them yet.

—Is that milk fresh?
—It is. Three hours ago it was grass!

A man accidentally dropped a lump of sugar down his wife's back. But not wishing to waste it, he poured a cup of coffee down after it.

He: That sponge cake we had for lunch was terrible.
She: I think I must have asked for the wrong sponges.

Guard the house, men! You take the left wing. You take the right wing. And I'll take the dark meat!

—I saw a pumpkin weighing five thousand pounds.
—That's nothing, I saw three police sleeping on one beat.

—I haven't tasted food for three days.
—Well, don't worry; it still tastes the same.

All the chickens that are killed to supply the demand for chicken salad would, if stored in a room eight feet square, die of loneliness.

—All right, come to tea and I'll bake you a lovely marble cake.
—Okay, I'll bring a chisel along.

—Have you got anchovy paste?
—No, but we've got LePages glue.

—There is good in everything.
—If you think so, open this egg.

—How did you like the pudding you had at our house last night?
—I thought it was mediocre.
—No, sir, it was tapioca.

—I bought a two-handed cheese.
—What's that?
—You hold the cheese in one hand and hold your nose with the other.

—Did you have chili or soup?
—I don't know. Whatever I had, it tasted like dishwater.
—Oh, you had soup. The chili tastes like hell.

—Remember the old days when we used to buy those big pies; and when we ate them, we used to get it all over our ears?
—Ah, those were the good old pioneer (pie-on-ear) days.

—He eats crackers in bed.
—Crackers!
—Yeah, fire crackers.
—I'd get a bang out of that.

After dwelling for an hour on the parts played by carbohydrates, proteins, and fats, respectively, in the upkeep of the body, the professor asked, "Now, what three foods are required to keep the body in health?" A student answered, "Breakfast, lunch, and dinner."

> When grapefruit is cut up
>   And eaten like pie,
> You get more in your mouth,
>   And less in your eye.

—Yes, I've eaten meat all my life.
—But do you think it has done you any good?
—Good? I feel as strong as an ox.
—That's strange. I've been eating fish for about three months, and I can't swim a stroke.

A man comes to the door.
Man: Pardon me, Ma'am, I'm hungry. Kin I have something to eat?
Woman: Here's a piece of cake I baked myself with some jam on top.
(Later: knock on door)
Man: The jam was swell, lady, here's your board back.

Sweet Tart, you're roll the world to me! I'm a well bread young man, and that's a good raisin why you should marry me. Be my batter half, and everything will pan out all right. Icing your praises night and day because I loaf you. Doughnut refuse me, sugar, or you're cruller than I think you are!

How those lunch rooms in New York order their food is sure funny. I sat down at a counter, and one customer said to the waitress: "Hey, girlie, ham sandwich me." Another customer said: "Apple pie me." A fellow on my right said: "Oh, Missy, coffee me." I was afraid to order. I wanted milk.

—Ya' like t' read?
—Ye'h.
—Wha'cha like t' read?
—Oh, Lil' Orphan Annie, Popeye, n' Flash Gord'n.
—Ya' like O. Henry?
—Naw, de nuts git in me teeth. [O. Henry, an author and a candy bar]

Cooking

She gave him a choice of food every night. He could take it or leave it.

He: Can you cook, dearie?
She: I don't know, but I used to make wonderful mud pies.

Wife: I'm afraid your dinner will be a bit burnt tonight, darling.
Husband: Oh, did they have a fire at the delicatessen?

Wife: Breakfast is ready, dear.
Husband: It can't be. I didn't hear you scrape the toast.

Hubby: Do you think I can make the toast myself while you're away?
Wife: Well, you'll have to scrape along as best you can.

I know a young wife who just worships her husband. She places burnt offerings before him every night.

My wife always reads poetry when she cooks breakfast. She reads Bacon and Waffles. She reads Browning and Making Toast and Burns. [Francis Bacon was an essayist, Robert Browning and Robert Burns poets.]

In one American prison, the convicts are allowed to have their wives bake them a home-made cake; however, if they have good conduct marks, they don't have to eat it.

Bride: I cooked the supper tonight, darling. Guess what you're going to get?
Groom: Indigestion?

Hungry Hubby: When do we eat?
Irritated Wife: There you go again! Don't you ever think of anything except your dinner?
Hungry Hubby: Sure I do, breakfast and lunch!

—It's a weight off the mind of the bridegroom when he finds out that his bride can cook.
—It certainly is, if the weight isn't transferred to elsewhere after she begins doing it.

Dieting

—And how is your husband getting on with his reducing exercises?
—You'd be surprised. That battleship 'e 'ad tattooed on 'is chest is now only a rowboat!

—What are you exercising for?
—I'm trying to keep slim.
—Why can't slim keep himself?

Eating

I can't take my girl into a kosher restaurant. She eats like a pig.

Two fellows were dunking and talking. One got so excited that he had his whole hand in the cup instead of the first two fingers.

Housemother at infirmary: How is Susie getting along?
Nurse: Just fine. She's been eating for a week.
Housemother: She must be getting pretty full.

My friend's father loved pigs' knuckles. He liked them so much nothing else mattered. One day he was enjoying the knuckles so much, he ate his arm off up to his elbow before he noticed.

> Little Jack Horner sat in a corner
> Eating his Christmas pie.

He stuck in his thumb and pulled out a plum,
And said, "Hell, I ordered peach."

Gluttony

—If you eat another bite, you'll bust.
—Hand me that cake, and get out of the way.

While shooting Zola's *Nana*, starring (of all people) Anna Sten, Samuel Goldwyn ate through eleven shots. Anna Sten, who had a personal interest in her "Sammy," told him he'd have stomach trouble if he kept that up much longer. He laughed and continued eating everything including baloney, pastrami, salami, etc. "You'll catch indigestion yet, from this!" burped Anna. "Hah! Don't I know dot!" squelched Sam, "but noo, dun't you know dot I'm seemply crazy about bicarbonate from sodah!"

FOREIGNERS

He's one of those hand-kissing foreigners. He lives a strictly hand to mouth existence.

—Did you know the French drink their coffee out of bowls?
—That's nothing. The Chinese drink their tea out of doors.

FORTUNE-TELLING

He was a crystal gazer and he married the girl 'cause she had a glass eye.

Fortune Teller: You wish to know about your future husband?
Lady: No. I wish to know the past of my present husband for future use.

Gypsy: I tell your fortune.
Man: How much?
Gypsy: Fifty cents.
Man: Correct.

She: They tell me you are a professor of palmistry.
He: None better.
She: Would you read my palm?
He: Yes . . . that line shows you will die when you are sixteen.
She: But I'm nineteen now.
He: Well, you'd better have that line fixed.

FRACTURED FAIRY TALES, RHYMES, AND STORIES

The old lady who lived in a shoe now has a daughter who lives with a heel.

Now, I'll tell you the story of my friend Alabama and his forty thieves.

Mary had a little lamb. The lamb and Mary are doing as well as can be expected.

The lamb that followed Mary was
    As pretty as you please.
But a cur once followed after it
    And now the fleece has fleas.

Father, dear father, come home with me now
The sheep's in the meadow, the hay's in the cow.
Little Boy Blue has found your corn,
And Little Red Riding Hood's pants are torn.

Jack and Jill went up the hill
But not for any water
The sun went down, the moon came up
Oh Mother, guide your daughter.

Jack and Jill went up the hill
To fetch a pail of water
Jack fell down and broke his crown
And Jill got a buck and a quarter.

Mary had a little lamb,
The saucy little elf
Every time it wagged its tail
It spanked its little self.

Mary had a steamboat
The steamboat had a bell
Mary went to heaven
And the steamboat went Toot Toot.

Mary had a little cow,
And oh, how it did stutter.
In place of every quart of milk
It gave a pound of butter.

Little Jack Horner sat in a corner
Having been given the shaft;
His pants were torn and what is more
He felt a terrible draft.

Mary, Mary quite contrary,
How does your garden grow?
But Mary got tough

And she answered real rough,
"Who in the hell wants to know?"

FRENCH

As they say in the French, it was very lousay.

GAMBLING

A gambler's wife was admiring small twins. The gambler assured her that before they were through, he'd have a full house instead of a small pair.

Cards

Poker song: Waiting on chips that never come in.

He's a poker hound. He'll sit all night with a pair of queens.

Boy, if dirt were trumps, what a hand you'd hold.

Shall we have a friendly game of cards? No, let's play bridge.

The bridge players' motto: early to bid, early to raise.

And another kind of bridge partner we usually draw, when we draw any, is the one who calls a spade two spades.

The only difference between bridge and dice is that your pants wear out in different places.

—Hello! Is this the city bridge department?
—Yes. What can we do for you?
—How many points do you get for a little slam?

Pinochle players go on forever, but crap shooters go like that: snap fingers.

Three men were playing pinochle. They started bidding when one of them clutched his cards and dropped dead. Another fellow looked at his cards and said, "He couldn't have won, anyhow."

Pro: Let's play that game called spire or turret.
Novice: What game is that?
Pro: Pinnacle. [Pinochle]

—I'm going to close your place up.
—What'll I do if I can't open?
—Pass! Maybe the next guy has a pair of jacks.

Finally, when all the money in front of them had been bet, Olaf called a halt. "I call," he announced. "What you got, Gus?" Gus exposed his hole card. "I got a jack," he declared triumphantly. "What you got?" Olaf looked very sad. "You win," he said, "I thought you were bluffing!"

I was invited to a home—wealthy people, millionaires. It was a poker party. The very first hand I had two pair; the host bet a dollar. I raised him; he raised me; I raised him; he raised me; and then I got that feeling. You know how you feel when you have nervous indigestion? So I said very meekly: "I call you, I have two pair, what have you?" He said: "I have three of a kind," and threw them face down into the discard. I said: "Wait a minute, let me see them, that's what I paid for, let me see them." He said: "Sir, did you mean to doubt my veracity? This is a gentleman's game, and as the host I want you to know that I don't doubt my guests and I don't expect my guests to doubt me. When someone in this game says he has threes or a straight or a flush, we accept his word as a gentleman." I said: "Oh, I didn't know that." Ha ha, I didn't lose another hand all night!

Horses

No matter how hungry a horse might be, he can't eat a bet.

I bet on a horse called Dream. Ha, did you ever see a dream walking?

He told me to put two dollars on his nose. I did, and he bit me.

In the old days if you wanted a horse to stand still, you tied him to a hitching post. Nowadays all you have to do is place a bet on him.

Bettor: That horse you gave me ran seventh. Absolutely last!
Tout: Shows how good he was. It took six horses to beat him.

Some of the horses we bet on run as though they had already been to the glue factory.

Gambler (boasting): I've got a bankroll that'll choke a horse.
Loser (begging): Fine! Go choke that one I bet on yesterday.

Guest: I guess you won't cash this check.
Clerk: If I could guess like that, I'd do nothing but play the horses.

—You know the horse that ran in the fifth race at Aqueduct?
—You know I'm not interested in horses.
—Oh, you'll be interested in this one. Your rent was on it.

I love to back horses. I'll never forget when I backed Swan Song in the Kentucky Derby, but he got scratched. Then I turned to dog races. I backed one dog, but it stopped and scratched itself.

One of those race track habitues who found out that dope sheets are written for dopes was heading home with a sour kisser, after guessing wrong all day. "You look ill," a pal remarked, "what's the matter?"

"Nothing," was the nimble retort, "I'm merely a victim of too much information."

A fellow went up to a bookie and wanted to bet on a race in which there were only three horses running. The bettor asked what were the odds on the longshot. The bookie told him he could have any odds that he wanted. So he said, "Make it ten to one," placed a one hundred dollar bet, and left. When he returned, the longshot had won. As the bettor was collecting his money, the bookmaker said, "Did you know that that horse you bet on belongs to me?" And the bettor said, "And did you know that the other two belong to me?"

A fellow got a tip on a horse and was told not to tell anyone, not even his own mother. He kept the secret and the day of the race drove to the track. Just before the race started, he went to the betting window and said, "Put this ten dollars on the fourth race." After watching his horse win, he returned to the window to collect on his horse, which had won at big odds. The clerk said, "You didn't tell me the name of the horse." And the guy replied, "I should tell you when I didn't even tell my own mother!"

Other Bets

—What happened? Have you had an accident?
—No, I bet Hans he couldn't carry me up a ladder on his back. And I won.

—I lost all my money gambling and I wanted to send Mom ten dollars.
—Serves you right!
—But you know, Mom will be heartbroken if she hears I was gambling.
—Here's ten, send it on.
—Make it fifteen, will ya? I wanna tell her I won!

—I just went into the hotel lobby and a fellow wanted to make me a bet that he knew the next world's heavyweight champ.
—Did you make the bet?
—No.
—Who took him up?
—The elevator man.

GARDENING

A gardener planting Mae West seed: for heaven's sake come up and see me sometime.

—Today, I saw a man running a steam roller over his plot.
—Sounds like he's raising mashed potatoes.

—Remember that cherry tree you sold me last fall?
—Yeah, how is it?
—A peach.

GERMANS

I asked a little German girl how she came by the name Alice. I explained that Alice was a very unusual name for a German girl. She said: "You see it happens like this. Ven I was born, before me in the family there were eight odder kids. I must haf been sick at the time because I vuz in bed vit Momma. Pappa, he comes home, he looks at me, und den he looks at der odder eight kids playing on the floor, und den again at me unt say, 'Momma, das iss alles!'"

A pair of portly Teutons met on the street one day and began talking about their sons. "Ach, hullo, Fritz," said the first. "Und wie geht's, wie geht's? And how iss it by your son, Otto?" "Ach ja, my son Otto is simply fine. He goes along very good in his new chob." "His new chob, eh? Vat kind off a position has he?" "He iss a butler." "A butler, eh? T'ink of leetle Otto a butler. Dot is very good. Iss he mit a chvell family?" "Family? V'y no. He's not mit any family." "Not mit any family. V'y I t'ought you said he iss a butler." "Sure he's a butler," answered Fritz proudly. "He's mit a ginger ale buttling company."

GOSSIP

Amy has ears like a steam shovel—always picking up the dirt.

Not all tellers work in banks.

This little girl comes from one of those small towns where there isn't much to see, but what you hear makes up for it.

—I don't tell all the gossip I hear.
—No, you haven't the time.

She: If you tell a man anything, it goes in one ear and out the other.
He: Well, tell a woman anything and it goes in both ears and out her mouth.

GREEKS

—What's Greek for boiled water?
—Soup.

GREENHORNS

My cousin just came over here from the old country, looking for work. He looked pretty ragged; he had long hair and needed a shave. Before I sent him to my friend for a job, I told him if he wanted to get it he'd have to make a good appearance. He'd have to smarten up a whole lot. So I gave him a buck and told him to go over to the barber shop. He went in and sat down on the footrest of the chair. The barber looked at him and said, "What do you want?" My cousin said, "I want fixing up a bit." The barber said, "Okay, but why are you sitting down there?" My cousin said, "Where are you going to sit?"

HARD TIMES AND THE DEPRESSION

It's a cinch to be honest with the income tax this year.

1931 finds us with fewer dollars, but more "sense."

Many of the upper classes are now on their uppers.

What this country is going to need is a good five cents.

T'hell with expense, give the canary another seed!

Another ten years of this depression and we'll all be dressed like Gandhi. [Gandhi wore a loincloth.]

This morning they had pawncakes. He had to pawn his watch to get the dough.

Things are so bad at my house that the wolf has to bring his own lunch.

When beer was five cents a glass, apples were sold only on fruit stands.

A song they used to sing: Ten cents a dance. It's now been reduced to a nickel.

I knew a fellow who was so hungry that he tried to take a bite out of a sandwich board.

He started in business on a shoestring, and now he's trying to get the shoestring back.

Things are so bad on the farm that the sparrows have to kneel down to eat the corn.

I was at a party the other night with three fellows: two real-estate men . . . and the other didn't have any money either.

—Business must be picking up.
—Yes, it's looking up. It's flat on its back.

—I haven't eaten for three days.
—That's no good; you must force yourself to eat.

—If things aren't better this year than last, I'll eat your hat.
—If things aren't better, I won't have a hat.

—I started life as a barefoot boy.
—Well, I wasn't born with my shoes on.

—Your kisses aren't what they used to be.
—Well, things are bad all over.

The depression is still with us because, as some wit remarked, the banks are carrying more people than the railroads . . .

Half the people are waiting for their ships to come in; the other half are waiting for their horses to come in.

A sign reads: "Danger! Men Working." A man comes on, sees it, erases the word "Danger," and writes "Hooray."

—Did your grandfather keep his promise and cut you off in his will?
—He did worse; he left me his farm!

—How's business?
—Terrible, even the people who never pay have stopped buying.

(Variation)
—Nu, Yussel, howz business?
—Even the pipple who dun't intend to pay are not buying.

I asked him how's business and he said, "Sh, don't speak so loudly of the dead." (*Or:* take off your hat when you speak of the dead.)

There are a great many people trying hard to live within their income and a great many trying to live without one.

(Variation)
My wife is trying to make me live within my income, and the income people are trying to make me live without one.

—Well, well, well! It if isn't old Joe Pennyfeather.
—Listen, just call me Joe Feather. I haven't a penny to my name.

Well, in the old days, it was the subways and the tenements that were crowded. Nowadays, it's the space behind the eight ball.

Why is it that when a family is fighting to keep the wolf from the door, the stork slips down the chimney?

Things are so rough with me that this morning I tripped over the wolf when I came out of the house.

(Variation)
Things are so bad, men are now howling at the wolves' door.

My brother was in the law business, but things got so bad he had to start taking pillow cases.

Things are so tough with him that he goes around with a blank expression hoping someone will give him a penny for his thoughts.

A luxury is anything that costs more than a dollar and that can't be bought on the installment plan.

In keeping with the times it has been suggested that the tune "Shine on Your Shoes" be changed to "Shine on Your Pants."

I'm so broke that my pants are threadbare. If I sit on a dime, I can tell you what it is, heads or tails. If things get much worse off, I'll be able to tell the date.

The words "In God We Trust" on our money should be changed to read: "Under new management."

The last few years, there has been a great deal of agitation about a new motto for the coin of the realm, and one newspaper suggests, "Abide With Me" and "I Need Thee Every Hour."

Hubby: Well I guess if the worst came to the worst we could go and live with your parents.
Wifey: That wouldn't be possible; they're living with their people.

—Mister, do you think that we will get out of this depression just because we got out of all the others?
—Well, sir, lots of folks drown that have been in the water before.

President Hoover's campaign against hoarding certainly is getting results. After listening to one of the radio speeches, our pup crawled behind the sofa and dragged out two slippers, a golf ball, and a bone.

—I know how to settle this unemployment problem. If we put all the men of the world on one island and all the women on another, we'd have everybody busy in no time.
—Well, what would they be doing?
—Why, boat-building.

A man enters selling apples. He cries, "Help the down and out!" Another man enters and buys the last two apples. The first man exits. The second walks downstage, looks at the newspaper, and says: "Gee, U.S. Steel dropped ten points. Help! Here! Buy my apples! Help the down and out!"

—Aha, hear that song he's playing over on the piano: "I've Got Five Dollars"?
—That's the new prosperity.
—Instead of on the piano, he should be playing it on the old-fashioned lyre.

He: Oh, sweetheart, I love you so much. Let's run away just as we planned.
She: But what about my husband?
He: He has a job, hasn't he? What more does he want in times like these?

A wealthy man went broke playing the market. When he got home that night, his wife showed him a beautiful mink coat she had just bought. He shouted at her to take it back, but she said, "I won't, I won't!" So he said, "All right, but you'll be the best dressed woman in the bread line."

My sister just came back from California and she says that one of the Chinese guides was taking her through Chinatown when they came upon a statuette of Buddha. One coolie approached the idol and said, "Buddha, my God, please give me a long life and wisdom." But it seemed as though her guide was of more modern vintage. He knelt before the statuette and humbly asked, "Buddha, can you spare a dime?"

HEAVEN AND HELL

Who wants to go to heaven since business went to hell?

—Suppose I died. What would become of you?
—I'd stay right here. The question is, what would become of you?

—I went through hell for that girl.
—So that's where you found her!

—Do you know that when I go to heaven I'm going to tell Bill Shakespeare that I don't believe he wrote all those plays.
—Ah, but suppose he doesn't happen to be in heaven?
—In that case you can tell him.

—I wish I had money to burn.
—You will have, if you take any with you when you die.

—Say, that worries me, I'll have an awful time getting my coat on over my wings.
—Your worry will be getting your pants over your tail.

After an argument about money.
—Here's the five dollars I owe you. But I want a receipt.
—What's the receipt for?
—When I die, and I reach the pearly gates, Peter is going to ask me if I paid back the five dollars I borrowed from you. And if I don't have the receipt, do you think I'm going all over hell looking for you?

A young man got terribly drunk and his friends tried scaring him by telling him that he was dead. It looked as if they succeeded because he passed out cold. His friends decided to carry on the hoax when he awoke. After a couple of hours, he came to, looked around, and asked, "Where am I?" One of his friends, in a weird voice, said, "You are now dead and no longer earthly." He said, "Listen, cut that out. If I were in heaven, how could I be hungry; and if I were in hell I wouldn't be cold."

HERO

What is a hero? A man who gets a piece of gold on his chest in exchange for a piece of lead in his pants.

HOBOES

—There goes a great track man.
—He looks like a hobo to me.
—He is.

HOTELS AND BOARDINGHOUSES

In Bridgeport, I slept on a three season bed. It had no spring in it.

Lovely hotel . . . built on a bluff . . . and operated along the same lines.

He's an admiral in the hotel. He has charge of all the vessels on the third floor.

First Chambermaid: Have you heard the story of the double bed? Second: Have I? Why, I made that up!

The hotel man told me I could have an inside or an outside room. I told him to give me an inside room 'cause it was raining outside.

—What was your mother's name before she was married?
—I think it must have been "Savoy." That's the name on our towels.

I'm not staying at the so-and-so hotel any more. After four weeks, I found out they didn't have bathrooms.

Clerk (to a young woman): We're all full now, but if you come back about midnight I can squeeze you in a little room upstairs.

—Do you dress for dinner at this hotel?
—What do you think we're running here . . . a nudist camp?

In my boarding house there's a sign in the bathroom. It says, "Please Clean Tub After Bathing Landlady."

I went to a hotel and asked the desk clerk if they had any rooms. He said that they did. I asked, "What price?" He said, "Six up to twelve." I said, "How much for all night?"

Lady: Can you give me a room and bath?
Clerk: I can give you a room, madam, but you will have to take your own bath.

—She was one of those girls who look for bugs.
—Oh, an entomologist.
—No, a chambermaid.

In the hotel this morning, an employee came right into my room. I said, "Look here, don't you have to be careful walking right into a room the way you just did? A lady might be undressing." He said, "That's all right, mister, I always look through the keyhole first."

Landlady: A professor formerly occupied this room, sir. He invented an explosive.
New Roomer: Ah! I suppose those spots on the ceiling are the explosive.
Landlady: No, that's the professor.

A young lady who had missed her train was stranded in a small country station. "Where can I spend the night?" she asked an old man nearby. "I dunno," he said. "I guess you'll hafter sleep with the station agent." "Sir," exclaimed the girl. "I'll have you know I'm a lady." "That's all right," said the old-timer, "so is the station agent."

The new hotel guest phoned down to the front desk and cried to the clerk:
—Dammit, I can't sleep!
—What's the trouble, sir? Is there too much noise?
—No, but I can't sleep.
—Is something wrong with the bed, sir?
—Oh, no, but I can't sleep.
—Well, what can I do for you? Send up some sleeping potion?
—Hell, no, just send up the key to my room. I'm locked out.

A landlord was interviewing a prospective tenant.
—You know we keep it very quiet and orderly here. Do you have any children?
—No.
—A piano, radio, or victrola?
—No.
—Do you play any musical instruments? Do you have a dog, cat, or parrot?
—No, but my fountain pen scratches a little sometimes.

—Whatsa matter, Joe? You look mad!
—Boy, I am mad! In fact, I'm burning up!
—What happened?

—Well, it was like this. We had hot cakes at the boarding house for breakfast, and I was stowing 'em away pretty good when the landlady ups and says: "Say, Joe Wonkus, do you know how many hot cakes you have et?" And I says back, "No, I don't know as how I've had any reason to count 'em." "Well," she snaps, "you've et twenty-seven, that's how many!" Well, sir, that just went all over me . . . counting 'em like that, the old hawk . . . and it made me so mad that I got up and left the table without eating my breakfast!

Rentals and Renters

The trouble with the average seaside boardinghouse is how to tell which is bed and which is board.

I was asked out to a party the other day and told to live it up. Boy, was I successful! They wanted to break their lease.

The landlord called for his rent, which was many weeks overdue. "I'm sorry," said the tenant, "but I can't pay you this week." "But you said that last week and several weeks before that," snapped the landlord. "Yes, and didn't I keep my word?" replied the tenant blandly.

HOUSES

—What happened to Mrs. Witter's husband?
—He accidentally swallowed a marble while he was sitting in the breakfast nook, and they had to operate to get him out.

HYPOCRISY

Bubbles ain't refined like me; she's coarse as hell.

The world's biggest hypocrite is the man who comes out of a theatre last so the others will think he sat in the first row.

ILLEGIBILITY

The height of illegibility is a cross-eyed man writing his name with a post office pen while wearing a pair of boxing gloves.

INCOMPETENCE

She married a guy who did ten years for arson, but he couldn't even get the kitchen fire started.

INFIDELITY

Many a happy home was broken up by an idle roomer.

Never let your right hand know who's holding your left.

Nothing but trouble ever seems to hatch out of a love nest.

Husbands are a kind of promissory note. One gets tired of meeting them.

—I have a clever wife.
—Mine finds out, too.

—They've been married for ten years, and she's still in love.
—Has her husband any idea who he is?

—Perhaps my husband's secretary would know where my husband is.
—Yes, she's with him.

She is a smart wife. She saw him kissing the maid and closed an eye to it. His left eye.

She: Will you take me for your lawfully wedded wife?
He: I don't think she'd care to have you around.

Angry Wife: Very well, now that I have a Frigidaire, see what you can do about a mechanical stenographer.

The husband who knows where his wife keeps her nickels has nothing on the husband who knows where the maid's quarters are.

She: You are a terrible flirt. Today I saw you with a woman I have never seen you with before.
He: That must have been my wife.

—Your husband looks like a brilliant man. I suppose he knows everything.
—Don't fool yourself. He doesn't suspect anything.

The husband came home unexpectedly in the middle of the day. His wife was bending over the washtub. He pinched her bottom. She said, "Leave two quarts and a pint of cream."

Husband: Did my wife say anything over the phone when you told her I'd be detained at the office and wouldn't be home till late?
Secretary: She said, "Can I depend on that?"

—Do you know your wife is telling everyone that you can't keep her in clothes?
—That's nothing. I bought her a home and I can't keep her in that, either.

A slightly intoxicated husband attempted to sneak in the house without disturbing his wife. On opening the door he discovered the old lady was sitting up. "Good evening, mother of three," said the husband with a sheepish grin. "Good evening, father of none," sarcastically replied the wife.

—Let's get together some night this week. I know a couple of nice girls.
—Great.

—How about Tuesday night?

—Sorry, I'm getting married Tuesday. But Wednesday will be okay.

The playboy held the girl in his arms. He kissed her tenderly at first. Then his ardor increased. The girl's eyes were closed. "Love me, honey?" she whispered. "Oh, yes, yes!" he whispered back. "Do you love me?" The girl drew him closer. "You know I do." There was a moment's silence while the playboy kissed her again. The girl looked at him. "Tell me," she whispered. "Do you love your wife?" "You bet I do," he whispered back. "Do you love your husband?" "I'm simply crazy about him," she admitted. The playboy sighed. He pressed the girl tightly to him. "Gosh," he breathed, "ain't love grand!"

A patient goes to his doctor and tells him that he's feeling depressed. The doctor replies that, whenever he feels blue, he goes home and hugs and kisses his wife, and that always cures him. The doctor tells the patient to do the same and return in a week. When the patient returns, the doctor asks him how he's feeling. The patient says, "Wonderful. I did just what you told me. And by the way, you've got a really swell house."

A tabloid newspaper, offering one dollar for each "embarrassing moment" letter accepted by the editor, is reported to have received the following epistle: "I work on an early night shift in a steel plant. I got home an hour early last night and there I found another man with my wife. I was very much embarrassed. Please send me two dollars as my wife was also embarrassed." The editor, so we are told, sent a check for three dollars admitting the possibility that the stranger, too, might have been embarrassed.

She: I'd make a splendid wife because I'm a very good house-keeper.

He: Do you cook?

She: Sure I cook, I can cook anything, and I can bake cookies.

He: Do you wash the floors?

She: Sure I wash the floors.

He: Can you sew buttons on a shirt?

She: Yes, and darn socks too.

He: Do you do all the housecleaning yourself? Do you wash yourself?

She: No, the laundryman does that for me.

The latest Broadway story concerns an actor who was very much in love with an actress in the same show. The actress was married, and her husband was around frequently. Both she and her lover, however, were very certain that hubby suspected nothing. The affair lasted for over a year, and only terminated when the actress died. The actor attended the funeral, and he wept loudly and long. The husband watched him curiously for a while, and then patted him on the back. "I know how you feel, old fellow," he murmured. "But don't cry. I'll get married again soon!"

Husband's Infidelity

Salesgirl: Could I interest you in a bathing suit?
Man: Yeah, but not so loud. That's my wife.

On the opening night of the bike races, a young man asked his wife if she'd mind if he attended. She said, "No, go ahead." He came home a week later and said, "Gee, it was a swell race."

—I've had enough! Next week I'm divorcing that faithless husband of mine!
—Ah, so you're part of a triangle?
—Triangle nothing! I'm part of an octangle!

A man was telling his wife about a business party he had just attended.
Man: The boss offered a new silk hat to any man who could honestly say that he had never kissed another woman.
Wife (looking around): Where's the silk hat?
Man: Well, dear, you know I look like hell in a silk hat.

A fellow was walking down the street with his wife when a beautiful blonde passed and said familiarly, "Hello, hon!" The man's wife asked, "Who is that hussy?" But the fellow walked on without answering. His wife kept pestering him until finally he said, "My God, will you be quiet. I'll have enough trouble explaining to her who you are."

A husband had journeyed from Minnesota to New York to see the sights of the big city. A few hours after his arrival in Manhattan, his wife grew restless and suspicious. She sent a telegram to her husband as follows: "John, dearie, remember you're a married man." Later in the day she received this reply: "Am sorry but your wire arrived one hour too late."

A preacher made the announcement in church that it had come to his attention that a certain person right there in the church was going around with another man's wife. He asked that man to stop it, and to confess by placing a five dollar bill on the plate. The collection plate was passed around, and when it came back there were fifteen five dollar bills on it and one two dollar bill with a note that the man was bringing the other three next week.

Wife's Infidelity

A man kissed his girl and said, "It must be wonderful for your husband to have a girl like you to call his very own."

—I hear you're a devil with the ladies.
—Ah, your wife tells you everything.

(Variation)
—You're a hound with the women, ain't you?
—Aw, gwan. Your wife tells you everything.

—Sorry I'm late, but I've just been setting a trap for my wife.
—That's bad. Who do you suspect?
—A mouse.

—You look worried.
—I am. A fellow wrote me and said if I didn't stay away from his wife, he'd run me out of town.
—Well, keep away from her.
—Yeah, but the darn fool didn't sign his name.

(Variation)
—A fellow wrote me a letter telling me to keep away from his wife.
—Well, why don't you?
—The darn fool didn't sign his name.

A man with a terrible sore throat and laryngitis goes to his doctor's house and knocks at the door. The doctor's wife answers the door. The man whispers, "Is the doctor in?" The wife whispers back, "No, come in."

(Variation)
I was very hoarse and went to the doctor's home. I could scarcely talk above a whisper. A beautiful nurse opened the door. I whispered, "Is the doctor in?" She said, "Sh! No, come on in!"

A woman on her death bed calls her husband to her side. She says, "Sweetheart, I have a confession to make. I haven't been true to you." He says, "Don't you think I know? Why do you suppose I gave you poison!"

The other morning, while my wife was sleeping, I heard a knock on the door. Putting on my wife's bathrobe, I went downstairs to see who it was. When I opened the door, the milkman gave me a great big kiss. I guess his wife and mine have the same bathrobe.

A man, looking for his wife, goes next door and finds her in the arms of his neighbor. The man furiously curses and shouts. The neighbor bawls out the husband and tells him, "Aw, run home and go to bed." The husband says, "That's what I'm mad about. Tell her to give me the key." (*Or:* "She's got the key.")

First Man: I tell you, I've kissed the girls at Vassar, kissed the ladies of Bryn Mawr, kissed the university beauty queen, but I've yet to get greater enjoyment than when I kiss my own wife.

Second Man (*enthusiastically*): By George, you're right!
(*Painful silence*)

A fellow had an argument with the janitor of his apartment house and told him he'd have him fired. The janitor said, "I don't care, I've already kissed every woman in the building except one." The fellow ran to his apartment. His wife saw he was agitated. He told her he'd had an argument with the janitor, who'd said that he had kissed every woman in the building but one. The wife said, "Don't worry yourself; I suppose it's that stuck up Mrs. Cohen."

> I wonder what became of Sally.
> I wonder if her old man is asleep.
> I wonder if I hadn't better leave town.
> I wonder where my baby is tonight.
> I wonder where I can get hold of a good specialist.
> I wonder what my wife will say when I get home.
> I wonder who's kissing her now.

This man came home late from the Elks one night and found his wife all excited and nervous, and, upon looking under the bed, he discovered a man. When he saw this tough-looking marble under the bed he said, "Hey, what are you doing under there?" And the man said, "Believe it or not, I'm only waiting—I mean I've just caught a rat." "Well," said the outraged husband, "what are you doing with it?" "I'm killing it," came the indignant reply. "Oh, I thought maybe you were kissing it. You have lipstick all over your face."

The new school teacher was making her first trip around the neighborhood. At the first house she visited she was met at the gate by a farmer and a little child.
Teacher: My, but your yard looks neat. It looks perfectly adorable with that white fence running around it.
Farmer (*proudly*): Yep, I made it myself, Miss.
Teacher: And that rose bower! It's a dream!
Farmer: Yep, I made it myself, Miss.
Teacher: I suppose you'll be sending your child to school? It's one of the cutest little tots I've seen!
Farmer: Yep, that's what the wife says, Miss!

INSANITY AND THE INSANE ASYLUM

I'm going to the insane asylum to get me a raving beauty.

(*Variation*)
She went back to the insane asylum. She was a raving beauty.

Next time that guy goes to an insane asylum, it won't be on visiting day.

He: I am crazy about you.
She: Well, run along, this is no insane asylum.

—You were drunk last night or I'm crazy.
—I'm sober this morning, and you're still crazy.

A prima donna sang a benefit for an insane asylum the other night. They were all crazy about her.

Nurse *(in insane asylum):* There is a man outside who wants to know if we have lost any male inmates.
Doctor: Why?
Nurse: He says that someone has run off with his wife.

Warden: So, you think you are sane now. If we give you your liberty will you leave liquor and women alone?
Inmate: I sure will.
Warden: You better stay here. You're still crazy.

Some college boys were visiting an insane asylum and one of them asked an inmate his name. The man replied, "George Washington." "Why," said one who had visited the place before, "the last time you said your name was Abe Lincoln." "Yeah," the inmate explained, "that was by my first wife."

A visitor to an asylum saw a patient using a dry brush on a piece of blank canvas.
—What does that represent?
—The Flight of the Children of Israel from Egypt.
—Where are the children of Israel?
—They have left.
—Where is the Red Sea?
—Rolled back.
—Where are the Egyptians?
—They're expected any minute.

INSULTS

Slogan for reformers: Let us pry.

There's always one flat tire at a blowout.

Don't mind him; he's just a good-natured slob.

You're about as useful as last year's phone numbers.

His dad was a train engineer. He was the first wreck.

He does lots of swimming. He knows every dive in town.

He has such an inferiority complex that he married a midget.

You may be a boon to your mother, but you're a baboon to me.

She has hoof and mouth disease; all she does is dance and eat.

I'll wash the dishes after dinner if you'll dry up during dinner.

He was brought up to be a sculptor, but turned out to be a chiseler.

Let's play hide and seek. I'll hide and if you find me, I'm lost!

You were cast in the same mold as your dad, only you're moldier.

You think he's a silly ass? You should see his brother Jack.

Her face is so sour that when she uses face cream, it curdles.

What would you charge to stand at the wrong end of a shooting gallery?

He's the kind of a guy who has to break in a new set of friends every year.

He: We'll meet again.
She: Yes, accidents do happen.

My girl is crazy about cats. Every time she looks at me she says, "Hello, puss."

—I want to go in the Army and get to be a mess sergeant.
—Well, you've got a good start. You're a mess already.

(Variation)
—I used to be a mess boy in the Army.
—You're not a boy now but you're still a mess.

—I saw your brother on the street this morning, but he didn't see me.
—Yeah, he told me.

—I'd even commit murder for you.
—Make it suicide.

He: I'd go through fire for you!
She: Well, try it sometime. You aren't any too hot at present.

She: Please, I'd like you to remember, I'm a lady.
He: Yeah, and I'm Napoleon.

Diner: Do you serve crabs here?
Waiter: Yes, sit down, we serve everybody.

—Ha, that's one of my dad's stale jokes.
—What are you, one of your mom's jokes?

—Everybody sniffs at that guy.
—They should. He's a bad egg.

—I make people happy wherever I go.
—You mean whenever you go.

—Does Bill still walk with that slouch of his?
—No, I hear he's going with better women now.

The meanest girl is the one who sent back her engagement ring in a box marked: "Glass—handle with care."

—Gee, I'm not myself today.
—Well, you got the best of the bargain.

I've nothing against him. I'm only saying that anyone who goes to his funeral should be forced to pay an amusement tax.

—When I speak, they jump!
—Oh, really? Are you a flea trainer?

What a busybody she is. The only thing she ever missed was her mother's wedding.

Anyone who didn't know this fellow would say he's a bum, and those who know him swear to it.

—I'm on my way to the museum.
—As a guest or part of a collection?

—Don't you remember me? You saved my life twenty years ago.
—Did I? I'm sorry.

—I've written a play about a rat.
—An autobiography?

Hello there! Same old Ed. Same old smile. Same old personality. Same old greeting. And same old suit.

—I wear this dress to tease.
—Tease who?

—I've worked for months on this play.
—All work and no play.

The burglar alarm sounded just as my agent stepped in his office the other morning.

Brown: I'm a self-made man.
Jones: That's what comes of employing cheap labor.

—I'm a self-made man.
—Yeah . . . who interrupted you?

—Is he reliable?
—Just as reliable as the speedometer on a used car.

—He speaks Mexican like a native.
—Yeah, like a native Bulgarian.

—My picture was in all the hometown papers last week.
—How much reward are they offering?

I know a girl who asked her boyfriend for a fur coat and found he didn't give a wrap for her.

You get worse every day, and, today, you're acting like it was tomorrow.

—My mother had an awful accident in Cleveland.
—I thought you were born in Pittsburgh.

—I always mix in the best circles.
—So that accounts for the dizzy look.

He: Don't you ever wish you were a man?
She: No, do you?

He: I passed your house last night.
She: Thanks—for passing.

—I had a terrible nightmare last night.
—I know, I saw you with her.

He: Where I come from, men are men.
She: I guess that's why they chased you out.

—I thought you were sending me a chicken.
—I was, but it got better.

I'm going to start calling you Piggy. You've got a long snoot, you're a little runt, and you're always squealing.

—Can you suggest anything that might help my appearance?
—Well, you might try a heavy veil.

—My face is my fortune.
—That's right; you should keep it in a vault.

He: My mother was very handsome.
She: Oh, so you take after your father.

—I wish I had lived in the Dark Ages.
—I don't blame you; you're a sight in the light.

—I listen in to all the beauty talks on the radio.
—You must be hard of hearing.

Here's Bill Upright. He says he doesn't smoke, drink, or gamble; you could almost say he's perfect . . . if he wasn't such a liar.

—Whipping kids doesn't do any good. When I was a kid they spanked me, and that was for being good.
—Well, they certainly cured you.

—When you were born, what did your mom and pop first say?
—Why bring that up?
—I thought so.

He: Oh, that's my foot. Please get off.
Straphanger: Why don't you put your foot where it belongs?
He: Don't tempt me, madam.

Frosh (*entertaining young miss*): Yes, that's my way. I always throw myself into anything I undertake.
Bored Young Miss: Marvelous, I suggest you go out and dig a well.

She: My boyfriend reminds me of seven rainy days.
He: Seven rainy days?
She: Yeah, awful week!

—Hey, is it true you told so-and-so I was a dirty double crosser?
—Why, no, I thought he knew it.

—We're going to live in a better neighborhood from now on.
—So are we.
—Are you moving, too?
—No, we're staying here.

—Did Sandy come through last night when his chorus girlfriend suggested a cold bottle and a bird?
—Well, he came halfway; he gave her the bird!

—I'm having chicken for supper at home tonight.
—Howdja like to have me for supper?
—No, I prefer chicken.

Soldier: I suppose you realize I have an imposing record.
Gal: Yes, I understand you've imposed on more people than any other fellow in the regiment.

Mr. Penny (*to servant*): Please announce Mr. and Mrs. Penny and daughter.
Butler (*loudly*): Three cents! [*See under* Wordplay ("Mr. Dollar").]

—You ugly looking mug! You dope! You bum! I could cut your throat! Just to look at you makes me sick in my stomach!
—You mean you don't like me?

Admirer: Tell me, you beautiful, gorgeous, divine, alluring creature, wouldn't you like to have me as a lover?
Actress: No, but I'd like to have you as a press agent.

—She reminds me of the sea.
—Howzat?
—She looks green and is sometimes awful rough.

—Where were you born?
—Washington, D.C. Why?
—I don't know why. I was asking you that.

Prof: All men descended from monkeys. Am I right, Mr. Smith?
Bored Student: Yeah, I guess so, but who kicked the ladder out from under you?

—What did you say?
—I didn't say anything. I merely raised my eyebrows.
—Yes, I heard.

—Say, did you ever ride a jackass?
—No.
—Well, get on to yourself.

—Do you know anything about a monkey?
—No.
—Then get wise to yourself.

—I know a game we can play—let's play house.
—But I don't know how to play that game.
—Oh, I'll teach you. You be the door, and I slam you.

Conceited Cuss: Supposing a real ugly-looking fellow tried to kiss you, would you object?
Blonde: Try me and see!

—I'm meeting the Duchess of Heifer.
—The Duchess of Heifer? A heifer is a cow.
—So you know the Duchess.

—How did your horse come in at the races yesterday?
—Oh, as usual, lost by a nose.
—Too bad; it's a pity you couldn't swap noses with him.

Man (describing a disaster): It was terrible. I stood there . . . my face as white . . . as white as your shirt. (Looks at friend's shirt.) Whiter!

—Darling, time seems to stand still when I'm with a clever girl like you.
—Well, no wonder. You've a face that would stop any clock.

She: Darling, will you love me when I grow old and ugly?
He (tenderly): Dearest, you may grow older, but you will never grow uglier.

—I wanna get rid of that woman. I wish you'd tell her a lot of lies about me.
—Why not tell her the truth?

Negro 1: You is so thin you could close one eye and pass as a needle.
Negro 2: Me? What about you? You is so thin your ma could feed you on grape juice and use you fo' a the'mometer.

—Gracious, it's been five years since I've seen you. You look lots older too.

—Really, my dear? I doubt if I would have recognized you . . . but for your coat.

One day she turned and saw that he was smiling at her. She smiled back at him. No, he didn't turn away; he didn't disappear. He looked at her more intently than before. "Smile like that again," he said. She blushed and dimpled. And he laughed and laughed. "Just as I thought," he said, "you look like a chipmunk."

(Variation)
"Smile that way again." She blushed and dimpled. "Just as I thought," he said. "You look like a chipmunk."

—Now listen to me! Your mother was an old cat, and your father was a bum, and your sister is in jail, and your brother is waiting the electric chair . . . and you . . . you . . .

—Now just a minute; don't get personal!

—Where will you be about six o'clock next Saturday?

—Well, I don't know. I think I could be outside the Roxy theatre about seven o'clock.

—Fine. I'll be in Philadelphia.

—Have you ever loved before?

—No, Oscar, I have often admired men for their strength, courage, beauty, or intelligence, but with you, Oscar, dear, it's all love, nothing else.

He: I dreamed of you last night.

She *(coldly)*: You don't say.

He: Yes; then I woke up, shut the window, and put an extra blanket on the bed.

—Say, I heard that you lost all your money and that you blamed me. That's what I get for helping you look for it.

—I didn't say you stole it. I said if you hadn't helped me look for it, I might have found it.

—You rat.

—What did you call me?

—A rat.

—You be careful. Some day you'll call that to someone who ain't and you'll get in trouble.

Frosh: I guess you've gone out with worse-looking fellows than I am, haven't you? *(No answer)* I say, I guess you've gone out with worse-looking fellows than me, haven't you?

Coed: I heard you the first time; I was trying to think.

Dog Jokes

—I just came from a dog show.
—Did you win a prize?

Collegiate Man: Give me a half a pound of dog meat.
Butcher: Should I wrap it up or will you eat it here?

—How did you meet the girl?
—She advertised for a dog she lost, and . . .
—And you answered.

—So you like college boys? Well, look me over.
—What for?
—I'm a West Pointer.
—Yeah? You look more like an Irish setter.

Husband and Wife

—My wife looks like a swan and sings like a nightingale.
—With my wife, it's just the opposite.

She: Isn't it wonderful that such a lovely silk dress should come from such an insignificant little worm.
He: That's no way to talk about your husband.

Moron Jokes

She's a disciple of zero—knows nothing.

You don't have to live in a tree to be a sap.

This girl's air-minded; that is, she's a bit flighty.

If I had your head, I'd go into the lumber business.

They named a town in New England after him: Marblehead.

Darling, I wish you were twins. Then you'd be only half as dumb.

Intelligence is written all over his face . . . with invisible ink!

"Send your head around some time for embalming," she said crushingly.

The stork that carried you should have been arrested for carrying dope.

You're very temperamental: ninety-nine percent temper, one percent mental.

—This liniment makes my arm smart.
—You should rub some on your head.

Blonde: I've just read your new script and I think it's awful.
Brunette: Oh, do you read?

Someone must have hit him on the head with a sponge and he got softening of the brain.

Guy: Last night I was completely wrapped in my thoughts.
Gal: Poor boy, you must have been cold.

—Don't worry, I can fill Eddie's shoes anytime.
—Yeah, but how about the other end?

—My stock in trade is my brains.
—Well, you've got a hell of a sample case.

—Everybody says I got a head like Lincoln. I got a long head.
—Yeah, you got a long head, like Lincoln, but his wasn't so thick!

—What's the idea telling everybody I'm a fool?
—I didn't know it was a secret!

—Do you think I should marry a man who's my intellectual equal?
—Why should you marry a moron when you might do better?

—I know a thing or two.
—Really? What's the other one?

—I fell off my horse last week and was knocked senseless.
—When do you expect to get better?

(Variation)
—I was knocked senseless.
—Oh, when do you expect to get better?

—I'm not as big a fool as I once was.
—No, have you been on a diet?

—Tell me, are sheep stupid?
—Yes, my lamb.

—My husband married for beauty and brains.
—Oh, then you've met his first wife.

—I never send a subordinate off on a fool's errand.
—No, it's so much better to go yourself.

—Englishmen wear monocles because of a weakness in one eye.
—Luckily, they haven't started making glass hats yet.

—He's one of this town's most substantial citizens.
—Yes, solid as a rock from head to foot.

—I just got this letter. It says, "Dear Bob . . . "
—Let me see. Yeah, but she spells "Bob" with two o's.

—I've changed my mind.
—Does the new one work any better?

—Do you know the height of stupidity?
—How tall are you?

—I got a bright idea out of a corner of my brain today.
—Ah! A stowaway.

—I only say what I know.
—Ah, one of those big, strong, silent men!

He once had an idea in his head, but it died from solitary confinement.

—Why, sir, is this called higher education?
—Because it's all over your head.

After a long explanation about some subject.
—Now are you learning anything?
—No, I'm listening to you.

—You should have a nice soft job.
—That's the truth. I've been looking for something soft all
my life.
—Yeah, and you never thought of looking under your hat.

(Variation)
—That's for me, a nice soft job. I've been looking for something
soft all my life.
—Did you ever think of looking under your hat?

—You know, last year the doctor told me if I didn't stop smoking
I'd be feebleminded.
—Why didn't you stop?

—We're intellectual opposites.
—How come?
—I'm intellectual, and you're the opposite.

—I call my girl Opium.
—But Opium—that's a dope.
—So's my girl.

Husband: Did you ever notice, my dear, that a loud talker is generally an ignorant person?
Wife: Well, you needn't shout so; I'm not deaf.

Graduate *(leaving college)*: Goodbye! I am indebted to you for all I
know.
Dean: Don't mention such a trifle.

She: Do you want to know something?
He: Sure.
She: Well, maybe some day you will!

Neighbor *(complaining):* Mr. Brown, have you spoken to your boy about mimicking me?
Father: Yes, I have. I told him not to act like a fool.

—If you were to stand with one foot on a dime, tell me what chain of stores you would represent.
—I give up.
—Kresge—nothing over ten cents.

He: Let's get married.
She: You don't want to get married to me. You ought to marry a smart, intelligent woman.
He: No, I want to marry you.

—Did you ever sit up with a dead person?
—Partly.
—What do you mean partly?
—He was dead from the ears up.

Talent

Some people have an inferiority complex when they really are inferior.

I never realized how much music there was in a riveting machine till I heard you play the clarinet.

You're one of those musicians who, if you can't B in harmony in A flat, you try another key.

She: Isn't it funny? I promised my mother I'd never be an actress, and here I am on stage.
He: That's okay, you kept your promise.

(Variation)
She: My father offered me fifty grand not to become an actress.
He: What did you do with his money?

She: I could dance on like this for ever.
He: Don't say that—you're bound to improve.

—His playing reminds me of Paderewski.
—But Paderewski isn't a violinist.
—Neither is he.

—Tell me, Mr. Lowry, do you drink?
—Only after I have a good program.
—Um, I guess you don't drink.

He: Whatever made you take up singing?
She: I did it to keep the wolf from the door.
He: Well, you certainly did what you set out to do. You'd keep a whole pack away.

She: Have you heard my last song?

He: I hope so.

She: Say, I'll have you know my mother says all men are liars.

He: Well, you have a gorgeous voice, but remember what your mother said.

—I was on a program and I thought of you often.

—What program was it?

—Major Bowes Amateur Hour.

—I get it . . . and those amateurs reminded you of me.

—Not all of 'em, just the ones who got the gong.

INSURANCE

The time allotted has expired. I got that off my insurance policy.

—I want to take out some insurance.

—Fire or life?

—Both. I have a wooden leg.

INTELLIGENCE

She: They tell me that you are a mental giant.

He: I am. My dad and I know almost all there is to know.

She: Well, tell me, what are the fundamental principles of numerology?

He: Oh, that's among the stuff Papa knows.

IRELAND AND THE IRISH

There's a great inventor . . . that Irishman whose name you see on everything: Pat Pending.

Two Irishmen were walking down the street, when Pat said to Mike, "Have you ever heard the story about the feet?" Mike said, "No." Pat said, "Be jabbers, you have two."

—So your name is Murphy, is it? Are you any relation to John Murphy?

—Well, distantly. You see he was the first child and I was the fifteenth.

Mulhern: Which would yez rather be in, Mike, an explosion or a collision?

Murphy: Why, in a collision, Pat. Because in a collision there yez are, but in an explosion, where are yez?

I went to a baseball game. The umpire announced, "Andy Cohen now batting for Seamus Kelly; Andy Cohen now batting for Seamus Kelly." A big Irishman stood up in the stands and yelled, "McNulty now leaving the grounds."

I went to the zoo today. There was an Irish nurse there with some children. They were looking at the kangaroos. She asked the keeper what they were. He said, "They're kangaroos, a native of Australia." The nurse said, "Good heavens, my sister married one of them."

A Jew and an Irishman were on board a ship bound for Ireland.
Irishman *(catching sight of his homeland):* Hurrah for Ireland.
Jew *(riled):* Hurrah, hell.
Irishman: That's right. Every man for his own country.

O'Brien was reading a letter for his friend Murphy, who was standing behind him with hands over O'Brien's ears. When Murphy was asked why, he explained, "I just got a letter from my girl and I can't read. So O'Brien's reading it for me; but I'm stopping his ears so that he can't hear what she's written me."

An Irishman was killed while working. His mates engaged in a lengthy discussion about who should break the news to Mrs. Clancy—and how. Fitzpatrick was elected. He went to the Clancy home and timidly rang the bell. When Mrs. Clancy opened the door, he asked, "Are you the widow Clancy?" She said, "I'm Mrs. Clancy, but I'm not a widow." He said, "No, what'll ya bet?"

An Irishman called O'Brien went out seeking a job. He saw a long line of men standing at the construction site waiting to be hired. So he got in line. Finally, he reached the point where the foreman was doing the hiring. The man in front of O'Brien was asked his trade and replied, "Mason and bricklayer." Next came O'Brien. When he was asked his trade he said, "Knights of Columbus and builder."

A fellow with two wooden legs entered a speakeasy and got very drunk. The barman, wishing to be rid of him, threw him into a telephone booth. About half an hour later, an Irishman who had had a few drinks decided to call his wife and tell her that he was working late. He opened the door of the telephone booth, stepped in, and yelled, "That's a foine place to put a wheelbarrow."

Before the plane took off, the pilot advised everyone to take his parachute. One big burly Irishman refused. The pilot told him, "You'd better have one, flying's not so good today." He still refused. So they started up. After about fifty miles, the plane went into a spin and the pilot gave orders for everyone to jump. All the passengers did, including the Irishman, who jumped last of all. As he went down, he passed the pilot and said, "You're just a sissy."

Two Irishmen were standing outside the Catholic church and saw the good priest come out carrying an umbrella. It was just starting to rain, so the good man loosened the strap on the umbrella, which was one of those newfangled kind that opens with the press of a button. He pressed the button, the umbrella flew open, and he walked away. One of the Irishmen slapped the other and said, "What a pity such a wonderful thing to happen and not a Protestant around to see it."

An Irishman, stewed to the gills, began to feel remorseful and went to confession. The priest surveyed his condition and said, "Go home like a good man. You haven't killed anyone, have you?" "Certainly not," mumbled the Irishman and staggered out. Just outside the church, he saw his friend heading in. He went over to him and said, "Shay, it's no use going in there. The good Father's only hearing murder cases today."

Pat had been drinking to excess for months. One day he was met by the priest. "Why don't you stop drinking," scolded the holy man, "and support your family as you should?" "I'll take the pledge right now, Father," Pat promised. "That's fine," smiled the priest. "But remember, Pat, if I ever see you drunk again, I'll have you excommunicated." Pat heeded the warning and kept sober for six months. Then he fell off the wagon. Staggering up the street, he saw the priest approaching. Just as he met him, Pat shouted at the top of his voice: "Make way for a Protestant!"

Billy O'Sullivan went to confession and told the priest that he had swiped a jug of "Minnesota thirteen" likker from old man Smith, and hid it in the culvert near the school house. Billy was given penance to do, and as soon as darkness fell the priest removed the jug and returned it to Smith. Well, Billy went looking for his jug, and when he found it gone he suspected Father O'Leary. The next Sunday, Billy had another sin to confess. He told the priest he had been out for a buggy ride with a widow. "What's her name?" asked Father O'Leary.

"Never you mind, Father. Remember that I told you where the jug was," said Billy.

ITALY AND ITALIANS

He used to run a laundry in Italy until they started wearing black shirts.

An American tourist drowned while touring Italy. He got drunk in Venice and tried to sleep in the gutter.

—Were you ever in Venice?
—Yeah.

—Did you like it?

—No, the darn place was flooded.

JANITORS

The janitor sent up a little heat, in token of his steam.

Our janitor looks as though butter wouldn't melt in his furnace.

JEWS

Goof, the smartest man in college, can speak Yiddish with one hand.

A Jewish fellow wanted to enter a synagogue to look for his brother. The doorman resisted, but finally let him in with the warning, "All right, you can go in, but don't let me catch you praying."

Ginsberg: What's the difference between a shilling and pence?
Goldberg: You can walk down the street without a shilling [but not without pants].

—I swallered a pan only yesterday und it hoits sometings turrible.
—Vat kind of a pan—a dishpan maybe or a frying pan perhaps?
—No, no. A fountain pan.

—Mulligan, Mulligan, Levy and Mulligan
—What's Levy doing in there?
—That's what the Mulligans want to know.

—Will the person who wins the schnozola contest be able to smoke a cigar under a shower?
—He ought to be able to. Sam Bloomenbaum smokes a cigarette under one now.

Two Jewish fellows with a heavy dialect. One of them is trying to think of a word in the middle of a sentence. As he is struggling and waving his arms, the other says the word: catastrophe. The other says. "That's it! You took the words right out of my hands."

An old Jewish man boarded a streetcar with his son and refused to pay the fare for the boy. The conductor said, "That kid is fourteen if he's a day. In fact, that kid looks at least fifteen years old." The old man said, "Can I help it if he worries?"

A New York theatrical agent heard of an all-Indian jazz band playing in a small town and he went there to book them. "Are all of you really Indians?" he asked. "If you are, I'm sure I can put you over big on Broadway." "Vat vould be the use of kiddin' mid you?" replied the chief. "Ve are all fool blodt."

An Irishman and a Jewish fellow are moved next to each other in a hospital. Next morning, the Jewish boy is going through the ceremony of laying "t'fillin." The Irishman says, "You can't beat these Jewish people. Look, he's here only two days and already he's taking his own blood pressure." [T'fillin: phylacteries; black straps that Orthodox Jews wrap around one arm for purposes of prayer]

In a forty-four story building, four Jewish guys were walking upstairs because the elevator was out of order. One of them said, "Okay, we each walk eleven floors and tell a story. That way we won't notice how bad it is." When they climbed the last eleven flights and reached the top, the fourth man said, "Oy, fellows, have I got a sad story for you. I forgot the key."

Two little boys, Jewish and Irish, always played together. One day the Irish boy's mother told him she didn't want him to play with little Abie. He asked her why and she told him. A few days later, the Irish boy was playing alone. The Jewish boy came up to him and said, "Come on, let's play together." The Irish boy said, "No, I can't play with you." The other said, "Aw, come on." But the other persisted, "No, I can't." The Jewish boy asked him why he wouldn't play, and the Irish kid said, "Mamma says I'm not to play with Jewish boys." Little Abie replied, "Aw, come on, we won't play for money."

A priest came upon some youths playing in the street, and thought he'd test them by offering a quarter to anyone who could tell him who was the best known patron saint. The kids began to think. One of them said, "St. Louis." The priest said, "Very good, but that's not the one I'm thinking of." Then he turned to a little Hebrew boy. "What do you say?" He replied, "St. Patrick." The priest said, "Excellent! You win the quarter. But tell me: why did you say St. Patrick? Surely you would think of Moses first." The kid replied, "Well, I did think of Moses first, but business is business."

A little Hebrew was on his way to the coast. A big burly cowboy got on the train out west and offered the Hebrew a ham sand-wich. "What kind of sandvitch?" asked the Hebrew. "Ham," said the cowboy. "Pork?" "Yeah." "No thanks." The cowboy offered him a cigar. "Sorry, I never could smoke." After a few more miles, the cowboy offered him a drink. The little guy said, "No thanks, I never drink." The cowboy knocked back a few drinks and offered the bottle again. The little guy refused, so the cow-boy pulled a gun and said, "Here, take a drink of this or I'll give you a dose of lead." The little guy said, "Vell, if it's a holdup, I'll take the sandwich too."

Three men in the same jail cell were awaiting execution, a Ger-man, an Irishman, and a Jewish fellow. The warden told them that since this was the eve of their execution, their last night to live, they could have for dinner whatever food they desired. When the warden asked the German what he wanted most, he said: "Vell, if it's all the zame by you, I vould like it a nice Viener schnitzel mit kartoffel." The warden said fine; then he turned to the Irishman. "Sure, an' I'd like some corned beef and cabbage." The warden agreed and turned to the Hebrew. "Vell, ahll tell you. I'd like some strawberries and cream." The warden said, "Sorry, strawberries aren't in season." So the Jewish chap said, "Dat's all right, I'll vait."

An orthodox Jew was walking down the street on the Sabbath, a day on which Jews are not supposed to handle any money until sunset. He saw a twenty dollar bill lying in the road, walked past it a few times, then around it, and finally he stepped on it. After a while a cop appeared and started to question him. "I've noticed you've been standing here for three hours. What's it all about?" The Jewish man said, "Am I hurting anybody? I'm not causing a disturbance, am I?" The cop replied, "Yes, you're causing a disturbance with me. I want to know why you're standing here, and if you don't tell me quick I'll hit you over the head with my billy club." The man wouldn't speak or move, so the cop hit him with the club. Then the Jewish man said, "Gee, it's dark, it must be night," and picked up the note.

A little Hebrew looking through the art gallery with a friend for a guide came to the picture of the Holy Family. He puzzled about it. He asked about each person in the picture.
—This is Joseph.
—But he has no shoes.
—Of course not, he was only a poor carpenter.
—And this one dressed in rags?
—Mary, the mother.
—And the child sitting on the bare floor with a crust of bread?
—Jesus.
—Huh, no rugs on the floor, only a crust of bread in the house, but they can have their pictures took!

Bennie Ginsberg, tired of his betrothed, decided to cancel the engagement in a diplomatic and gentlemanly manner.
Bennie: Ve vere nefer meant to be mates. By us is too difference de temperaments. Ve vill hunly be bickering weet fighting.
Sadie: Vy, Bennie, you got wrung de idea. Ve luffink itch odder like two turdle doves.
Bennie: Rilly, Sadie mine dollink, ve'll nefer agree, end will be by us ull de time freection.
Sadie: No, Bennie. It'll be like Rumeo with Jooliat. I'll making a poifect wife end it'll nefer be a quarrel.

Bennie *(earnestly):* Sadie, I'm tellink you by us will be nottink but arguments wit quarreling!

Sadie *(sharply):* But, Bennie, I say . . .

Bennie *(yelling):* See, vot did I tell you! Ve're fighting ullraddy!

Jews, Business, and Money

I have a friend who lives on next to nothing. He has the hat check privilege in a synagogue.

The only thing that Henry Ford has against the Hebrew race is that they can get more for a used Ford than he can get for a new one.

—Nu, Yussel, howz business?

—Once the store burns down, I'll be fine.

Two Jewish fellows met on the street. One of them said, "Hello, Abe, congratulations. I hear you had a fifty thousand dollar fire." And the other fellow said, "Sh, it's tomorrow."

Mr. Meefoofksy was frequently contacted about a long overdue account. So he phoned the sender of the dunning letters and said, "Stop sending letters and all the time asking for do moneh. I do business only one way. Eeder I pay . . . hor I dunt."

Ginsberg went into the art business. He said that he was buying and selling pictures. He bought one for twenty-five dollars and sold it for fifty, saying he didn't know the name of the picture, but it portrayed three fellows: one had a fife, one had a drum, and the other had a headache.

Abie Nussbaum and Pat Casey had just returned from the funeral of their mutual friend, Mike O'Brien. In life, Mike was a man of means, and consequently the ceremonies had been elaborate. "Tall me sometink," asked Abie. "How much deed dot whole funeral costed?" "Well, Abie," said Pat, "the casket cost $5,000. The limousines for the procession ran to another $1,000. The flowers were valued at $3,000, and the cost of the tombstone would be no less than $20,000." "Hmm," hmm'd Abie, "dere's no gattink avay from it. You gantiles certainly know how to live!"

When Murphy learned that Goldstein, with whom he had had some business dealings, had folded up, he hurried over to see if he couldn't obtain a settlement of his account. Goldstein, after promising to save Murphy from loss, finally offered to make him a preferred creditor. The Irishman agreed to this and went home. But after thinking the matter over that night, he was somewhat dubious about the plan so the next morning he called upon Goldstein. "Just what do yez mean by makin' me a preferred creditor?" he asked. "Vell," said Goldstein, "I tell you vot it iss. You

know now dot you von't gat anyt'ing, vile all de odder creditors
von't know it for sixty days."

Abe and Moe met on the street. Abe asked Moe about the family.
Moe: My son, Irving, he has a wonderful office in Wall Street,
with clerks and lots of help.
Abe: And Sam?
Moe: He's got a beautiful store. He changed his name to
McIntosh, and his business is growing by leaps and bounds.
Abe: And what about Isaac? I don't suppose he ever amounted to
much. What is he doing?
Abe: Oh, Isaac, he's still got that little store on Delancey Street.
Still the same old Isaac. If it wasn't for him, we'd all be starving.

A young Jewish boy went into a fancy Jewish clothing store. *(He
gives a description of the store.)* He looks at a suit and says, "Say,
I'm lovin' this swoot. How much cost a suit like this?" The salesman says, "This is one of those fency stores that don't ask two
prices. (*Or:* we don't have two prices.) I'm not asking twenty-
three dollars, twenty-two, twenty-one. This suit you shall have it
for twenty dollars." The young fellow responds, "I wouldn't buy
clothes where there're two prices. So I wouldn't offer you seven,
eight, or nine dollars, but ten I will positively give—" And the
clerk says, "Sold!"

Done with a Jewish dialect. Little Abie worked in a cloak and suit
factory. He and the boss had been pals for years. He went into
the boss's office to ask for a raise.
Abie: For a few more dollars a week I'm asking. Look how long
I've worked here for nothing practically. I ask just three dollars
more a week.
Boss: Huh, three dollars a week? Do you realize, Abie, that
means twelve a month. That means 144 dollars more out of my
pocket on the year. In five years 720. In ten years, 1440. In twenty-
five years 3600 dollars you take out of my pocket. In thirty years
it means—oh, my god, I'm bankrupt!

Shapiro and Levy were partners in a suit and cloak business.
Business began to fall off terribly. Bills were coming due; creditors were threatening; and there was no money to be gotten
anywhere. One day Shapiro said to his partner, "Levy, O'm
disgosted. I tink O'm goink hum. You take care on de store."
He left, and the next day he received a phone call from his partner. "Shapiro, com on don to de store, kvick. I ken't tell you de
trobble over de phun. Com on don kvick." Shapiro jumped into
his car and went tearing down the road at fifty miles per hour.
Suddenly, a cop drew up to him and ordered him to pull over
to the curb. "Where do you think you're going, to a fire?" he

demanded. Shapiro leaned over the side of the car, and whispered, "I tink so!"

Jews and Germany

A Jewish man, trying to buy an international hook-up on radio in Germany, paid a fabulous price for one word: HELP.

(Variation)
In Germany, a Hebrew was trying to buy time on the radio. They took his money and allowed him to say one word, "Help."

Hitler: What's your name?
Culprit: Abraham MacBromovitz an' tis a bra bricht night we're 'aving.

A Hebrew artist was engaged to make a portrait of Hitler. When it was shown to the hanging committee and the dictator, he shouted, "What's the idea of showing only the back of my head in the picture?" The artist replied, "I thought any man who does the things you've done would be ashamed to show his face."

In Germany, two little Jewish fellows were arrested, brought into court, and charged with making derogatory statements about the dictator. One of the Jews said in their defense that they didn't mention a name. They merely said, "That damn fool dictator." The judge said, "You're guilty. There's only one damn fool dictator."

Jews in Palestine

In Palestine, a Jewish delegation called on the British High Commissioner to thank him for putting an end to the war between the Arabs and the Jews. The spokesman, a little Hebrew, thanked the High Commissioner for the land that the Jews received, but complained that now that they had the land, they had no seeds to plant. The next day, they got the seeds. A few days later, the delegation, led by the little Hebrew, came asking for farm implements. The next day they got the implements. A few days later, they rushed into the Commissioner's office again. They thanked him for the wonderful treatment—the land, the seeds, the farm tools. "What's the trouble now?" asked the High Commissioner. The little Hebrew replied, "We can't get those Arabs to work."

Jewish Pronunciation

—Do you know anything about Texas?
—Yeah, I know the Texes are much worse this year.

Jewish Pronunciations
Atom—the first man (Adam)
Collar—shade, hue (Color)

Column—serene, peaceful (Calm)
Comb—to arrive (Come)
Dais—periods of time (Days)
Expanse—cost (Expense)
Guess—motor fuel (Gas)
Hearse—that girl's (Hers)
Hymns—that fellow's (His)
Impotent—big shot (Important)
Jerk—a humorous anecdote (Joke)
Lips—jumps (Leaps)
Pasture—a church official (Pastor)
Pence—an article of male attire (Pants)
Phase—physiognomy, countenance, visage, puss (Face)
Pig—to select (Pick)
Pip—to look slyly (Peep)
Raid—a color (Red)
Ride—correct (Right)
Sang—was submerged (Sunk)
Seed—observed (Seen)
Ship—a wool-bearing animal (Sheep)
Shoe—yes, indeed (Sure)
Slip—to slumber (Sleep)
Violate—a dainty flower (Violet)

Yiddish

The girls over in Paris were chic, but over here they're chikkar.
[*Chikkar* is Yiddish for "drunk."]

The boys on the team opposing Notre Dame decided to give their
signals in Yiddish. On the field, they started calling the numbers
and right away they lost yardage. This happened several times
until McLaughlin of Notre Dame shouted across the line,
"Gornischt helfin." [Yiddish: "It won't help."]

Two salesmen were comparing notes.
One: I don't have much luck selling in Jewish communities.
Two: That's my best trade. You have to know some Yiddish
words. They love it when you can speak a little of their language.
One: But how can you remember the words?
Two *(pointing to his head)*: I keep them up here in my tuchis.
[Note: *tuchis* in Yiddish means "backside, derrière."]

JOKES

It's a wisecrack that knows its own father.

A pun is a joke at which everyone groans because they didn't
think of it first.

—That comedian always makes the same joke.
—Yeah, he's got a one crack mind.

—I'll get by. My jokes will keep me in my old age.
—Well, that's only fair. You've kept them in THEIR old age.

—I'll tell a little parlor story.
—Wait a minute. I'd better hear it first. *(He whispers in her ear; she laughs.)* You must have heard that in a pool parlor.

—I'll bet you I can make you say, "No, I haven't." Aw, I'm probably just wasting my time. You've heard this one before.
—No, I haven't.

When an Englishman is told a joke, he laughs three times: first, to be polite, second, when the joke is explained, and third, when he catches on. When a German is told a joke, he laughs twice: first, to be polite, and second, when the joke is explained. He doesn't catch on. When a Frenchman is told a joke, he laughs once: he catches on immediately. When an American is told a joke, he doesn't laugh at all: he's heard it before. *(Pause)* Oh, well, you're an American, aren't you?

LANGUAGE

First Grammar Lesson: Never end a sentence with a proposition.

—Say, do you know the King's English?
—Well, so he should be.

—That guy ought to be hung.
—Hanged you mean.
—No, hanging's too good for him.

—Let's go to a new place and dine. You know, away from the hoi polloi.
—Swell, I'm sick and tired of eating that Chinese food.

—What will you have, sir?
—Consommé, bouillon, hors d'oeuvres, fricasse poulet, pommes de terre au gratin, demitasse des glacés—and tell dat mug in the corner to keep his lamps offa me moll, see!

Uncle: I have went. That's wrong, isn't it?
Nephew: Yes, uncle.
Uncle: Why is it wrong?
Nephew: Because you ain't went yet!

LATIN AMERICA

A Latin American diplomat is a person who pours banana oil on troubled waters.

—They gave the president of the South American republic the customary salute of twenty-one guns, but I'm afraid it was a failure.
—How so?
—They missed him.

LAUGHTER

He who laughs last must have had a mouthful.

—And do you mean to say that you laughed in the face of death?
—Laughed? I thought I'd die!

LAUNDRY

I had trouble with the laundry but got it all ironed out.

—Your laundry just came back.
—Thanks.
—They wouldn't take it.

LAW

Courtroom

—You can take your choice, ten dollars or ten days.
—I'll take the ten dollars.

Judge: What brought you here?
Man: Five cops and a patrol wagon.

Judge: We've located your wife, but she won't talk.
Husband: That's not my wife.

Judge: Your wife sez you gave her two black eyes and a broken nose.
Husband: Don't mind her, judge, she's punch-drunk.

Magistrate: Why did you throw a hot flatiron at your husband?
Wife: Well, it's my motto to strike while the iron is hot.

Judge: I fine you one dollar and ten cents for beating your wife.
Prisoner: I don't object to the dollar, but what is the dime for?
Judge: That's the federal tax on amusements.

Attorney: Your Honor, your bull pup has chewed up the Bible.
Judge (grumbling): We can't adjourn to get a new Bible. Just have the witness kiss the dog.

A bank president stole eighty thousand bucks. The judge shouted at him, "Why did you steal eighty thousand dollars?" He said, "'cause I was hungry."

—You've been in jail for stealing, drinking, gambling and bigamy. What have you to say for yourself?
—Well, none of us is perfect.

—You know one man's word is as good as another's.
—Yeah, did you ever appear in a traffic court with a policeman against you?

Judge *(to prisoner):* What, you here again?
Prisoner: Yes, sir.
Judge: Aren't you ashamed to be seen here?
Prisoner: No, sir! What's good enough for you is good enough for me!

Judge: The policeman says that you were traveling at a speed of sixty miles an hour.
Prisoner: It was necessary, Your Honor. I had stolen the car.
Judge: Oh, that's different. Case dismissed.

Judge *(in traffic court):* I'll let you off with a fine this time, but another day I'll send you to jail.
Weatherman: That is exactly what I predicted.
Judge: What do you mean?
Weatherman: Fine today—cooler tomorrow.

A case that was brought before the local magistrate involved the rightful ownership of an eight-day clock. After hearing both sides of the argument, the judge turned to the prosecutor. "You get the clock," he told him gravely. "Look here, what do I get?" complained the defendant furiously. "You get the eight days," snapped the judge.

—You see that girl? She just received two thousand dollars for a short love story.
—Good heavens, that's a lot of money for a short story. Did she sell the movie rights?
—No, she told it to a jury.

—Do you know any of the jurymen?
—Yes, I know more than half of them.
—Are you willing to swear you know more than half of them?
—If it comes to that, I'm willing to swear I know more than all of them put together.

Judge: Now, John, tell us why you insulted this lady.
John: Well, Yur Honor, I picked this lady up in my cab and took her to where she wanted to go an' when she got out she gave me the exact change and no more, an' I sez under my breath, "You stingy ol' hen," and she heard me.
Judge: Perhaps, John, you can tell us just what is your idea of a lady.
John: Well, Yur Honor, I picked up a lady the other day an' took her to her destination an' she gave me a five dollar bill an' me bein' an honest man I reaches fur me change, but sez she, "aw,

t'hell with the change, go buy yourself a shot o' gin." Now, that's what I considers a lady.

Ole, the night porter, was testifying before the jury after the big bank robbery.
Attorney *(thundering):* You say that at midnight you were cleaning the office, and eight masked men brushed past you and went on into the vault room with revolvers drawn?
Ole: Yah.
Attorney: And a moment later a terrific explosion blew the vault door off, and the same men went out past you carrying currency and bonds?
Ole: Yah.
Attorney: Well, what did you do then?
Ole: Aye put down my mop.
Attorney: Yes, but then what did you do?
Ole: Vell, aye say to myself, "Dis bane hell of a way to run a bank!"

Lawyers

Before this fellow was an actor, he was a lawyer. He defended eleven murderers, and not one is in prison now. They all got the chair.

Lawyer: When did the robbery occur?
Man: I think it began—
Lawyer *(interrupting):* We don't care what you think, we only want to know what you know.
Man: Sorry, but I can't talk without thinking. I'm not a lawyer.

LAXATIVES

—Do you use Pluto water?
—Yeah, I'm a regular fellow.

—That guy's old man is a millionaire laxative king.
—Hah, a plutocrat.

—Say, Lisa, is you gonna drink that whole bottle of Pluto water?
—Ain't gonna do nothin' else but.
—Oh, yes you is!

—I heard that Bing Crosby was going on a program sponsored by Ex-Lax.
—It'll be very short, just two announcements and BING.

—You know, one thing that always has the power to move me is Brahms's first symphony. Those concluding chords to the first movement get hold of something inside of you. They grasp you in its mood. They give you the feeling of wilderness. They loosen up something, something inside of you.
—Yeah, Brahms is swell, but didja ever try Ex-lax?

LAZINESS

I got him a job as a street cleaner, but he didn't have any push.

He's so lazy he tried to get a job as laundryman in a nudist colony.

The only thing that can lay down on the job and get results is a hen.

He's so lazy that he sits up all night to keep from washing his face in the morning.

—When did your husband lose his inclination for work?
—Don't ask me, we've been married for only six years.

He never did a thing in his life; and he didn't do that well. You might say that he belonged to the No-Ability.

—If you're not tired, why are you resting?
—I'm resting just in case I get tired.

Stenographer: Hey, come back here! The boss wants to see you.
Office Boy: Did he ask for me personally?
Stenographer: No, he said he'd like to see the fellow who could loaf eight hours a day and get paid for it.

Two fathers of college seniors were discussing their sons.
—Why, my son is so lazy he wants to open an ice factory in Alaska.
—Why, man, my son would like to get a job with your son as bookkeeper.

—Does your husband work, Mrs. Briggs?
—Oh, yes. He sells toy balloons when there is a parade in town. What does your husband do?
—My husband sells smoked glasses when there is an eclipse of the sun.

Weary Willie and Dusty Rhoades were reclining upon the grassy slope near the water tank. The usually talkative Willie was very quiet and had been that way for a half hour.
Dusty: Say, wot's eatin' youse? You ain't said a word for ever since we been layin' here!
Willie: I wuz jest thinkin, that I wisht I was a coal miner so's I could go on strike with them others!

LIBRARIES

One place you don't find an endurance sitting contest . . . the library on Saturday evening.

LIES AND LIARS

The love that lies in a woman's eyes lies and lies and lies.

She was born in the hill country and hasn't been on the level since.

He's a second-story man. If you don't believe his first, he's always got a second.

He: My wife writes fiction.
She: That's nothing. My husband talks it.

—I wish I could say the same about you.
—You could if you lied like me.

—Do you know what happens to little boys who tell lies?
—Sure, they travel half-fare.

He: You are the first girl I ever kissed.
She: And you're the first man I ever kissed.
He: I'd never marry a liar. (*Or:* I don't like a liar.)
She: I would. (*Or:* I do.)

—Say, what makes you so healthy?
—I take a cold bath every morning.
—Did you take one this morning?
—No, there was no hot water.

Freshman *(to a group of bystanders):* When I returned to my room in the hotel after I had gone to the show, I found a beautiful woman asleep in my bed. So I quietly went to the lobby and slept on the divan. Now what would you have done?
Another Frosh: The same thing you did, only I wouldn't have lied about it.

> Me hate he
> Me hate he
> Me wish he were die
> Him tell I
> Him love I
> But damn he, him lie.

LIFE INSURANCE

Life insurance is like fun. The older you get, the more it costs.

LIFE'S LESSONS

Be it ever so homely, there's no face like your own.

What the world needs is more starters and fewer cranks.

Variety is the spice of life . . . but don't get too spicy.

A pessimist is one who wears a belt and suspenders at the same time.

The man who starts out to borrow trouble finds that his credit is always good.

(Variation)
Your credit is always good if you want to borrow trouble.

If you want your opinions to be valued, don't throw them around as if you didn't value them.

An expert says that seventy percent of the dreams we have in sleep are unpleasant. Hell, that's not much better than being awake.

A psychologist says that we should never do any difficult task before breakfast. That's when we perform our hardest one—getting up.

One reason why Chinese generals dislike losing face is that their head usually goes with it.

Some folks say the world is round. Some say it's flat. Others say it's crooked.

—The older a fellow gets, the more he learns.
—But when he gets old, what he learns ain't so important.

—Do you think it will stop raining?
—It always has.

I read that the best way to get the most out of life is to fall in love with a beautiful woman or a great problem. Why not choose the former and get both?

Willie: Pop, what do they mean when they talk about the ups and downs of life?
Pop: The giving ups and the paying downs.

You can fool some of the people all the time and all of the people some of the time, and the rest of the time somebody else will fool them.

LOGIC

—Your dog bit me.
—He did not!
—Prove it!
—First, my dog has no teeth; second, he is not ferocious; third, he is particular whom he bites; fourth, I have no dog.

LOSERS

He was one of those breezy guys—everybody gave him the air.

He's the kinda fellow you don't like at first, and then you gradually grow to hate.

LOVE

Love is the tenth word in a telegram.

Puppy love is the beginning of a dog's life.

It's better to have loved and lost—much better.

She's always making love to people. Perpetual emotion.

Calf love is only half love, but who wants to be a cow?

A short love story. He falls. She falls. Niagara Falls.

She: Oh, Hector, I love you so.
He: So what?

I don't think I really love you. The only times I think of you are days . . . and nights.

She: Do you believe in love at first sight?
He: Yeah—and at every other opportunity.

A literary critic says there is too much love in fiction. Judging by the large number of breach-of-promise cases, I'd have to say the reverse is also true.

Fiction, we're told, could not survive without matrimony. Well, I can tell you: matrimony can't get along without fiction.

I completely ran out of synonyms for the word love. So I telephoned a pal and asked, "What is a synonym for love?" To which my pal replied, "What the hell is a synonym?"

—I know a man who didn't know how to read or write. At the age of forty, he met a woman and for love of her made a scholar of himself in two years.
—I know a scholar of forty who made a fool of himself in two days—for a woman.

The lovesick swain chewed his pen for a moment. Then came inspiration. "My own darling Nell," he wrote feverishly, "every minute that I am away from you seems a century. I would sacrifice my life for one glimpse of your beautiful face. I would crawl ten thousand miles across a fiery desert for just one look into your adorable blue eyes. I would swim the seven seas to lay my heart at your feet. I would fight an army for one of your smiles. Believe me, my adored one, there is nothing on this earth that I would not dare do for you."

—Joe

"P.S. I'll be over Wednesday night if it isn't raining too hard."

MANNERS

Boy, has he got good manners. You should see the way he runs the bread around his plate. He cleans it perfectly.

If a man offers a woman his seat, she admires his politeness; if he does not, she admires his nerve.

MARRIAGE, DIVORCE, AND ALIMONY
In General

She knocked him out to keep him in.

A wife is usually a man's booin' companion.

His wife always backs him up—into a corner.

She was married in a garage and she can't back out.

You don't have to go to Europe to marry abroad.

The ideal marriage: his ugliness made her speechless.

Two may live as cheaply as one, but not nearly as quietly.

Love is a ski ride down a hill; marriage is the climb back.

One way to keep your wife at home . . . nail her to the floor.

He got an awful fright on his wedding day—and he's still got her.

Marriage is a wonderful institution. No family should be without it.

His wife has a will of her own, and he's waiting around to collect it.

He calls her his little ballplayer because she was thrown out at home.

She calls him her time-clock. Every time he comes home she punches him.

I bought my wife a ten-foot fence for her birthday and she can't get over it.

He's so clever he convinced his wife that a woman looks fat in a fur coat.

The only time her husband gets a chance to open his mouth is when he yawns.

I'm sending my wife on a vacation to the Thousand Isles, a week on each Isle.

He and his wife are inseparable. It takes six people to drag 'em apart.

(Variation)
This young man is married—really married. He and his charming wife are inseparable. It takes six people to drag 'em apart.

He thinks he married a magician. She can turn anything into an argument.

All of which reminds us of the henpeck's version: All's fear in love and war.

As soon as I get married I'm going to retire—even if it's a noon wedding.

Marriage is just like leaving a call at the hotel. You get a ring and wake up.

Marriage is like a three-ring circus: engagement ring, wedding ring, and suffer-ing.

Bride: Just think, John, we don't have to pull down the shades; we're married now.

I never take my troubles home with me from the office. I don't have to. They're there.

When a man of sixty marries a girl of twenty, it's like buying a book for someone else to read.

He's a great fellow, but he made two big mistakes in his life: his first and second wives.

They've been married a year but they're still courting. She has him in court every other week.

Much of the lost faith in heaven may be owing to the belief that marriages are made there.

When a fellow can no longer afford to take his girl around and show her a good time, he marries her.

Most young men find it hard to settle down before marriage. And most find it hard to settle up after it.

She was fond of games. When he came home at night, she'd take out the rolling pin and play knock rummy.

His name was Underwood and her name Remington. She said, "I could never marry you; you're not my type." [Underwood and Remington were typewriters.]

I read that a Spanish toreador is giving up bullfighting to get married. Well, of course, he knows best.

No girl (or: man) should marry if she doesn't have a sense of humor. The trouble is that if she has, she probably won't.

There's a new electrical gadget that in seven minutes will remove all the wrinkles from any tie—except the marital one.

Marriage for a girl is just like a mousetrap: easy to get into, hard to get out of, and the husband is a piece of cheese.

Wife: A letter came for you marked "Private and Personal."
Husband: What did it say?

—I don't intend to be married until I am thirty.
—I don't intend to be thirty until I'm married.

—My wife is so irritable, the least thing starts her off.
—You're lucky. Mine's a self-starter.

—My wife tells me that she is all unstrung. What shall I do?
—Send her a wire.

—Which is the more important, a man's wife or his trousers?
—Well, there are lots of places a man can go without his wife.

—And is your daughter happily married?
—Oh, yes. Her husband is scared to death of her.

—Do clever men make the best husbands?
—Clever men don't become husbands.

Husband: But, my angel . . .
Wife: One moment, please . . . is that a hope or a compliment?

—You worm! What do you mean by coming home at this hour?
—Every other place was shut, my love.

—Your silver anniversary, is it? Congratulations old man!
—Yes, that's the first twenty-five years of it over.

—Gosh, your wife sure has a changeable temper, hasn't she?
—Yes, sometimes it's bad and sometimes it's worse.

—Should a father of forty-five marry again?
—No, that's enough children for any man.

—You told me before you were married, you were well off.
—I was, but I didn't realize it.

—Does your wife like housework?
—She likes to do nothing better.

—Your wife dresses well. Why don't you?
—That's why.

—How long did you know your wife before you married her?
—I didn't know her. I only thought I did.

—If you come home drunk again, I'll never speak to you.
—Lead a man not into temptation.

—You struck me when I was sick.
—I'm not big enough to hit you when you're well.

—Allow me to present my wife.
—No thanks, I have one. That's enough.

(Variation)
Allow me to present to you my wife. You keep her, I don't
want her.

—I've half a mind to get married.
—That's all you need.

—Am I still the light of your life?
—Quit kidding. I just paid a nine dollar electric bill this morning.

First Girl: For a husband I want a young go-getter.
Second Girl: Well, I prefer an already gotter.

—In which state do women have the greatest rights?
—The state of matrimony.

—Do you know what the world's greatest example is of double
jeopardy?
—Marriage.

I'd like to come back to life as my wife's first husband, because
then I'd know how to be perfect.

—My daughter's getting a man's wages now.
—I know. I was at the wedding.

—I didn't know my hubby had so much money till our wed-
ding day.
—How did he happen to let the cat out of the bag?
—Oh, he said he intended to retire as soon as we were married.

—Why don't you put your foot down and let the wife know
who's boss in your house.
—I don't have to. She knows who's boss.

Groom: These biscuits are just like the ones mother used to make.
Bride: Really?
Groom: Yes, that's why father left her.

—I have one thing to tell you before I marry you. I'm a very poor
cook.
—That's all right. I'm not working so there'll be nothing to cook.

When a man has been married a year, he wishes he'd remained a
bachelor. When he has been married twelve years, he wishes his
father had.

Young men are being told that if they want to marry, they should
make a little money first. Afterward, they'll have to make a little
money last.

—I've been married once too often.
—How often have you been married?
—Once.

—This note says that a man is planning to run off with my wife.
—And will you shoot him?
—Yes. If he changes his mind!

A drunk staggered into the police station and confessed that he
had pushed his wife out of a ten-story window. "Did you kill
her?" asked the sergeant. "I don't think sho. Thash why I wanna
be locked up."

—Dear, you can't imagine how I worry when you're away.
—Oh, you shouldn't do that. I'll always return, you know.
—Yes, that's what I worry about.

Wife: The couple next door seem to be very devoted. He kisses
her every time they meet. Why don't you do that?
Husband: I don't know her well enough yet.

Don't worry if your wife turns cold toward you. The cooing may
last only until the end of the honeymoon, but the billing will go
on forever.

—What did he do when his wife ran away?
—He ran away too—in case she changed her mind and wanted to
come back.

After the wedding ceremony, a pal took the groom to one side
and asked, "What made you marry an ugly dame like that?" He
said, "You've no need to whisper. She's deaf too."

Before marriage you always remember to "Say It With Flowers."
After you're married, you realize there's lots of things you can't
say with flowers.

—Do you believe in the old saying, "Marry in haste and repent at
leisure?"
—No. When a man's married he has no leisure.

Before and after marriage: she used to stay up half the night waiting for him to go home; now she waits up half the night waiting
for him to come home.

He: Honey, I bought a lovely present for you, a cute little marmo-
set. Do you know what that is, a lovely little pet monkey.
She: That's great, now I won't miss you so much.

He: I'm tired of married life. Why didn't some idiot propose to
you before you married me.
She: An idiot did, and I married him.

He: I want to marry a rich girl.
She: Why?
He: So I can give her all she wants.

—Are you happily married?
—Yes, I'm happy. I've got the finest wife in the country.
—Well, a man can be happy with a wife in the country.

I just read where a man has invented a machine where you drop a nickel and get a wife. Now, if the guy would only invent one where you can drop your wife and get a nickel.

—My wife had a dream last night and thought she was married to a millionaire.
—You're lucky. Mine thinks that in the daytime.

—Was your married life very unhappy?
—Very unhappy.
—A case of December wedded to May?
—No, Labor Day wedded to the Day of Rest.

—I can't marry him, Mother, he's an atheist and doesn't believe there is a hell.
—Marry him, my dear, and between us, we'll convince him that he's wrong.

—We have been married a year and never quarrel. If a difference of opinion arises and I am right, Felix always gives in immediately.
—And if he is right?
—That never occurs.

Wife *(angrily to her drunken husband):* I suppose you expect me to believe you came straight home from the office.
Husband: Sure I did. I *(hic)* came home jusht like the crow flies.
Wife: So I see. Stopping frequently for a little corn.

—Some guy broke into my house the other night.
—Did he get anything?
—Did he get anything! I'll say he did; my wife thought that it was me!

—Listen, Mazie, my husband sits around the house and won't talk to me.
—He has probably deserted you, but can't afford to live any place else just now.

—And what time did you get in last night?
—At a quarter of twelve.
—Nonsense; I heard the clock strike three.
—Well, three is a quarter of twelve.

—My hubby and I went shopping and we're having an awful fight about this expensive underwear.
—Will it end in a draw?
—Yes, in my bureau drawers.

—That operatic tenor in the apartment next to mine is driving me nuts.
—But I'll bet your wife is crazy about him.
—Yeah, that's what's driving me nuts!

A fellow had a terrible crash right outside the theatre. When asked where he lived, he said he didn't know. When asked his name, he said he didn't know. When asked was he married, he said, "No, this is the worst accident I ever had."

—I get seventy-five dollars a week and my wife gets seventy-five dollars a week, too.
—Gee, doesn't that make a hundred and fifty?
—No, I get it first and she gets it afterward.

He: I just read in the paper about a man out west who exchanged his wife for a horse.
She: That's terrible. You wouldn't do that with me, would you, hon?
He: No, but I'd hate anyone to tempt me with a good car.

—Marital squabbles are distasteful. You and your wife should live as one.
—Hell, we live as ten.
—How do you mean?
—I'm the nought and she's the one. *(Or the reverse)*

—Mary has a wonderful husband.
—Yes? Houzat?
—Why, he helps her do all the work. Monday he washed the dishes with her. Tuesday he dusted with her. And tomorrow he is going to mop the floor with her.

—Delighted to have met you. Come over one evening soon and bring your husband.
—Oh yes, I've been married for the best part of a year.
—But I thought you were married only about ten days ago.
—Yes.

—Do you see Emma often?
—Oh, yes, quite frequently.
—Is she happily married?
—Is she? I should say so. Why, that girl is so happily married she has to go to the theatre for a good cry.

A group of traveling men were discussing the pet names they had for their wives. "I call mine Compass," said the first, "because she has such good points." "Mine's Crystal," stated the second, "she's always on the watch." "I call mine Daily," sighed a third, "because if I didn't she'd get suspicious."

She: Hello, Hal, glad to see you.
He: The same with you. How's things about town?
She: I suppose you heard that Jimmy married Peggy.
He: Is that so? What on earth made Jimmy marry Peggy?
She: Peggy.

She: What's the matter? You don't look well.
He: I was out very late last night.
She: What does your wife say when you come home late?
He: Why, I'm not married.
She: Then why do you go home late?

He: I'm going to go out drinking.
She: Why is that?
He: Oh, last night I came home, and I threw an axe at the wife and missed her.
She: Gee, you should cut out liquor, if that's the way you carry on.
He: I'll have to cut it out; it's spoiling my aim.

The old martinet was lecturing his nephew. "I've never known such a generation," said the old fellow. "You modern boys want too much." The boy was tactfully silent. "Do you know what I was getting when I married your aunt?" asked the uncle. "No," replied the nephew, realizing the time had come to terminate the argument, "and I bet you didn't either."

About a year after Jim Smith got married, his wife said to him one night: "Jim, you do not speak so affectionately to me as you used to when we were first married. I fear you have ceased to love me." "Ceased to love you?" growled the man. "There you go again. Why, I love you more than life itself. Now, shut up and let me read the baseball news."

A cook went to the mistress of the house to tell her she was leaving. The mistress wanted to know why. Did she want more money? Did she object to the working conditions?
Cook: No, not that. I'm going to be married.
Mistress (amazed): Married!
Cook: Yes, do you remember I went to a funeral a short time ago? Well, I'm going to marry the corpse's husband. He said that day, I was the life of the party.

She: You know, you are very brave wanting to marry me.
He: Why is that?
She: My first husband died very soon after marrying me.
He: Yes?
She: And the second took poison; and the third is in an insane asylum. Don't you think I'm a seductive woman?
He: You're not seductive, you're a plague.

—For being so nice, I'm going to give you a mink wrap.
—How sweet of you. What a lovely man you are.
—But there's one condition.
—There usually is.
—No, before I give it to you, you must promise to darn my socks.
—Please, I don't darn anyone's socks.
—Okay, you don't give a darn, I don't give a wrap.

(Variation)
Husband: I won't buy you an evening wrap because you won't even darn my socks. So if you don't give a darn, I don't give a wrap.

One man makes a bet with a second that if Harry were told that his wife ran away, he would break down and cry. The second man says that in this day and age it is improbable. So the two men bet. Harry enters, and they tell him. He thinks it over for a minute, looks very serious, asks to use the phone, calls up friends and tells them that the bridge game is off tonight. They won't have a fourth hand. The second man, ready to pay off the bet, decides to let Harry know that it's only a joke. On being told, Harry breaks out crying.

One night, the wife discovered her husband standing over the baby's crib. Silently she watched him. As he stood looking down on the sleeping infant, she saw in his face a mixture of emotions—rapture, doubt, admiration, despair, ecstasy, incredulity. Touched and wondering at this unusual parental attitude and conflicting emotions, the wife with eyes glistening arose and slipped her arms around him. "A penny for your thoughts," she said in a voice tremulous. He blurted them out. "For the life of me, I can't see how anyone can make a crib like that for three forty-nine."

A man is writing a letter to his son.
Dear Son,
    Marriage is a wonderful institution if you find the right mate. The best advice I can give you is to compare your girl to your mother, with whom I have been so ideally happy for the past thirty years. If she can even approximate your dear mother's homemaking, housekeeping, and always even temper, you are a lucky young man, and I give you my blessing and advise you to grab her at once.
                                        Your loving Father
P.S. Your mother just left the room. Don't be a damn fool. Stay single.

One man is telling another about his marriage woes. His wife is always jealous and distrustful. The other tells him to pull himself together, make a fuss over her, and smother her with kindness.

He says, "Buy her some flowers or candy. Instead of berating her all the time, be gentle and considerate." The unhappy husband returns home with a bouquet of flowers. His wife, who has been crying, looks up and flies into a worse fit. He asks what's wrong. She says, "The landlord has been asking for the rent. The grocer wants his bill paid. The baby is sick. There's no money in the house. Everything's wrong, and now look at you: you come home drunk!"

He: I hear your sister is engaged to be married again.
She: Yes, but we're going to put a stop to it.
He: Yeah? What's the matter with her fiancé this time?
She: Well, you remember her first husband was a jeweler. He gave her thousands and thousands of dollars worth of jewelry and cutlery.
He: Yes? Well, what's wrong with that?
She: Then her second husband . . . he was a furrier and he gave her a house full of furs.
He: Well, so what?
She: Well, now she's engaged to an admiral, and we have no room around the house for battleships.

Hen-Pecked Husbands

He who hesitates is bossed.

Charlie's a real home fellow. Every place he goes, his wife goes with him. He has to take her. (*Or:* Every place he goes, he takes his wife along. He has to.)

—When he says a thing he means it. Every time he speaks, his wife jumps.
—Yes, she jumps all over him.

—When I got married, I swore I'd be boss or know the reason why.
—And now?
—Now I know the reason why.

—It's true, isn't it, that the hand that rocks the cradle rules the world?
—I don't find it so.
—G'wan! You know your wife is the boss.
—Yes, but being boss she makes me rock the cradle.

(Variation)
He: The hand that rocks the cradle is the hand that rules the world.
She: Well, come in the house and rule the world a while. I'm tired.

He: In my house, I'm boss.
She: Don't kid me, I heard differently.
He: You're mistaken. Only yesterday my wife chased me into the closet and dared me to come out.
She: And did you come out?
He: I should say not! I'm the boss of my house.

Marrying for Money

—If I marry you, will you let me still keep my job at the office?
—Will I let you? Dearest, I'm depending on it.

—John dear, I'm to be in amateur theatricals. What will people say when they see me in tights?
—They'll probably say I married you for your money.

He: Will you marry me?
She: No. I'm afraid not.
He: Oh, come on, be a support.

She: How does it feel to be marrying an heiress?
He: Great! Every time I kiss her I feel as if I were clipping the coupon off a government bond.

She: My fiancé lost all his money in Wall Street.
He: I bet you feel sorry for him.
She: Yes, he'll miss me.

She: My father made his fortune when he was a young man. Would you like to know how he did it?
He: Not particularly. But I should like to know if he still has it.

Marriage Proposals

The four-wheel brake song: four-wheel brake the news to mother.

Suitor: I want your daughter for my wife.
Father: All right, I'll trade you.

Suitor: Sir, I want your daughter for my wife.
Father: What does your wife want with my daughter?

(Variation)
He: Darling, I want you for my wife.
She: What's your wife want me for?

The only difficult thing about proposing to a girl under a beautiful moon is to keep from making a success of it.

Doris was in love and anxious to hear the news.
She: So you've seen daddy, darling? Did he behave like a lamb?
He: Absolutely! Every time I spoke he said, "Bah!"

He: Will you marry me?
She: You! Why, you couldn't keep me in handkerchiefs.
He: Say, you're not going to have a cold all your life, are you?

(Variation)
Father: You'll never marry my daughter, young man, you couldn't keep her in handkerchiefs.
Suitor: Gee whiz, she ain't gonna have that cold all her life, is she?

He: Marry me, proud beauty, and I'll make you the happiest woman in forty-eight states.
She: 'Fraid not, handsome. I don't want to live in a trailer.

She: It was leap year. I proposed marriage to a fellow on a river bank.
He: What happened?
She: He leaped.

Bachelor: How many times did you ask your wife to marry you before she consented?
Married Man: Once too often.

He: Lois, I want to marry you!
She: Yes, but have you seen Dad?
He: Oh yeah, often. But I want to marry you anyhow.

A young man asked the father of his girlfriend for her hand. After questioning the young man for a long time, the father congratulated him and said, "Well, I suppose you must seal it with a kiss." The suitor kissed the old man.

He: Wantelope?
She: Cantaloupe.
He: Oh, honeydew.
She: I'd have to write to Secretary Mellon about it.

He: You're worth a million dollars, aren't you?
She: Yes—what of it?
He: Will you marry me?
She: I should say not. But why do you ask?
He: I just wanted to know what it feels like to lose a million.

He: I'm awfully crazy about you.
She: That's so sweet of you.
He: Will you marry me?
She: Sure, but you will have to wait.
He: Why?
She: I want my first marriage to be for love.

He: Do you remember when you and I were eighteen, and on every date I used to ask you to marry me?

She: Yes . . . how wonderful.
He: And do you remember how you used to refuse me?
She: Yes.
He: Those were the happiest days of my life. (*Or:* Those are my happiest memories.)

A young woman told her boyfriend that her father would be dropping by his office to see for himself whether the boyfriend was successful enough to marry his daughter. The boyfriend, never having met the woman's father, keenly awaited his arrival. When he saw a man being ushered in, he quickly picked up the telephone and said: "Sell my two hundred shares of Buick and buy Dupont stock. Take the five thousand from my diamond account and buy gold. And if you hear that the price of silver has gone down, buy me a hundred shares." Then he turned to the man and asked if he could help him. "I don't have much time," said the boyfriend, "as you can see, I'm very busy." The man replied, "I'm from the telephone company . . . here to repair the phone. It's been out-of-order since yesterday."

Separation, Divorce, and Alimony

So long, dear, I'll sue you later.

Who pays the woman who pays?

Putting water in a leaking radiator is like paying alimony.

Reno is where the cream of society goes through the separator.

They're issuing marriage licenses now with a ticket for Reno attached.

She left me for a crazy reason. She was crazy about someone else.

A woman lost two hundred pounds all in one day. Her husband left her.

Have you heard of the sword swallower who divorced his wife because she was always looking daggers at him?

Lots of women are willing to exchange their wedding gowns for divorce suits without waiting for alterations.

She: I think I'll get a divorce.
He: You'll have to give me two weeks' notice.

—What did you divorce your husband for?
—Two hundred dollars a month.

—I hope you weren't excited when you asked your husband for alimony.
—Not at all. I was cool and collected.

—His wife divorced him on account of flat feet.
—How come?
—He was always getting his feet in the wrong flat.

A famous woman star had just received her fifth divorce. Her husband couldn't pay alimony, so the court awarded her his family mansion. She quipped, "One more husband and I'll have the place furnished."

—I had a little sister, but we're divorced now.
—Two children divorced?
—Yes, Ma's got sis and Pa's got me.

"I'm going home to Mother," sobbed the young bride. "Fine, I'll go along with you," said the irritated husband. "Then we can both get a square meal."

MEANNESS

Some people sing for money, I sing for spite.

He's a meany. He hates a nickel 'cause it ain't a dime.

That guy is so mean, if he were a ghost he wouldn't even give you a fright.

—Why did you kick that man while he was down?
—He started to get up.

Some men were standing at a bar convinced that the grim fellow at the end of the bar was a wild man, a gun man, a mean drunk, or worse. They asked him to have a drink, and he said, "Okay, then I'll take an ice-cream soda."

MEDICINE AND HEALTH

Have you heard the aspirin story . . . the one about the three Bayers?

—Is the west coast a good place for rheumatism?
—Yes, that's where I got mine.

If you give your body as much care as your automobile, you'll be able to get up any hill in high.

—The secret of good health is to eat garlic every day.
—How do you mean, a secret?

—What do you do to get soft white hands?
—Nothing.

—I don't feel good.
—See a doctor.
—I did. He told me to take one pill three times a day, but how can you do that?

Salesman: Is your drugstore doing anything to help the sale of the firm's dyspepsia tablets?
Pharmacist: Say! You ought to taste some of the new sundaes we're putting out.

—Sit down and tell me all about it.
—I can't.
—You can't tell me about it?
—No, I can't sit down.

—You look all tired out.
—I am. I skipped all last night.
—Are you in training?
—No, doctor's orders. He gave me medicine and on the bottle it said, "Take two nights running and skip one night."

(Variation)
—What's all that noise in the bedroom?
—That's my wife. The doctor told my wife to take medicine two nights in a row and skip a night. This is the night she skips.

—What's the matter?
—Got dyspepsia.
—Don't you enjoy your meals?
—Enjoy my meals? My meals are merely guideposts to take medicine before or after!

Dangerous Dan McCrobe

A bunch of germs were hitting it up
In the bronchial saloon;
Two bugs on the edge of the larynx
Were jazzing a rag-time tune.
Back in the teeth, in a solo game,
Sat dangerous Ack-Kerchoo;
And watching his pulse was his light of love—
The lady that's known as Flu.

Dentists

I was at the dentist, and he drilled so much my mouth feels like a parade ground.

(Variation)
My mouth feels like a parade ground. I've just been to the dentist and had him drilling on it all morning.

Dentist: I'd have that tooth pulled out if it were mine.
Patient: So would I, if it was yours.

A scientist says that a snail has a thousand teeth. Its rate of progress would suggest that it is on its way to the dentist.

My friends tell me to keep a cheerful, open face. But when paying a visit to the dentist, I find it difficult to keep it cheerful and open at the same time.

—Why so happy this morning when I saw you?
—I was just coming back from the dentist.
—What had you to be happy about?
—He wasn't home.

A taxi driver had been working hard all day with a terrible tooth-ache. He finally dragged himself to a dentist and said: "Oh Doc, quick pull it out. It has me crazy. I can't stand the pain." The doctor turned to get his instruments and immediately the exhausted taxi driver started to doze off. The dentist nudged him and said: "Do you want gas?" The taxi driver said: "Yeah, and see how my oil is too."

Doctors

The chiropractors' song: "We Maim to Please."

Give a chiropodist an inch and he'll take a foot.

I got my operation very cheap. The doctor was holding a removal sale.

Dad had an operation, and Mom is suing the Doc—for opening her male.

He said he was sick as a dog, so she sent for a veterinary.

(Variation)
I ate so many hot dogs, I got sick as a dog and had to be treated by a veterinary.

(Variation)
—The man who's sick is in the house, doctor.
—But I'm a veterinary.
—That's all right. He's sick as a dog.

A chiropractor is a man who gets paid for what any other man would get slapped for.

Doctors say that people who take cold baths in the winter never have rheumatism. But then they have cold baths!

Teeth are the things you have out just before the doctor decides it was your tonsils.

My doctor recommended butter as a cure for my lumbago. Every morning, I just give myself a pat on the back.

He: You're engaged to a doctor, eh? Has he got any money?
She: What do you think—I'm getting married for my health?

Doc: What you need is a shock, something to stir up your emotions.
Patient: I'll probably get it, Doc, when your bill comes.

—Do you suffer from gout?
—Well, I certainly don't enjoy it.

He put his bed on top of the stove before going to sleep. The doc told him to try hot springs for his rheumatism.

—You've been in and out of that tub all day.
—Well the doctor told me to take a pill every half hour in water.

—Doctor, can you help me? My name is Crumfuss.
—Sorry, I can't do a thing for that.

Patient: Doctor, sometimes I feel like killing myself. What should I do?
Doctor: Leave that to me.

Doctor (to obese patient): A medicine ball would be good for you.
Woman: I never go to those doctors' dances.

A fat man got sick and called the doctor. He asked for something to put him back on his feet. The doctor said, "I'll be right up with a derrick."

Doctors say the man who doesn't drink lives twice as long as the man who does. But the guy who does drink sees twice as much. So it's all even.

—Doctor, that corn cure was wonderful.
—It worked, eh?
—Yeah, now can you give me something to bring back the toes.

A man was not feeling good and went to a doctor. The doc took out his watch, felt the man's pulse, stared at him for a moment, and said: "Either you're dead or my watch has stopped."

Doctor: I'm sorry, old fellow, but I'll have to put you on a special diet with a special nurse.
Patient: That's all right, Doc, but what kind of a couch is a diet?

Patient: The first doctor I had did nothing but listen to my heartbeats.
Doctor: Yes, your chest has all the earmarks of a dirty quack.

Doctor: You should take a bath before you retire.
Patient: But doctor, I don't expect to retire for another twenty years yet.

—How are you making out with that girl I saw you with yesterday?
—I had to give her up. Doctor's orders.

—You had to give her up, doctor's orders?

—Yeah, she was the doctor's wife.

—Doctor, I've been misbehaving and my conscience is troubling me.

—I see, and since I'm a psychiatrist you want something to strengthen your will power?

—No, something to weaken my conscience.

Patient: It's a peculiar ailment, Doc. I keep dreaming that I've been shipwrecked with thousands of beautiful girls. This has been going on every night for weeks.

Doctor: But you sleep all right, don't you?

Patient: Yeah, but damn it, Doc, I can't get any rest!

Patient: What do you think is wrong with me, doctor?

Doctor: You need a minor operation, which will cost about twenty-five dollars.

Patient: Are you sure it is not a dangerous operation?

Doctor: I should say so. You couldn't buy a serious operation for less than a hundred and fifty dollars.

(Variation)

Patient: Will the operation be serious, Doc?

Doc: No, you can't buy a serious operation under fifty bucks.

The doctor of a country village had two children who were acknowledged by the inhabitants as being the prettiest little girls in the district. While the two children were out walking one day, they happened to pass quite near two small boys; one lived in the village and the other was a visitor. "I say," said the latter to his friend, "who are those little girls?" "They are the doctor's children," replied the village boy. "He always keeps the best for himself."

A young doctor was assigned to his first confinement case by his college professor and instructed to report immediately after the child was born. A few hours later came the news that the baby had died. The following day, the professor met the doctor and tried to console him. "Don't worry," he said, "that happens to the best of us. It's not the doctor's fault because a child dies. You did your best, didn't you?" "I know," cried the beginner; "it wouldn't be so bad if it was only the baby, but to make matters worse the mother also died this morning." "Well, don't let that worry you; it happens every day," assured the prof. "But tell me, is the father all right?"

Flatulence

Too bad anti-knock gas can't be taken internally.

Health

—Another exercise that's good for your health is skipping rope.
—I suppose so, but I hate to give up my cigar.

—How did you break your leg?
—I threw a cigarette in a manhole and stepped on it.

—You can't have any fun in a hospital. Only the surgeons are allowed to cut up.

A doctor passing through the hospital ward:
—Good moaning, boys, good moaning.

After a visit to a famous foreign scientist, whose wonderful microscopes proved that there are always some living organisms to be found preying on the human body, an American turned to him and said: "Sir, I came here believing myself to be an individual; I leave knowing myself to be a community."

Visitor at a private hospital: May I see Lieutenant Barker, please?
Matron: We do not allow ordinary visiting. May I ask if you're a relative?
Visitor *(boldly)*: Oh, yes. I'm his sister.
Matron: Dear me! I'm very glad to meet you. I'm his mother.

Hospitals

A woman patient, covered with a sheet, was lying on a gurney in a corridor waiting to be wheeled into the operating room. Men in white coats repeatedly came down the hall, looked her over, lifted up the sheet, and walked on. The next time a man came along, looked at her, and lifted up the sheet, the woman asked, "Please, doctor, tell me: when are they going to operate?" He replied, "I'm no doctor. I'm a painter here."

Illness

Boy, you look like "Death Takes a Holiday."

She was chilled to the bone and got a cold in her head.

When you look at him, you realize his wife is practically a widow.

The difference between a cold and La Grippe is twenty-five dollars.

—We have a case of measles at home.
—How many measles are there in a case?

—Junior's face is all swollen. Is that a symptom of mumps?
—That's not a symptom . . . that's mumps!

My friend said, "Ed, how is your cold?" I replied, "My cold is doing fine. I'm the guy who's getting the worst of it."

—What are you taking for your cold?
—Make me an offer.

He went to the hospital to play for a sick friend. But before he got finished tuning up, his friend died.

His asthma is so bad two neighbors got up in the middle of the night to go to work. They thought it was the six o'clock whistle.

—Joe's ill.
—What's wrong with him?
—Asthma.
—I just did, you darn fool, what's wrong with him?

—Well, so long, I'm goin' fishin'
—You got worms?
—Yeah, but I'm goin' anyhow.

—Why John, you've got a white coat on your tongue!
—A white coat? My goodness!
—Shame on you, wearing sport clothes this time of the year.

—Honest, I'm beginning to think you have kleptomania. Why don't you do something about it?
—I am. I'm taking things for it.

—The doctor is here to examine you.
—I can't see him.
—How come?
—I'm ill.

I met a chap who asked me how my brother was. I told him my brother was sick. This chap is interested in Christian Science and went on to tell me that my brother only thinks he's sick and said, "Now you go right home and tell him that he only thinks he's sick." He left me and I went home. When I saw the chap some time later, he asked me how my brother was getting along so I told him, "Oh! He only thinks he's dead."

A man who had been bitten by a dog found that his wounds didn't heal and consulted a doctor. The physician, alarmed by the appearance of the wound, had the dog caught and examined. The dog had rabies. As it was too late to give the man a serum, the doctor told him he would have to die of hydrophobia. The poor man sat down at a desk and began writing. The physician sought to comfort him. "Perhaps it will not happen quickly," he said. "You needn't make your will now." "I'm not making my will," replied the man. "I'm writing out a list of people I'm going to bite."

Medicine and Tonic

A young bride walked into a drugstore and approached a clerk timidly. "That baby tonic you advertised," she began, "does it really make babies bigger and stronger?" "We sell lots of it," replied the druggist, "and we've never had a complaint." "Well. I'll take a bottle," said the bride after a moment, paid for it, and went out. Five minutes later she was back. She got the druggist into a corner and whispered into his ear: "I forgot to ask you about this baby tonic," she said under her breath. "Who takes it, me or my husband?"

Nurses

—Doctor, don't you remember me? You saved my life twenty years ago.
—Did I? I'm sorry.

The doctor was questioning the new nurse about her latest patient. "Have you kept a chart of his progress?" the doctor asked. The nurse blushingly replied, "No, but I can show you my diary."

—My uncle is going to be in the hospital a long time.
—Goodness, did you see the doctor?
—No, I saw the nurse.

—I've been operated on for my liver, kidneys, tonsils, appendix—
—Stop! That's enough outta you. First, I'll give you an X-ray.
—What's that for?
—I'd like to know what people see in you.

Operations

He couldn't have a minor operation because he was over twenty-one.

—I can't afford an operation now.
—No, you'll just have to talk about the old one for another year.

I must run along now; a friend of mine is being operated on for appendicitis and I want to be there for the opening.

—Sure I'll operate on you. What have you got?
—Appendicitis!
—Lemme see . . . how do you do that?
—You're a surgeon and you never did an appendix operation?
—Well, one, but that was on the side.

—Tell us about your operation, Major. Was it serious?
—Was it serious! Why, they used so much catgut in sewing me up that my stomach doesn't growl any more—it meows!

Pregnancy and Maternity

Her dad was a baker, so she always had a bun in the oven.

Teenager Audrey went to the doctor who told her that she was going to have a baby. Audrey laughed and laughed. She knew that wasn't possible because she wasn't married!

—Where are you working these days?
—Over at the maternity ward.
—How is it?
—Oh, they just about kid the life out of me.

—After the birth, I fainted. They brought me to. So I fainted again.
—Why?
—Well, they brought me two more.

A new doctor entered the maternity ward and asked each woman when the blessed event was expected to take place. Each gave the same date. Coming to the last woman, the doctor said, "I suppose yours is expected on February 9th, too." She said, "No, I missed the picnic."

MEMORY

She used to work in Woolworth's but she got the sack for forgetting the prices.

—I've swallowed my collar button.
—Good, for once you'll know where it is.

There're three things I can really brag about: first, my good memory, and I forget what the other two are.

I knew a guy who was so absent-minded that he went into a restaurant and started talking to a doughnut and dunked the waitress.

I'll tell you how absent-minded I've become. Last night, I went for an auto ride with my wife—and I parked.

—Washington sure must have had a great memory.
—Why do you think he had a great memory?
—Well, they built a big monument to it.

—My wife has the worst memory in the world.
—She forgets everything, eh?
—No, she remembers everything.

We were brought up together. Our families have been friends for years. I know her as well as I do my own sister. What's that girl's name again?

—Why do you have that string around your finger?
—My wife put it there to remind me to mail her letter.
—Did you do it?
—No, she forgot to give me the letter.

—I'm a lightning calculator.
—What's that?
—I remember numbers. Just write down a lot of figures, and I'll memorize them, add them, and give you the answer.
—Well, I can't use you right now, but I'd like you to give me a ring next week. Maybe I could use you then.
—Where should I call you?
—Call me at Wickland 2-7975.
—Would you mind writing it down?

MEN

I see her only on rainy nights. She calls me her rainbeau.

Some men are like tubes of toothpaste. You have to give them a squeeze to get anything out of them.

—Are you the kind of man who makes the best of things?
—You bet! I make the best cocktails, the best chorus girls, and the best of alibis.

Bachelors

A bachelor is a man who never makes the same mistake once.

A bachelor is a guy who didn't have a car when he was young.

A bachelor is a man who makes mistakes without marrying them.

A bachelor is a selfish man who is cheating some worthy woman out of alimony.

MEXICO

I just heard that Mexico postponed its yearly revolution until after the tourist season.

In Mexico (*or:* Latin America), the problem is whether they can keep their New Year's revolutions.

In any story of a Mexican (*or:* Latin American) candidate running, it is necessary to specify in what direction.

MIDGETS

Pity the poor little midget at whose hanging the military band played "Swingy Little Thingy."

MODESTY

She wouldn't tell a story about crude oil 'cause it wasn't refined.

1494

 Jokes

Carol's so modest that she turned the bureau around so the drawers wouldn't show.

MONEY

Make money first, and then make it last.

Out of debt, out of danger, if your brakes are good.

The only thing you can buy now for five cents is a wrong number.

I was just reading a book with the saddest ending—my bank book.

I'm dancing with tears in my eyes, 'cause it's ten cents a dance.

I'll love you when your money is gone, but I won't be with you.

There is no friend as faithful as a good book, especially a bank-book.

The greatest after-dinner speech I ever heard came from a friend: give me the check.

A certain fellow was so crooked he couldn't even work on a straight salary.

Jake, the artist, says: you can always draw the queens, if you have the jack.

You know what the definition of economy is? A reduction in some other fellow's salary.

The man who lives within his income never gets as much credit as the man who doesn't.

According to an economist, money is the people's servant. Yeah, here today and gone tomorrow.

I know a big sporting goods store that is selling tennis rackets for hitting checks that bounce back.

The remarkable thing is not that money makes fools of great people, but that it makes great people of fools.

—That was a slave bracelet you gave me, wasn't it, honey?
—Yes, I had to slave for five months to get the money to buy it.

—I wish I had money to burn.
—You will have, if you take any with you when you die.

They're very rich. I was out to their house and they had fruit on the table—and no one in the house was sick.

She: I keep my money in my stocking.
He: That's one place it'll draw interest.

—Get my broker.
—Yes, sir, stock or pawn?

—Have you seen the new thousand dollar bills yet?
—No, I haven't seen the old ones yet.

—If I were to give you this twenty dollar bill, what would you do?
—I'd drop dead.
—Yeah? Well, then, I'm going to save your life.

Have you heard of the circus performer who earns his living by letting a gorilla hug him? That's my idea of being hard pressed for cash.

Last week, I dreamed a guy owed me ten bucks. When I woke up, I found it was true. Now I daren't go to sleep lest I dream he paid me.

One argument for reducing the war debts is that we won't lose so much when we fail to collect.

—I hear that you sold your property for a song.
—Yes, I got nothing but notes for it.

Found: A roll of five dollar bills. Will the owner please form a line at the north entrance of Madison Square Garden.

Professor: Where is the capital of the United States?
Student: All over the world.

In the early days, the Indians were noted for giving things and then trying to take them back. Nowadays it's the finance companies.

—I just lit my pipe with a ten-dollar bill.
—You must be a millionaire.
—Naw, it's easier to burn it than pay it.

—All them millionaires . . . their money is tainted . . . all of it!
—Ow d'yer mean, tainted?
—Well, 'taint yours, an' 'taint mine, is it?

Someone needs to invent a new fountain pen called Save-the-Sucker. It will automatically stop the flow of ink the second the point is placed on a dotted line.

First Show Girl: I'm divorcing Andrew. You don't know what I've gone through, living with him.
Second Show Girl: Five-hundred-thousand dollars, wasn't it?

—Dirty gold! Bad Gold! Rotten gold! Stupid gold!
—What are you doing?
—I'm panning gold.

He: Darling, I must make a confession. I once stole fifty thousand dollars.
She: I hope you still have it.

—Say, buddy, could you spare a buck?
—What's the idea asking for a dollar; won't a dime do?
—Hey, I didn't ask you your business, did I?

All this talk about national deficit is Dutch to me. They talk about forty or fifty billion dollars. Ha, when they get over $22.50, I'm lost.

Great bunch around here. We were all out at a party together. After a couple of drinks, a buddy lit his cigar with a five dollar bill; then another buddy, not to be outdone, used a ten dollar bill. But they couldn't top me. I used a hundred. But mine was a check.

Julius Tannen, in *Shoot the Works,* tells of a fellow he met whose salary had been cut till it was only two dollars a day. The impoverished fellow asked, "How can a man be a Christian on two dollars a day?" "How can he be anything else?" asked Julius.

—I saw in the paper that in some out-of-the-way corners of the world, the natives still use fish for money.
—What a sloppy job they must have getting chewing-gum from a slot machine.

Young husband: I'm glad you're so impressed, dear, by all these explanations I have been giving you about banking and economics.
Young wife: Yes, darling. It seems wonderful that anybody should know as much as you do about money without having any.

—I was out with a man last night who said he'd sell me some oil stock at half price.
—Isn't there something fishy about that?
—Yeah, he thinks I'm a sucker.

A son bought his father a three-hundred dollar camel's hair coat for a birthday present. His father objected to such extravagance. So he wrote his father that he bought the coat for fifteen dollars. The father wired back, "Thanks for the coat. I sold it for eighteen dollars. P.S. Please send me three coats immediately."

It's a funny world. If a man gets money, he's a grafter. If he keeps it, he's a capitalist. If he spends it, he's a playboy. If he doesn't get it, he's a ne'er-do-well. If he tries to get it, he's a Communist. If he doesn't try to get it, he lacks ambition. If he gets it without working for it, he's a parasite. And if he accumulates it after a lifetime of hard work, he's a sucker.

Two fellows met on the street, one of them looking very depressed. The other asked him what was the matter. The depressed fellow said, "It looks like I'm bankrupt. Business is bad and the creditors are making my life a misery." The other said, "Oh, never mind, the creditors can't take what you've settled on your wife. What? You've nothing settled on your wife? Well, I guess you have settled money on your daughters. What? No settlements? Well, I expect you have some fire insurance. You haven't?" The depressed man said: "As you can see, I'm bankrupt." The other man said, "Bankrupt, hell, you're ruined."

MONOCLES

A monocle is a pane of glass worn in one eye in order that its wearer may not see at one time any more than he is able to understand.

MOTHERS-IN-LAW

There're two sides to every question—my wife's and my mother's.

Wife: How about having mother for lunch today, dear?
Husband (brightly): By all means, dear; let's have her stewed.

Say, Doc, my wife's mother has ptomaine poisoning. If you're passing this way sometime next week or the week after, you might call in.

A fellow was arrested for driving without lights, but the cops let him off. He told the officer he was looking for his mother-in-law.

—My mother-in-law has visited my home only once since I got married.
—You sure are lucky.
—Luck, nothing! She's never left!

—I'm having trouble with the wife.
—You told me your wife was a pearl.
—The trouble is with Mother of Pearl.

Photographer: Don't assume such a fierce expression. Look pleasant.
Murphy: Not on your life. My wife is going to send one of these pictures to her mother, and if I look pleasant she'll come down on a visit.

Young Bride: Oh, I'll bet that's mother calling again.
Young Hubby: Gosh, if a man's wise he'll choose a girl who comes from the right sort of home.
Young Bride: Why, what do you mean?
Young Hubby: An orphans' home.

A fellow went to a lawyer and asked him how much it would cost to get a man off who had shot someone. The lawyer quoted a price. After the two men haggled a while, they agreed on a fee. As the fellow was leaving the lawyer's office, he said, "Stay right here. I'm going to shoot my mother-in-law."

MOVIES

I know a director who's always trying to make a little extra.

The picture he made was so bad that he had to have retakes before it was thrown out.

After a movie preview:
—Well, what did you think of it?
—I think you've got a fortune in that picture.
—You think so?
—Yeah, and you'll never get it back.

Ah, dear old Capri. Lovely isle in the romantic Mediterranean. Palm fronds kissing the lilting waves. Little jewel set in a platinum sea where one thinks of nothing but love and romance. Ha, I'll never forget the last time I saw dear old Capri . . . in the newsreel.

Hollywood

Hollywood: the home of the wits. Well, maybe they're half right.

In Hollywood, they do things in a big way. Why, only today I saw a flea with two dogs on it.

Movie Stars

I have a letter here. I think it's from Clara Bow. *(He smells it.)* No, it's from Tom Mix. [Tom Mix played cowboy roles.]

—What becomes of the stars in the day time?
—Most of 'em sleep till noon!

I know a Hollywood couple who have been married so long that their lawyers are starving.

When these Hollywood actresses leave for Reno, their farewell words are: "Till we mate again."

Judge: When your husband became a film star, you say he transferred his affections to another?
Wife: Yes, your Honor, to himself!

—Now be careful 'cause everything you say will be held against you.
—Everything I say will be held against me?
—Yes, sir.
—All right, Greta Garbo.

Movie Ushers

—What good are all these robots going to be?
—Well, they may loosen a few screws and make them into movie ushers.

—He just leads women on and then leaves them in the dark.
—Oh, a heartbreaker.
—No, a movie usher.

MUSIC AND MUSICIANS

American song: "Did you ever rip a seam walking?"

They put bridges on violins to get the music across.

He was collecting fares. He said he's a guest conductor.

The only one who gets anywhere letting things slide is the trombone player.

Tin Pan Alley turns out twenty-five thousand different popular songs a year. Thank goodness, they have different names.

A modern composer (*or:* artist) has been saying that the public doesn't realize what he's doing. I doubt that his luck will last.

Neighbor: Where's your brother, Freddie?
Freddie: He's in the house playing a duet. I finished first.

—There's something musical about that guy.
—Yeah, he goes out fit as a fiddle and comes home tight as a drum. [*See* Women Drinkers.]

—I play the organ.
—Yes, and if things don't improve, I'll have to play one too.

—You don't play any good music on that drum of yours.
—No, but I certainly drown out a lot of bad music.

—Do you know the sextet from "Lucia"?
—No, but I know the quintet from Canada.

—Now I'll play "Tea for Two."
—You're playing flat, Eddie; that's sour. That's tea with lemon.

—He's a wonderful conductor. He used to be with the Metropolitan.
—I used to know a lot of conductors with the New York Central.

—Can't you hold a note longer than that?
—You should know. I've been holding a note of yours for a year.

—I was a musician once.
—Well, anyone can be a musician once.

Virtuoso: That man just paid four thousand dollars for a Whistler.
Seamstress: And you can get a Singer for about fifty.

I used to practice all night and, believe me, some of the neighbors sat up all night to hear me.

—My boyfriend plays his violin under my window every night in his night shirt.
—I get it, "Serenade in the Nightie."

She: You know, I studied opera. I played the part of Carmen, the Flower of Spain.
He: Look me over. I played Gold Medal, the Flour of Minneapolis.

—What's the book the leader keeps looking at?
—That's the score of the overture.
—Oh, really, who's winning?

A piano player was telling me there are eighty-six notes on a piano. On mine at home there must be eighty-four. I know there are two notes due yet.

A village band was blowing their lungs out on the parade ground and had finished a number when the leader called to them, "Washington Post March next." The trombone player said, "Hell, I just got through playing that."

She: What is the name of that piece the orchestra is playing?
He: I don't know; let's ask one of the boys in the orchestra.
She *(to pianist):* What's that you're playing?
Pianist: A piano, lady—a piano!

(Variation)
—I played a solo on the piano.
—What did you play?
—The piano, you dope!

One day in a big theatre, a famous conductor was leading the symphony. In two places in the music, he had to have a big trumpet blast. The orchestra led up to the first climax, but the trumpet blast was missing. Nevertheless, the conductor continued. The second time, he waited for the blast, but it never came. After taking several bows, the conductor left the stage in search of the trumpet player. He heard two men arguing. The porter was telling the trumpeter, "You can't blow that damn thing here, I tell ya, there's a concert going on."

Saxophones

A pint and a half of prussic acid, swallowed rapidly, will kill the average saxophone player.

A music critic said that saxophone players are born, not made. Another argument for birth control.

—After you learned to play the saxophone did you receive any offers?
—Yes, several of my neighbors offered to shoot me.

—My brother plays the sax.
—That's nothing, my brother's a musician.

Jailbird: Baby, was it my saxophone that got me here, or my tap dancing?
Lovey Dovey: Your darn tootin'!

—Hey, your wife ran off with a sax player.
—Well, what about it?
—You don't seem so excited.
—I'm not. See, he was driving us crazy, and we tossed up who should get rid of him, and she lost.

Singers, Singing, and the Voice

I know a singer who had his voice lifted so that he could be heard in the balcony.

A true music lover is a man who, upon hearing a soprano in a bathroom, puts his ear to the keyhole.

—This fellow is a singer from way back.
—Well, the farther back he sings from me the better I'll like it.

My voice is improving. I used to get complaints from the apartment two doors away. Now they complain in the next building.

—Why did you get thrown out of the glee club?
—For singing.

—I saw a man without hands play a piano.
—That's nothing, I know a girl without a voice who sings.

—I sing for pleasure.
—Yeah, whose pleasure?

—I got my voice from my father.
—I guess the old man was glad to get rid of it.

She: Your singing carries me back to my girlhood days.
He: I was always told I had a voice that carried a long way.

—My uncle says you're a better singer than accordion player.
—That so! He heard me sing?
—Naw, he heard you play the accordion!

Soprano: Then you think I sang that song at too slow a tempo?

Contralto: Yes, the faster you sing it, the less time the audience has to endure it.

—When you sing like that, I just stand and wonder.
—Wonder what?
—Why you sing like that.

—If I sing this song at the concert tonight, do you think I'll get a big hand?
—Yeah! Right over your mouth.

—I used to be in a choir where they had ten thousand sopranos and ten thousand altos. And that's all.
—But what about the tenors and bassos?
—Oh, I sang both.

—I once sang before a very eminent judge.
—Yes?
—And when I finished he shouted, "Fine, fine!"
—And did you have to pay it?

A patient in the hospital ward was dying. "I have but one last request to make," he gasped. "Get me a famous radio team to sing 'Sonny Boy' outside the door. Have them sing it eight times." The hospital called the team in question, and they agreed to grant the dying man's plea. Arriving there shortly after midnight, they began to sing "Sonny Boy." They sang it eight times and departed. In the morning the doctor arrived and met one of the nurses in the hall. "Well," smiled the doctor, "How is the patient who made that peculiar request?" "He's entirely recovered," replied the nurse. "He left the hospital at six this morning. But the other twenty-three patients in the ward died during the night!"

NAMES

Mulligan: he's an awful stew.

We call her Autumn. Everything falls for her.

He called his girl Pearl. He met her in a dive.

I call her Bicarbonate. She's always after meals.

I want you to meet the Hawk Brothers—Moe and Tommy.

They called her Agnes when she was born, but she grew up to be a Helen [hellion].

—Say, why do you call your girl postscript?
—For short. Her name is Wilhemina Crumpacker.

They call her "Opportunity," because the boys are always trying to take advantage of her.

After a busy day being called upon every minute, a kid with a difficult name—Algernon—said, "It's a good thing I don't have one of those short names like Jim."

He: Is that your given name?
She: Yes, why?
He: Well, give it back as soon as you can.

—I've just become engaged to an Irishman.
—Oh, really?
—No, O'Reilly.

—What's your name?
—Here's my card.
—It's obliterated.
—No, it's Doakes.

He: What's your name, little girl?
She: Annie.
He: Annie what?
She: Anything.

Sweet Young Thing: Did my father order some coal this morning?
Coalman: This load of coal is for a Mr. Zell.
Sweet Young Thing: That's fine, I'm Gladys Zell [glad as hell].
Coalman: So am I.

—Say, mister, what's your name?
—I don't know.
—Why don't you know?
—I'm not myself right now.

Guide: On our right we have the palatial home of Mr. Gould.
Old Lady: John Jay Gould?
Guide: No, Arthur Gould. And on the left is the residence of Mr. Vanderbilt.
Old Lady: Cornelius Vanderbilt?
Guide: No, Reginald Vanderbilt. And in front is the First Church of Christ. *(To old lady)* Now's your chance.

—What else happened on the trip, Baron?
—Vell, Sharlie, vit me vus my frent . . . vot iss his name . . . its starts mit a zee.
—Oh, you mean Zimmerman.
—Ach no, my gootness, mit a Z.
—Oh, you mean Z.
—Oh, my gootness, such dumbness. Mit a Z . . . Z.
—Oh, a C.
—Ya, Z. Och, I haf it: O'Neal!

NEW JERSEY

He's a great artist. He's what you call a globe-trotter. He has appeared in every part of the civilized world and also in some parts of Jersey.

NEWSPAPERS

A reporter was covering a rape case and writing lengthy articles about it. The editor continually bawled him out for being too wordy. "Write it shorter," he repeated. Finally, the reporter came back with three words: screw and bolt.

—I read O. O. McIntyre regularly, but for the life of me I can't remember what his initials stand for.
—Odd.
—Yes, isn't it?

When the plumber makes a mistake he charges twice for it.
When a lawyer makes a mistake, it is just what he wants, because he has a chance to try the case all over again.
When the carpenter makes a mistake, it is just what he expected.
When a doctor makes a mistake, he buries it.
When a judge makes a mistake, it becomes the law of the land.
When a preacher makes a mistake, nobody knows the difference.
But when an editor makes a mistake . . . my God!

NEW YEAR'S GREETINGS

A Dismal New Year to:

Well-meaning bores who try to pin me down
To calling on their friends when out of town;

The host who tunes-in on a blaring station
And then insists on making conversation;

The old blocks from whose over-zealous lips
Come mile-long anecdotes about their quips.

To these, and others equally as drear,
I wish a grim and wholly wretched year!

A Dolorous New Year to:

The oafs who sit behind me at the play
Repeating every word the actors say;

The tippler and his jewelled and ermined mate
Who stumble down the aisle a half-hour late;

The ring-tailed gent, with soft, off-center brain,
Who ogles at my paper on the train;

The man who, when I'm buying cigarettes,
Plugs razor blades, knives, soap, and books in sets.

A double pox on all those lunatics!
And may they have a lousy '36!

A Desolate New Year to:

The owners of all tea rooms, pseudo-swank,
Where atmosphere is great and menu rank;

The taxi-driver of the wolfish mien
Who honks his horn before the light turns green;

Those sophomoric, Class of '14 croakers
Who try to drag me to alumni smokers;

To hundreds just as bad, and maybe worse,
Including those who air their ills in verse
I wish an insupportable, severe,
Exasperating, trouble-haunted year!

NIGHTCLUBS

I worked in a nightclub. One of those new affairs, semi-basement and sewer.

Nightclubs are full of G-men: gabbers, grabbers, grafters, gassers, gangsters, gamblers, gyppers, and gorillas. The only kind of a G-man that doesn't visit our place is a gentleman.

NOISE

A noisy and hilariously exuberant party was shouting its way through the evening and well into the next morning. A Negro orchestra was filling the air with blaring notes. A telephone shrilled in the next room and the host left to answer it. A few minutes later, he returned and, after calling for silence, made the announcement: "Folks, I'm sorry, but next door there is a lady who is very ill. They just called up, and I think we ought to tone this party down." Immediately there was a lessening of the noise. This went on for fifteen minutes and the phone rang again. The host left and quickly returned. "It's okay. Make all the noise you want to. She's dead!"

NUDITY

A nudist went around the golf course in nothing.

He was as careful as a nudist crossing a barbed-wire fence.

He's a strict nudist. He won't even have dressing on his sandwich.

He used to hide behind his mother's skirt, but she joined a nudist colony.

A nudist camp doesn't really need a cook, because they eat all their meals raw.

I know a nudist who won't even stick his tongue out because it has a coat on it.

I'm giving a little party at the nudist camp. Come over if you've got nothing on.

I heard of a nudist camp where the girls wear only beads . . . of perspiration.

She: Can I entertain you in any way, shape, or form?
He: Well, the last two methods sound promising.

—So you and Jane did a lot of needlework while at the nudist colony?
—Yes, I'd take splinters out of her and she'd take 'em out of me.

She used to be with Artists and Models, but she gave it up as it was just a bare existence.

(Variation)
This young lady used to be an artist's model but she quit. It was only a bare existence.

—How did things go at the nudist colony?
—Oh, everything came off all right.

He: Hey, hold it! There's no swimming allowed here.
She: Why couldn't you tell me before I got undressed?
He: Well, there's no law against that.

—Say, Peggy, is it true you're going into the new Earl Carroll show?
—No, I'm not in the NUDE for working.

—I used to sell underthings to nudist colonies.
—What kind of underthings?
—Cushions, Dodo, cushions.

I know two girls who once carelessly undressed before an open window. One caught a bad cold, and the other caught a rich bachelor who lived across the street.

While I was dancing with her, her dress fell off, and do you know every man in the room turned into a sailor. When I turned around, all I could see were Popeyes.

—What's all the excitement about?
—A girl was playing a violin solo and her string broke.
—A string on her violin?
—No, on her pajamas.

OBSCENITY

A New York judge ruled that a certain novel was not obscene. The publishers are expected to appeal the case.

OLD MAIDS

An old maid is just a YES girl who never had a chance to talk.

An old maid locked herself in her room and played strip solitaire.

Four old maids were in a Turkish bath—playing bridge for the rubber.

I knew an old maid who dreamt that she slept in a house with seven Gables.

Old maids always kiss each other when they meet—just to keep in practice.

An old maid is a girl who slept through the preliminaries while waiting for the main event.

Judy's an old maid, because, when she was a girl, she fell asleep during the preliminaries.

An old maid went to a fancy dress ball dressed as a postage stamp. She made up her mind she was going to get stuck on some male.

Burglar: Don't be scared, lady, all I want is your money.
Old Maid: Oh, go away. You are just like all the other men.

An old maid entered the bus, slid into the crowded rear seat, and murmured in a general voice, "It's all right, you may squeeze me all you please."

Niece: Auntie, do you peep under the bed at night and then say your prayers?
Spinster Aunt: No, I say my prayers and then peep under the bed!

First Old Maid: If you had your choice of all the great lovers of the screen, which one would you prefer?
Second Old Maid: The one who could get here the quickest!

One old maid shouted, "Help, quick, I've got a cramp." Another old maid came running and then said sadly, "Oh, for goodness sake, I thought you said a tramp."

Old Maid (phoning from the hotel room): This room has a chink in the wall.
Clerk: Well, what do you want for two-fifty—a couple of gigolos? [Chink was a derogatory term for a Chinese person.]

An old maid wanted to get a man, so she went to Sweden 'cause she read that's where the matches are made. Then she went to

the Swiss Alps to the Vale of Echoes and shouted, "I love you."
When the echo came back, she blushed.

Two old maids were sitting in an insane asylum. They had been
there for years. One of them sighed and said, "My, wouldn't it be
nice if we were going to a party tonight where there were lots of
people and dancing, and we were each escorted by a big handsome man." The other said, "Gee, now that you're talking sense,
you'll be out of here soon!"

—I understand your old-maid friend found a burglar in her room
the other night.
—Yes. He kissed her and then stole a ten-dollar bill she had on
the mantel.
—Of course she notified the police?
—Not on your life! Every night now she leaves a twenty-dollar
bill on the mantel.

A spinster, who'd moved opposite an athletic club, complained to
the landlady about the men running around the pool naked. The
landlady accordingly visited the old maid's room to investigate.
"Why, I don't see any men there," said the landlady. "Look,
they've got about three-fourths of every window screened. You
can't see a thing." Snipped the spinster, "Oh yeah? Well, just you
get up on this table and see if you can't!"

A widow, a flapper, and an old maid lived in the same boarding
house. Each had a date with a young man. The question arose
who would be kissed most. They decided on a sign. Each one on
coming down to breakfast would say "Good morning" for each
kiss she had received. The flapper came down blushing and said,
"G-o-o-o-d m-m-m-o-o-orning. He kissed me just once but that
was plenty." The widow came in and said, "Oh, good morning,
good morning, good morning, good morning, good morning."
The old maid entered dramatically. The other two women were
full of expectancy. The old maid said, "Hullo."

OPPORTUNITY

Two knocks.
—Who's that?
—Probably opportunity.
—Nope, opportunities are like eggs; they come only one at a
time.

OPTIMISM AND OPTIMISTS

The height of optimism: Looking in the cuckoo clock for eggs.

An optimist is one who puts two cents on a letter and marks it
rush.

An optimist is a man who does not care what happens, if it does not happen to him.

An optimist is a man who thinks his wife has quit cigarettes when he starts finding cigar butts around the house.

I have a friend who's an eternal optimist. He always looks on the bright side of things. The other day, he bought a pair of shoes without even trying them on. When he got home he found a big nail sticking up in the heel. Did he take them back? I should say not. He said, "I suppose the nail is there to keep the foot from sliding forward."

PAINTERS

—I'm a painter. I draw under a very famous artist.
—Oh, just an underdrawer.

—He's an outdoor painter.
—Landscape?
—No, fire escape.

—I'm a painter; I paint ships.
—I wonder: would you like to give me some lessons?
—Sure. I can teach you how to paint ships.
—But I don't want to paint ships. I want to paint some relations.
—Sorry, I can't teach you how to paint relations, but I can teach you how to paint ships.
—Heck, I don't want to know how to paint ships.
—Why not?
—I want to paint my relations.
—All right, then, I'll teach you how to paint your relations; but they'll look like ships.

PARTIES

A dry sense of humor has saved many a party from being all wet.

A fellow was going to a house warming so he took one of his old flames.

People who live in glass houses shouldn't throw stones—or parties either.

I was invited to a girl's house. She phoned me and said, "Come on up. We're going to throw a party." I was the party!

PAWN SHOPS

Calling a pawnshop: Hello, hello, Mr. Goldfarb! Will you take a look at my watch and tell me the time.

She *(anxious to impress):* I've just put my furs into cold storage.

He: Cold storage! Ha! Jolly good. Never heard it called that before. My cuff links and gold watch are there too.

PEDESTRIANS

The only rights pedestrians have are the last rites.

—How did you come to knock that pedestrian down?
—I didn't. I pulled up to let him cross the street, and he fainted.

(Variation)
—Hey, did you run over that guy?
—No, I stopped to let him pass, and he fainted from the shock.

—You ran into me with your car! You saw me crossing the street, didn't you?
—No, I closed my eyes. I can't bear to see anyone suffer.

PEEPING TOMS

I asked a friend of mine to go window shopping with me. He said, "What do you mean, window shopping? No one goes to bed this early."

A wise guy who knows how many itches there are in a mosquito can also tell the number of peeps in a keyhole.

—My window was open and a man peeked in while I was dressing.
—Did he get an eyeful?
—I'll say! An eyeful of fist!

—What's the matter? You look weary.
—I am. I'm leg weary.
—What from, walking?
—No, looking.

PERFUME AND SMELLS

—I just followed a skunk into a hole and discovered gold.
—U-reeka!
—I know it.

—Smell that? I can get it wholesale. I know the makers.
—Smells like a stable.
—It is, and I know the horse.

—What's that perfume? It's lovely.
—Oh, I get it very cheap. I know the salesman. What's that cologne you're using?
—Oh that. It's just a little odor. See, I live over a stable . . . and I know the horse.

PHILADELPHIA

She wanted to be a trained nurse, but she came from Philadelphia and the chloroform kept her awake.

PHOTOGRAPHS AND PHOTOGRAPHERS

Photographers get all the blame for nature's dirty work.

I'm going to have some X-ray pictures taken. If they come out good I'll let you have one.

You know those pictures parents have taken when you're a little baby, sprawled out on a cushion? Well, my mother had one of me, and she lost it. So she just wired me that she wishes I'd have another one taken.

PLAGIARISM

I was listening to the radio in order to steal some gags. Some of them came so fast, I almost dropped my pencil.

I understand there is a humor magazine that is having its contributors mail their jokes directly to the homes of the radio comedians.

[See also the poem about King Tut and joke stealing in the introduction.]

POLICE

Never race with a motor cop.

Any detective believes that clues make the man.

That cop is so dumb he arrested a cross-eyed man for looking crooked.

He's been arrested so often, he calls the police patrol his town car.

—I see where all the police are going to be vaccinated.
—Why? They never catch anything.

—Ever been pinched for going too fast?
—No but I've been slapped.

Cop (to a drunken woman): Come on, you'll have to accompany me.
She: All right, what are you going to sing?

—I see they pinched one of the local cops with a whole car full of moonshine.
—Corn on the cop, eh?

Stranger (in small town): So you're the chief of police! Glad to know you. I wonder if I could also shake hands with the fire chief?
Police Chief: Sure. Just wait till I change hats.

A Russian was being led off to execution by a squad of Bolshevik soldiers, on a rainy morning. "What brutes you Bolsheviks are," grumbled the doomed man, "to march me through the rain like this." "How about us?" retorted one of the squad. "We have to march back."

Mistress: The last maid I had was too fond of policemen, Mary. I shall expect you to avoid them.
New Maid: Don't worry about that, ma'am. I 'ates the sight of 'em. My father's a burglar.

Cop: Where's my police whistle?
Man: I dunno, it was here a minute ago.
Cop: Is that thing lost again? Aw shucks, now I gotta buy another box of crackerjacks!

There had been an auto accident. The policeman arrived to take notes. "Look here," said one of the drivers angrily, "I clearly had the right of way. This man here"—he pointed to the other driver—"ran into me. Now you say that I was to blame." "And you certainly were," insisted the policeman. "But why, officer?" pleaded the driver. "Because his father is mayor; his brother is chief of police; and I'm courting his sister."

If a dog bites a man it's news, but if a dog bites a cop it's not news; it's a blessing!

Caught Speeding

Cops are a hardworking lot, and a cheerful bunch. Especially traffic cops. They're always whistling at their work.

(Variation)
She's got a boyfriend who's the happiest man in the world. He whistles all day. He's a traffic cop.

Cop: You were going sixty.
Ed: Don't be foolish, I wasn't going even forty. In fact, this car won't go thirty. I don't think I was even doing twenty. Probably not even ten miles an hour.
Cop: All right, here's a ticket for parking.

THE POLISH

—Her dad was a Pole.
—Yes? North or South?

—Did you ever hear of a wooden wedding?
—That's when two Poles get married.

POLITICS AND POLITICIANS

A lame duck is a Congressman whose goose is cooked.

It used to be called gift of gab. Now it's grift and grab.

Nowadays, Republican rallies are held in a telephone booth.

The world has almost every kind of government except the kind they promised to be.

What our government needs is a good political matador. One adept in handling the bull.

A conservative is someone who wants the rules enforced so that nobody can take his pile the way he got it.

The Democrats hadn't had the Republicans worried for years until they offered to cooperate with them.

Although he started out life with the handicap of being unable to tell a lie, George Washington got pretty far in politics.

A doctor told a politician: "Congratulations, it's triplets." The father-politician replied, "I demand a recount."

A new use has been discovered for the dial telephone. The government is going to use it to teach congressmen how to count to ten.

A statesman is a man who wants to do something for his country. A politician is one who wants the country to do something for him.

The acoustics in the House of Representatives are said to be so bad that almost all the speeches can be clearly heard.

If all the copies of the *Congressional Record* were piled up and burned, the resultant heat would run the New York subways for a week.

Poor Politicians. They're getting ten thousand a year, but it costs thirty a year to live. And they end up saving a hundred thousand a year.

Some of the people can fool you all of the time and all of the people can fool you some of the time, but the rest of the time you have to fool yourself.

Speaking about those big dirigibles . . . they're just gas bags. The government ought to stop building them and the people ought to stop electing them.

This young lady danced in Washington last week before members of the House of Congress. I've heard it was one of the most successful movements (*or:* motions) brought before the house in years.

Country Gentleman: Here, hold my horse for a minute.
Senator from Kentucky: Sir, I am a member of Congress.
Country Gentleman: That's all right. I'll trust you.

It's hard to predict which party will win, what with the Democrats always letting the cat out of the bag, and the Republicans always getting left holding it.

Captain: Don't you know that the sea is full of sharks?
Sailor: Yes, sir, but sharks don't worry me. I am tattooed.
Captain: What has that to do with it?
Sailor: On my back I have tattooed "The Americans won the war," and even a shark can't swallow that.

A couple couldn't decide what their son was cut out to do, so they thought they would give him a test. They placed a Bible, some money, and a bottle of liquor in his room and watched him, figuring that if he took the book first, he would become a journalist or writer, if he took the money, he would eventually be a businessman, and if he took the liquor he would become a bum. When the boy entered his room, he put the money in his pocket, drank the liquor, and started to read the Bible. Seeing this, the father declared: "That boy is going to be a politician."

A ward heeler was out rounding up information on the new voters when he came to the home of a family that had just moved in. "How do you do," he grinned when the lady came to the door. "I'm making a canvass of the neighborhood and would like to know your political affiliations." "My which?" asked Mrs. Murphy. "What party do you belong to?" "Oh, he's in there. But he's busy just now." "I mean, is your husband a Democrat?" "No, I don't think so," said Mrs. Murphy. "A Republican, then?" "Nope." "Well, is your husband a technocrat?" "Wait, I'll ask him." Mrs. Murphy lifted her voice loudly, and called to her husband: "Are you a technocrat?" [taking a crap] "Naw," came the muffled answer, "just shaving."

POPULARITY

A popular person is one who enjoys being bored.

PRISON

Thirty days hath September, April, June, and my uncle for speeding.

He held his last job for four years, with two off for good behavior.

—Are you back in jail again?
—Yeah! Any mail?

—Officer, is Sing Sing the place you go for life?
—Naw, it's always pretty dead up there.

—I graduated with two degrees from Penn State.
—Yeah, and got the third degree at State Pen.

—What did you go to jail for?
—Well, I wanted to be a warden, but figured I'd start at the bottom.

Prison Warden: You say you have a complaint to make? Well, what is it?
Convict: There ain't enough exits, sir.

—Hello, Bill, I'm glad to see you. What on earth have you been doing for the past three months?
—Ninety days.

A welfare worker said to a jailed convict, "I hope you'll let me help you when you get out of here." He replied, "Sorry, madame, I always woik alone."

Mean Warden: Up knave, and be off to your vocal lesson!
Disgusted Convict: Oh, I'm getting sick and tired of this perpetual Sing Sing all the time.

—I'm sick and tired of trying to reduce. I've been bending and twisting for two hours.
—That's nothing. My brother just finished a four-year stretch.

A murderer was about to meet his doom, and the prison chaplain asked him: "Is there one last favor I can do for you?" The man thought for a moment. "Yes, sir. I'm terribly afraid. Will you hold my hand while I'm in the chair?"

The execution date was set for October 1929.
Executioner: We're going to give you anything you want for your last meal.
Condemned: All right; can I have some champagne?
Executioner: Sure. Any particular vintage?
Condemned: Yes, 1984!

—For stealing a million bucks he'll get at least a five-year sentence.
—That means he'll do about three months in jail under the current parole system.

—How long were you in jail?
—Two months.
—What was the charge?
—No charge . . . everything free.

He: Where is your husband?
She: On the road.

He: Can't he get away from his work and visit you?
She: Oh, no! There are men with rifles watching him.

First Jail Bird: What are you in for?
Second Jail Bird: Rocking my wife to sleep.
First: But they can't put you in here for that.
Second: But you ain't seen the size of them rocks.

Visitor: And what's your name, my good man?
Prisoner: Nine, seven, four, two.
Visitor: Is that your real name?
Prisoner: Naw, dat's just me pen name.

—My uncle got a week in jail for loitering.
—That's nothing. My dad got three years in the pen just for sneezing in a bank.
—Sneezing in a bank?
—Yes, he waked the night watchman.

At the turn of the century, when women's dresses brought up the rear for a yard or two, a famous social worker was visiting at Sing Sing. To demonstrate how the convicts were locked up at night, the warden escorted her into one of the cell tiers and ordered the doors opened, then closed. In the process of locking, the tail of her dress caught in one of the doors. She tugged at it gently and, being unable to release it, turned to the convict in the cell and asked, "Will you please lift my skirt?" The man shook his head mournfully. "Madam," he replied, "for doing that, I am doing this."

PROHIBITION

We call our cow Carolina 'cause she's dry.

The new anthem: "Three cheers for the red wine and brew."

They'll broadcast the end of Prohibition on a coast to coast hiccup.

Opportunity knocks at your door, but the prohibition agent busts right in.

Wonder when the government will let some real brewers muscle in on the beer racket.

Prohibition is as foolish as the law against concealed weapons in a nudist colony.

It's not a question of bringing back beer; it is a question of bringing back good beer.

Some of the politicians favor calling off the Prohibition battle on account of wet grounds.

While his friend watched, a judge tried some cases. Later, the judge asked, "What was the case worth?" His friend replied, "I wouldn't give you more than six bucks a pint."

—Do you think since Prohibition that liquor tastes better 'cause it's illegal?
—No, 'cause it's liquor.

—I miss my bathtub.
—On the contrary, I think showers are much better.
—They're all right, but I can't make beer in a shower.

In a town out west where the liquor question is no question at all, no one knew that the water had been shut off for a week until they had a fire.

Wharton School tactics are driving men to drink and dribble. The other day a vacationing student walked up to a bank teller and pulled out two twenty-dollar bills. Thrusting the money through the window, he asked bluntly enough, "I want two cases." The teller sized up the well-groomed chap and then sympathetically inquired, "Two cases of what, sir?" "I don't know what you call it," replied the student, "but the sign in the window says two and a half percent, and I'm willing to try anything." [Wharton is the famous business school at the University of Pennsylvania.]

PROSTITUTION

We used to go to school together. She was the teacher. She used to teach us to take two from three, three from five, six from ten. Now she takes ten from one, twenty from another.

"I'm sorry," said the girl at the theatre ticket booth, "but that two-dollar bill is counterfeit." Stunned, the woman stood motionless. "My God!" she whispered, "I've been seduced."

A beautiful girl was sitting dejectedly outside a booking office. A friend asked her what was wrong. She replied: "When I got my first cut in salary I said: 'There go my dollar lunches!' When I got my second cut I said: 'There go my silk stockings!' And now with my third cut, I say: 'Here goes my amateur standing!'"

PROVERBS

People who carry glass bottles should not sit on stone benches.

You can't drive a nail with a sponge, no matter how you soak it.

RACE

—What race has the dominating influence in America?
—The Kentucky Derby.

RADIO

N.B.C. Noisy but Consistent.

Static makes many a radio program a pleasure.

Please turn off that cheese program; the house is getting full of mice.

According to radio artists who depend on a fickle public, it's Air Today and Gone Tomorrow!

—What does Kate Smith wear on her broadcasts?
—A nationwide hook-up.

—Do you think the radio will ever take the place of the newspaper?
—No, you can't swat flies with a radio.

We've always wanted to visit a big radio station, particularly to see the room where they age jokes.

We always get our early morning exercise from the radio. Somebody turns it on, and we have to get up and turn it off.

Crimes are now being reenacted on the radio. And many of them go on under the name of dance music.

Einstein can't decide whether the universe is static or dynamic. We can—we own a radio.

Radio reception has been found to be better underground than above. Here is the answer to the question: "Death, where is thy sting?"
[Variation for punch line: "Alas, there is no escape."]

I just got a radio. It's great. I can get all stations: *(Mention one or two radio stations and)* Times Square, 72nd Street, and the Pennsylvania. Gee, it's great.

—Last week when my uncle listened to your program, he nearly choked to death.
—I'll admit it was funny, but he didn't have to choke to death.
—Yeah? Well, you try holding YOUR nose for thirty minutes!

—I have a good soprano voice and would like to sing over the radio. What would you suggest?
—Buy a bullet-proof vest and travel to and from the studio in an armored car.

She asked her husband to tune in on a certain broadcasting station and copy a recipe that was to be given at that hour by a culinary expert. He tried to do so, but another station, which was broadcasting physical culture exercises at the same time, interfered considerably. This is what he took down. "Hands on hips, place one cup of flour on the shoulders, raise knees and depress toes and mix thoroughly in one-half cup of milk. Repeat six times. Inhale quickly one-half teaspoonful of baking powder, lower the legs and mash two hard-boiled eggs in a sieve. Exhale, breathe naturally, and sift in a bowl. Attention! Lie flat on the floor and roll the white of an egg backward and forward until it comes to a boil. In ten minutes remove from the fire and rub smartly with a rough towel. Breathe naturally, sprinkle with pepper, dress in warm flannels, and serve with soup."

REINCARNATION

—Reincarnation is an interesting subject.
—Yes, but it has me worried. Wouldn't it be funny if, when I died, I came back as a skunk.
—Don't worry about it; you can't be the same thing twice.

RESOLUTIONS

The things that get the most breaks in this world are good resolutions.

Believing that in self-denial the soul is born, and that they will aid in my quest for the fuller life, I do hereby swear to firmly and diligently abide by the following resolutions for the year _____:
1. I will smoke no cigarettes manufactured by Eskimos.
2. I will drink no intoxicating liquors in church or airplanes.
3. I will play at games of chance with men only—unless there happen to be women and children present who want to play.
4. I will not eat little babies unless I get terribly hungry.
5. I will attend school regularly except on days when I cut classes.
6. I will do all I can to keep from breaking my neck or either of my legs.
7. I will not run around with wild women over eighty years old.
8. I will not play with snakes or wildcats.
9. I will not bet on horse races on February 29th.

RESTAURANTS

A bird in the hand is bad table manners.

The percolator fell over and strained its coffee.

We give you your choice of food: take it or leave it.

This is windmill soup. You get some if it goes around.

He paid the bill so often they began to take him for an after-dinner mint.

I asked the waiter to pass me a nutcracker and he handed me a beer bottle.

Sole usually stands for fish or leather. In this restaurant it stands for both.

I just saw a terrible fight in a restaurant: two cooks were beating up an egg.

I know a cafe that furnishes gigolos to unattended ladies. There's no lover charge.

—What's the matter with the egg . . . was it boiled too long?
—No, too late.

(Variation)
—Do you think those eggs were cooked long enough?
—Yeah, but not soon enough.

A fellow complained that his cocoa was cold, so the waiter told him to put his hat on.

You could hardly tell the guests from the waiters, except that the waiters were sober.

We haven't got lump sugar. Here's the granulated. If you don't like it, you can lump it.

I just went to a restaurant and no one was there. A sign on the window said, "Home Cooking."

In a restaurant, a man was complaining about the egg being bad. The waiter said, "Please, sir, don't blame me. I only laid the table."

I went into a restaurant. When I sat down, I said to the waitress, "Hello, how's the chicken?" She said, "Fine, how's the kid?"

—Please have my chops lean.
—Yes, sir, which way?

Joe *(at Mexican restaurant):* Two orders of Carnicero Lleno, please.
Waiter: Sorry, sir, that's the proprietor.

—Where's the paper plate I gave you your pie on?
—I must have eaten it. I thought that lower crust was kinda tough.

Waiter: It must be kind of difficult to eat soup with a mustache.
Customer: Yeah, it's quite a strain.

—These are the best eggs we've had for years.
—Well, bring me some you haven't had so long.

—Do you want those eggs turned over?
—Yes, to the museum.

—A sign on the restaurant says, "French spoken here." Who speaks it?
—Just the customers.

—I don't care for these shellfish; they don't look very good to me.
—Well, if you're eating on the looks, why didn't you buy gold-fish?

—This is marble cake.
—Pass me the chisel.

The waiter: Steak medium or well done, sir?
Absent-minded parson: Well done, thou good and faithful servant!

Waiter: Would you like to drink Canada Dry, sir?
Student: Yeah, but I'm only here for the weekend.

Diner: This salad tastes putrid. Do you wash the lettuce?
Cook: Yes, even with soap.

Customer: Say, waiter, I ordered pumpkin pie and you gave me apple.
Waiter: That's all right. All the pies are punk in here.

—Waiter, are the grapefruit fresh?
—Yes, sir, one just spit in that gentleman's eye.

—Waiter, waiter, there's a button in my salad.
—It must have come off in the dressing.

—Waiter, two eggs, please! Boil them four minutes.
—Yes, sir, be ready in half a second, sir.

—I want a couple of hard-boiled eggs to take out.
—Mamie and I don't get off till ten. You'll have to wait.

—Waiter, there's a fly in my soup!
—That's all right, sir, it won't drink much.

—Waiter, there's a fly in my soup!
—That's quite all right, sir, it can swim.

—Waiter, there's a fly in my soup!
—That's all right, sir, it's not hot enough to burn him.

—Waiter, there's a fly in my soup!
—Well, let the poor thing have a little fun.

—Waiter, there's a fly in my soup!
—I might add that it's a Drosophila Melangaster, sir.

—Waiter, there's a fly in my soup!
—It's "flies" to me, "gnats" to you!

—Waiter, there's a fly in my soup!
—You'll usually find them quite tasteless, sir.

—Waiter, there's a fly in my soup!
—You see, sir, our cook used to be a tailor.

—Waiter, there's a fly in my soup!
—Not so loud, sir, everybody'll want one.

—Waiter, there's a fly in my soup!
—That's all right, sir, he's housebroken.

—Waiter, there's a fly in my soup!
—It will be all right, sir, if you'll strain the soup with your teeth.

She: But why are we dining in a cafeteria?
He: Because the doctor says I must take a long walk before every meal.

(Variation)
For the benefit of those who would take a long walk before breakfast, it's suggested that they eat in cafeterias.

—I read where a man ate twenty pounds of sausage in ten minutes. What would you call that? A record?
—No, baloney!

Diner: Here, waitress, take this chicken away. It's as tough as a paving stone.
Waitress: Maybe it's a Plymouth rock, sir.

Waiter: Here is some very good canvas-back duck, sir.
Businessman *(after some chewing):* Here, take this canvas back and bring me the duck.

A restaurant charged me four dollars for a meal. I gave the waiter ten bucks and told him to keep the change because I was going to take a toothpick.

—What is it you wish, sir?
—Well, originally I came in for breakfast, but if dinner is ready I'll take that.

—You must have a very clean kitchen here.
—Oh, we have, sir.
—Yeah, everything I eat tastes of soap.

—Gosh, am I hungry! I'll have another steak.
—Wait a minute, we didn't serve steak.
—Who carved a hole in the table?

—Waiter, why do you keep laughing?
—I laugh all the time. It's good for my liver.
—I wish you'd laugh for my steak. I ordered it an hour ago.

—This is strawberry shortcake.
—Where are the strawberries?
—That's what we're short of.

Nowadays in a drug store, you eat at one counter, where you get your indigestion, and then go on to the next counter, where they give you a prescription to put you right.

—I want some beer, waiter.
—Yes, sir, pale?
—No, just a glass will do.

I went into a little Greek restaurant and asked what kind of pie they had. The Greek started to recite, and also to count on his fingers, "We've got apple pie, peach pie, plum pie, cherry pie." I asked him, "What does the thumb represent?" He said, "Oh that, that's cake."

A lady bustled into the station coffee shop and curtly called to the waiter. "Bring me a cup of coffee and make it snappy. My train leaves in five minutes." A lanky cowpuncher arose and handed her his cup. "Take mine, lady, it's already saucered and blown."

Diner: I know of nothing more exasperating than to find a hair in my soup.
Waiter: Well, it would be worse, wouldn't it, to have the soup in your hair?

—Did Clarice enjoy her date with Harry, the wrestler, at that ritzy restaurant?
—She was never so embarrassed in her life. When he started to eat his soup, five couples got up and began dancing.

—How do you make your beef stew?
—With onions, carrots, and potatoes.
—Where do you get the beef?
—From the customers.

A man was hired as a cook in a restaurant. The manager asked him if he had had much experience. "Yes, sir, I was an officer's cook two years and wounded twice." The manager tasted the soup the man had made and said: "You're lucky, man. It's a wonder they didn't kill you."

Lawyer: This man says that you put horse meat in your rabbit stew. Is that true?
Defendant: Well, we make it fifty-fifty.
Lawyer: Whaddaya mean, fifty-fifty?
Defendant: One horse to one rabbit.

I took my father into a restaurant. He's not used to eating in those places. We both ordered. He asked for just a small steak, a filet mignon. When the waiter brought it, the old man asked, "Is this a filet mignon?" The waiter said, "Yes, our best." My father said, "Take it away, and bring me a steak. At home, I leave more than that."

—I'm sorry, but I haven't money enough to pay for that meal.
—That's all right, we write your name on the wall, and next time you come . . . pay for it.
—Don't write my name up. Everyone coming in will see it.
—No, they won't. Your overcoat will be hanging over it.

—Who beat you up?
—You see, it's this way. I took my girl to a restaurant and she found a fly in her soup. She called the waiter and said: "Get this insect out of here."
—So what?
—So what? He threw me down a flight of stairs.

After studying the menu for a long time, the man finally decided on his order.
—I'll tell you vat I vant. Gimme, pliz, a nice toikey sendwich.
The proprietor shook his head.
—Today, I ain't got no toikey.
—Dot's too bed. I vanted toikey. Vell, den, gimme, pliz, a chicken sendwich.
Again the proprietor shook his head.
—Dot's how it goes. Today I ain't got no chicken sendwich neither.
—Vot! No toikey and no chicken? You certainly should hev it chicken!
The proprietor finally grew angry.
—Leesten dope, eff I would have had chicken, you'd 'a' got your toikey sendwich!

RÉSUMÉ

If anyone would like my records, he can get them at the nearest police station.

REVOLVING DOOR

A fellow landed in the hospital because he started through a revolving door and changed his mind.

RIDDLES

Automobile Accidents

I was run over by a car this morning and wasn't hurt. You know why? I was standing under a bridge.

Boomerang

What do you call a boomerang that doesn't work? A stick.

Clocks

—If a man smashed a clock, could he be accused of killing time?
—Not if he could prove that the clock struck first.

Clothing

Why do a pilgrim's pants always fall down? Because they wear their belt buckle on their hat.

College

How many Harvard students does it take to change a tire? Two. One to hold the drinks and one to call dad.

Cows

What do you get from a pampered cow? Spoiled milk.

—Why does cream cost more than milk?
—Oh, because it's harder for the cows to sit on the small bottles.

Dogs

Where do you find a dog with no legs? Right where you left him.

What do you get when you cross a pit bull with a collie? A dog that runs for help—after it bites your leg off.

—How far can a dog run into the woods?
—As far as he wants to, I suppose.
—Not on your life. After he passes the middle he is running out.

Fish

What did the fish say when it hit a concrete wall? "Dam!"

Food

What's the best way to raise corned beef and cabbage? With a knife and a fork.

What's the difference between roast beef and pea soup? Anyone can roast beef.

Frogs

Three frogs were sitting on a lily pad. Two of them took a notion to jump off. How many were left? Answer—three! Because they only took a notion.

Heaven and Hell

How do you get holy water? You boil the hell out of it.

Hoboes

—How is a hobo just like a cigar lighter?
—Don't know.
—Well, a hobo won't work. If he doesn't work, he's a politician. If he's a politician, he gives away cigars. And if he gives away one cigar, he is a cigar lighter. If he is a cigar lighter, he won't work. And if he won't work, he's a hobo.

Horse

—I have a horse without a tail and I want to sell him, but I'll have to sell him wholesale.
—Why?
—Because I can't retail him.

Inimitable People

—Who are the most imitated people?
—I don't know.
—Inimitable persons.

Insects

—What is the difference between a spider and a fly?
—You can't sew a button on a spider.

Kissing

Why is a kiss over a telephone like a straw hat? Because neither is felt.

Movies

You know what Priscilla asked the talkie star who had a double do his signing for him? "Why don't you squeak for yourself, John?"

Music

Why do bagpipers walk when they play? They're trying to get away from the noise.

Pedestrians

You know how crazy people get through the forest? They take the psycho path.

Rabbits

How do you catch a unique rabbit? Unique up on it.
How do you catch a tame rabbit? Tame way, unique up on it.

Romance, Garden Variety

Do you know what a garden romance is? An old tomato married to a dead beet.

Shipwreck

What lies at the bottom of the ocean and twitches? A nervous wreck.

Snakes

—What's the difference between a snake and a flea?
—A snake crawls on its own stomach, but a flea's not so particular.

Spanish

What do you call four bullfighters in quicksand? Quatro sinko.

Telephones

Why are there so many Smiths in the phone book? They all have phones.

Truck Driver

—He drove straight to his goal. He looked neither to right nor left. He pressed forward, moved by a definite purpose. Neither friend nor foe could turn him from his course. All who crossed his path did so at their own peril. What would you call such a man?
—A truck driver!

Vampires

What do you get when you cross a snowman with a vampire? Frostbite.

Widows

—What weeds are easiest to kill?
—Widows' weeds. You have only to say "Wilt Thou?" and they wilt.

SCOTLAND AND SCOTS

A Scotsman was found dead in a pay-as-you-leave car.

Scotch Chicken: a frankfurter with a feather in it.

He's as happy as a Scotsman at a free-for-all fight.

A Scotsman phoned the poorhouse and reversed the charges.

A Scotsman found a bottle of iodine, so he cut his finger.

A taxi was smashed in Scotland. Eighteen people were killed.

I just heard there is a terrible epidemic of grippe in Scotland.

A Scottish kid took his balloon to get a vulcanized patch on it.

Scotsmen lead good lives so they won't have to pay for their sins.

One good thing about a Scotsman: he never gives his friends away.

A Scotsman went next door and turned on the gas to commit suicide.

A Scotsman gave his wife a new spring outfit—a pair of rubber heels.

I telephoned a Scotsman for a donation and he sent me his best wishes.

A Scotsman's friend asked for a stiff drink, so he put starch in it.

A Scotsman shot his wife for washing out his lather *(shaving)* brush.

You know what a clutching movement on a song is called? Scotch palsy.

A Scotsman married the half-witted girl because she was fifty percent off.

A Scotsman married a rosy-cheeked girl so he wouldn't have to buy rouge.

I have a request here written in shorthand. I guess it's from a Scotsman.

Did you hear about the Scottish athlete who hated to loosen up his muscles?

Then there was the Scotsman who bought the car because the clutch was thrown in.

The good old Scottish remedy for seasickness: hold a sixpence between your teeth.

A man was selling sandwiches in the street and two Scotsmen took a bite at him.

A Scotsman used a straightjacket for a nightgown, so he'd be sure to sleep tight.

I know a Scotsman who carries a fiddle around so he won't have to have his hair cut.

A Scotsman went on his honeymoon alone because his wife had seen Niagara Falls.

I just saw a terrible accident at the baseball game. A Scotsman fell out of a tree.

The Scots don't like drinking from the bottle because you've got to tip the bottle.

It will be a Scotsman who will find a way to condense shampoo suds back into soap.

Then there's the Scottish sheik who gave his sweetie moth balls to put in her hope chest.

A kid swallowed a penny so his parents let him keep it for Christmas. (*Or:* his birthday)

A Scotsman walked twelve miles to see the ballgame and was too tired to climb the fence.

A Scotsman got a present of a box of corn pads, so he went out and bought tight shoes.

A fellow asked a Scotsman for something for a cup of coffee. He gave him a lump of sugar.

—What is your idea of rigid economy?
—A dead Scotsman.

He: For two cents I'd kiss you.
She: Migawd, a Scotch gigolo!

—What started the Grand Canyon?
—A Scotsman lost a penny in a ditch.

A Scotsman put green glasses on his horse and fed him straw to make him believe it was grass.

Our Scottish landlady is so stingy that she heats our knives so we can't use so much butter.

A Scotsman bought a car and expected to run it cheaper because his wife had gas on the stomach.

A Scotsman went to the Grand Hotel because he thought he could get away with a couple of towels.

A Scotsman started biting his fingernails when his doctor told him he needed more iron in his system.

Then there is the Scotsman who moved next door to the church because he was so fond of rice pudding.

I know a Scotsman who wanted to smoke monogrammed cigarettes. So he changed his name to Chesterfield.

A Scotsman bought a car with free wheeling and took it back when he found out he had to buy gas and oil.

A Scots murderer upon entering the death chamber complained to the warden that he was being overcharged.

The Scots are such good golfers because they realize the fewer times they hit the ball the longer it will last.

A Scotsman went outside at Christmas, fired a shot, came in, and told the kids that Santa had committed suicide.

A Scotsman's wife was running a fever of 105, so he had her moved into the basement and used her to heat the house.

Once there was a Scotsman who was so tight that he put boric acid in his grapefruit in order to get a free eyewash.

Clerk: And you get an extra pair of pants with this suit.
Scotsman: Throw in an extra coat and I'll take it.

A Scotsman was invited out to tea. He was asked how many lumps of sugar with his tea. He said, "How many do ye give?"

A Scotsman hoped it would be a damp night Christmas eve, so he could have a rattle in his chest to take home to the kiddies.

Have you heard of the lady who asked a Scottish tenor to sing as he'd never sung before? She asked him to sing for charity.

A Scotsman was celebrating his golden wedding so he took along his friend Goldberg; and Goldberg brought along a goldfish.

A terrible thing just happened in Scotland. A little boy killed his father and mother so he could go to the orphans' picnic.

Wedding Guest: Isn't this your fourth daughter getting married?
Canny Scot: Aye, and our rice is getting a wee bit dirty.

A Scottish wife almost fainted when her aviator husband did a loop. She remembered she'd left some loose change in his pocket.

A Scot took his little boy to church one Sunday morning and told him to take bigger strides to save the new shoes he was wearing.

And then there was the Scotsman who died on the way to the electric chair. He happened to think that he was paying for his crime.

A Scotsman came to America. He came on one boat and his baggage on the next boat, so that if one sank he wouldn't lose everything.

A Scotsman wouldn't let his daughter go to school because she had to pay attention and didn't receive any interest from the principal.

Another theory has been advanced as to why George Washington stood up in the boat. He was Scottish and had just had his pants pressed.

I recently stayed in a swank London hotel and saw a Scotsman holding on to his shoelaces while the valet tried to get them for cleaning.

Then there was the Scotsman who, when asked what he had clenched in his fist, answered: "My wife's false teeth. She's been eating between meals."

Driver of overturned taxi *(to Scottish passenger):* Are you hurt, sir?
Scot: Don't be a bothering about my being hurt, man. Stop that wee clock of yours.

A Scotswoman bought her son a pair of glasses because he was shortsighted and told him to take them off when he wasn't looking at anything.

A Scot bought two tickets for a raffle. With the first he won a thousand dollars; then he cried because he'd wasted his money on the second.

A Scot went to the doctor to have an examination and was told he had too much sugar in his system. The next morning he cried into his grapefruit.

A Scotsman wanted to go into the pictures for half price because he had only one eye. The Scottish manager asked him double price saying it would take him twice as long to see the show.

A Scotsman visiting New York said, "It's wonderful here. Free parks. Free museums. Free picture galleries. And the restaurant I go to always has a quarter under the plate for a surprise."

A Scotsman, sending his wife to a theatre to see an illusionist, advised her, "Listen Maggie, when he comes to that trick where he makes twenty omelettes with one egg, watch verra close."

—Hear about the Scotsman who wanted his money back?
—No, what was the matter?
—He bought a score card at the game, and the team scored.

—Why, said McPherson, this car has such swell brakes I can stop her on a dime.
—Yeah, and you probably would, if you saw one!

Gloria: I'm going downtown and exchange the present Sandy gave me for Christmas.
Gladys: I've got to go to the five-and-ten, too.

A Scotsman living on the outskirts of Chicago became engaged to a girl who got so fat that he wanted to break off the engagement. But the girl couldn't get the ring off, so he had to marry her.

A Scotsman called up his doctor in great agitation. "Come at once!" he cried breathlessly, "Ma wee child has swallowed a saxpence!" "How old is it?" asked the medico. "1894!" wailed the Scot.

A Scotsman took his girl to the free city art exhibit, told her to walk quickly, and then pointed out that by so doing they got the effect of watching moving pictures.

A Scots boy asked his girl in a picture theatre the other day if she would care for some chewing gum. She answered, "Indeed I would, Jock." "All right," said he, "feel under your seat."

A young man in a Scots family swallowed a fountain pen. His father was telling someone about it, and the party asked, "Whatever did you do about it?" The father said, "Well, we have had to use a pencil."

A big-hearted Scotsman waited at the stage entrance of a theatre where the Siamese Twins were playing. When they came out, he whispered to one of them, "If you can get away, I'll treat you to a drink."

A Scottish traveling salesman, held up in the Orkney Islands by a bad storm, telegraphed to his firm in Aberdeen: MAROONED HERE BY STORM WIRE INSTRUCTIONS. The reply came: START SUMMER VACATION AS FROM YESTERDAY.

Coming over on the boat, we took a collection and on counting up we found ten dollars and three cents on the plate. I said, "It looks like we have a Scotsman here among us." A voice from the back said, "You're wrong, there's three of us."

It is rumored that on Lindbergh's recent flight across the Atlantic he experienced much trouble. His engine tore loose, the nuts and bolts began to fall, and the wings flopped. Then he crossed Scotland and everything tightened up.

—It will be just too bad if Herb ever gets sick, because his folks have a Scottish doctor.
—What has being Scottish got to do with it?
—He is so tight that he will never treat a patient.

(Variation)
You know why Scotsmen are not good doctors? They won't treat their patients.

—Ye wouldna buy your sweetie a ring at the five-and-ten, would ye, Sandy?
—Na, mon, it's better to gang to the twenty-five-cent store and get her a guid one.

—McTavish *(at box office):* Will ye kindly return me the amount I paid for amusement tax?
—Box Officer: Why, sir?
—McTavish: I wasna amused.

A Scotsman, an Irishman, a German, and a Jew were eating dinner together. When the meal was finished and the waiter came with the bill the Scotsman promptly said that he would take it. The next day a Jewish ventriloquist was found murdered.

"Your wife needs a change," said the doctor. "Salt air will cure her." The next time the physician called, he found the Scotsman sitting by the bedside fanning his wife with a herring.

Scotsman *(at football stadium gate):* What are the prices of your seats?
Gate Keeper: Students, fifty cents, all others, seventy-five cents; and programs, ten cents.
Scotsman: I'll sit on a program, please.

Two old Scotsmen sat by the road puffing solemnly at their pipes. "There's no' much pleasure in smoking, Donald," said Sandy. "Hoo dae ye mak' that oot?" questioned Donald. "Weel, if ye're smoking ye ain bacca, ye're thinking o' the awful expense, and if ye're smoking some ither body's y'r pipe's rammed saw ticht it winna draw."

Scotsman: My lad, are you to be my caddie?
Caddie: Yes, sir.
Scotsman: And how are you at finding lost balls?
Caddie: Very good, sir.
Scotsman: Well, look around and find one and we'll start the game.

A man boarded a cross-country train, gave the pullman porter half of a five-dollar bill, and told him if the service was good he'd give him the other half when they reached their destination. He went into the drawing room and discovered his friend, a Scotsman, biting a nickel in two.

Sandy McGregor gazed at the sign on the hat cleaner's doorway, gazed until he was purple in the face. "Two dollars and a quarter for cleanin' a little hat! Oh, the robbers!" So he went along and finally came to a Turkish Bath. The sign said, "Turkish Bath, $1.50." Inside went Sandy and paid his money. "Take off your clothes," said the attendant. "Sure," said Sandy. "But I'm wearin' ma hat!"

Sandy: My wife dreamt last night she went to a sale and spent two dollars for a dress.
Jock: What did you do?
Sandy: Well, it was so wasteful, I made her go back to sleep and buy it for a dollar ninety-eight.

Sandy MacGregor (all Scotsmen are Sandy MacGregors) was in the wilds of Africa hunting beasts of the jungle. One day as Sandy was walking up a hill he came face to face with a ferocious lion. The lion gave a healthy leap right at Sandy, and Sandy ducked. Then he ran. My, how Sandy ran! Far up the hill. Finally he turned around and looked down in a small open space where the lion was. And what do you think the lion was doing? Practicing small jumps.

A couple went into a restaurant in Glasgow and ordered a sandwich. The waiter brought the sandwich and put it on the table. The husband proceeded to cut it in half, putting one half on his plate and giving the other half to his wife. The husband began to eat and the wife watched him. The waiter, seeing that the woman wasn't eating, went to her and asked her if there was anything wrong with her half. She told him, "No, it's all right. I'm waiting until my husband gets through with the teeth."

McPherson's condition was critical and his wife was much anguished at having to leave him to go to the neighbors to call a doctor. As she looked down at his shrunken form, her hard face softened, and tears spilled over her cheeks. Pulling herself together with an effort, she put on her old bonnet, dabbed at her eyes with the back of her hand, and went over to say goodbye to her husband. "Now remember, Angus, no extravagance. If you feel yourself going, blow out the light."

SECRETS

—She told me that you told her the secret I told you not to tell her.
—I told her not to tell you I told her.
—Well, don't tell her that I told you she told me.

SERVANTS

—Do you ever have trouble with your maid?
—No, my wife watches me all the time.

In this period of domestic scarcity, the old axiom, "No man can serve two masters," may be changed to read, "No man can master two servants."

A man tells his wife he's going to spank their son because he won't go to sleep. The wife hears spanking and enters. "My dear," she says, "that's the maid's room."

Wife: Darling, the new maid has burned the bacon and eggs. Wouldn't you be satisfied with a couple of kisses for breakfast?
Hubby: Sure, bring her in.

Mistress *(to Butler):* You stand at the door and call the guests names as they enter.
Butler: Okay, I've been waiting a long time to do this.

—I've been asked for a reference for our last maid, and I've
told them she's lazy, unpunctual, and impertinent. Anything
else to add?
—Well, say something in her favor . . . that she sleeps well and
has a great appetite.

Mother *(encouragingly):* Remember, Junior, that after all your
father isn't such a hard man to get along with.
Junior: He seems to think so, too.
Mother: Did he tell you that?
Junior: No, I heard him tell it to the maid.

A matron was having trouble getting a nursemaid. One evening a
domestic agency sent a new girl. After instructing her to feed,
bathe, and put the children to bed, the harassed housewife opti-
mistically departed for a round of bridge at a neighbor's. Returning later, she asked how the children had behaved. "Oh, fine,"
confided the maid, "all except that big red-headed boy. He fought
like a wildcat when I tried to give him a bath." "Red-headed
boy!?" shrieked the lady-of-the-house. "My gawd, that was my
husband!"

SEX

Where there's boarders, there's roomers.

Frigidaire will never replace the ice man.

You never smoked in bed before you were married, Henry!

Do you know the milk song? A boy and a girl condensing.

A man can have only one wife, but an iceman has his pick.

If the covers are too short, your fiddlesticks outta the bed.

She's crazy about indoor sports, if they don't stay too late.

She used to go with the landlord, now she goes with the lease.

Helen is sure speedy. She makes at least forty MALES an hour.

She's the kind of girl you want to dance with in the worst way.

Many a man has been stung trying to get a little honey for himself.

She was a good girl as good girls go; and as good girls go, she
went.

A girl who gets into too much hot water is generally all
washed up.

Muriel of the cigar counter says the bigger they are the harder
they maul.

He's so fast that he puts out the light and is in bed before the room is dark.

When a girl knows her love-making from A to Z, you hear O's in the parlor.

Many a girl has had a close shave by working her sweetie into a lather.

Crowbar girl: her face is nothing to crow about, but she bars nothing.

She is the kind of a girl that five minutes with her and you're a man with a past.

Most any girl can make a man look sheepish merely by pulling the wool over his eyes.

—Let's teach the girl right from wrong.
—You teach her what's right.

I didn't have such a hot time with that girl last night. I guess I had too much will power.

She is the kind of a girl you like to take home to your mother—when your mother isn't home.

Little Tu Yung Tu went riding with a baseball player the other evening and then came home and pitched and tossed all night.

He: What could be worse than a man without a country?
She: A country without a man.

—You're a very nice girl, you know.
—Yes, I know, and I'm getting tired of it.

He: I bet I know what you're thinking about.
She: Well, you don't act like it.

He: You can never tell about a girl.
She: And if you can, you shouldn't.

Many a fellow who thinks he sees the love light burning in his girl's eyes finds that it's only her "stop" light.

A young man takes his girl into a florist's store and shows her a fig tree. The leaves are about the size of a silver dollar. The girl looks at the leaves and murmurs: "I thought they were larger."

She: He said some terrible things to me, things not fit for a gentleman to hear.
He: Did he? Tell me.

—I just went out hunting in the woods with my girl.
—Did you get anything?
—Yes, and two rabbits.

—In this play, I want you to play an old woman. Did you ever play an old woman?
—No, but I've played a lot of old men.

—Listen, what you do is your biz.
—Yeah, and what you do is your biz.
—But what we do is nobody's business.

—You don't love me as much as you used to. Haven't I always played fair with you?
—Yeah, you're fair, but I like 'em warmer.

—I sure like to take experienced girls home.
—Why, I'm no experienced girl.
—No, and you ain't home yet.

A legend of India: When a man dies, forty girls dance nude around the body for forty days. If he doesn't get up, then they know damn well he's dead.

Man (to zoo keeper): Aren't the monkeys coming out today?
Keeper: No; this is their mating season.
Man: Won't they come out for peanuts?
Keeper: Would you?

Coed: Would you like a drink?
Elderly Woman: Most certainly not. I would sooner commit adultery than drink that vile stuff.
Coed: Well, who wouldn't? [See Fast Women under Women.]

Jack: Next to a beautiful girl, what do you think is the most interesting thing in the world?
Jim: When I'm next to a beautiful girl, I'm not thinking about statistics.

I was asking for records in a store. The girl said the prices were fifty cents, seventy-five cents, and a dollar. I asked, "What can I get for half a buck?" She said, "One Summer Night." "And for seventy-five cents?" "Indian Summer." "What about a dollar?" I asked. She said, "You'd be surprised."

Boy: May I call on you tonight?
Girl: All right.
Boy: What time?
Girl: Well, I'm in bed at nine-thirty.
Boy: I'll be around at ten.

He: How did you start in this business?
She: Well, I used to be a chorus girl getting seventy-five dollars a week.
He: Yeah? And what else did you do?
She: Nothing. I just shouted, "Hip, hip, hooray!"
He: Oh, I see: twenty-five for the hooray, and fifty for the hips.

He: That was a lovely hat you had on yesterday.
She: Yes, my husband bought that for me.
He: And that fur coat, did your husband give you that, too? And that lovely diamond ring?
She: He gave me that, too.
He: And those two lovely babies I saw you out with?
She: They're my sister's.

> There was a little girl
> Who had a little curl
> Right in the middle of her forehead.
> When she was good
> She was very very good
> But when she was bad—
> She became very popular.

The newlyweds on their honeymoon had the drawing room. The groom gave the negro porter a dollar not to tell anybody on the train they were bride and groom. When the happy couple went to the diner for breakfast next morning all the passengers snickered knowingly. The groom called the porter and demanded: "Did you tell anybody on the train we were just married?" "No, sir," said the dusky porter, "I told 'em you all was just good friends."

> Here's to the men!
> When I meet 'em, I like 'em
> When I like 'em, I kiss 'em
> When I kiss 'em, I love 'em
> When I love 'em, I let 'em
> When I let 'em, I lose 'em
> Goldurn 'em.

The little dark-haired Italian girl was suing her husband for annulment on the grounds that, as the lawyers so quaintly put it, the marriage had never been consummated. The hearing was before a very dignified-looking judge. "Did you ever live with your husband?" questioned the girl's attorney. "No," she replied. The judge found this hard to believe. "Do you mean to say," he barked, "that you never resided with your husband at all?" The girl hung her head. She blushed. And then she spoke. "Only once, in Grant Park, your Honor."

The senator from the west sat in the lobby of a New York hotel admiring the scenery. Two young women of the night approached him.
Girl One: Good evening, you look lonesome.
Senator: I am.
Girl Two: Well, forget it. Come along with us, and we'll show you a good time.

Senator *(sighing):* I can't do it. It's too late.
Girl One: Aw, it ain't late. It's only nine o'clock.
Senator: But I didn't mean that. I meant twenty years.

Homosexuality

[A male homosexual was called a nance.]
—That nance mumbles constantly.
—Yes, he's always talking to herself.

Two fellows were sitting in a cafe talking about their respective
talents as lovers, bragging about how they satisfied their wives. A
nance at another table had finally heard enough and said, "What
sort of place is this?"

—Have you a fairy godmother?
—Why, of course not.
—How is it that you haven't got a fairy godmother? I have one
and so has everyone except you.
—I haven't a fairy godmother, but I have an uncle I'm not so
sure of.

Kissing

Never try to kiss a girl; either kiss her or don't.

He kissed her on the cheek and died of painter's colic.

Kisses are like pickles in a bottle. The first is hard to get but the
rest come easy.

He: What would I have to give you for one little kiss?
She: Chloroform.

—That was a nice kiss.
—You said a mouthful.

She: Freshy, who told you you could kiss me?
He: Everybody.

—Darling, they say that too much kissing affects the mind.
—You're crazy!

—If you make another mistake in grammar, I'm going to kiss you.
—You ain't neither!

She used to be a private secretary, but she left 'cause she caught
the boss kissing his wife.

I asked her for a kiss and she said, "Oui, oui." After I kissed her
she said, "WHEEEeeee."

—Am I the nicest girl you ever kissed?
—As a matter of tact, yes.

Never let a fool kiss you, and never let a kiss fool you. And don't mistake asthma for passion.

Asking the modern girl for a kiss is like sneaking into a speakeasy and asking for a Coca Cola.

—I'll bet if I kissed you for an hour, you'd yell for help.
—Not unless you needed it.

He: Would a kiss be out of place?
She: Not if you're careful.

Girl: Mmm, where'd you learn to kiss like that?
Hick: By clucking at horses.

He: They tell me you stutter when you're about to be kissed.
She: Y-y-y-yes, th'that's right!

She said, "I want a kiss for every time a light appears." Then she started bringing in lightning bugs.

—If I don't kiss a girl, she walks back.
—And if you do, she staggers back.

—Kisses are the language of love.
—Well, why don't you say something?

—You give such crazy kisses.
—That's because my lips are cracked.

He: For two cents I'd kiss you.
She: Do you have change for a nickel?

—Am I the only man (or: the first man) you ever kissed?
—You certainly are, and the nicest too.

She: I'm telling you for the last time, you can't kiss me.
He: Ah, I knew you'd weaken eventually!

She: You had no business to kiss me.
He: That wasn't business, it was pleasure.

—What're the chances of getting a kiss?
—What do you think I'm running, a punch board?

He: If I kissed you, would you scream?
She: Well, if you did it right, I don't see how I could.

She: I'll be frank with you. You're not the first man I ever kissed.
He: I'll be frank with you. You've got a lot to learn.

(Variation)
He: I'll be frank with you. You're not the first girl I ever kissed.
She: I'll be equally frank with you. You've got a lot to learn.

He: Every time I kiss you I feel like a hundred bucks.
She: Well, don't try to become a millionaire in one night.

He: What would you do if I should kiss you?
She: I should call father. *(He kisses her.)* "Sweet Daddy!"

Gertrude: I never let boys kiss me except when they say goodnight.
Hugh: Well, goodnight! Goodnight! Goodnight! Goodnight!

Sue: Doesn't your boyfriend get tired of seeing you every evening?
Mae: Of course not. Every time he kisses me he feels like a new man.

—Do you ever kiss any of the girls in the cloak room?
—That's my business.
—How's business?

He: Talking about kisses, what shape is a kiss?
She: I don't know; what shape is it?
He: Let me give you one and I'll call it square.

Gal: It's terrible, but nine men out of ten don't know how to kiss.
Guy: Let me kiss you.
Gal: Oh, dear. Ten men out of ten don't know how to kiss!

She: Daddy offered me five hundred dollars to promise not to kiss before I was twenty.
He: What did you do with the money?

[*See* Insults *under* Talent.]

Sue: I hear when you kissed the bashful chap, it brought out the beast in him.
Mae: Yes, the jackass!

He: Here, let me give you one of those submarine kisses.
She: What are they like?
He: All wet, and never come up for air.

Young Artist: You are the first of my models I have ever kissed.
Model: How many have you had?
Young Artist: An apple, a banana, a bouquet, and you.

Mazie: A man tried to kiss me last night.
Daisy: Did you slap his face?
Mazie: I should say I did—when he got through.

Mae: My sweetie just gave me a rainbow kiss.
Sue: What the devil is that?
Mae: Oh, the kind that comes after a storm!

She: You're the nicest boy I ever kissed.
He: Tell that to the Marines.
She: I have. Dozens of 'em.

Jack *(covering her eyes)*: If you can't guess who it is in three guesses, I'm going to kiss you.
Jane: Jack Frost . . . Davy Jones . . . Santa Claus.

She: Don't you dare try to kiss me or I'll yell for my father.
He: Where is he?
She: In South America.

He: That rouge is coming off your lips.
She: Why, it is not.
He: Oh, yes it is . . . I've made up my mind!

She: When you keep on kissing me, it makes me tremble from head to foot.
He: Yes, and when you tremble from head to foot, it makes me keep on kissing you!

Mother: Emily, your hair is all mussed up. Did that young man kiss you against your will?
Emily: He thinks he did, Mother.

Father: How dare you! Before you kiss my daughter you should ask me if it's all right.
Suitor: It's too late, I already kissed her, and believe me, it's all right.

The first time a man kisses a girl she is surprised. The second time she is angry. The third time she is pleased. And the fourth time she is waiting.

Shakespeare kisses: For five dollars, as you like it. For ten dollars, a midsummer night's dream kiss. For twenty dollars, measure for measure. And for fifty dollars, Julius Caesar [seize her].

He: Give me a kiss.
She: I won't.
He: Gee, but you're stingy.
She: No, I'm particular.

—Is it easy to kiss Jane?
—Like falling off a log.
—Where did you get the black eye?
—I fell off a log.

"Let me kiss those tears away, sweetheart," he begged tenderly. She fell into his arms, and he was very busy for a few moments. But the tears flowed on. "Will nothing stop them?" he asked, breathlessly. "No," she murmured. "It's hay fever, but go on with the treatment."

He: What would you do if someone kissed you?
She: I'd yell.

He: You'd yell if I kissed you?
She: Well, I'm still a little hoarse from last night.

—You've been married for years and yet you go around kissing
girls. Why?
—I'm old enough to realize the difference between reluctant assistance and wholehearted cooperation.

He: Do you believe kissing is unhealthy?
She: I couldn't say. I've never . . .
He: You've never been kissed?
She: I've never been sick.

Sue: Do you know, Dick kissed me twice last night before I could
stop him!
Mae: Gracious! What cheek!
Sue: Both!

She fell back into his arms. He looked down into her eyes and then
their lips met. Suddenly she turned and spoke, "You know, Jack, I
have never done anything like this before." He replied, "Certainly,
Marie, but what an awful lot of experience you must have inherited."

He: If you won't give me a long, lingering, kiss, will you give me
a short one?
She: I can't give you a kiss of any sort today.
He: And why not?
She: I'm out of sorts today.

Wife: Every one of your friends tried to kiss me at the party last
night.
Husband: Well, what do you want me to do? Make them all
apologize to you?
Wife: No, I want you to throw another party.

"Darling," he murmured, happily, "you are the only girl I ever
kissed."
"I believe you," sighed the girl. He kissed her again.
"And you are the only girl who believes what I say," went on the
foolish fellow, absent-mindedly.

Jack: May I kiss you, Audrey?
Audrey: Before I answer that tell me if you have ever kissed a girl
before?
Jack: Never.
Audrey: That's all right, then; I don't like men who kiss and tell
about it.

At the bazaar, a girl was selling kisses. A sign said "kisses: fifty
cents, seventy-five cents, and one dollar." Two fellows were discussing the sign.

—What was the difference?
—Well, for fifty cents, you kissed her. For seventy-five cents, she kissed you.
—What about the dollar ones?
—Oh, you just grabbed her and held on!
—Did she know how to kiss?
—Did she? Did you ever have an ether cone pushed over your face in a hospital? Wow!

Lover Boy

He's a man about town and a fool about women.

(Variation)
I'm a man about town and a fool about women.

I know a man who's an office holder. He holds every girl in the office.

—My girl's a brick.
—Mine's a hard baby, too.

She: Next to me who do you think of most?
He: Next to you, I don't think.

Sue: I use this lipstick to keep the chap off my lips.
Mae: What's his name? [*See* Cosmetics *under* Appearance.]

Suitor: Darling, you are everything to me.
She: Umm . . . hold everything!

He's a hound after the girls. He's one of those fellows who thinks a knee is a joint, and a joint is a place of entertainment.

Young lady *(in a drugstore):* Have you any Life Buoy?
Young clerk: Set the pace, lady! Set the pace!

—Do you want to be known as a lady killer?
—Lady killer? I don't even cripple 'em.

—I got a real kick out of kissing Jane, last night.
—Any more than usual?
—Yeah, the old man caught me.

She: Are you Santa Claus?
He: No.
She: Then leave my stocking alone.

He: And another thing, baby, I give advice to the lovelorn.
She: Honestly? What do you tell them?
He: My phone number.

He: When I grab you in my arms like this, honey, doesn't something within seem to snap?
She: Yes, usually my shoulder strap.

—I sat next to a swell-looking blonde in the movies last night and nearly talked her into having a date with me.
—What happened? Did she change her mind?
—No, she changed her seat!

A boy was walking down the street wheeling two bicycles, when he met a pal.
Pal: Where'd you get the two bikes?
Boy: My girl and I were out for a ride, and we stopped under a tree to rest. After a while I kissed her. "That's nice," she said. So I put my arm around her waist and asked her how that was. "Great," she said. Then I kissed her on the cheek and squeezed her, and she said: "Oh, boy! You can have anything I got." So I took her bicycle.

Petting

Her father kept a pet shop, and could she attend to business!

She: Oh, Jack, will you teach me how to pet?
He: Oh sure—in ten squeezy lessons.

He: Baby, I can read you like a book.
She: Okay, but lay off the Braille method.

He: A nice girl shouldn't hold a young man's hand.
She: A nice girl has to.

(Variation)
—When you go out with a girl, does she hold your hands?
—Yes, but that doesn't stop me.

The Month's Best Music Hit: "I don't mind your looking up my family tree, but let my limbs alone."

She: I suppose, handsome, you think you can pet any woman in town?
He: Oh, no. I have to take some of them to the country.

She: How is it that you pet so divinely after you've taken a few drinks?
He: That's because I drink rubbing alcohol.

Cried the irate flapper in a parked car: "Just because you're studying the piano doesn't mean you're going to practice your five-finger exercises on me."

He: I'm a tired man.
She: You poor fellow. Let's do some petting.
He: Naw, that's what I'm tired of.

She: I know a guy who can always find good places to pet.
He: How so?
She: He studied anatomy.

She: Oh, you don't love me any more!
He: How come you say that, dearie?
She: Well, when you change gears now, your hand never slips off the lever onto my knee!

Probably you haven't heard of the girl who told her sweetie she didn't care to pet for three good reasons. "First," she explained, "you'd think less of me. Second, I'd think less of you. And third," she added with a sort of regretful glance, "I always get a headache."

SHAVING

When he shaves, he makes faces at himself in the mirror.

I just shaved myself . . . and talked myself into a shampoo.

With all the men resorting to safety-razors, all the barbers can do is shave their expenses.

Barber: Was your tie red when you came in here?
Sucker: No, it wasn't!
Barber: Gosh, I must have cut your throat.

Victim: Say, I need a glass of water after that shave.
Barber: What's the matter, sir?
Victim: Oh, I just want to see if my face will still hold water.

Victim: Are you the barber who shaved me last week?
Barber: Yeah.
Victim: Well, give me chloroform.

Peach-fuzz kid: Mother, I think I'll shave.
Mother: You will not.
Father: Go ahead. She'll never know the difference.

SLEEP

'Tis better to have rolled and tossed than never to have slept at all.

I had a terrible time last night. I dreamt I was awake and when I woke up I was asleep.

—I haven't slept for days.
—What's the matter?
—I sleep nights.

One day the boss asked this guy why he was always late for work. The fellow replied, "I have a room that catches the sun about five or six o'clock in the morning. It wakes me up. But since I don't have to be at the office until nine, I pull down the shade, go back to bed, and somehow always oversleep." The boss told him to paint his windows black and warned that if he was late again, he'd be fired. That night, the fellow painted his windows black and went to bed. When he awoke, he looked at the clock, saw it was time to get up, dressed, and went to the office. He arrived on time and took off his coat. The boss walked in and said, "Well, you're fired!" The fellow couldn't understand it. He looked at the clock and said, "Say boss, I'm on time, ain't I?" The boss said, "Yeah, but where were you Monday and Tuesday?"

Sleepwalking

A woman in the presence of one man is admiring another.
—I think he is gorgeous.
—Did you dream about him last night?
—Yes.
—Did you dream you were out auto riding with him?
—Yes. How did you guess? (*Or:* How did you know?)
—I saw you walking in your sleep.

She: I dreamt you and I were out riding in the country.
He: Yes?
She: And we ran out of gas.
He: Yes?
She: And you started to caress me.
He: Yes? Go on.
She: And then I woke up . . . and I was walking in my sleep.

Talking in One's Sleep

He mumbled a few words in church and was married. He mumbled a few words in his sleep and was divorced.

—Jack, you've been married a long time. How on earth do you make your wife pay attention to you?
—That's easy. I pretend I'm talking in my sleep.

(Variation)
—Does your husband talk in his sleep?
—No, and it's terribly exasperating. He just grins.

(Variation)
The husband who talks in his sleep may easily ruin his wife's nerves—especially if she can't quite hear what he's saying.

A fellow who was crazy about golf and his wife who loved auction sales both talked in their sleep. One night, the fellow shouted, "Fore!" and his wife shouted, "Four and a quarter."

SMOKING AND TOBACCO

Twinkle, twinkle, cheap cigar, how I wonder what you are.

—I know a girl who swallows swords.
—That's nothing, I know one who inhales Camels.

—How do you like this new lighter?
—Pretty well; how many cigarettes do you get on a gallon?

—I'll buy a revolver and blow my brains out.
—Don't! Just buy some snuff, sneeze, and you'll blow 'em out.

A heavy smoker, who was always dropping hot ashes on his slacks, bought a suit with two pairs of pants—and then burnt a hole in the coat.

—I get dizzy spells from cigarettes.
—From inhaling them?
—No! From bending down to pick em up!

Movie Actress: I'll endorse your cigarettes for no less than fifty million dollars.
Cigarette Magnate: I'll see you inhale first.

He: Where did you learn to smoke?
She: In Paris. Why?
He: A good thing you didn't go to Norway. They smoke herrings there.

Betty: I'd rather you wouldn't.
Willy: Aw, please, just one!
Betty: But what will mother say if . . . ?
Willy: If I take just one, your mother'll never know.
Betty: Oh, yes, she will; she has all her cigarettes counted.

SPAIN AND SPANIARDS

Frenchman: You have to fill in the nationality blank also, sir. You are a Spaniard, n'est ce pas?
Spaniard: No, sir, I'm English. My mother and father were English.
Frenchman: But you were born in Spain.
Spaniard: That's nothing. If your dog had pups in the china closet, would you call them soup plates?

SPEECH

Dialects

—He was a blessing in disguise.
—Oh, you mean, in the life of dis guy's.

—He's a connoisseur.
—What's he kinda sore about?

—Hello, honey, I'm glad to see ya'all.
—I'm glad to see you all too, or any part of ya.

—Your mother certainly has a lot of poise.
—Yes and she had three girls too!

—Martin Beck? [theatre impresario]
—No, he won't be back till four.

—Give me a sentence with the word "inventor."
—Inventor, I wear heavy underwear.

I was asked to use a sentence with the word "vicious" in it. "Best vicious for a Happy Christmas." Then I was asked to use a sentence with the word "cigarette." "Cigarette life if you don't weaken."

—Tell me where you work.
—I woik in Des Moines.
—Really, I've always wanted to meet one of you miners.

Little Boy: Papa, vat's a vacuum?
Father: A vacuum is a void, Sammy.
Little Boy: I know, papa, but vat's the void mean?

—Have you heard the new locksmith's song?
—No, I'll bet it's a peep!
—Latch keys *(let's kiss)* and make up.

—My father and mother were killed by Indians.
—Orphan?
—No, only once.

—I'm getting so I can't sleep.
—Insomnia?
—Yeah, and in the winter, too!

"I'm afraid," responded the cashier with part of one eye on the check, "you haven't endorsed it correctly." "Indeed!" "No; it's made out to Gertrude H. Grey and you've written just Gertrude Grey." "But Gertrude Grey is my name." "Ah, but you don't quite understand me," barked the exasperated cashier. "What I mean to say is, you left out the H." "Oh, so I have," she exclaimed with a sweet, sugary smile as she took out her pen and wrote: Age, twenty-one.

Grammar

She: I love animals. I'd like to go to the zoo—will you take me?
He: Can't we go somewhere else? I don't want to see the animals.
She: But I want the animals to see you.
He: No, let's go out rowing.
She: Can you row a bike?
He: Row a bike? Who ever heard of rowing a bike?
She: Don't be like that. I once rode [rowed] one.

Impediments

—I've had kidley trouble.
—Kidley trouble: what's that?

—Kidley trouble.
—You mean kidney trouble.
—Well, diddle I just say that?

Lisping

Sally *(lisping):* I've got a Sherlock Holmth tooth.
Harry: What sort of a tooth is that?
Sally: S'looth.

Stuttering

—Did you ever attend a school for stuttering?
—N-no, I j-j-just p-picked it up.

—D-d-darling I l-l-love y-y-you.
—Oh, George, say it again.
—I j-j-just said it th-th-three t-t-times the f-f-first time.

—What's your name?
—B-b-b-b-b-Benjamin Yates.
—Why B-b-b-b-b-Benjamin?
—The parson who christened me stuttered.

A fellow asked the trainman to let him off at 14th Street.
The train whizzed on to sixty-first, and finally the fellow said,
"H-h-hey, I wanted to get off at 14th." The trainman said,
"Th-th-th-that's what you get for acting smart!"

Two stuttering blacksmiths had finished heating a piece of
pig iron, and one placed it upon the anvil with a pair of tongs.
"H-h-h-h-hit it," he stuttered to his helper. "Wh-wh-wh-wh-
where?" asked the other. "Aw, h-h-h-h-hell, we'll have to
h-h-h-h-heat it again now."

A stuttering chap decided to buy a parrot. He bought a young
bird, which the clerk guaranteed would develop into a fine talker.
The buyer came back six weeks later and said, "I don't want this
p-p-parrot, the d-darn thing s-s-stutters." The clerk replied, "He
doesn't stutter, he just hesssitates in his speech."

A fellow went to a doctor to be cured of his stuttering. Some
time later, he met a friend who asked him how the cure was
proceeding. He said, "Gee, I'm doing great. I can say Peter Piper
picked a peck of pickled peppers." His friend said, "Say, that's
great." The stuttering guy said, "It's okay, b-b-but I'm having a
hell of a t-t-time fitting it into conversation."

Tongue-Tied

Customer: I want a pair of spec-rimmed hornicles . . . I mean sporn-
himmed rectacles . . . pshaw! I mean hick-remmend spornacles.

Clerk: I know what you mean, sir. You mean a pair of rim-sporned hectacles.

SPITTING

—Who's that closemouthed brother over there?
—He ain't closemouthed. He's just waiting for the janitor to come back with the spittoon.

SPONGERS AND SPONGING

—Would you like to have dinner with me tonight?
—I'd love it.
—All right, tell your mother we'll be up at six.

—Give me a match, Bill.
—Here it is.
—Well, can you beat that? I've forgotten my cigarettes.
—'S'too bad, gimme back my match.

—Gotta match?
—Sure.
—Gimme a cigarette.
—Want me to light it for ya?
—If ya don't mind.
—How ya fixed for spittin'?

SPORTS

He talks three languages: horse racing, baseball, and golf.

His first girlfriend was a swimmer, his second a great tennis player, and third a golfer. He had a girl in every sport.

—I can tell you the score of the game before it starts.
—Betcha can't. What is it?
—Nothing to nothing—before it starts.

—Do you ever play golf?
—No, I get terrible blisters on my hands.
—What about basketball . . . do you play that?
—No, I get terrible blisters on my feet.
—Do you ever ride a bike?

Baseball

You don't have to be a baseball fan to be batty.

I'm going to buy those Brooklyn Dodgers some silk stockings. That's the only way they'll get runs.

And then there's Washington, first in war, first in peace, and near the bottom in the American League.

First Baseball Player: You didn't do so well with that millionaire's daughter, hey?

Second Baseball Player: Terrible—no hits, no runs, no heiress!

Boxing

Pity the poor palooka who never knows where the next melee is coming from.

Most boxers need more experience, but many of them already know the ropes.

Gene Tunney's *(or any successful boxer's)* new song: Every clout has a silver lining.

—Why are those two fighters fighting back to back?
—They're so lousy they're ashamed to face each other.

—You say you can't go through with the fight? Why, what's come over you?
—Goose pimples.

Have you heard about the absent-minded heavyweight fighter who took his girl to a dance and dropped to the floor in the middle of a waltz?

The son of the bearded lady had a match with a member of the House of David, but he couldn't hit his opponent because he reminded him of his mother.

He was a sissy referee. When a man was knocked out he used to count one, two, buckle my shoe, three, four, shut the door, five, six, pick up sticks.

Boxing Instructor *(after first lesson):* Now, have you any questions to ask?

Beginner *(dazed):* Yes, how much is your correspondence course?

—I'm one of those curfew fighters.
—Curfew fighters? What's that?
—When I strikes you go to sleep.

—Boy, I gave him the old one, three, one, three.
—You mean one, two.
—Oh no, I mean one, three. I got the second one. Boy, I had that guy all covered with blood—my blood!

Two second-raters were fighting a bout at a small club. At the end of the first round, the cluck who had taken a pounding staggered to his corner, ready to quit. "Don't be nuts," screamed his manager, "why he ain't laid a glove on you." He lasted out the second round, walked stiffly back to his stool and before he could protest, the manager whispered: "Didn't I tell you? He didn't even lay a hand on yuh!" The third round was particularly trying for the battered second-rater. Gloves rattled off him like hail off a tin roof, and he was just able to get to the corner under his own power. Looking up at his manager through swollen eyes, the chump screamed: "I know, I know, he ain't laying a glove on me! Then keep your eye on the referee, because somebody in that ring is giving me a hell of a lacing."

Fishing

Just got back from a fishing trip. If the fish were biting they were biting one another.

—Do you know a single fish lays five million eggs a year?
—How about the married ones?

—Where yuh goin'?
—Fishin'.
—What fer?
—Oh, just for the halibut.

Beginner (who had never fished before): Oh, I've got a bite. Now what do I do?
Fisherman: Reel in your line.
Beginner: I've done that. The fish is tight against the end of the pole. Now what do I do?
Fisherman (disgusted): Climb up the rod and stab it!

Football

Well, gents, step up and hear the football song: "After the Ball Was Over."

Football players may be strong, silent men and full of grit, but so are a lot of street cleaners.

A coach at a midwestern college was bawling out his players: "You guys play like a bunch of amateurs."

A football coach is a fellow who is always willing to lay down your life for his school.

You could tell he was a football player; he kept making forward passes all night.

—What good is our Army and Navy? We spend a lot of money on them and don't get a thing for it.
—You poor fish, don't we have an Army-Navy game?

Football captain (roaring with rage): Say you dumb duck, who the hell told you to paint that blankety-blank bench?
Manager: The coach, sir.
Captain: Looks nice, doesn't it?

Golf

He plays golf like a tailor. He presses with his irons.

Too many golfers use the woods even when using the irons.

Heard on the golf course: "Don't shoot that birdie, it might be somebody's par."

A fellow put twelve golf balls under a sitting hen and hatched out four eagles and a birdie.

The Audubon Society says that birds are naturally attracted to golf courses. But I've never been able to get a birdie on one.

—How is Dub getting on with his golf?
—Pretty good. He hit a ball in one today.

A new golf club with a peculiar hook on the end is now on the market. It is thought that this may enable a golfer to play a lost ball from the pocket of his caddie.

Two pinochle enthusiasts took up golf and went out with a couple of good players, who started to talk the money game. One of the card players said, "Sure I'll play for money. What shall we make it, a nickel a hundred?"

—Why do you play golf so much?
—It keeps me fit.
—What for?
—Golf.

A fellow was teeing off at the first hole, and about three foursomes were waiting for him. At the first stroke, which had a world of power behind it, he missed the ball completely. The waiting crowd shifted on its feet. Once more he missed the teed ball. This happened four times. The crowds were embarrassed, but not so the chap with the club. With an engaging smile, he turned on them all. "Tough course," he remarked.

A novice at golf went out with a pro for his first lesson. After an hour of instruction from the pro, the novice swung at the ball and made a great drive, which reached the edge of the green. The pro told him how to pitch the ball up onto the green to the flag. The novice hit it within six inches of the pin. Asking the pro what to do next, he was told which club to use to putt the ball into the hole. The novice said, "Why didn't you tell me that back there?"

A fellow had just bought a dozen new golf balls. He told the caddie that today he intended to track down any balls that landed in the rough. On his first stroke, he hit into ten-foot brush. The fellow said that he would find that ball if it took him all day. They took separate paths looking for the ball. After about an hour, the fellow calls out "Caddie, caddie!" The caddie replied, "What is it? Have you found the ball?" The fellow said, "To hell with the ball. Now I'm lost. Come and find me!"

A villain with a HOOK nose and CLUB feet is after a GREEN girl. He invites her to a CUP of TEE. "There's a HOLE IN ONE of your stockings," he observes. "Don't LIE to me," she retorts, "and I'll tell PAR if you get ROUGH." He APPROACHES. "This is not a FAIRWAY to treat me," she sobs. The villain HAZARD deathly scared. The hero DRIVES up in his CADDIE-lac, PUTT, PUTT! "STYMIE came," thinks the girl. The hero SWINGS at the villain and TOPS him with an IRON. "See the BIRDIE," gasps the villain. "Quite a MATCH," says the girl. "He might be FOURSOME, but not for me," replied the hero and offers her a diamond ring. "DIVOT here," she cries.

Gymnastics

Woman student: I'll stand on my head or bust.
Gym instructor: Never mind, just stand on your head.

Horseback Riding

—So you'd like me to come around to dinner any time after I've been horseback riding?
—Yes, it's a standing invitation.

Lil: Think I'll take up horseback riding, it will increase my social standing.
Helen: I don't know about the social part, but it sure will increase your standing.

An Englishman on a visit to the west decided to go horseback riding. The hostler who was to attend him asked: "Do you prefer an English saddle or a western?" "What's the difference?" he asked. "The Western saddle has a horn," replied the attendant. "I don't think I'll need the horn," said the Englishman. "I don't intend to ride in heavy traffic."

(Variation)
The first time I went to a ranch, some cowboys told me to go down and find a green horse. I could find red ones, black ones, and gray ones, but I couldn't find a green one. Finally, someone explained. When I brought it in, they told me I'd have to break it in myself. I tried for hours but I couldn't even bend it. Before I got on the horse, one fellow came to me and asked if I wanted a saddle with a horn. I said, "What? Do you have so much traffic down here?" (*Or:* "No, I don't need one, I'm not going where there's any traffic.")

Horse Racing

—Do you take the time on your racehorse?
—No, he takes his own time.

Talking of horse racing, I wonder if you realized there are one hundred and fifty ways of losing a race—and I know a horse that knows all of them.

Legalizing four percent beer will not only provide employment for several million men, but it will also take thousands of brewery horses off the racetracks in this country.

Horses got more sense than humans. You see fifty thousand people cheering five horses running a race. Didya ever see five men running a race with fifty thousand horses cheering?

—I was a jockey but used only one stirrup.
—One stirrup? Then you could only drive him on one side.
—That's right; but I figure if one side goes, the other will.

(Variation)
A jockey was wearing a stirrup on one foot. Asked why, he said, "Well, I figure if one side of the horse goes the other has to."

—Ascot, where all the wonderful races are.
—Ascot?
—You must have heard of Ascot.
—Ascot? Oh, yeah, Ascot rhythm [I'z got rhythm].

—The horse I was riding wanted to go one way and I wanted to go the other.
—Who won?
—He tossed me for it.

—I'm going fishing.
—Where are you going?
—Saratoga.
—There's no fishing there. That's where they have the horse racing.
—Well, I just heard they got the biggest suckers up there.

Hunting

Duck hunting isn't always what it's quacked up to be.

Rowing

I think rowing is very good for developing the arms. You ride a lot too, don't ya?

Swimming

—How is it that women learn to swim more easily than men?
—Who wants to teach a man to swim anyway?

—I used to be a life saver.
—What flavor?

He: Can you swim?
She: The last time I went in the ocean, I had six lifeguards out after me.
He: Out of your depth?
She: No, out of my bathing suit.

—Do you take to water naturally?
—Certainly. In the family, mother has water on the knee, Pa has a floating kidney . . .
—And you have water on the brain.
—Well, sometimes my head does swim.

Wrestling

So I grabbed him by the wrist, pinned his arm in a grip of steel, twisted his leg around his neck, and the next thing I knew, I was flat on my back!

STINGINESS

A cheapskate doesn't cut much ice.

He knew when to stop drinking: when it was his turn to buy.

—I'd like to propose a toast.
—No toast for me, you cheapskate. I want a regular meal.

When you read a newspaper over somebody else's shoulder, you're too darn close [stingy] to buy one.

She: Thanks for the present.
He: Oh, it's nothing.
She: That's what I thought, but mother wants me to thank you just the same.

She: I'm hungry.
He: What?
She: I said I was hungry.
He: Sure, I'll take you home. This car makes so much noise that I thought you said you were hungry.

At a hotel resort, a man complained about the bill. Asking about the charges for meals, he said, "I had no meals here." The manager replied, "That's your own fault; they were here if you wanted to eat them." The man said, "Well, I'm going to sue you for fooling around with my wife." The manager said, "I never fooled with your wife." The man said, "Well, she was right here."

STOCKS, BONDS, AND WALL STREET

We thought the stock market had a slow leak, but it's a blowout.

A friend of mine who was a stockbroker has taken up bee-keeping. He said he'd been stung every other way.

No, there ain't any use tryin' to interest her in nothin'. All her money's invested in Public Futility Bonds!

Stocks have been so low since the fateful crash that it wouldn't be surprising if brokers hired midgets as markers.

—Were you one of the many fooling with the stock market?
—Not me, I was serious; the market did the fooling.

I bought some shares of stock and they fell so low they landed in the help-wanted column. There's a new stock out now, and they give a headache powder with every share.

Two Wall Street brokers on holiday ran into each other at Atlantic City. They spent the next few days together, and one day went in for a swim. Some distance from shore, one called to the other, "Say, can you float alone?" The other said, "Why must you talk business when you're on vacation?" [See under Borrowing and Lending.]

After having been examined, a man left his doctor's office, got on the elevator, and said to himself, "God, can you imagine it? Diabetes at forty-two, diabetes at forty-two." Another fellow in the elevator, who had just left his broker's office, said, "That's nothing. What about General Motors at sixty!"

News of the Day in Wall Street: Trading was very slow today in spite of the new developments in Eastman Kodak. Maxwell House Coffee opened weak but this is not grounds for worry, except to the poor birds who had to drink it. Consolidated Gas made a steady rise owing to an extra session of Congress, while Simmons Beds were very active. American Can got the most trade as usual, with Ingersoll Watch a close second. There was a distinct rally around the rails (the brass ones) with Am Com Alcohol doing a brisk business. F & J (Frank and Jacks) opened strong but closed quickly on account of revenue agents. Checker Cab did a heavy business on account of the rain, as did United Rubber. Houdaille absorbed some punishment, Goodyear skidded off, and Otis Elevator dropped right out of the bottom of the page.

STORES

His earliest plaything: from the dry-goods store he got his notions.

Customer: Can you show me some satin bloomers?
Sales Clerk: Don't you want some bloomers that weren't sat in?

You never see wooden Indians in front of cigar stores any more. They're all in department stores as complaint managers now.

I went into a candy store and asked for ten cents worth of mixed candy. The salesgirl handed me two pieces and said, "Here, mix 'em yourself."

Customer: Are those eggs strictly fresh?
German shopkeeper *(to his clerk):* Feel those eggs, Jake, and see if they're cool enough to sell yet.

This fellow was such a good salesman that when a woman came into his store to buy a suit to bury her husband in, he talked her into an extra pair of trousers.

My wife and I went shopping in a department store. I lost her and looked all over. Finally, I found her in a new fur coat in the fur department.

Customer: I don't want those crackers. Someone told me that the rats ran over them.
Grocer: That isn't true because the cat sleeps in the box every night.

—I just put fifteen cents into that machine and out came a pack of cigs.
—That's nothing. I just put in a couple of slugs and out came the owner.

(Variation)
—Marvelous things, these automatic machines. I've just put a shilling into one and out came a packet of cigarettes and a halfpenny change!
—That's nothing. I once put a button into one, and out came the tobacconist.

—Charge it.
—What name?
—Zazvorkinski.
—Take it for nothing. I wouldn't write Zazvorkinski and potassium permanganate for no nickel.

I went into a store to buy some fruit and the proprietor charged me a buck twenty-five for six oranges. I said that's rather expensive and handed him a buck and a half. The proprietor said that's twenty-five cents too much. I said, "Oh! That's all right. I stepped on a grape on the way in."

My brother Louie went to a store where they give you a gift with every purchase. He bought a sixty dollar suit for forty cash and wrote a twenty dollar I.O.U. He then asked for his gift. The owner offered him a necktie. Louie said, "What, after spending sixty bucks, a necktie?" "All right," said the owner, "I'll tell you what I'll do. I'll give you back your I.O.U." Louie said, "Forget it, I'll take the tie."

Today I went to a department store to buy a book. Because of the heat, I took off my hat. I was looking around for someone to serve me, when a lady came up to me with a book in her hand and gave me two dollars. Then I went into the shoe department and hadn't been there more than a few minutes when a fellow came up to me with eight dollars and walked off with a pair of shoes. In the furnishing section, a lady picked up a bit of carpet and handed me five dollars. Tomorrow, I'm going to hang around the piano department.

My uncle has a shoe store. I went around to see him. While we were talking, a fellow tried on a pair of shoes. He said, "They're fine. How much?" Uncle said, "Seven dollars." The fellow said, "I'll give you five." Uncle said, "Wait a minute! This is strictly a one-price place. Give me six dollars and take the shoes." The fellow said, "Gee, the shoes are fine. They fit fine, they look fine, but I have only five dollars with me. Give me the shoes and I'll bring you a dollar tomorrow." I was surprised to see my uncle wrap up a pair of shoes and give them to him. After the man left, I said, "Uncle, how do you know that man will come back?" And he said, "Don't be silly, I gave him two left shoes."

STUPIDITY

The bigger the heads, the bigger the vacuum.

She thinks a refinery is a school of etiquette.

She's so dumb that she gave herself a surprise party!

Don't forget to phone me, even if it's only a postcard.

A dumb coed thought the Pied Piper was a drunken plumber.

She went to school and took a four year-course in ignorance.

He was so dumb that he yelled for the author at a Shakespearean play.

You've got an entirely new brain. It must be that you never used it.

Prof: What is a vacuum?
Student: I have it in my head but I can't think of it just now.

His parents had to apply for extradition papers to get him out of school.

She's so dumb, she thinks that a weather bureau is part of a bedroom suite.

He tried to keep the mice out of the yard by planting pussy willow in the garden.

My girl is so dumb she went to the dog races and tried to get a bet on the rabbit.

We have a janitor. He's so dumb he thinks a third degree is the right heat.

Lots of people who have one-track minds don't have them in the right direction.

A boy sent his girlfriend a blank postcard because they weren't speaking.

She's so dumb she refused a leopard skin coat 'cause every spot shows up on it.

She's so dumb that she bought a sunlight lamp to give the kid a tanning.

She says that she's going to take swimming lessons this summer and learn the sunstroke.

A kid came upon dozens of milk cans and ran all the way home to tell his mother he'd found a cow's nest.

I didn't have to put a stamp on the letter. I slipped it in the mail box when nobody was looking.

I'm no dumb cluck. I can do something a chicken can't do—lay an egg on the kitchen stove without getting my feet burnt.

—I live by my wits.
—No wonder you look so hungry.

Soldier: I captured twenty-seven Germans during that one afternoon.
Girl: Dear me, are you allowed to keep all you catch?

—I'll give you a wallop!
—Don't bother. I wouldn't know how to eat it anyway.

—A transparency is something you can see through.
—Oh, a keyhole.

—There's a salesman waiting outside, sir—a man with a mustache.
—Tell him I've got a mustache.

Doctor: Do you sleep with your mouth open?
Patient: I've never noticed, but I'll look tonight when I'm asleep.

—Someday the worm will turn.
—But why would it turn? It's the same on both sides, isn't it?

You gotta take that washin' machine back, Paw. Every time I put the baby in to wash 'im, the paddles beat him black and blue.

Landlady: She's not in. Do you want to leave a message?
Man: Yeah, just say that Sam didn't call.

—Won't you join me in a cup of tea?
—Well, you get in and I'll see if there is any room left.

—Have you ever heard of the Sesquicentennial?
—No. What's the name of it?

He lived dumb and died dumb. The last dumb thing he ever did was blow the gas out before going to bed.

—Where does steel wool come from?
—Off the sheep on the Iron Mountains, of course.

And did you hear of the stenographer who didn't mail the circular letters because she couldn't find any round envelopes?

I just can't seem to waken him. I've been hitting him on the head with a club and he won't waken.

—Do you know anything about Peoria?
—Yes, four out of five have it.

—Have you lived there all your life?
—Not yet.

Curious Old Lady: Why, you've lost your leg, haven't you?
Cripple: Well, damned if I haven't.

—And now how far is your house from the station?
—Only a five-minute walk if you run.

—Why are you weeping?
—I've just washed my face and can't do a thing with it.

—I know a guy who keeps racing pigeons.
—He must get terribly out of breath (or: winded).

—Do you know how to make a venetian blind?
—Yes, throw pepper in his eyes.

—There's a smell in the kitchen like burning cloth.
—It's all right. I'm cooking the potatoes with their jackets on 'em.

He's so dumb that when he met his friend just out of prison on his birthday, he wished him many happy returns.

He's such a dope that the other day he rubbed mustard on his feet because he said mustard is good for hot dogs. [See Feet under Appearance.]

—My boat makes ten knots an hour.
—Who unties the knots?

—Birds eat a lot of fruit.
—That's crazy, how can they get the tins open?

—I think you're dumb.
—Yeah, well I'm not as dumb as you think you are.

—What is it makes the Tower of Pisa lean?
—Worry over the thoughts of how near it is to falling, I guess.

—Clancy, guard all the exits.
—Yes, sir, how about the entrance?

—Mother, there's a blind man at the back door.
—Tell him that we don't want any.

—Brigid, did you turn on the gas under the stove as I told you?
—Yes'm, can't you smell it?

Man: Now understand, that kind of conduct around here is taboo!
Dope: Taboo or not taboo, that is the question.

—You're so dumb you think General Motors was in the French army.
—All right, smarty, I'll ask you: what army was he in?

Any student who throws a lit cigarette on the floor should be kicked to death by a jackass, and I should like to be the one to do it.

—What's the idea of the Greens having French lessons?
—They've adopted a French baby and want to understand what it says when it begins to talk.

Son: Ma, I bought the Statue of Liberty, ain't I lucky?
Ma: Such an idiot for a son I should have. How are you gonna bring it home?

—Why, you don't even know what a vacuum is.
—I certainly do. It's where the pope lives.
—Er, I didn't think you knew.

—Do you know that fish is a brain food?
—What does it taste like?
—I don't know. (*Or:* I never eat it.)

My girl is so dumb, she asked me what I wanted for my birthday and I said, "Corona, Corona," and she bought me a couple of portable typewriters.

—So you have been abroad? Did you have mal de mer when you were crossing?
—Naw, I was so sick I couldn't eat a thing.

—Fool, what do you mean by boiling that benzene? There will be an accident.
—Heck, it's a good thing everyone isn't as superstitious as you are.

My brother is a doctor. Boy, is he smart. For three months, he treated a fellow for yellow jaundice before he found out he was a Chinaman.

First Sleuth: What makes you think he's terribly dumb?
Second Sleuth: He saw a sign "Murderer Wanted" and applied for the job.

Buddy worked for years in a grocery store, but he got sacked when the boss asked him to go lay some eggs in the window. He said he couldn't.

—Just think, Jane has gone back to Arizona for her lungs.
—Poor dear, she's so absent-minded, she's always forgetting something.

He's a very nice boy, but a trifle dumb. Going on vacation last year, he had very little to pack, so he went for one of those over-night bags. He meant to be away for a week; he therefore bought seven.

Customer: I want to see some mirrors.
Clerk: Hand mirrors, sir?
Customer: Naw, I want one I can see my face in.

A kid brought me a telegram. I was in bed. He said, "Telegram, Mr. Lowry." I said, "Will you slip it under the door, son." He said, "I can't, it's on a tray."

—This tonic is no good.
—What's the matter?
—All the directions it gives are for adults, and I never had them.

—Did dopey Joey get the letter with the check from his mother?
—Yes, but the outside of the envelope said, "Please return in five days," so he had to send it right back.

—Pardon me, does this train stop at Tenth Street?
—Yes, watch me and get off one station before I do.
—Thank you.

"Would ya believe it," moaned one. "They say this girl from the Bronx got a new Rolls Royce from some old geezer, and she told the guy she didn't know how to thank him for it!"

A suburbanite tells us that at last he has hit on a plan to keep the ants out of the sugar container. His method is to fill the sugar container with salt.

—Isn't it strange that when people get frozen they rub their limbs with snow until circulation comes back.
—Gee, what do they do in summer when there's no snow?

—Hello! Say, you look just like the person who was here last week.
—I was here last week.
—Oh, that accounts for the resemblance.

—Painting that barn I got good and hot.
—What are you doing with all the clothes on?
—It says here on the can: use three coats.

—I want a book, please.
—Something light?
—It doesn't matter, my husband will carry it.

Gentleman (annoyed): Idiots!
Kid: Mama, what are idiots? Are they people?
Mother (absently): Yes, sonny, people just like you and me.

Mom: Don't use such bad words.
Son: Shakespeare used them.
Mom: Well, don't play with him.

—I've just been reading Wells's Outline of History . . . and it makes me realize how puny and insignificant man is.
—Did you have to read a book to find that out?

—Let's play that game where you stick your head in a tub of water and you keep it there till someone kisses you.
—Aw, no, Peg, I played that game at a party once, and if my mother hadn't been there I would have drowned.

—If the largest ocean liner were placed on its end beside the Empire State Building, how do you suppose it would stack up?
—The furniture and everything else inside of it would be in a devil of a mess.

Author: This is the plot of my story. A midnight scene. Two burglars creep stealthily toward the house. They climb a wall and force open a window and enter the room. The clock strikes one.
She (breathlessly): Which one?

It was dusk when she stopped at the roadside garage. "I want a quart of red oil," she said. The man gasped and hesitated. "Give me a quart of red oil," she repeated. "A q-quart of r-r-red oil?" "Certainly," she said. "My tail light has gone out!"

—Can you swim?
—No.
—Why?
—I ain't in the water.

—What?
—What did you say?
—I didn't say anything.
—Oh, I didn't hear you.

—I don't know how to answer this question.
—What is it?
—It says, "Who was your mother before she was married?" and I didn't have any mother before she was married.

—Where were you born?
—Australia.
—What part?
—All of me.

Boy: Fireman, fireman, our house is on fire.
Fire Laddie: Did you put water on it?
Boy: Oh, yes, sir.
Fire Laddie: Sorry! But that's all we can do.

—I'm going to be a picture star, and my dad's going to be president.
—How's that?
—Well, when I told Dad I was going to be a picture star, he said, "When you get to be a picture star, I'll be president of the U.S."

—Know how to tell a he bird from a she bird?
—Nope. Give up.
—Pull its tail. If he chirps it's a he bird. If she chirps, it's a she bird.

A young lady entered the stationery store and asked for a pound tin of floor wax. "I'm sorry, miss," said the clerk, "all we carry is sealing wax." "Don't be silly," she snapped, "who'd want to wax a ceiling?"

—We've got a splendid swimming pool. Today we had a party and one fellow went right up the highest diving board and dove right in.
—Gee, sounds like fun.
—I'll say—and tomorrow we're putting water in it.

—Have you seen George lately?
—Yes. Just the other day I thought I saw him across the street, and he thought he saw me; but when we got to one another . . . can you imagine . . . it was neither of us!

—My neighbor has his children shoot off their fireworks on July third.
—Why is that?
—He says so many children get hurt shooting on the Fourth.

—Would you rather die with your shoes on or your shoes off?
—I'd rather die with them on.
—How come?
—So I don't stub my toe when I kick the bucket.

—Which is the other side of the road?
—Why, right over there.
—Are you sure?
—Certainly it's over there.
—That's funny. A fellow over there told me it was over here.

—You act like a cannibal. Do you know what a cannibal is?
—No, but it sounds elegant, and I want to be one.
—Well, a cannibal is someone who eats people. For instance, if you ate your mother and dad what would you be?
—An orphan.

A lady took her little son and his nurse for a swim in the sea. As the lady entered the water, the nurse stayed right with her. When the water was up to the mother's neck, she turned and asked the nurse, "Where's little Johnny?" The nurse said, "He's okay, madam, I have hold of his hand."

I went into an ice cream parlor and asked: "What kind of ice cream do you have?" The girl, suffering from a bad cold, said *(imitate the speech of someone with a bad cold):* "We have vanilla and strawberry." I said: "Have you tutti-frutti?" She said: "No." Finally, I said: "Have you laryngitis?" She said: "I told you. We have only vanilla and strawberry."

One day, a backwoods mountaineer found a mirror that a tourist had lost. He picked it up, looked in it, and said, "Well, if it ain't my old dad. Never knew he had his picture took." Bringing the mirror home, he hung it in his attic. One night, his wife saw it, looked into it, and said, "Hmm, so that's the old hag he's been chasin'."

—What town in Connecticut reminds you of a Biblical character?
—I don't know.
—Middletown, Conn.
—How so?
—Simple. Just drop the i-d-d-l-e-t-o-w-n and add o-s-e-s and you have Moses.

—I had a narrow escape last night.
—How?
—Got up in the middle of the night . . . saw something white and shot at it. I turned on the light and saw it was my shirt.
—Don't see any narrow escape in that.
—Why, suppose I hadn't taken my shirt off before I'd gone to bed!

A friend said to me, "Did you ever hear the story about the deaf man who said to another fellow, 'I hear you're drinking again,' and the other man replied, 'I thought you couldn't hear?'" "No," I said. "Tell it to me."

"Why, I just did tell it to you," he grumbled. So I thanked him and went on my way.

So dumb as to think that:

Sing Sing is a lullaby.

the Mexican border pays rent.

July 4th was an English king.

a mushroom is a place to make love.

New Year's Eve is Adam's second wife.

Andrew Mellon is another kind of cantaloupe.

Einstein is a glass of beer.

there are springs in the ocean bed.

the League of Nations is a baseball team.

a goblet is a sailor's kid (or: child).

Hamlet is something good to eat.

a sap from the trees is an ignorant backwoodsman.

a run around is a small roadster.

you need a key to open an armlock.

you have to water an industrial plant.

a bridle path is for newly married couples.

the bank keeps liquid assets in a bottle.

Tennessee is a Chinese tennis game.

a guy with eight faces would be an octopus.

an apartment with more than one bath is a distillery.

panhandlers are people who work in hardware stores.

you phone a taxidermist for a mounted policeman.

Western Union is Cowboy Underwear.

SUICIDE

Suicide is unnatural. It's the last thing a man would do.

Groom: For two cents, my good woman, I'd kiss you to death.
Bride: Hooray, I've got a nickel! I want to commit suicide!

—The coroner pronounced it suicide.
—Well, how do you pronounce it?

He jumped from the tenth story window. He was going to jump from the thirty-fifth but he lost his nerve.

—What are you doing tonight? Come on, let's go to a show and take our minds off this Depression.
—Sorry, I can't. I got a bridge date.
—Okay, come on, I'll jump off with you.

A Central Park policeman suddenly noticed a man splashing about in a pool exhibiting an enormous Swimming-Positively-Forbidden sign. Walking to the edge of the water, he shouted: "I'm going to arrest you as soon as you come out." "Ha-ha-ha!" came the chortled reply, "I'm not coming out—I'm committing suicide."

SUNBURN AND SUNTAN

I knew a girl who couldn't get suntanned on the beach because her husband had her shadowed.

She: Say, you have a suntan. Did you get that in Atlantic City?
He: Yes, but you've got a tan too. Where did you get yours?
She: Walgreens.

—I got a terrific sunburn.
—Where did you get burnt?
—On my-ami.
—I mean whereabouts did you suffer most?
—On the beach . . . right in the middle of February. Funny how you go through life without a friend, and, as soon as you get sunburnt, everybody wants to slap you on the back. For years I've wanted a family . . . and now when I get a little sun I don't want it.

SWEDES

A Swede wanted a bottle of liquor and was asked did he want Squirrel or Black Crow. He said, "I tink I take the squirrel. I don't wanna fly, I just wanta jump around a little."

TALKERS

Have you heard of the ventriloquist who threw his voice in the ashcan when he got married?

A train announcer married a telephone operator, and their kids were fifteen before they began to talk.

—When a man starts to talk, he never stops to think.
—And when a woman starts, she never thinks to stop.

—Did they take an X-ray of your wife's jaw at the hospital?
—They tried to, but they got a moving picture.

She's very talkative. Her tongue goes 1500 revolutions a minute while her brain stays in neutral.

He studied seven languages and then he married a woman who wouldn't let him open his mouth.

(Variation)
He studied for years to learn eight languages and be a radio announcer; and then his wife wouldn't let him open his trap.

She: You talked in your sleep all night.
He: Do you begrudge me those few words?

—That wife of yours can talk a mile a minute.
—Yes, she's the fastest back-seat driver in the country.

—Will you stop rambling and get to the gist of it.
—Gist a minute, gist a minute!

My wife wouldn't be any good on radio. She wouldn't stop talking long enough for station announcements.

If a girl wants a strong, silent man she should get herself a north-woods hunter. They don't open their traps more than three times a year.

—Why did you hit your wife on the jaw?
—It was getting late and I wanted to shut everything up for the night.

—Do you know why they call our language the mother tongue?
—I don't know.
—Probably because father never gets a chance to use it.

—I tell you that baby of mine is a wonder. Think of it, eight months old and he can talk!
—Pshaw! I've known men who curse the day they were born.

—Exercise like this constantly, Felix, if you want to look like Johnny Weissmuller. Constant exercise will enlarge any part of the body.
—Then why doesn't my wife look like Joe E. Brown?

The little man hurried into the hospital, anxiety on his face. "My wife did not keep an appointment to meet me," he said, "and I believe a woman answering her description was injured in a motor accident and brought here." "A woman was admitted three hours ago," he was told, "but she hasn't spoken yet." The little man turned to leave. "That's not my wife," he said, reflectively.

TATTOOS

I know a temperamental tattoo artist who always does his best work on an empty stomach.

Coed: I want you to tattoo a cat on my knee.
Tattooer: Nope, I'll tattoo a giraffe or nothing.

I know a big strong man who has the United States tattooed on his chest. He has such a big expansion that when he takes a deep breath, Mexico joins the Union.

TAXES

Have you heard the income tax song: "Why not take all of me?"

I'm trying to make a deal with the government to give them my whole income, if they'll give me the tax.

TAXIS

Cab drivers in New York love their job. They never miss a thing.

I know a New York cabby who has a five-piece band in his taxi. He can't afford a radio.

—Can you think of anything worse than raining cats and dogs?
—Yeah, hailing taxis.

Conditions may be getting better, but taxi-drivers tell us that they're hardly making enough to pay for the damage they do to other cars.

A drunk got in a cab.
Cabby: Where to?
Drunk: What streets you got?
Cabby: Plenty.
Drunk: Gimme 'em all.
After the cabby drove for several hours, the drunk asked how much he owed.
Cabby: Seven dollars and fifty cents.
Drunk (mumbling): Turn around and drive back to thirty-five cents.

—Say, it didn't take you long to get here.
—Well, you know those streamlined taxis?
—Yes.
—The ones with the radio . . .
—Yes.
—With the funny hood so you don't know which way they're going?
—Yes.
—They go sixty miles an hour . . .
—Yes.
—Well, I came on the subway.

TELEPHONES AND TELEGRAMS

Asking for the number on the phone: two ate one chestnut.

Listen operator, that's the third wrong number you've given me. I'm telephoning, not broadcasting.

—I wonder who this telegram is from?
—Western Union. I recognize the handwriting.

—What's an appropriate gift for a telephone operator?
—Why not give her some earrings?

Two telegrams:
She: Lonesome, send for me.
He: Broke, send for me.

—What is that little booth out there? I just put a nickel in it.
—That's a telephone booth.
—My god, I've been robbed.

—What should I say to the operator when I lose a nickel in the telephone?
—That's an embarrassing question.

The telephone rang, and the mistress of the house told the maid to answer the phone. The maid did. "Yes'm," she told the caller, "yes'm. It sure is." Then she hung up. Again the phone rang and again the maid answered. "Yes'm, yes'm. It sure is." Again she hung up, and again the same thing happened. Finally, the mistress asked, "What is it?" The maid said, "Gee, this young lady keeps callin', and all for nothin' at all." The mistress asked, "What do you mean?" And the maid responded, "Well, first she wanted to know, 'Is this Mrs. Perkins's apartment?' And I said, 'Yes'm.' Then she said, 'Is Mrs. Perkins home?' And I said, 'Yes'm.' Then she said, 'Is Senator Perkins her brother?' And I said, 'Yes'm.' And then she said, 'It's long distance to Washington.' And I said, 'It sure is.'"

(Variation)
Telephone Operator: Is this one, seven, four, nine?
Maid: Yassum.
T.O.: Is this Mrs. Blotz's residence?
Maid: Yassum.
T.O.: Long distance from Washington.
Maid: Heh! Heh! Yassum, hit sho' is.

—Hello, is this Mr. Goldfarb?
—Yes.
—This is Mr. Shneck's office. Will you please hold the wire?
(Pause)
—Hello, is this Mr. Goldfarb?
—Yes.
—This is Mr. Shneck's private secretary. Hold the line a minute please.
(Pause)
—Hello, is this Goldfarb?

—Yes.
—Well, this is Shneck. Goldfarb, you stink!

TEXAS

The Vermonter replied to the Texan that it would be a very easy task. "The only thing that you will have to do," said he, "is to lay a two-inch pipe from your city to the Gulf of Mexico. Then if you fellows can suck as hard as you can blow, you will have it a seaport inside half an hour."

TIME

—You probably don't remember me, but ten years ago you gave me a message to deliver.
—Oh, so you brought the answer?

—Pardon me, have you got the right time?
—Yeah.
—Thanks.

—Well, I'm gonna take a nap. Wake me at two o'clock.
—But it's three o'clock now.
—Darn it, I overslept.

TIPPING

Tourist (having looked over historic castle, to butler): We've made a stupid mistake. I tipped his lordship instead of you.
Butler: That's awkward. I'll never get it now.

TOMBSTONE INSCRIPTION

Here lies the body of Mary Brown,
A girl who knew no terrors.
Born a good girl, died a good girl— No runs, no hits, no errors.

TRAINS AND TROLLEYS

A locomotive is not afraid of an automobile.

Streetcar gag: Those that run . . . run much faster.

She: I'd much rather ride in a train than in a rumble.
He: Why is that?
She: Well, as yet, I haven't heard of an engineer hugging a fireman.

I boarded a streetcar this morning. After we rode awhile, the conductor looked at me as if I hadn't paid my fare. When we got downtown, I asked him which end of the car I should exit from. He rudely said, "Make up your mind. Both ends stop."

—Where you from?
—Whoosisville, Virginia.

—One of those jerk towns where everyone goes to meet the train?
—What train?

> A maiden entered a crowded car,
>   And firmly grasped a strap.
> And every time they hit a bump
>   She sat on a different lap.

I boarded a trolley this morning, and a fellow started to misbehave and make threats. The conductor came over and took hold of the fellow in order to throw him off. "Hey, let go of me," said the fellow, "or I'll turn everything on this car upside down." A little nervous old lady in the corner said, "Please, let me off quick."

A green brakeman on the Colorado Mudline was making his first trip to Ute Pass. They were going up a very steep grade, and with unusual difficulty the engineer succeeded in reaching the top. At the Cascade station, looking out of his cab, the engineer saw the new brakeman and said with a sigh of relief: "I tell you what, my lad, we had a job to get up there, didn't we?" "We certainly did," said the brakeman, "and if I hadn't put on the brakes, we'd have slipped back."

Two friends meet in Chicago. One is going to New York, the other to Los Angeles. They get to talking, marvelling over the wonders of modern invention. After talking for about an hour, they look out the train and find it going. One says, "There, that just shows you how the modern world has progressed. Here we are travelling on the same train—and you're going to Los Angeles, while I'm on my way to New York."

My kid sister was going to visit some of our relatives out of town. Mother gave her a long lecture about speaking to people in the station and on the train and warned her especially not to tell any men where she was headed. As she walked through the gate, the attendant asked her where she was going. But she refused to say. He got very angry and bullied her. Finally, she told him she was going to Los Angeles. He then pushed her on to the rear end of the train. Just as it was pulling out, she yelled after him, "Ha, Ha, smarty, I'm going to New York."

I came here on that special guaranteed train from St. Louis. You know, the one on which they pay you for every hour you are late. Somehow we lost an hour and a half, and the conductor was walking up and down the aisle, fuming as if it were his money. The engineer had the throttle wide open and was pressing to make up the lost time, when suddenly we came to a little junction in Pennsylvania. There in the middle of the track stood a man waving a lantern. The engineer blew the whistle, but he wouldn't move. He stood there defiantly. Why this guy was a brakeman, I'll never know. Maybe it was the red flag that enticed him. Anyway, the train stopped, and the conductor came tearing up to the brakeman and said: "Do you know that we are an hour and a half late, and you're making us even later?" The brakeman put his hand on his hip and said: "That's just it. Where have you been?"

—I saw a terrible thing.
—What?
—An old lady was standing on the railroad tracks. The train was coming hell for leather, and she didn't move. There she stood. Nearer and nearer came the express, and still the old lady stood on the tracks, directly in the path of the onrushing train. Closer it came and still she didn't move. Hurtling on, eighty miles an hour, the bell ringing madly and the siren blowing, it came down the track. And still she didn't move. On and on, and then finally the sickening moment, when the train reached the point where she was standing on the railroad tracks.
—What happened then?
—Then she moved!

TRAVEL AND VACATIONS

—Will it take Bill long to pack for the holiday vacation?
—Pack? Why, when Bill buttons his coat his trunk is locked!

—It's useful to be baldheaded. On my journeys I needn't take a hairbrush or comb!
—Have your teeth out. Then you won't need a toothbrush!

—So you went to *(mention some local spot)* on your vacation; how did you enjoy it?
—That's about the deadest place on earth. Why, they have to put bells on the cows to keep them from falling asleep.

TWINS

Bill: The girl I am married to has a twin sister.
Mae: Gee! How do you tell 'em apart?
Bill: I don't try; it's up to the other one to look out for herself.

Unice and Inice are twins. They look so much alike you can't tell them apart. Unice has teeth, Inice hasn't. If you put your fingers in Inice's mouth and she bites you, it's Unice.

UMBRELLAS

—Yesterday, I saw five men standing under one umbrella and not one of them got a drop of water on him.
—That must have been a big umbrella.
—No, just the ordinary size. It wasn't raining.

My mother went hunting through the house for an umbrella and found a half dozen that needed repairing. She asked me to take them downtown to have them mended. It took three hours for the man to do the job, and just to kill a little time, I went into a restaurant to have a bite to eat. As I was leaving, I accidentally picked up an old lady's umbrella. She came running after me and said: "Here, you, you know that umbrella doesn't belong to you; now give it to me." I felt embarrassed, apologized, and returned the umbrella. A couple hours later, I was riding home in the bus with mother's six umbrellas under my arm. I suddenly looked up and saw this same old lady sitting opposite me. She looked over and smiled and said: "You had a good day, didn't you?"

Shortly after a traveling salesman checked out of a Minneapolis hotel he discovered that he had left his umbrella behind. He went up to recover the lost article. He went hurriedly down the hall and was about to try the door of his room when he over-heard the conversation of some newlyweds inside.
—Whose little eyebrows are those?
—Yours.
—Whose little eyes are those?
—Yours.
—Whose little nose is that?
—Yours.
—Whose little lips are those?
—Yours.
—And whose little neck?
—Yours.
At this point the impatient salesman could stand it no longer. "Hey, you," he shouted, "when you come to an umbrella, that's mine!"

WEATHER

Snow is beautiful if you are watching the other fellow shovel it.

It was so cold up there, a little dog wagged its tail, and broke it off.

The other night I went to a house warming and we nearly froze to death.

He's the kind of a fellow who was born in a fog, and everything he touches is mist [missed].

I was up in Montreal one winter and the snow was so deep they had to jack up the cow to milk it.

Say, I did a show in Duluth. It was so cold up there I had to wear my heavy underwear when I took a bath.

It was so cold up in the country that I woke up during the night and heard my teeth chattering on the dresser.

It was so cold last night that the blanket and sheet were fightin' to see which one got underneath to keep warm.

"Yes," mused the returned Arctic explorer, "at one time we came within an inch of freezing to death. Luckily, however . . . " He gazed reflectively at the ceiling. "We had the presence of mind to fall into a heated discussion."

WILLS

—Where there's a will there's a wait.
—Where there's a will there's a why.

A fellow just died and left all he had to an orphan's home. He left ten children.

—Did that millionaire grandfather of yours remember you when he made his will?
—He must have; he left me out.

WISHFUL THINKING

—What would you do if you were on guard one night and you felt a pair of arms around your neck and someone squeezing you?
—I would say, "Let go . . . honey."

—It's lovely to be able to go home, put on my slippers, slip into a robe, sit in my favorite chair, and ring the butler for a drink.
—You must be rich to have a butler to ring for.
—I don't have a butler, but I love to hear the bell ring.

WOMEN

Lady Luck is as fickle as the rest of her sex.

Time tells on a man, but it shouts at a woman.

All women are puzzles, so why not give them up?

This girl is a very fine type. Her dad's a printer.

If you make light of a girl's clothes, she'll burn up.

She's a French model. Well, fifty million Frenchmen can't be wrong.

You've heard about cooling plants? Well, here's the little girl who wrecks 'em.

"If a girl can't get silk stockings," sighs Sheila, "she should pray for rayon."

Girls who wear cotton stockings are either over-confident or don't give a darn.

It doesn't do any good to spank a girl after she's sixteen, but it's lots of fun.

One half of the women today are working women, and the other half are working men.

The girl who thinks she's too good for any man, may be right; and she may be left.

The only things some girls can ever get straight are the seams of their stockings.

A man never gets into trouble chasing women. It's after they're caught that the trouble begins.

Do you know why girls are not good at explanations? They aren't anxious to make themselves plain.

—What's the difference between a girl and a cop?
—When a cop says "stop" he means it.

Do you know the definition of a modern girl? She builds her castles in the air, but leaves out the kitchen.

She: I wish the Good Lord had made me a man.
He: Probably he has, but you haven't found him yet.

An expert calculates that eighty percent of American women artificially shape their eyebrows. That must take some pluck.

Experts say that women's feet are two sizes larger than they were twenty years ago. That comes from their trying to fill men's shoes.

"No woman is truly beautiful," says Flo Ziegfeld, "when she is half-starved or angular or bony." But no doubt she still has her points.

She: Do you like vain girls or the other kind?
He: What other kind?

—Have you no little peach preserved for you?
—Preserved? The ones I get are pickled!

—Isn't it a wonderful thing to see a girl grow into womanhood?
—It is. So many of them these days want to grow into manhood.

—What's the difference between a phone and a woman?
—They both repeat what they hear, but a phone repeats correctly.

—A woman can make a fool of you in ten minutes.
—Ah, yes, but think of those ten minutes.

The modern miss isn't nearly so much concerned with what a man stands for as what he'll fall for.

She: Aren't you wild about bathing beauties?
He: Can't say I ever bathed one.

About the only difference between a cutie and an old maid is that a cutie goes out with the Johnnies and an old maid sits home with the willies.

Woman: You said this dress had fast color; but after the first washing, the color all came out.
Cleaner: Well, ain't that fast enough?

A girl may wear a golf skirt and not go golfing, or wear a bathing suit and not go near the water, but when she puts on a wedding gown, kid, she means business.

—Why does a woman take the name of a man she marries?
—Well, she takes everything else, so why shouldn't she have that? (*Or:* She may as well have it, since she takes everything else.)

Optimist: After all, old boy, we've got to admit it; the most beautiful thing in the world is woman.
Cynic: Yes, when she has money.

Woman is like a rainbow. She gets green with envy, white with fear, purple with rage; sometimes she's tickled pink, other times she sees red. And she's apt to be blue anytime.

> Woman's hair, woman's hair,
> It sets my heart aflutter,
> But how it makes me sick
> To find it in the butter.

> I thought that I would never see,
> A dame who could get the best of me,
> And though only God can make a tree,
> A dame has made a monkey out of me.

> The girl I left behind me
>   I think of night and day,
> For if she ever found me
>   There'd sure be hell to pay.

The census taker asked the woman if she was married. She said her husband had died five years ago. When he asked her how many children she had, and their ages, she replied, "Five, ages one to five." The census taker said, "But I thought your husband was dead." The woman replied, "He is, I ain't."

If she didn't have her hair bobbed,
If she didn't daub with paint,
If she had her dresses made to reach
To where the dresses ain't.
If she didn't have that baby voice,
And spoke just as she should,
Do you think she'd be as popular?
Ah, like fun she would.

A drunk wandered into a women's-rights meeting, arriving just in time to hear the speaker extolling the women who were a credit to their sex. She shouted, "Look at the women lawyers of today!" Falling in with the spirit of the thing, he shouted, "Hooray for those women lawyers." The speaker went on, "Look at all the brilliant women who are in politics!" The fellow hollered, "Hooray for those women politicians." Concluding her talk, the speaker said, "Women are as useful in the business world as men. There is very little difference in the sexes." The drunk shouted, "Hooray for the little bit o' difference."

Bad men want their women
To be like cigarettes.
Just so many, all slender and trim
In a case—
Waiting in a row
To be selected, set aflame, and
When their fire has died,
Discarded.

More fastidious men
Prefer women like cigars:
These are more exclusive,
Look better and last longer;
If the brand is good,
They aren't given away!

Good men treat women
Like pipes,
And become more attached to them
The older they become!
When the flame is burnt out
They still look after them.
Knock them gently
(But lovingly)
And care for them always—
No man shares his pipe.

Blondes

You can never tell a blonde by the color of her hair.

He is eyeing a blonde and his wife strikes while the eyeing is hot.

Hal: What's the matter with George? He looks terribly emaciated.
Sal: Oh, he's suffering from high-blonde pressure.

He: Gentlemen prefer blondes.
She: How silly, I am not a blonde.
He: I am not a gentleman.

Hal: Boy, oh boy! That was some blonde with you last night.
Where did you get her?
Sal: Dunno. I just opened my billfold and there she was.

A fellow was about to strike his wife when a second man
entered and bawled him out. The wife cried, "I have no milk
for the babies, and he won't give me a penny." The husband
gave her a penny and the other man told him that he ought to
be ashamed. "You have some nerve! Your children and wife are
starving, and you won't lift a finger to help them." The wife
complained, "That's not all! He's got a date with two beautiful
blondes, and he's on his way to meet them right now." The
stranger was horrified. Turning to the husband, he said, "You
would leave your wife and run after two other women? Surely,
what I'm hearing can't be true!" The husband said, "Yeah, it's
true. What are you going to do about it?" The other fellow pulled
out a gun and shot the woman, saying, "Let's go! Where are
those two blondes?"

Fast Women

Lover boy, I'll give you just twenty minutes to take your arm
away.

Some fast young ladies take twenty-five years to reach the age of
nineteen.

(Variation)
That girl is very fast, yes indeed. It took her thirty-five years to
reach nineteen.

He: Why do you like the cold weather?
She: It brings chaps to my lips.

He: How old are you?
She: Old enough to know you better.

Sue: Jim has always been a perfect gentleman with me.
Mae: Yes, he bores me, too.

Lost—a lead pencil by Marjorie Weats, blonde, blue eyes, good dancer. Finder please return or call Waverly 9998 between the hours of seven and nine P.M.

A man wandered into a tennis tournament the other day and sat down on a bench. "Whose game?" he asked. A young thing sitting next to him looked up hopefully. "I am," she replied.

Siren: You look sweet enough to eat.
Weasel: But you're a vegetarian!
Siren: Yes, but you're the apple of my eye, big boy!

A man stepped up to a single lady in the hotel lobby.
Man: Are you looking for a particular person?
Woman: I'm satisfied, if you are.

Woman: Porter!
Porter: Yes, madam, what is it you wish?
Woman: I just found two strange men in my apartment and I want you to put one of them out.

He: Did Tom hand you that "sister and brother" stuff last night?
She: Yeah, he said he'd love me like a brother.
He: Did he?
She: I dunno. Didn't seem any different from the rest of the boys.

Redhead: I hate that man.
Blonde: Why, what'd he do?
Red: Well, we were parked, and he said I couldn't whistle. Just to show him, I puckered up my mouth just as round and sweet as I could, and what do you suppose he did?
Blonde (blushing): How should I know?
Red: Well, the darn fool just let me whistle!

An old-fashioned lady saw a girl puffing on a cigarette and spoke to her indignantly, saying it was a disgrace to see a young girl smoking. The girl said, "What are you talking about? Everyone smokes these days. Where have you been hiding?" The old lady, now feeling insulted, said, "I'm ashamed of you. Why, before I'd smoke I'd rather go up to the first man who comes along and kiss him." The girl replied, "Who the hell wouldn't!"

(Variation)
A girl and an elderly woman were waiting for the other members of the party to arrive. "Have a cigarette?" asked the girl, offering her case. The older woman looked at her in extreme annoyance. "Smoke a cigarette!" she cried indignantly. "Good gracious, I'd rather kiss the first man who came along." "So would I," retorted her companion, "but have one while you're waiting."

Flappers

Be careful of a mule backways, a bull frontways, and a flapper always.

The main difference between a radio and a flapper is that there's usually something on the radio.

You know flapper dresses didn't particularly appeal to me at first, but I can see through them now.

According to Flapper Fanny, the Whiz Bang style expert, the last word this season in pajamas is "good night!"

On top of a crowded bus in Chicago, the conductor shouted to the passengers: "Low bridge! Everyone keep his seat and face to the front." A gay little flapper up forward turned around, smiled sweetly, and said, "My dear, you know that can't be done."

Gold Diggers

A gold digger is a girl who robs Peter to play Paul!

He calls her his treasure. All he does is dig for her.

She: There goes Sarah. She picks her boyfriends.
He: She does—picks 'em clean.

Heaven will protect the working girl, but who will protect the guy she's working?

When a Chinese prince told an American gold digger, "I've got a Yen for you," she said, "How much is that in American money?"

She's somewhat of an after-dinner speaker. It seems that whenever she speaks to you, she's after her dinner.

A Hollywood girl doesn't marry for money alone. She also hopes that Cupid will shoot her with a Pierce-Arrow [a luxury automobile no longer manufactured].

Mae: Was it a case of love at first sight?
Sue: Absolutely! The first time I saw him in his Rolls-Royce.

He: My sweet, would you like a wristwatch with twenty-one jewels?
She: No, I have a watch. Just give me the twenty-one jewels.

He: Why are you so cold toward me?
She: Because I never got that fur coat you promised me.

He: If I had a million dollars do you know where I'd be?
She: Yes, you'd be on our honeymoon.

He: Only a mother could love a face like yours.
She: I'm about to inherit a fortune.
He: I am about to become a mother.

Tom: Freda, your heart is like glass. No one can make any impression on it.
Freda: Someone might, if he tried with a diamond.

Mae: The man I marry must have something that Clark Gable's got.
Sue: A swell personality?
Mae: No, a swell income.

Mae: They say you married him because his aunt left him a fortune.
Sue: That's a lie. I'd have married him just the same whoever had left it to him.

Mae: So you're going to persuade your sugar daddy to give you a diamond bracelet, are you?
Sue: Yes, I'm out for my pound of flash.

Hal: So you broke off your engagement with Mary.
Sal: She wouldn't have me.
Hal: Well, did you tell her about your rich uncle?
Sal: Yes, and now she's my aunt.

Hal: I hear that since you've been in the contracting business you've become a woman hater.
Sal: I've spent the first half of my life digging ditches, and the second half ditching diggers.

Spendthrift Women

She was a human dynamo. Everything she had on was charged.

Her parents wanted her to marry a plumber because she was such a drain.

The modern woman has been tried and found wanting—everything under the sun.

I don't go for her, she's too biased. Every time you go out with her, it's bias this, bias that.

She believes in capital punishment. She's been punishing her husband's capital for years.

Woman's Honor

My girl won't go any place without her Ma, and Ma goes every place.

He: You look bad tonight, girlie.
She: Well . . . the mud on my shoes proves that I'm not.

WORDPLAY

She gave him a beautiful belt for Christmas—right in the mouth.

My mother told me if I could strike a happy medium, I'd be successful.

She swallowed a tack and now she has a nail growing out of her big toe.

My brother fell in a tub of cement and he was never so mortified in his life.

Definition of the word "eclipse": When he sees a joke in the paper eclipse it out!

He: Why do you always answer a question by asking another?
She: Do I?

Sal: Do you use Williams Shaving Cream?
Hal: No, he's not living with me any more.

Woman: Would you give ten cents to help the Old Ladies' Home?
Man: What! Are they out again?

She: I've been walking since I was ten weeks old.
He: Gee, you must be tired out.

She: I feel giddy tonight.
He: All right, giddy up.

He: Once I had my arm broken in two places.
She: You ought to keep away from those places.

She: I bought some skin soap.
He: Well, what am I expected to do, break out in a rash?

—What are children of the Czar called, mister?
—Czardines, sir.

—What's the matter with the garbage man?
—He's down in the dumps.

John: I hear you were out with a spiritualist last night. Have you known him long?
Beatrice: Sure, he's an old psychic [sidekick] of mine.

—Do you know any operettas?
—Yes, I know two telephone operators. (*Or:* Sure I know lots of 'em: telephone operators.)

Mr. Dollar (*arriving at a dinner party with family*): Please announce Mr. and Mrs. Dollar and daughter.
New Butler (*announcing in loud voice*): Three bucks.

—What's that thing an angel has around his head?
—Halo.
—Hello, yourself.

—What's the China Clipper's first stop?
—Hawaii.
—Pretty good. How're you?

—How would you describe the inside of an empty tube?
—Hollow.
—Hello.

—What's the antonym for lower?
—Higher.
—Hiya.

—What would you do if a fire broke out?
—Holler.
—Hello.

—What keeps bugs out of radiators?
—Gratings.
—Greetings, friend, greetings.

—I was shipwrecked for a whole week.
—My, my, do tell.
—Lived the week on a can of sardines.
—Tsk, tsk, how could you move around?

—Do you know art?
—Art who?
—Artesian.
—Sure, I know artesian well.

—I never heard of rules like that.
—It's according to Hoyle.
—What Hoyle?
—Banana Hoyle!

> My Analyze over the ocean
> My Analyze over the sea
> Oh, who will go over the ocean
> And bring back my Anatomy.

Alice: What's your father's occupation, Bill?
Bill: My father's a cop, but I'm no flop.
Alice: Well, my father's a baker, but I'm no Quaker.
Fred: My father's a chauffeur, but I'm no loafer.
Helen: Er—ah, my father's a surgeon.

Assuming a Napoleonic pose.
—Whatever are you doing?
—I'm posing for animal crackers.
—Why, that's silly.
—Silly? When you were a kid, didn't you ever play Statues?
—Oh, Statues, sure. You mean you dress up in some funny
clothes and then I come in and say, "Isdatyou?"

Questions and Fractured Answers

- In order to see a mosque you've got to (a) catch a mosquito, (b) drink a lot of muscatel, (c) go to Moscow.
- When you need glasses you visit (a) an optimist, (b) an occultist, (c) a speculator.
- A myth ith (a) a virgin if you lithp, (b) a thythtem for beating the horthes, (c) a female moth.
- In Venice they go around in (a) gladiolas, (b) Gwendolyns, (c) gorgonzolas.
- Umbilicus means (a) being very bilious, (b) something that looks like an umbrella, (c) not eager to fight.
- Some famous ornamental flowers are known as (a) spittoonias, (b) salivas, (c) cuspidorias.
- Bronchial means (a) going to the Bronx, (b) of a bronze color, (c) an unbroken horse.
- Stupendous means (a) very stupid, (b) having many steps, (c) bending way over.
- Gargoyles are (a) something for rinsing the throat, (b) girls who belong to the G.A.R., (c) sunglasses.
- A ruminant means (a) one who is a rum addict, (b) one who lives in furnished rooms, (c) a native of Rumania.
- If you have a sick cow you call in (a) a vegetarian, (b) a ventriloquist, (c) a vestryman.
- A polygon is (a) a dead parrot, (b) a man with many wives, (c) a cube with twelve sides.
- The poll tax was (a) a tax on barber poles, (b) an axe for killing poultry, (c) a box of carpet nails from Poland.
- Cleopatra was bitten by (a) an ass, (b) an aspirant, (c) asthma.
- A cluster of stars in the sky is called (a) a conversation, (b) a consultation, (c) a constipation.

Otter—To give voice to your thoughts (Utter)
Pack—A fourth of a bushel (Peck)
Palfrey—A tower in which a bell is hung (Belfry)
Paunch—To beat or strike (Punch)
Pauper—A male parent (Papa)
Pause—Father's (Pa's)
Pepper—A printed news journal (Paper)
Petition—A wall or other barrier separating one part of a room from another (Partition)
Phase—The anterior portion of the head; visage; countenance (Face)
Pigeon—The act of tossing something (Pitchin')
Pillow—A great wave of the sea (Billow)
Pitch—A fruit known for its fuzzy skin (Peach)
Plush—A reddening; as of the face, from modesty, shame or confusion (Blush)
Poach—A covered structure on the front of a house (Porch)

WORK

His work can be described in three words: phenomenal.

Our Motto: Anything worth doing is worth overdoing.

About the only thing that can lay down on the job and get results is a hen.

What a lucky guy! He's got a wife and a cigarette lighter and they both work.

Once a manicure girl married a dentist, and ever since they've been fighting tooth and nail.

—Don't forget, I'm an honor student in biology.
—Yeah, how are you on Fryology, Patchology, and Scrubology?

—What made you so late quitting last night?
—I wasn't doing anything, and I couldn't tell when I was through.

Ambition is a thing to be shunned. Take the example of the street cleaner who was over-ambitious and had his face kicked in.

We've just received a report from Pawtucket concerning a farmer who crossed his bees with lightning bugs so as to make 'em work at night.

—My wife told me to demand a raise from you.
—All right, I'll ask my wife if I can give it to you.

Boss: Would you care if I gave you only fifteen dollars a week to start?
Gertie: Huh, for that I couldn't even START caring!

Press Agent: And when the director told his assistant his services were no longer required, what did the poor fellow say?
Cameraman: He said, "What? After all these yeahs?"

—Say, I hear you're a detective. Is that true?
—Is it true? See that heel? *(He points to his shoe.)* I ran that down.

—I want you to meet my husband. He makes his living with his pen.
—Oh, so he's a writer?
—No. He raises pigs.

—I wanna buy a baseball, a bat, and a glove.
—What's the idea?
—My boss said if I'll play ball, we'll get along fine.

Son: Father, I've a notion to settle down and go in for raising chickens.
Father: Better try owls. Their hours would suit you better.

A house painter was working to the rhythm of the song he was singing. His boss came up to him and said, "If you must sing, instead of singing slow songs, sing something like 'Yankee Doodle Dandy.'"

Prospect: Did you say you were selling insurance for a living?
College graduate: Yes.
Prospect: Have you sold anything yet?
College graduate: Yes, my saxophone, my watch, and my overcoat.

A department-store buyer and a salesman met in hell. The salesman said, "Well, here I am right on time for that appointment." The buyer said, "I don't know what you mean." The salesman said, "Remember the last time you saw me at your office? You said you'd see me in hell, and here I am."

I used to usher at a theatre that was neat as a pin and so strict that the manager would fire you if you dropped lint on the floor or showed up one minute late. Well, I arrived late one morning and the manager asked, "Where have you been?" I said, "Sorry, sir, I went down to the river to spit."

Boss: Late again!
Clerk: Well, my wife presented me with a baby last night!
Boss: She would have done a lot better with an alarm clock.
Clerk: Come to think of it, that would have been quite an achievement.

—Last summer, I was working on a farm and I used to get more milk than anyone else on the farm. I was the best milker.
—How is that?
—Oh, I had pull.

(Variation)
—I used to work on a farm. I got more milk than any of the other farmhands. I had pull.

(Variation)
—When I worked on a farm, I used to milk the cows naturally.
—Well, is there any other way?

Jones was coming for the first time to see how his worthless son, who had been sent out on a farm to work, was behaving himself. He met the owner of the farm and immediately became anxious to learn whether or not his son had proved a success. His first question was: "How's the boy gettin' along?" "Well," said the farmer, "he broke two spade handles yesterday and one to-day." "What, workin' so hard?" "No, leanin' on 'em."

The difference between an economist and a broker is simply this: An economist is a man who knows a great deal about very little; and as time goes on he knows more and more about less and less, until finally the good man knows EVERYTHING about

NOTHING. Whereas a broker is a man who knows a little bit about a great deal; and as time goes on HE knows less and less about more and more, until finally HE knows NOTHING about EVERYTHING.

They worked on adjoining jobs and were becoming the best of friends. One midnight they ate "lunch" together. Each opened his little tin dinner pail and brought out food evidently prepared by the good wife at home. "Didn't you bring no coffee with your lunch?" questioned the first night watchman upon seeing its absence in the other's dinner pail. "Naw," replied the second watchman, "if I did, I wouldn't sleep a wink all night."

Business conditions are in a terrible state. The tailoring business is only just sew sew, and the carpet trade is held down by tax. The barbers are only just scraping along; the butchers are trying to make both ends meet; and in the hotels, even the elevator boys are having their ups and downs. The carpenters are nailing everything they can get their hands on. Most of the radio business is in the hands of receivers, and the undertaking business is just dead. In fact, the only people who are making dough are the bakers. Given the state of the nation, I didn't know what to do with my savings. So I asked around and was told that if I put my money into a bank for fifteen years, I'd be able to retire. But the bank must have heard about it, because they retired last week.

Looking for Work

"These," remarked the unsuccessful job hunter, "are the times that try men's soles."

When a girl is looking for a job as a stenographer, her best references are a pair of shapely legs.

No wonder the southern winter resorts didn't do any business this season. Most of the people who went down there were looking for jobs.

A young Filipino saw in a newspaper an ad reading: "Wanted—A saxophone in good condition." Not long afterward he called at the address and said to the advertiser: "I want to accept the position as saxophone. I've never been a saxophone, but I think I can do it and I am in good condition."

Menial Jobs

—I just got a job in the mining business.
—Gold mining?
—No, calcimining.

—I have a good job polishing those big round doors.
—Oh, revolving doors.
—No, cuspidors.

She: I have a new job, but I don't like it.
He: Well, you've made your bed, now lie in it.
She: Gee! I can't do that. I'm a chambermaid.

Bill: My brother is working with five thousand men
under him.
John: Where?
Bill: Mowing lawns in a cemetery.

A woman was scolding a hobo who was beating her rugs.
"You're not hitting them hard enough." He replied, "What do
you want for a dime (*or:* a meal), a sandstorm?"

—I tell ya I'm a panhandler.
—A panhandler isn't a job.
—I tell ya it is a job. I'm a panhandler in a hospital.

—Louie broke his leg yesterday.
—Too bad; how did it happen?
—He got a job as a window washer and he stepped back to
admire his work.

—How do you like your new job?
—Snap.
—Why, what do you do?
—Sort rubber bands.

No Work

My girl worked in the movies for three years, but they have men
ushers now.

My brother doesn't like to work, so I got him a job trimming century plants.

My brother used to be a salesman, but he lost out 'cause he took
orders from no one.

—Do you want a meal badly enough to work for it?
—I said I was hungry, not desperate.

—They advertise a book here that'll save me half my work.
—Better get two of them.

I once had a job cutting dogs' tails but I lost it. The dogs got
wise, and every time I came around, they'd sit down.

—Say, do you know where I can get a position?
—What kind of a position?
—Reclining.

—My brother helps my dad.
—What does your dad do?
—He's out of work.

Student: I have called to see about getting a job.
Boss: But I do all the work myself.
Student: Perfect, when can I start?

Doctor: I'm afraid I have bad news for you. You will never be
able to work again.
Graduate: What do you mean bad news?

—'Ows your 'usband feeling since the accident?
—Well, dearie, e's 'eaps better now, since the doctor told 'im 'e'd
never be able to work again!

Gentleman in Top Hat: You haven't had a job since Easter, have
you? What are you?
Tramp: A hot-cross bun maker, sir.

—I was with my last employer nine years.
—Any references?
—No, I bit my keeper.

—What are you doing now?
—I'm an ex-porter.
—An exporter?
—Yeah, I was just fired from the Pullman Company.

Women Workers

Just because she's a salesgirl doesn't mean she has to give out
samples.

This girl is double-jointed. She works here and doubles in a joint
across the street.

Mae: The boss is having me do a little filing today.
Sue: Why is that?
Mae: Because I scratched him the last time he tried to kiss me.

This girl used to be in "A Night in Venice," "A Night in Spain,"
Ten Nights in a Barroom." But she quit and now she's on day
work. (*Or:* But she quit and plans to go into day work.)

Sophisticated Sadie had applied for and obtained a job at
Cohen's Department Store as a cloak model.
Sadie: And what will my salary be?
Cohen: I will giff you twenty-five dollars a week mitt pleasure.
Sadie: Not a chance, mister; mitt that, it's thirty-five.

PART TWO

MC Material:
Biz, Jokes, Routines,
and Skits

ACKNOWLEDGMENTS

I hope I made it perfectly clear that the dresses were sent to us from the *(name a local dress shop)*. They provided the dresses and we had them filled.

Announce who furnished all the dresses, shoes, clothes, and accessories. Then say, "Jewelry from the *(name the local city)* Plate Glass Company."

AUDIENCES AND AUDIENCE BIZ

This gag will entertain every kid from 6 to 60.

A bird in the hand is worth two from the audience.

Will someone please call out one number, and I will guess what it is.

The last time we did this act, people were actually crying, crying for their money back.

Come to the show next week and the week after and the week after that. Bring the whole family. Be my guest. All you have to do is buy a ticket.

The last time we did this act, the people laughed so hard they fell right out into the aisles. I don't want anybody to get hurt here, so fellows, open your vests, loosen your belt, sit back, and relax. Girls . . . just do the best that you can.

The night I played Hartford, the audience was so small, they all went home in one taxi. The manager said it was because I was an elite dog. Hell, I'll eat anything. In Boston, the theatre was so exclusive the usher had to pay to get in, and we had to send out to get a fourth for bridge.

You know, it's amusing to stand up here and watch the reaction of the men when a beautiful woman comes on stage. The wives are bored, but the husbands are all attentive and leaning out of their chairs. There'll be many an argument tonight on the way home. I got my hell last night.

(After trying to get someone in the band to tell a gag and having it spoiled, the MC tells the fellow to sit down.)
MC: If I was as dumb as you I'd sue my mom and pop. I'll tell it with someone from the audience and get better results. *(He tries to get a girl to come on stage.)* You don't want to tell a joke with me? All right, I've had better girls than you say no to me. You're not the first to refuse me. *(Finally, he brings a girl on stage and invites her to tell the gag about a black hen laying a white egg.)* Girl: I don't know it. What should I say? *(The MC whispers in her ear)* Well, what's funny about that?

MC: Well, can you do it?

(Enter carrying a camera under your arm.)
I suppose you folks are wondering what this camera has to do
with the show. Well, I'll tell you. I want to get a picture of the
audience while they're laughing. This idea may sound silly, but
there's a reason, and a good reason. Here it is. You see, I have an
uncle living in California who is worth millions. He thinks that
as an entertainer I am a good plumber's helper. Now, if I can
prove to him that I am not the failure that he thinks I am, I will
be in line for a lot of dough. So I want to get a picture of the audience, while they are laughing, to send to my uncle. So I'm going
to tell a joke now and when you laugh, I'm going to take your picture. *(He tells a bum gag.)* There were two Irishmen walking down
the street. Pat said to Mike, "Have you ever heard the story about
the feet?" Mike said, "No." Pat said, "Be jabbers, you have two."
*(You laugh extravagantly and get ready to snap a picture. The audience
is virtually silent. You look up and disgustedly say)* Listen, I have to
get a picture of the audience while they're laughing. It's for my
uncle, you see. So the idea is this: I'm going to tell a joke, and
when you laugh, I'm going to take your picture. Get that? All
right, here we go. There were two Jewish fellows who met on the
street one day. One of them said, "Hello, Abe, congratulations. I
hear you had a fifty thousand dollar fire." And the other fellow
said, "Sh! it's tomorrow." *(Repeat the business of laughing while
the audience is quiet.)* You folks don't seem to get the idea of this
thing. I have to get a picture for my uncle *(by this time you are
getting sore)*, so I'm going to tell a story and when you laugh I'm
going to take your picture, if I have to stay here all day. A fellow
got a hot tip on a horse called Blue Belle in the fourth race. He
put twenty dollars on it, and about five o'clock he called up the
bookmaker and said, "How did Blue Belle do in the fourth race?"
The bookmaker said, "He was in the fifth race, too; they couldn't
wait for him any longer." *(Same result. Introduce next act.)* The
next act is . . . *(Immediately following the act, bow. Then walk down
to the footlights with a very sarcastic look on your face. Hold up the
camera and just stand there silently looking at them. This effect invites
laughter. Then very quietly and sarcastically begin.)* I have to get a
picture for my uncle, etc.

BAND BIZ

When the cat's away, the Mice-tro will play.

He's as busy as a one-fingered clarinet player.

Hold on to your seats, I'm gonna sing.

You sound like a Zulu trying to sing "Tea for Two."

I'm going to sing two songs at once, my first and last.

If my voice should crack, it's simply my youth. My voice is changing.

(The band plays a number and skips a few bars.)
Aha, I never did like that part.

(The MC comes on after a slow number and fires two shots.)
No one's going to sleep while I'm here.

The band will play with verve, zest, gusto, gustave, and the rest of the musicians' union.

All the members of the band interrupt one another as each person tries to introduce the band.

The MC announces to the audience that the boys lean toward classical music. Then all the boys lean over.

On an encore, have the MC conduct the band but no music comes out.
Rather, the audience sees a great deal of soundless motion.

I studied violin five years. I fiddled away five of the best years of my life.

I used to take fiddle lessons. Oh, I got so I could scrape like mad. My tutor was a wonderful man. Before I'd been going to him two weeks, he had me in the second position.

(Ed blows off key.)
Huh, always the case when you borrow these things. *(Ed then plays the part properly.)* Say, wasn't that terrible?

That guy plays with feeling. He could play "Lead, Kindly Light" and before you'd know it, you'd be all lit up.

Let me tell ya about our trumpet player. Last week, he blew so hard that he blew three women right out of their seats.

(A drummer drops his bells.)
They're his sleigh bells. If he drops them again, I'll slay him.

This is a little number. The third movement from "Not Paying the Rent."

Say, do I know all the operas? I knew Madame Butterfly when she was a caterpillar.

I have a brother who plays piano by ear and an uncle who fiddles with his whiskers.

You've heard of the composer Rubinoff? Well, I'm his brother Mazeltoff. [*Mazel toff* in Yiddish means "congratulations."]

First I played Beethoven, then I went to Mozart, and then the piano went Bach.

The only thing I really play is "Chopsticks." I'll have a go at anything you'd like to ask for, but it'll sound like "Chopsticks."

We have a soloist in the band who plays trumpet, trombone, drums, horses, chorus girls. He played piano for a while, but he switched. He figured a trumpet was easier than a piano to play in the streets.

Ed: Remember, I'm a musician.
Band Member: You don't look like a musician.
Ed: It's bad enough being one without having to look like one.

Yesterday, when we played this number, a fellow fell asleep. I shouted to the fellow beside him, "Mister, will you wake that man up?" and he said, "Wake him up yourself. You put him to sleep."

(The MC points to the bass or tuba.)
Imagine taking that big thing to a party and then nobody asks you to play.

(Ed tries to play a trombone.)
Some fellows play this thing by ear. I've all I can do to play it with my mouth.

(Ed is tuning up.)
Would you mind giving me a sour note. Just blow off key. (Someone does.) All right, that's as near as I ever get.

(After a band number)
Say, the boys are doing much better since they learned to read music.

Stroke a ukelele round the head. Run your hand down to the shoulders, hips, neck, etc., telling the audience what a wonderful uke it is. Then just put hand on the bottom or pat it a few times.

The MC announces that the boys in the band are going to play this next number with lots of pep—and spirit. All the boys pull out a bottle.

(The MC says to the band members)
Keep your eyes on the music, boys, at least one eye. I'll do all the watching, and tell you about it later.

(The MC kids the boys in the band about wearing white suits.)
I have a suit like that. It's at home. I sleep in it. (Or: "My brother has a suit like that. He works for the city.")

Introducing a song, or person, or skit, etc., try to catch an imaginary fly. Finally slap your hands together and say: "That's the last show you'll ever see for nothing."

I was just reading in the paper where some philosopher says all men with big mouths are liars. What do you think, fellows? *(They all cover their mouths; or they all pucker up their mouths.)*

I went out hunting and took the clarinet along so I could play and the hunters wouldn't shoot at me in mistake for a deer. They shot me for playing.

A man comes out to play an instrument. As he starts, the spot moves all over the set. He shouts, "Hey, Cockeye, here I am!" Shortly into his number, the light goes out. A moment later it comes back on to find the man holding a different instrument.

(Ed is playing two saxophones at once.)
Pucker your mouth and say, "I could never do that." Then stretch your mouth wide open and say, "I was just thinking Joe E. Brown could play eleven at once—if he could play."

The MC brags about the band being so peppy and willing. He says that they're always practicing, always wanting to show off their stuff. He gives the cue and stamps his foot to start the number. But only the tuba plays; the rest are sound asleep.

The MC enters, sings, sits down at the piano, and plays. A musician throws a half dollar on the stage and asks him to stop playing. While the MC retrieves the coin, the piano continues to play. The MC says: "Nobody believed me when I first sat down to play."

The stage is dark, except for a spot on the leader. He brags about the boys being so ambitious that they just can't wait to perform. The spot then picks out the boys, disclosing one reading a paper, one sleeping, one plucking his eyebrows, and several playing cards.

The MC announces that next week he is going to do a trick. He will cut a woman singer in half. The top half he will give away and the bottom half he will throw to the dogs. All the band members yell, "Woof, woof!"

(Variation)
The MC tells the female singer, "I have a good mind to tear you limb from limb and throw you to the dogs." All the band members stand up and bark.

MC: Why do you play with one hand?
Musician: To guard with the other. I blow the notes in, but don't guarantee what comes out. Funny thing, sometimes I'm three notes ahead of what's coming out. They don't make these keys fast enough for me.

MC: You see our cello player over there? He met a girl who was crazy about him. She played the cello, too. One day, she invited

him to her house. He played for her, and she was so thrilled that
she said he could have anything he wanted. The next day he
came to work with two cellos.

MC: Hey, what's this? Do you always have things like this lying
around on the floor? Fellows, has anyone lost a roll of ten dollar
bills? Has anyone lost a roll of bills?
Band Member: Yes!
MC: You, okay, here's the rubber band.

MC: Say, Mr. Bones, I'm sorry to have to reprimand you in front
of such a distinguished audience, but I passed your house last
night and saw you hugging and kissing your wife in front of an
open window at twelve o'clock midnight. Bones: The joke's on
you 'cause I wasn't home till two-thirty.

At the end of a band number, the leader holds a long chord.
He gives the hold sign with his baton and then turns round to
the audience, leaving the band holding the chord. After a minute,
he reminds himself that he left the band and turns round for the
downbeat—and all the band fall down.

The MC hands each of the band members a flower. One boy, however, is left out. He begins to beef. The MC explains the impossi-
bility of finding another flower at this moment. The boy still
complains, until one of the other band members gets up, says
he'll settle the whole thing, and shoots the boy without a flower.

(Variation)
The MC passes out flowers to the boys in the band. One doesn't
get any and starts to shout. Another boy says he shall have a
flower, shoots him, and hands him a lily.

The MC wears a red necktie. At some point during the orchestra's
playing, the musicians break into bird whistles and light nance
comedy. Someone calls out a nance expression. The MC looks
round and wonders what it is all about. Then he looks down at
his necktie and tears it off. [Homosexual men were reputed to
wear red ties.]

Acting like a nance, a fellow compliments those big masculine
types who have just sung Rudolf Friml's "Vagabond King" with
the chorus behind them. As he sings the song, he is overcome
and faints. In the spirit of the show must go on, one of the
chorus boys jumps in and ends the song, a la nance style.

One of the players in the band wants to tell a joke. The MC says,
"No, we've heard that one before." The player starts to tell a joke
about a farmer's daughter. The MC interrupts and says, "No. Try
another." But when the player starts another, the MC stops him
again, saying, "No, we've heard that here. You'll get razzed." The
player responds, "I've heard that here before."

MC: Mr. Tambo will sing "After You're Gone." *(Tambo sings.)*
Whatever made you take up singing?
Tambo: I had to take up singing to keep the wolf from the door.
(Mr. Bones guffaws.)
MC: What are you laughing at?
Bones: With a voice like his, he could keep the whole pack away.

The MC announces the opening band number (or encore). He
says that it will be done in the slow-motion style. He then goes
into a slow-motion beat with his foot. The boys bring up their instruments in slow motion. The MC conducts very slowly. One or
two of the boys take solos in slow motion. After this snail's pace,
the MC calls for an ultra-rapid pace. All the boys play doubly fast,
including the conductor, who works like lightning.

The leader holds up his palm on which he supports an imaginary
flea. He asks the flea to do tricks and then describes them. Suddenly the flea flies off. The drummer says that the flea has come
to rest on his drum; after a pause, he says that the flea has run
off. The leader finds it on his coat, picks it off, and tries to make
it do tricks again. "He can't do 'em," says the leader, "this is not
Alexander!" All the boys leap up from their seats and scratch.

Have the band play some very big classical overture. The MC bor-
rows a fiddle from one of the boys in the band and stands ready
to play. As soon as the band has played the intro, the MC, just on
the end of a musical phrase, goes down front as though to play.
The fiddle is under his chin but the hanky is on the opposite
shoulder. The bandleader says, "No, not yet." He repeats this line
a few times. Finally, he says, "Now!" But when the MC starts to
play, the fiddle breaks in half. *(It is hinged.)*

The band members wear tin helmets. The leader acts like the
chief mechanic. He turns on the juice at a switchboard. First, he
turns slowly and the men play accordingly, that is, mechanically
and slowly. Then he turns the juice on faster and the men play
faster, until they are in full swing. One man, however, begins to
run down. The leader goes over with an oil can and greases him
under an arm. Then the man resumes his former "health." For a
finish, have a powder box under one of the men's chairs and
blow a fuse.

MC *(to the singer):* I wonder why you're so small.
She: I stopped growing when I was ten, six years ago.
MC: Six years ago—boys!—six years since she stopped growing.
(To violinist) Say, how old are you? Viol: I'm fourteen.
MC *(to drummer):* How old are you? Drum: Oh, I'm thirteen.
She: How old are you, Ed?
MC: I'll be born next Wednesday.

(The MC runs on stage and throws cigars to the musicians. The band-leader gestures, as if to say, "What's going on?")
MC: Hello! Hurray! Hello! Have a cigar; have another; have a cigar.
BL: Hey, Eddie, why all the generosity?
MC: Do you remember when I met you yesterday? I told you I was going to be married today. Today's the wedding day.
BL: Yeah!
MC: Well, it's off! *(Throwing more cigars)* Hurray!

(Blackout. Two men enter with flashlights. They shine the lights on each other, disclosing that they are wearing burglars' masks.)
—Where is that safe?
—Right over there.
(They supposedly open the safe and come down front with a paper.)
—Ha, you found the paper!
—Yes.
—What does it say?
—Ed Lowry's band number this week is . . .

(Variation)
(Blackout. The curtains open. Two men with flashlights; they are ostensibly burglars.) Patter: "Did you locate it?" "Not yet." "I know that it's here." "How much do you think it's worth?" "Who knows?" Finally one says, "Here it is. The show this week is . . . "

A disturbance on the side of the stage: there's a fellow with a gun in one hand and a clarinet in the another. A stagehand is struggling with him. The fellow says he's been trying to get an audition for months, and adds disparagingly, "I can't even get an audition from *(give the name of the bandleader)*. And we all know what he sounds like." The fellow is therefore going to shoot himself. The MC grabs the gun, holds it, and says, "I know *(he gives the bandleader's name)*, and he'll hire you if I say so. Go ahead and play for me, right here and now." He plays badly off key. The MC shoots him. Blackout.

The MC announces that this is going to be a celebration-night performance. He says, "I'm going to give away some little presents. Here're some lollipops for the kiddies." *(He distributes them. If he finds two children sitting together, he says)* "Aw, go on, give her a lick." *(Pause)* "And now for the ladies, beautiful roses." *(He hands out some roses. To a single woman he says)* "Madame, please don't tell your husband who gave you this." *(Once the roses are gone, he announces)* "Now, here's something for the men." *(He runs off stage and returns rolling a beer barrel. The band members all jump up and make a rush for the presumed free distribution of beer.)*

MC: Before I started playing this I was a wallflower. I was never asked out any place, but now that I can play it, it's a different

story. Only last night, I was asked out of a swell party. All the
boys laughed when I started to play. You see, there aren't enough
notes on this instrument . . . two notes due on it right now. *(Plays
the instrument badly.)* Funny, I blow in the sweetest things and it
comes out terrible. So I learned how to play with one hand. I'm
no fool. I have the other free to defend myself. I used to play one
of those big saxophones, but gave it up. Who wants one of those
big things dangling around when you're trying to run away?

In the middle of a number, one of the boys in the band hisses
to attract the MC's attention. The boy points to his wrist watch.
The MC ignores him and tries to cover up so the audience won't
notice. The boy repeats the same hissing and pointing again and
again. The MC cracks a joke about rattlers in the pit or a gas leak.
The boy then shows his watch to one of the other band members, and the other boy takes up the hissing to attract the attention of the MC Finally, the MC can't stand it any longer and stops
the band. Both boys point to their watches. At last, the MC understands. He takes out a bottle and spoon, pours himself a dose
from the bottle, and puts the bottle back in his pocket.

A man in the band wants to sing. The bandleader invites him to
come down front. The singer does a bar or two of song, and a
man walks on stage saying that he's from some coat firm and
either wants payment on the coat or else he takes the coat. The
singer says he hasn't got the money. So he loses his coat. In succession, different people come in to take his jacket, vest and tie,
and shoes. At last someone comes in from a pants company and
wants his pants. The singer goes off and comes back a minute
later with an umbrella in front of him. *(His trousers are rolled up,
showing bare legs.)* The farce is completed when a man comes
in and asks for the umbrella. The two men then fight over the
umbrella.

(Variation)
Just before the opening number (or in the middle of a musical
number), the installment collector comes on stage and accosts
one of the musicians. "Pay me my money or give me back the
coat, hat, vest, shoes, shirt, and tie." The collector takes the performer off stage. The performer returns holding an umbrella. His
trousers are rolled up, giving the impression that the collector
has taken his pants.

One of the musicians comes down front and says, "I want to
dance." The MC says, "This is no time to come down like this. It's
show time. The program is set." The musician replies, "Well, I
want to dance." The MC says, "All right, go ahead." After about
two bad steps, the MC brings him his instrument and sends him
back to the stand. He gets back to the stand and during the
announcement stands up and makes motions behind the band-

leader asking the audience to applaud for his dancing. The leader turns around and tells him what a terrible dancer he is, but tells him he can have a second chance if he'll sing. Standing in front of the backdrop, the musician sings, first in bass, then in a high falsetto. Someone drags him off. The leader rubs his hands and says, "Here today and gone tomorrow."

MC: This is official straw hat day. At a certain hour during the day, a whistle will blow, and when it does, anyone caught still wearing his derby will be chastised. We have some peculiar boys in our band. In fact several of them actually regard their old hats with affection, and they have asked me wouldn't I please permit them to wear their derby hats during the show. I'm sure you folks don't object, do you? Go ahead, boys, put on your hats. *(The boys put on trick hats, each one with an invisible string attached from his hat to a baton in the flies.)* Now that the boys are happy, let's get on with the show and forget about hats. *(He starts to tell a gag when suddenly a whistle blows and every hat flies off and up to the flies. Simultaneously each man grabs a straw hat and puts it on.)*

(Argument: the MC owes one of the boys in the band two dollars.)
One: Remember, we took two girls out and the bill was eight dollars. The girls paid two dollars each. And I paid for you and me.
MC: I haven't the two dollars in these clothes.
One: What do you mean in THESE clothes?
MC: Well, here's a dollar and I'll owe you a dollar.
(A second band member pipes up.)
Two *(to the first band member):* Where are the two bucks you owe me?
Boy *(to the second band member):* Here, take this and I'll owe you a dollar.
(The second band member takes the dollar and hands it to the MC.)
Two: Here's the dollar I owe you.
(The MC passes it to number one, who hands it to number two.)

(A young man is seeking employment as a violinist.)
Man: I just came from my Music College graduation ceremony and I'd love to join your orchestra. Today, I just got my diploma, my M.D.
MC: What's that stand for: mentally deficient or musically deficient?
Man: If you'll play some of the higher types of music I'll be glad to let you share my talents.
MC: Do you know any Tchaikovsky junk? I love his latest success, "Springtime in the Rockies." You know I played cello for years, but I cut it out, it was getting me all bowlegged. Then I started to play the big bass viol, and it was VILE. I finally got disgusted. I carried that big thing to a party one night, and no one asked me to play.

Man: May I have an "A?" *(Pizzicato "A")* No, No, give me capital A. *(Plays arpeggios on the fiddle.)*

MC: Now he's trying to show off. Do you know any of Rachmaninoff's numbers?

Man: Yes.

MC: Which one do you prefer?

Man: "Walking My Baby Back Home." And I'll have two choruses: make the first chorus pizzicato with a little fortissimo thrown in and the second chorus S.O.S.

MC: What does that mean?

Man: Same only softer. If I get too cute stop me. *(He fiddles with his whiskers, and someone in the band plays the music.)*

A spotlight illuminates the MC or bandleader, who takes a clarinet or banjo from one of the boys in the band, telling him, "Let me have that. I'll just show you how it ought to be played." He goes down front and says, "I was never asked out any place, but since I took up the clarinet *(or:* banjo) only last night I was asked out of a swell place. All the boys are jealous. They play for money, I play for spite. They all laughed when I picked up the clarinet, but when I started to play. . . . " He "plays" and shortly into the song puts down the clarinet to sing. But the playing continues, because a boy from the band has actually been playing from the start. Then the lights black out. In every break of the music, he shouts for the lights to come up. "How can I play in the dark?" He keeps repeating this, and the music still plays: a solo on the clarinet *(or:* banjo). Finally, the lights come up and he is discovered holding a trombone.

Three men, preferably in Indian blankets, bring a letter to the MC, who reads it aloud. The text of the letter is that the three men are musicians who do not speak English. They are replacing the three men who just left the band. The MC tells them that they will have to know some English and that he'll teach them a phrase each, so they will be able to get by. He teaches the first Indian "The three of us," the second, "For fifty dollars," and the third, "That's what we all want." After they all sing, he leaves them. Two men enter, arguing; one pulls out a gun and shoots the other. The stricken man falls to the ground, as his assailant runs off stage. A cop dashes in, goes over to the body, and questions the three men. He asks them in turn, "Who did this?" Number one answers, "The three of us." The cop asks number two, "What did you do this for?" The second man answers, "Fifty dollars." He asks the last man, "You know what you'll get for this—the chair!" And he answers, "That's what we all want."

—Was it you I heard playing between shows?
—Yes, I was playing a little.

—Little is right! Do you know what I'd do if I played the sax like that?
—No, what would you do?
—I'd take some lessons.
—That's not nice. You know I'm trying to get ahead.
—You need one.
—Now listen here, I won't stand for that. I paid a lot to learn how to play the sax.
—Yeah, well, you ought to see my brother about it.
—Why, is he a music teacher?
—No, he's a lawyer. He'll get your money back.
—You know, I've got a great instrument here. Two thousand wouldn't buy this instrument.
—I guess not. I'm one of them.

—Viola, I love you. I want you tuba mine. I lay my harp at your feet.
—Aw, quit stringing me along. You don't get to first bass with me.
—Say, I'm tired of playing second fiddle! You've got too many guys bowing you around.
—Oh, what a violin sinuation! What brass! Why did you piccolo thing like that to say to me? I ought to give you a baton the head!
—Yeah? Gee, I'm trebling all over!
—You'd better tremolo-ver what you said. I'm liable to drum you yet.
—Oh, but suite, let's give this a rest.
—Oh! Trying to snare me in double quick time, eh? Well, quit horning in. Gwan! Blow!
—Well, fife not been a chump! After all the do I've spent a music you! That's a scaly trick!
—Say, I'm tired of listening to your chorus language. You're not so sharp. I'm leaving you flat!
—Well, I'll be—!
—Which B?

(This musical routine is done with the bandleader, and according to colors.)
White Gardenia: White
Am I Blue: Blue
Yes, Bananas: Yellow
Mazeltoff: Gold
Red Hot Mamma: Red
Silver Threads: Silver
Old Gray Mare: Gray
Tan Little Fingers: Tan
Body and Soul: Flesh
Pink Lady: Pink
Henna Doesn't Live Here Hennamore: Henna

I'm a Dreamer, Orange We All: Orange
Black Bottom: Black
Irish Reel: Green
Orchid to You: Orchid

(A musician in the band makes a commotion, attracts the MC's attention, comes down front, and explains.)
Mus: One of the girls in the last act is walking around in her sleep. She's a somnambulist. And not only that, she takes things.
MC: You mean she's a thief?
Mus: No, no, not a thief really. She always returns the things that she takes when she's finished with them.
(At this point, the girl enters with her arms extended as though she's walking in her sleep. She takes a watch from one of the boys in the band and strolls away with it.)
Mus: Don't worry, she always brings back what she's taken when she's finished with it.
(A moment later, the girl returns, puts her arm around one of the boys in the band, and starts to walk off with him.)
MC: Hey, where's she taking you?
Boy: Don't worry, she'll bring me back when she's finished with me.
[Additions to this routine: (1) the boy leaves his money with the MC before leaving; (2) she takes the watch and the MC says, "Next, she'll give him the works."]

The MC starts to tell a gag about two Jews. One of the boys interrupts, saying he resents it. Then the MC starts to tell a gag about two Germans, but one of the boys interrupts, saying he resents it. Then the MC starts to tell a gag about two Italians, but one of the boys interrupts, saying he resents it. Finally, the MC starts to tell a gag about two girls, and one of the boys does a nance, saying, "Hey, there, I resent that." *[See under Routines]*

(Variation)
MC: I just heard the funniest story. It's about two Jewish boys. It seems two Jewish boys were walking down Delancey Street—
Boy 1 *(interrupting):* Hey, wait a minute! I resent that.
MC: You resent what?
Boy 1: Any reference to the Jewish people.
MC: What are you raving about? I haven't said anything anyone could take offence at. I think I know enough about people's feelings not to offend. Sit down! Ladies and Gentlemen, I apologize for him. I'm sorry. I really had a very funny story, but I won't attempt to tell it now. There may be other people just like him. *(Stalls a minute.)* Gee, that burns me, this was probably the funniest story you ever heard. *(Laughs hysterically.)* I have it. Two Italians were walking down the street, and this one wop said to the

other— Boy 2 (*interrupting*): Hey! (*Have the boy go through a whole string of Italian words, ending up with*) You lay off the Italians, you get me? (*Then have him gesture as if cutting someone's throat.*)

MC: This must be a frame-up! Believe me, folks, I'm sorry. It's a shame. You're the ones who are being cheated. (*Gets hysterical.*) I scream every time I hear it. Last night I got up in the middle of the night to laugh at it. I have it! Two Germans (*etc.*) . . .

Boy 3 (*interrupting*): Hey! (*He goes through the same routine as the other, preferably in German.*)

MC (*He goes through the same routine of apologizing. In the middle of his speech, he pauses and hits on an idea.*): I have it! There were two girls walking down— Drummer (*doing a nance dance with his hand on his hip*): Hey, you, just wait a second!

(*The MC trips back and kisses him on the forehead.*)

(*Note: Pick out boys in the band skilled at dialects; or if any of them are identified as being of a certain nationality, pick them. Jews, Germans, and Italians are the best to get comedy from, especially the Italians. The throat-cutting business never fails to bring down the house.*)

ENTRANCES

Opening gag: Walk on wearing a hat. Look for some place to hang it. Finding none, tear up the hat.

I hope you won't mind me carrying my hat (*or:* coat), but I see some strange actors out there and this is safer.

EXIT LINES

Goodbye . . . and write me sometime, if it's only a check.

Goodbye . . . and give me a ring sometime, if it's only a postcard.

I wasn't born here, but I promise you, if it ever happens again, I'll see that this is the place.

(*MC to the bandleader*)
You take care of things while I just go finish a nap that I'd started before I came on.

The young lady will reappear later in the show, and on her next appearance she will sing a duet—with three other people.

Now I'm going to look for myself for a few minutes. Jack, if you happen to see me around while I'm gone, just hold me till I get back.

Later in the show, this girl is going to be the bride and I'm going to be the broom . . . I mean groom. The boys all throw rice and old shoes. During the last show, one of the boys threw a shoe and left his foot in it.

FRACTURED FAIRY TALES
A Knight and a Fair Damsel

I had a fairy tale prepared, but I won't have time to tell it 'cause when I look it over it's too long. Anyway, I can give you the theme of the thing. Away back in the days when men were men and only women wore red ties, there was a terrible knight, a dirty knight. Well, one stormy night, he jumped on his horse and galloped to the castle where the golden-haired princess lived. And just to show that he was a gentleman, he kidnapped the blonde and rode away with her. They galloped away into the night, and as he rode, she pleaded with him and said, "Please, surely you're not going to hold me for ransom." And the bold knight said, "Hell no! Let Ransom hold his own women."

Little Red Riding Hood

Would you like to hear a bedtime story? Once upon a time, a long time ago, dere lived a little girl about seventeen years of old age. I tink her name was Little Red Riding Hood. One day she was going trew da woods to see her grandmother. She was carrying a basket of different kinds of vegetables, when all of a sudden, for no reason at all, along came a hanibal, and dis hanibal was a wollef. Da wollef walked right up to Little Red Riding Hood and said, "Where you going, kid?" She said, "To whom are you speaking?" The wollef said, "Don't get fresh. Speak normal. Where are you going?" She said, "Well, if you must know, I'm going to see my grandmother, who lives in the woods. I'm bringing her a basket of vegetables." The wollef said, "I'll tell you what I'll do. I'll run you a race to your grandmama's house." (*Aside to the audience:* "You know, Little Red Riding Hood she was hignorant because the wollef had four legs and he could run twice in the same place while Little Red Riding Hood could run only once.") "All right," she said, "I'll took you up." So dey ran the race and da wollef got dere first. He walked up to da grandmama's door and stood on his hind legs and mid his front hands he gave a konock on the door. "Who stays there?" said the grandmama. "It's I am your grandchildren, Little Red Riding Hood." (*Aside to the audience:* "Of course, it was the wollef.") "Come in," said da grandmama. So the wollef went in and jumped on da bed and ate up da grandma. Den the wollef put on the grandma's pajamas and jumped in da bed and pulled da sheets up over his eyebrows. Pretty soon along came little Riding Hood Red. She too gave a konock on the door. "Come in," said the wollef, and she said, "Oh Grandmama, what long eyebrows you have." The wollef said, "All the better to look into you from, my dear." "Oh Grandmama, what long arms you have. What are dese for?" "All

the better to hug you, my dear." "Oh Grandmama, what long teef
you have, what are dese for?" And the wollef said, "All the better
to eat you, my dear." Just den the wollef jumped out of de bed
and was going to eat up Little Redding Ride Hood. But along
came Gaspipe Jake da Plumber from *(cite the local town)* and
heard a wrestling match goin' on da inside. Quick, like a flash
of tunder, he jumped in da house and pulled from his pocket
a penknife and cut da gizzards from da wollef. Den he said,
"Where you live, kid? I got ortermobile outside. I'll took you
home." So she got in the ortermobile and walked home. Dots a
cute story, no?

INTRODUCTIONS

It's a great show so far. Well, this next act will put a stop to that.

The MC enters with a piece of rope in his hand and says, "I either
found the rope or lost a horse."

This is the most exclusive theatre *(or:* party, *etc.)* in town—
everybody's welcome.

Remember last week? We had the smallest midgets in the world.
Well, this week we have some smaller still.

I'm not your usual MC who comes out here and bores you for
hours with anecdotes and gags. No, I introduce the other fellows
and let them do it.

I always believe in starting off a show by singing a song myself,
because after I've finished, then you can really appreciate how
clever the other people really are.

(Introducing an Arab act)
Immediately after this performance, the boys will be in the lobby
selling Oriental rugs and statues.

As the MC is introducing an act, he pauses. Off to one side, a husband is talking to his wife. A blonde woman passes. The husband
leaves his wife, takes the woman by the arm, and exits. The MC
says, "Blondes make the best husbands," and continues the introduction.

Men

He's a very popular boy . . . welcome in every home but his own.

Introducing the answer to a maiden's prayer, um, um, um . . .

(Introducing a pretended drunk) A graduate from ginger ale high.

There's something flower-like about you; you're always getting
potted.

(Introducing three men)
Three Roman tailors: Coatus, Pantus, and Vestus.

His stage name might not mean a whole lot to you, but he works in radio under the name of Bernie.

His first name is William; his last name is Not. So we call him Will Not for short, and Won't for shorter.

Before he came into the band, he used to be on the stage. He and another fellow did an act as male impersonators.

Famous men are known by their last names, for example, Jolson, Cantor, Barrymore, Roosevelt. Now I wish to introduce JOE Doakes.

Now I want you to meet a big butter and egg man. I shouldn't say butter and egg man, because where he comes from he's the whole cheese.

So-and-so will now come on the stage with that nonsensical little ballad entitled, "Oh, the boys call her 'Bunny' because she has a hare lip."

I want you to meet a real Irishman. It's a pleasure to introduce a countryman of mine. I came from Ireland, too—Rhode Island. (*Or* Coney Island)

Come on now, make a speech. Tell them all you know. It won't take more than a minute. Now, if you make the speech with me, it won't take any longer.

Let me introduce our arranger. He used to arrange all the dates for the boys in the band. Now he's married and they have to make their own arrangements.

I want you to meet two boys. I don't know whether to say they are singers or dancers. Those who hear them sing say they are dancers, and those who see them dance say they are singers.

He writes songs under assumed names: Irving Berlin. (*Or:* I write songs under an assumed name: Irving Berlin. *Or:* I write a lot of songs, but I always write under an assumed name: Irving Berlin.)

(Intro for a couple when one is large and the other small) For example, introduce a cute little fellow. Then go to the entrance and look down at the floor to bring the next person on. The laughter issues when a big person walks out.

(A man dressed as an Indian enters.)
Ed *(to Indian):* What's your name?
Man: White Rock.

Ed: White Rock?

Man: Yeah. Me good IN-GIN.

Women

She's a cute little mite—dynamite.

This little lady was Miss America in 1812.

If this girl isn't sweet, then magazine covers lie.

She has those Gloria Swanson eyes, and Clara Bow legs.

She is a Sunkist girl—kissed by every son in California.

She used to go to school with me. She was my schoolteacher.

This girl was in George White's Follies and Ziegfeld's Scandals.

We call her Pauline Revere. She's always going on midnight rides.

They call her the sweetheart of the air. She hangs around the flying field.

Legs by Steinway, shoes by Hanan, body by Fisher, and necks by the hour.

She's a nice girl. She was once taken for Greta Garbo—and once for grand larceny.

The girls are going to do a hot number, and I mean hot. When it rains on them, it sizzles.

Ha, there's flaming Mamie. She's so hot that even when she goes in for a swim the fishes have to come up for air.

Do you notice this little girl? She has her hose turned inside out. She is so hot they have to turn the hose on her.

She is from the south, and she says she feels cold up here. So let's make it hot for her.

Wait until you see these girls. Oh boy! Every day they make them more beautiful, and I keep getting older.

Have all you boys got your ice packs ready; is the cooling system on? Okay, then, let the parade of beautiful women begin. (*Or:* Let's go ahead with the beauty contest.)

This girl's a very good singer. Her dad's a plumber and, boy, has she got pipes.

This next young lady is a very unusual type. She doesn't carry her mother with her.

This is little Flat Tire, boys, she's been given the air by every motorist in town.

Here's a charming young lady who always jumps when you make a bad move: Miss Checkers.

She's the kind of girl who can make you feel she's taking dinner with you instead of from you. [*also under* Dating and Courtship *in* Part One]

The last boy who kissed this girl, please stand up. *(The whole band rises.)* Oh, it's a convention.

Last night, Myrtle's husband was in the audience, and when she shot herself, he got up and cheered.

Hello, darling! My sweetheart, how are you? You look beautiful. *(He hugs her.)* Darling, tell me: what's your name?

These are the Foster girls. When I say Foster girls, I don't mean he is the father of all these girls. He is just the producer.

This young lady was with Artists and Models, Ziegfeld's Follies, George White's Scandals, and several other scandals—er, I mean shows.

She's one of those girls you wouldn't be a bit afraid to take home to meet your mother and sisters, but I'd hate to trust her with the old man.

Wait till you see this girl. Boy, is she beautiful. I'm not asking you. I'm telling you. She dresses right next door to me, just a thin wall separates us. I don't know what that wall is made of, but I wish you could see my penknife.

Let me introduce Mae Joyce. She's not really related in any way to Peggy Joyce. You know how Peggy gets married and, naturally, changes her name? Then three or four months later she re-Joyces. Well, Mae hasn't learned any of those tricks yet. But she's doing the best she can.

Ed: This next girl is so beautiful and talented, it's a miracle she's still single. I'll try to get her to marry me. I'll ask her to elope. *(The girl enters.)* Sweetheart, will you elope with me?
She: Cantaloupe.
Ed: Honey-Dew.

Ed: For her next number I've had 4,865 requests.
She: Really? That many?
Ed: Well, I've had 150 requests at least.
She: Honest?
Ed: Er, I've had a request from your mother that I ask you to sing.

(The MC reads from a card.)
I don't have to write things down. I remember every word.
Now to present a memorable young lady who has the Grace of

Garbo . . . the pulchritude of Bow . . . the charm of Swanson . . . and the poise of . . . ? *(He looks at both sides of the card. It's not written down, and he can't remember.)* Umm . . .

She: Your introductions annoy me so much, I could tear you limb from limb.
Ed: I know you really care for me.
She: What would you do if you found your right leg out in the lobby, your left leg in the operator's booth, your hair hanging on the chandelier, and your schnozzle in the balcony?
Ed: I'd say, that's me all over.

MC: I met a young lady you all know. She was here before and you received her with lots of . . . of . . . of . . . lots of applause. In fact, you clapped your hands. I found her out in Hollywood. She was fooling around with the pictures. Yes, she was playing with a lot of photographs. She got on her bicycle and here she is. *(During her number, she picks a flower and walks toward the MC. But at the last moment, she passes him by and hands the flower to the drummer.)* Gee, how I hate drummers!

Ed *(introducing a female performer and wooing her):* Wouldn't you like to go out and dine with me?
She: Yes, but I'll have to take mother along.
Ed: What?
She: Oh, I take mother along everywhere I go.
Ed: Is she here with you now—right in this theatre? Is she out there now?
She: Yes.
Ed: Ladies and gentlemen, this little girl will sing a song for you.

Clothing

Has that girl lost her dress or am I seeing things?

(A man enters.)
Did you get a whistle with that suit?

(A woman enters with a very tight skirt.)
Don't mind the way she walks. She's not going any place particular.

(A man enters in a dress suit.)
Take no notice of that suit. He was never a waiter in his life.

(A woman enters wearing a backless dress.)
Gee, from where I'm standing you're naked.

(Walking with someone modeling bridal clothes)
I sure feel funny every time I get married.

She's wearing a coming-out dress. She wouldn't dare come out of it any further.

(Variation)
—That's a lovely dress you have on.
—Like it? It's a coming-out dress.
—Yeah, well, don't come out of it any further or you'll get pinched.

(A woman enters in a backless dress.)
Say, that's a beautiful dress. Let's hope you never put it on back to front.

(Introducing a risqué costume number)
Wait till you see these costumes; they just arrived here this morning from Paris. They were brought over here by a carrier pigeon.

—That's a pretty barbed-wire dress you have on, Mary.
—What do you mean, barbed wire?
—Oh, it protects the property but does not obstruct the view.

Dancers

She's a great dancer. Wait till you see the way she kicks the back of her head. I think that's what's the matter with her.

These girls are wonderful toe dancers. When I say they're toe dancers, I don't mean they have to depend on their toes for a living. They each have a couple of heels to fall back on. I'm not one of them.

These boys are the greatest dancers in the country. They may not be so hot in the city, but in the country, oh boy!

I say this boy is a great dancer. Recently he took part in a big ensemble dance at Madison Square Garden. There were fifty fellows dancing at one time and he was the only one in step.

This is a special dance arrangement. It's for married couples only. Therefore it'll be very short.

Twins

(Two girls enter dressed alike.)
The one in the red dress is the older.

Are they cute? We should call them the tonsil sisters. Everyone wants to take them out.

I think they're twins. I'm not positive of both of them, but I'm sure the one on the right is.

These kids are really twins. I know both of their mothers. They're not only twins, they're sisters, too.

These kids are twins and they both have the same name. Both of their names are Agnes, except Helen. Her name is Jenny.

LETTERS

Today, I received the following letter. "The other night, I brought my mother-in-law to see your show and she nearly died laughing. I am inviting her again, so, for God's sakes, be hilarious."

(Variation)
I received a letter. "Dear Mr. Lowry, My wife (*or* mother-in-law) has just seen your show and says, if you sing again, she will pack up and leave. Enclosed you will find fifty dollars. Let your conscience be your guide."

I received the following letter. "Dear Eddie, Since you went away, a barber has come to live at our house. He is very good-looking and very nice to me. Last night, he bought me a pair of silk stockings and took me out to the pictures. He expects to be here till you get back. May God bless you and keep you from your loving wife."

(A man enters reading a letter.)
He: The scoundrel! To write like that to me! How insulting!
(He angrily tears the letter into tiny pieces.)
She: What does it say?
He *(throwing the pieces on the floor):* Just read that!

Louie: I'm terribly burned. I've been insulted.
Ed: Insulted by whom?
Louie: By our momma.
Ed: Why, our momma is three thousand miles away.
Louie: Yeah, well, a letter came this morning addressed in Mom's writing. I opened it. It was written to you. Do you understand?
Ed: Yes, but where does the insult come in?
Louie: In the P.S. that's where it came in. It said. "P.S. Louie, don't fail to give this letter to Eddie."

MC BIZ

See that fellow? A woodpecker caught him without his hat.

I see by tomorrow morning's paper that this show is a terrific success.

I was in Hollywood for a long time and finally made up my mind to come east—and make a personal disappearance.

A fellow came to the door and said, "Does Mr. Lowry live here?" My mother said, "Yes, bring him in."

I went to a fancy party. The only way you could tell the guests from the waiters was that the waiters were sober.

I'm very much in demand. Three companies after me: the telephone company, the gas company, and the insurance company.

I want to mention that it's illegal to send threatening letters through the mail. I hope my tailor is in the audience.

Funny how people get attached to you in this town. I wasn't here five weeks before I was attached. First my car, then the furniture, then the house.

I've got swell friends. They're so glad of my success in the windy city that they sent me a telegram. "We hope you remain in Chicago for a long time. Your friends in New York."

I was invited to a luncheon today at *(give some location)*. They did it up right. *(With a great flourish, he pulls out a handkerchief, and spoons fall on the floor. He looks around, embarrassed.)* Say, there should be a salt cellar some place.

(Variation)
I was invited to a luncheon today but I'll be darned if I can remember where. I just can't think of the place. *(He reflects for a moment. Then he pulls a spoon out of his pocket and looks at it.)* Oh yes, I ate at the *(give the location)*.

The MC holds up a check and asks if there's a Mr. So and So in the house. A fellow shouts. The MC asks him if this is his handwriting. The fellow says he can't see it from there. The MC stretches the check. "Now can you see?"

(Harry Lauder Telephone Gag: The telephone rings.) Hello! Who? Harry Lauder! Well for the love of mike, what are you doing here? Do you a favor? I'll be delighted. What is it? What? No, I couldn't do that. No, I'm sorry, it wouldn't be fair to the management. That's too bad. If you're sore, use Sloan's Liniment. Well, I won't do it. Goodbye. *(Hangs up)* Well, can you beat that guy? He wants me to leave the receiver off the hook, so he can listen in to the show!

Chat-up Lines and Flirting

He: Gee, you look like a million dollars.
She: Yes, and I'm just as hard to make.

She: Stop it! What kind of girl do you think I am?
He: Give me time, I'm trying to find out.

She: Say, Freshie, I'd like to be your mother.
He: I'll speak to the old man about it.

He: Do you want to be the kind of girl men look up to?
She: No, I want to be the kind of girl men look round at.

She: I wouldn't walk a step for the best man on earth.
He: You don't have to; you've got him right with you.

He: I think I've got a flat tire.
She: I think that makes us even.

She: Pardon me, I've got indigestion.
He: Acute indigestion?
She: Oh, now, all the boys say that.

She: I've taken up selling as a sideline. Do you think I could interest you in a Ford?
He: You . . . you could interest me any place.

He *(at eleven P.M.):* Did you know I could imitate any bird you can name?
She: No, I didn't. Can you imitate a homing pigeon?

He: So you won't go out with me?
She: No, I like a man who has known hardship, the outdoor life, hunger, and despair.
He: Oh, I get ya. You want a bum.

He: Say, you're a good looking kid, you know it?
She: Aw, you'd say that even if you didn't think it.
He: Well, that makes us even, 'cause you'd think it even if I didn't say it.

He: Say, that's a nice pair of stockings you have on.
She: Yes, I got them in Paris. They cost only two dollars a pair and over here you couldn't touch them for less than ten dollars.
He: How did you know what I was thinking?

She: What's the matter with your jaw?
He: A girl I was with last night cracked a smile.
She: What has that got to do with your jaw?
He: It was my smile she cracked.

She *(fresh):* Hello, baby!
He: Say, I don't know you.
She: Haw, come on, sweet daddy.
He: I'm growing fast.

He: I suppose you're like all the rest of 'em—hungry.
She: Well, I would like a bite.
He: Where, on the back of the neck? (*Or to bandleader:* Say, Joe, come and give this lady a bite on the back of the neck.)

He: Give me your phone number and I'll call you up.
She: Oh, it's in the phone book.
He: Splendid, I'll call you. What's your name?
She: That's in the phone book, too.

He: I'm crazy about you. Have you ever kissed a man before?
She: Yes.

He: Tell me who he is; I'll thrash him.
She: Don't try, he may be too many for you.

She: I can read your mind like a book.
He: No, you can't.
She: Yes, I can.
He: All right, then, go ahead and slap my face.

She: Stop! Don't do that! Stop, leave me alone. Stop! If you do,
I'll scream. Stop!
He: What is this? What do you think you're doing—sending a
telegram?

*(The MC gives a girl a bouquet. She throws her arms around him, kiss-
ing and hugging him. He breaks away and starts to leave.)*
She: Oh, gee, I'm sorry. Are you running away 'cause I offended
you?
He: Don't be a sill. I'm going for more flowers.

She: Just imagine, Eddie, to think that I'm the first girl you ever
said that to!
Ed: Yes, darling, isn't it wonderful?
She: Yes, and to think that you think I believe that.

Ed: The last time I went to Coney Island I flirted with a girl, and
she called a policeman.
Man: You're lucky. The last time I flirted with a girl she called a
clergyman.

He: Who gave you that flower?
She: I don't know if I should tell you.
He: Come on, tell me.
She: Well . . . it was a certain boy in your band.
He: Say, none of those boys are certain.

He: Oh, what I could do to you.
She: Oh, and what I could do to you.
He: Just what do you mean?
She: I don't mean what you think I mean.
He: What do you think I think you mean?
She: Do you think I think what you think you think?
He: Oh, what I could say to you.
She: Oh, what I could say to you.
He: If I wasn't afraid of you, I'd kiss you.
She: You mean like this? *(The girl kisses the man, who falls into a
trance.)* I know exactly what you're thinking about. *(This statement
shakes the man out of his trance.)* You're thinking of taking me to
Mamaroneck, spending a nice weekend, having a lovely time
swimming, and enjoying the pleasures of life.
He: No, I wasn't thinking of that, but it's a damn good idea.

Clothing

See this suit . . . comes from Paris . . . made by Shmattay.
[*Shmattah* in Yiddish means "rag."]

I like these pants. Of course they are a little shabby, but you can't
get pants in a restaurant.

The MC pulls up his socks three times. The third time, he thumps
his leg and says, "Now swell."

How do you like this suit? It looks good, doesn't it? Can you
imagine that someone suggested I should rent a dress suit? But
why should I when I have one that looks as though it were
rented?

Reach down and plant the idea that your sock is coming down:
roll it and adjust it a couple of times just to plant the idea that
the sock is there. After the idea is well planted, pull up your trouser leg and discover that the sock isn't there. (Or pull up the
other trouser leg and mug surprise at having no sock there.)

(A woman performer enters and rags the MC.)
Woman: You look like a bum. Look at those socks! *(The MC
removes his socks.)* Look at that suit! *(He removes his coat.)* What
a terrible tie! *(He removes his tie.)* That shirt is awful! *(She pulls the
shirt off him.)* Hey, get a look at those pants.
MC *(dropping his pants):* You call me a bum? Now come on: show
us what you've got!

—Gee, Estelle, you look sweet. Boy, you look sweet enough to eat.
—I do eat, Eddie.
—No, no, I mean the dress, it looks marvelous. Is that one of
those Paris creations?
—Yes, I got it at the Galleries Lafayette.
—Get a load of my suit. Just because you're here, I got all decked
out in my confirmation suit; and it isn't rented. I bought it on
the mezzanine of the Boston Flea Market.
—Why didn't you rent one?
—Why should I, when I have this suit that looks just like a
rented one?

Compliments, Fishing for

—Eddie, Eddie, do you love me?
—I'll say.
—Do you think I'm beautiful?
—Uh huh.
—Are my eyes the loveliest you've ever seen?
—Yep.
—My mouth like a rosebud?

—Sure.

—And my figure divine?

—Uh huh.

—Oh Eddie, you say the nicest things. Tell me some more.

Dating

She: I have a surprise for you this evening. I've prepared a nice supper for us both and I want you to come out to my house after the show.

Ed: Really? Well, Myrtle, that's darn nice of you.

She: You bet. It is nice of me. I'm a nice girl.

Ed: I'll say you are. You're a real nice girl.

She: Yeah, a real nice girl. Now you won't want to come.

Ed: Say, if you're blue it's your own fault. Every time I see you, I ask you to go out with me, and you refuse. Why is that?

She: Oh, Eddy, I don't know.

Ed: Well, if you don't go out with me this time, they'll be dragging the river for my body—but they won't find me.

She: How do you mean? Why won't they find you?

Ed: 'Cause I'll be home in bed.

(Variation)

She: I'll certainly not go out with you, and that's final!

Ed: All right, then, tomorrow night they'll be dragging the river for my body, but they'll not find me.

She: What do you mean? Why not?

Ed: Because I'll be home in bed.

Debts

(Settling a hundred dollar debt. Start to pay off.)

Ed: Five dollars, ten, fifteen, twenty. How old are you?

Man: I'm thirty.

Ed: Thirty, thirty-five, forty . . . how old is your father?

Man: He's fifty-five.

Ed: Fifty-five, sixty . . . how old is your grandfather?

Man: He's eighty.

Ed: Eighty-five, ninety-five, a hundred.

Drinking

Off Stage: two shots

She: What's that?

He: My father. He always takes a couple of shots before he goes to bed.

Fan Mail

She: Ed, I'll tell you a secret if you'll promise not to tell the sponsor.

Ed: I won't tell.

She: I've been writing half your fan mail.

Ed: You have? Well, I'll tell you a little secret, too, if you'll promise not to tell the sponsors.

She: What?

Ed: I've been writing the other half!

Fast Women

She: Put your arms around me, make love to me, kiss me, hug me . . .

Ed *(nervous):* Please, don't be like that.

She: Oh, Eddie, squeeze me. Press me to you. Why can't you make love to me, Eddie?

Ed: Well, you see, it's just that . . . I don't know if I should.

She *(tough):* Listen, didn't your ma tell you anything?

Fitness

She: One thing about you, Eddie, you always look fit and well. That girlish figure . . . how do you manage it?

Ed: Well, since you ask, I'll tell you the secret. It's all due to swimming.

She: Swimming keeps you like that?

Ed: Absolutely! It is the finest exercise in the world; you use every muscle in your body when you swim. Just look at all the finest swimmers in the world, Ederle and Weissmuller, for example. They all have wonderful physiques and fine figures—and they all swim.

She: Yes, but did you ever get a look at a duck?

Infidelity

Man *(enters):* Mr. Lowry, I have something terrible to tell you. I just saw your wife off stage in the arms of a stranger.

Ed: You did, eh? *(He exits and returns.)* Say, you're wrong. That's no stranger, that's my cousin.

Man: Oh, and I suppose if she told you it's the cow that brings the milk to your house, you'd believe her.

(Or he comes back rubbing his hands after firing two shots off stage. "Well, now I'm a widower.")

Insults

He: I followed the chimpanzee act and got a great reception.

She: Yeah, the audience thought it was the chimp back for an encore.

Ed: I understand you said that I was the most naturally good-looking man at the party.

She: That's what I like, plain Ed Lowry. No after-shaving lotion, no powder, no facial massage. None of those things for beauty. No sir, you just wear a mask.

Kissing

(The MC is making up to a girl.)
MC: I don't know what people see in pawing over a girl like you. I bet some of them kiss you like this. *(He kisses her.)* Think that means anything to me? You bet your life it does!

Ed: Give me a little kiss. *(The girl doesn't move.)* Aw, come on, give me a little kiss. *(She remains motionless.)* Didn't you hear me, give me a kiss. *(The same)* Say, are you deaf?
She: No, are you paralyzed?

Ed: I've been working on a picture all day, and am I tired. The most trying part of the day was when I tried to kiss the leading lady.
She: What was wrong with that, Ed?
Ed: I wasn't in the scene!

She: Are you going to kiss me?
He: Well, since you say it like that . . . but tell me, why do you want me to kiss you?
She: Well, I want to be able to brag to the girls back home. If I tell them I kissed you, it will be a feather in my cap.
He: Come on, I'll make you into an Indian Princess.

She *(running out on stage):* Oh, Ed, a big fat man just tried to squeeze me in the alley.
Ed: What's that? A big fat man? Wonder who that was.
She: His name is Sam Watson.
Ed: Here, what's this? How do you happen to know his name?
She: Well, don't you think I can read? *(She pulls out a watch.)*

He: I've been learning magic since you were last here. I'll bet you a nickel I can kiss you without touching your lips.
She: I'll bet you can't.
He: All right, it's a bet.
(He kisses her on the lips.)
She: Aha, you touched me.
He: Aw, you win your nickel.

She: And if I sit over in that nice dark corner with you, will you promise not to hug me?
He: Yes.
She: And will you promise not to kiss me?
He: Yes.
She: And will you promise not to . . .
He: Yes.
She: Then what do you want me to go over there for?

He: Do you like to neck or pet?
She: No.
He: Well, tell me, what would you do if I reached over and gave you a little kiss?
She: I'd scream.
He: Oh yeah?
(He grabs the girl, kisses her passionately, and then lets her go. She very feebly whispers.)
She: Whoopee.

Lies and Liars

He: Do you smoke?
She: I should say not.
He: Do you drink?
She: No, I don't.
He: Do you pet?
She: No, I don't.
He: Do you kiss?
She: Of course not!
He: I know what you do do.
She: What? Tell me.
He: You tell lies.

Love

She: Tell me—how much do you care for me?
He: Well, now that you ask me, I can't exactly tell you, 'cause love isn't one of those things you can weigh. But I care for you a whole lot.
She: But tell me, would you go through any danger for me? Would you? Would you go through fire and water for me?
He: Hey, wait a minute! If that's the sort of guy you want, you'd better get a fireman.

Mothers-in-Law

(A man comes running across the stage.)
MC: Where are you going?
Man: My mother-in-law is terribly sick from eating cucumbers.
MC: Well, are you rushing for a doctor?
Man: Doctor, hell, I'm going for some more cucumbers.

Pertness

When a cute kid like you gets as fresh as you do someone ought to put you right over their knee and spank you. Furthermore, I'd like to be the one to do it!

Secrets

—She told me that you told her the secret I told you not to tell her.

—I told her not to tell you I told her.
—Well, don't tell her that I told you she told me.

Man: Mr. Lowry, I've just come here secretly.
Ed: Yes?
Man: On a very secret mission.
Ed: Yes, yes.
Man: I've got a secret order for you.
Ed: What is it?
Man: I can't tell you, it's a secret.

Sex

(The MC and a girl are in a tight embrace. A woman enters.)
Woman: Excuse me, I didn't mean to intrude.
MC: Oh that's all right. Peggy and I were just reminiscing.
Woman: Oh, is that what they call it now?

—I went out riding with a girl yesterday.
—And?
—Well, I asked her for a little hug.
—And what did she say, Ed?
—She said, "I thought so."
—Well?
—I got a little further and asked her for a kiss.
—What did she say?
—She said, "I thought so."
—Oh, Ed . . .
—A little further and I asked for a hug and a kiss.
—What then?
—Do you really want to hear the rest?
—I thought so!

Stupidity

She: Is that a fresh chrysanthemum you have in your coat?
He: That's not a chrysanthemum, that's a carnation.
She: No, Eddie, you're wrong, it's a chrysanthemum.
He: You're crazy, it's a carnation. Well, how do you spell chrysan-
themum, anyhow?
She: I guess you're right: it's a carnation.

MELODRAMAS

Tradition

Through the darkness, through the blinding snow, she struggled
on, each struggling footstep a heart-rending effort. Wild thoughts
surged through her brain. Her father, her mother . . . were they
still alive? Would they forgive and forget? Would they? At last.
The old home. The old door. She stumbled on . . . to collapse in
a faint on the threshold. "My daughter!" sobbed her mother.

"Mother!" murmured the girl. "Where . . . where is your child?" demanded her father. "Father," she stammered, "I . . . I have no child." "No child?" shrieked the old man. "Ain't you got no respeck for tradition?" And the old man booted her back into the cold, cold night.

Late Delivery

A mother is telling her little girl how long it's been since her father left them. The girl asks her mother whether she would like to have her father return. The mother hedges her answer and indicates that she and her husband had a troubled marriage. At that moment, a burglar enters and backs into the room. The woman screams; he turns; and they recognize each other. "My God, my husband," she says; and he replies, "My wife!" He tells her he's going to shoot her at the count of three. Then she'll be dead and out of his way forever. He counts one, two, and then the little girl jumps between them. He recoils and asks who she is. The mother tells him that she is his daughter who arrived shortly after he left. Blackout. In the next scene, a barroom, the men are drinking and carousing. A woman rushes in and whips out a gun. One man turns round and says, "My wife!" She says, "My husband! But you won't be for long, because I came to kill you. When I count three, you'll be dead: one, two—" A little boy suddenly jumps between them. She shows surprise and asks her husband who this person is. He tells her, "That's your son, he came just after you left."

MONOLOGUES

The Candle

A travelling man knocked at the door of a farmer's house, and an old man, with a protruding upper lip, came to the door. The travelling man, who talked out of the left side of his mouth, asked for a room, and the old man said, "I don't know if we have one, but I'll call my wife and she'll tell you." The old man called his wife, an old German woman, with a long under lip, and asked her, "Have we got a room for this young man?" The old lady said, "Sure, I think we can take him in. Come inside and our boy will show you up to your room." She called her son, who talked out of the right side of his mouth. He got a lighted candle and showed the travelling man to his room. The boy asked the salesman if everything was okay. The man said yes, and the boy left the candle and departed. After undressing, the man tried to blow the candle out. *(Mime the action.)* He couldn't get it to extinguish, so he called the boy back and asked him to blow the candle out. The boy tried *(biz)* but couldn't; so he called his mother and she tried *(biz)*. She couldn't either; so she called in the old man and he tried *(biz)*. When he failed, the salesman said, "Oh, T'ell with it, let it burn."

Exaggerating

From now on, there's going to be no shouting about the shows and telling lies about what the attractions are. No exaggerations. I'm going to be truthful. You are my friends, and I'm not going to lie to you. I'm not going to announce that our Amazon contraltos are petite little sopranos. If they're good, I'll give it this *(thumbs up)*; if not, I'll give it this *(thumbs down)*. I'm not going to lose my friends through lying about the shows. Let *(cite local sponsor)* look after themselves. *(Off stage:* "Hiss, hiss.") What's this? Is there a snake in the house? Oh, a wire! *(He takes the telegram.)* Let's see: "Dear Mr. Lowry, we intend to raise your salary if the crowds warrant it." Say, that's fine. *(He comes down stage full of enthusiasm.)* Now, folks, you're going to see the greatest show on earth. Last week we had the greatest dancer on earth. Well, this week we have one who's even better.

The Flea

Consider the flea. It has, as you may be quite surprised to learn, its prejudices, desires, ambitions, and Freudian complexes. It even has its own sex life. Take, for example, a young, adolescent, male flea. There's the rub. This particular flea is going about his business on a nice white doggie. Suddenly he passes a young lady flea of his own age. You know the type—short skirts and painted lips and pretty legs, etc. He tips his hat and she gives him that what-are-you-waiting-for look. In a sec, the poor flea falls for her and off they start, picking their way carefully between the nice white hairs of Mrs. Zilch's nice white doggie. Of course she says she hasn't been kissed before. Pretty soon they get tired of kissing, so the question arises, what next? Plenty, brother, plenty. They walk some more until they get to a very furry part of the nice white doggie. This is known to the fleas as the woods. Well, they kiss a little more and get tired of it again. That's all, except that in a very short while the nice white doggie starts to scratch very hard. *Very* hard.

A Goiter

I'll tell you how I happened to become an actor. I was in love with a girl—crazy, daffy about her. She said the man she married would have to buy her a string of genuine pearls. She had a peculiar weakness for pearls. I went from town to town always with one thought in mind: this string of pearls. Each time I got enough money I would buy one pearl for the necklace. Finally I had a string just big enough to fit tightly around her neck. It measured so closely it would just barely clasp together. I'll never forget that last night. I finished in *(local town)*, jumped on the train, all the while picturing myself putting this beautiful necklace around her neck. When we reached the station I jumped into a cab, arrived at her house, dashed up the stairs, rang that bell, and when she opened the door . . . she had a goiter!

Hard Times

(A man enters eating an apple.)
Nothing like helping a worthy cause. A fellow down the street was stuck with a whole barrel of apples, so he gave me three for a nickel. Funny what a lot of trouble an apple caused. Don't remember the details. I was really only a kid at the time. I think Adam told Eve he was going to take a bite of the apple and she said, "I don't care A-Dam." It wasn't the apple that caused the trouble, it was a green pear. Really, conditions are tough all over. Midgets are even selling crab apples. In Chicago the gangsters are selling pineapples. I saw a fellow yesterday who had only two apples left and he wanted me to buy them, but I didn't. I figured if I bought his last two apples, he'd be unemployed again.

Ima Hound

I couldn't sleep last night on account of lying awake. But I'm glad I did stay awake because I wrote a great drama—a real drama—called *The Miracle. (To the bandleader)* You're in it, Dave. The opening scene shows Dave buying drinks for all the boys in the band—the miracle! The girl in the show is the heroine. Her name is Ima Hound. Now Ima is a pure little girl who has never had any experience except the eight or nine times she was out with fellows in the band. Last night she was out with Dave, and now she's experienced. There comes into Ima's life Brigham Young's nephew, Gettem. This Gettem Young is a professional tattooer, and he has evil designs on Ima. One night, he comes to Ima's house. I had better describe the house first. It's one of those places where if you want to go from the kitchen to the dining room, or from the living room to the parlor, you stay right where you are. Well, Gettem comes there one night and asks for Ima's hand. But the old man gives him the boot. He says, "Go and make your fortune, then you can marry my daughter." So Gettem packs his clothes and jumps on a train for New York. Now there is another fellow who loves Ima. His name is Herbie Halitosis, and Ima loves him, but he doesn't know it. Even his best friends won't tell him. He's an architect, and naturally he has plans. He sneaks up one night and kidnaps Ima. He holds her for ransom, but Ransom doesn't show up. They are sitting around without anything to do, so they get married. Then we have Pathos. Gettem hasn't been able to get employment in New York, so he opens a shoeshine stand. The scene shifts back to Utah and shows Gettem's father, old man Young, working in the hayfields. On the other side of the stage it shows Gettem shining shoes. The play has a moral. Yes, sir, it shows the old man making hay while the son shines. But everybody in New York has started wearing overshoes, and business is poor for Gettem, and he isn't making any money, and he is hungry, so the curtain comes down with a roll.

Herbert Hoover

American farmers were doing pretty well till Congress started to give them relief. Then Europe. They were doing pretty well, and we gave them relief and put a stop to their progress. I went to a banquet to entertain President Hoover. He spoke to me; he said, "Get out of my way." Finally, he recognized me and I told him a couple of jokes. He got hysterical. Just picture Hoover or Coolidge getting hysterical. *(Sudden laugh and then deadpan)* The president got up to talk. As soon as he opened his mouth, two moths flew out. The banquet hall—what a place! You couldn't tell the waiters from the guests, except the waiters were coherent. Hoover said the depression had cost us three billion dollars. I don't think it was worth that much. One thing we can boast about is that the Reds didn't get into the government—but the government got into the red.

Mexico

It used to be that in Mexico they'd elect a president in the morning, murder him in the afternoon, and bury him at night. The newspapers would print the election and the death notice in the same issue. It's no longer possible for a president to hide in Mexico; all the hiding holes have been used up. Most times down there half the people are out in the streets fighting and the other half are in the house hiding, afraid to come out. I wasn't afraid. I just didn't care to come out. I'm not interested in politics. I used to read the paper three times a day to see who was president. Politics are different in Mexico. A president down there has always to run twice—once for president and once for his life. The faster he can run the longer he lives. *(Or:* the longer he's president)

The Moth and the Flame

The setting for this story is a swank clothing store on Franklin Avenue. It's strictly a one-price place, but no reasonable offer is ever refused. In the opening scene, you see a little boy playing on the sidewalk with matches, and his daddy says, "The street is not the place to play with matches; if you must play with matches, come inside the store." The place operates under the name of Goodfriend, Goodfriend, Goodfriend, and Brother. Now Izzie Goodfriend became bad friends with the other Goodfriends. He went to the three Goodfriend brothers and he said, "I'm going to buy you out, sell you out, or kick you out. Tomorrow Izzie Goodfriend starts in business together with himself alone." It seems Izzie caught Sam cheating in a poker game. Sam said, "How do you know I cheated?" and Izzie said, "Don't be silly, I know what cards I dealt you." Anyhow, Izzie opens right next door, and he does great business, until the three mean brothers make him take down a sign he had over his door. It read, "Main Entrance." Now comes the sad part of the little playlet. Poor Izzie is suffering because not only is business bad, but he is in the store all by himself. To kill time he plays solitaire. The other three brothers play pinochle, and they won't even allow Izzie to kibitz. One day, during a stretch of bad business, a widow comes into the store to buy a suit to bury her husband in. After Izzie has talked her into buying two pair of pants, they become very friendly. The widow's name is Bella Donna. He gets Bella Donna plastered and she gets stuck on him. Bella gets a job as a hostess in a dance hall where they dance with tears in their eyes 'cause it's ten cents a dance. Now before this scene takes place, three months elapse—so if you folks have any place to go, go ahead. Bella is working very hard, and Izzie notices that every night a different fellow brings her home. So he definitely decides that Bella is a good girl. He proposes, and she accepts with the provision that she won't become Mrs. Goodfriend unless Izzie consents to her continuing her friendship with all her old, good friends. Izzie says that will be okay if she will bring them into his store to buy their suits. Well, business gets so good that Izzie goes around killing fire bugs. He allowed the fire insurance policy to lapse. Now comes the dirty work. The three mean brothers get hold of a trained moth and deliberately send this moth into Izzie's store with malicious intent. It's one of those sentimental moths. It sits around all day and cries. Did you ever see a moth ball? Well, anyhow, while the two mean brothers are chuckling over the havoc the moth is going to create in Izzie's store, Bella makes friends with the moth and trains him so he will sit down only on the buttons. Now one day while Bella is out, Izzie sees the moth squatting on a camel's hair coat, and, as he makes a lunge for the moth, he kicks over the lamp. The place bursts into flames, and the moth flies into the mean brothers' store. Izzie flies out into the street, and yells, "Whoopee!" That's the story of the Moth and the Flame.

Movies

Up and up and up went little Annie McAnnie, eighteen-year-old aviatrix. She was smiling happily at the start. At one thousand feet she still was smiling. The air began to get thinner and she breathed more rapidly. At twenty-five hundred feet Annie's smile began to fade. Soon her lips were clamped tightly together.

Happy confidence was replaced by flickering doubts. These increased as she climbed higher and higher. Once Annie felt dizzy, faint. She felt she could climb no higher. Then she gritted her teeth and kept on. She couldn't give up now. Be a quitter? Not little Annie McAnnie, "The Sweetheart of the Clouds." And then, hardly conscious of what was going on, she knew she was at the top. With a weak sigh she relaxed in the seat. But in a moment she was herself again. "Just about what I might have expected from you!" she snapped to the boyfriend. "The last row in the top balcony! And if there ever was a picture I wanted to see close up it's this one!"

Paul Revere

You all remember reading in your history books how Paul Revere sat in a tavern and guzzled some beer, when suddenly he got an inspiration and leaped on his horse and started riding around town, knocking on doors. History says he knocked on doors all night. But you can't fool me. I know this neighborhood. Someone must have said, "Come in." He was plenty smart. He'd knock on a door, and if a man's voice answered, he'd leap back on his horse and shout, "The Redcoats are coming," and then he'd start galloping again. He'd gallop and gallop until he reached *(cite a local bridge)*, and, as he was crossing the bridge, he looked down into the river, and there he saw George Washington standing up in his canoe. You've seen the picture of Washington crossing the river and standing up in his canoe. He couldn't sit down; his pants were too tight. After a few more minutes of galloping, he landed out in the woods, and there he saw Abe Lincoln's log cabin. He knocked on the door, and the door fell in. Then he yelled, "Hello, Abe," and Abe said, "I'm not here." So he said, "Where are you, Abe?" and Abe replied, "I'm down the road in the mud with a blind pig." Soon as Paul heard "blind pig," which means the same as speakeasy, he galloped down the road, and there he saw Abraham in the mud struggling with a blind pig. Paul walked right into the mud, and the pig got up and walked out. Paul was all covered with mud. He rode on and on till he came to Betsy Ross's shack. He knocked on the door, but she didn't answer. She was busy making a flag or something. And then he heard voices. So he shouted, "Betsy, I know you're there. Why don't you answer?" and that's where those famous lines came from when she said, "Cromwell is here." He said, "Oh, yeah." He broke down the door and started to wrestle with Cromwell, who tore Paul's clothes off him, and that made Paul bearer. *(Aside:* "I just shoved that in.") They got mud all over the floor. Betsy kicked them both out, gathered up all the mud from the floor, opened a beauty parlor, and that was the beginning of the mud pack.

Prohibition

You want I should undress the public? I stand here on a wet *(anti-Prohibition)* platform. *(Steps to one side, as if the platform were actually wet.)* I am for the public and against the people. Take back in the revolution, when Patrick Henry was knocking on all the doors. For what was he knocking? For what? Beer! They fought the revolution for liberty. Then they got the liberty, and we got the Statue. Then came the Great War. The war was warring and the bullets were bulleting and the cannons were cannoning. The flag was flying from the stiff—that is, staff—and while the bugles were bugling what happened? Montreal became America's filling station and all over on the fences they wrote "Drink Canada Dry." Is that fair? Drink Canada dry. I've tried. You can't do it. Then comes the big wind, I mean draught, and everybody gets a uniform and goes over there. They all go over there. And for what? For what they go over there? For what? Beer! And did we get it? No! That's just it. U.S. stands for United Suckers. Over in Germany they have real beer, and we think we won the war. No beer, no work! That's my position.

Reincarnation

Two fellows, very good friends, both believed in the hereafter and reincarnation. One of them died. About ten years later, the surviving friend was walking along the street when a voice called his name, "Jakey!" Now there was only one man who called him Jakey, his pal of years ago. But when he looked around, all he could see was a milk wagon and an old decrepit horse standing with it. He was going to walk on, when again he heard his name called. This time, he walked back a ways. Nearing the horse, he heard the voice say, "Jakey, don't you know me? I'm your pal, Hienie." Jakey said, "Oh my goodness, you've come back as a horse. What's it like being a horse?" Hienie said, "It's terrible! Why, my owner gets me up and out on the streets at six in the morning. I deliver milk till about two or three in the afternoon and then go to work hauling a baggage wagon. I don't get through with that till night, and then I go to the stable to eat oats and other slops." Jakey said, "That's awful! I'm going to talk to your owner, whoever it is, and give him the best telling off he ever had in his life." Hienie replied, "My goodness, don't go tell him I'm your pal, or he'll have me shouting 'Milk!'"

The Three Old Maids

This is a story about three old maids who lived in a hut way out in a dark forest. One day, they went for a walk, and when they had gone, a tramp came to their hut and went in. On the table, he saw three meals that the old maids had set out for when they returned. He tasted one and didn't like it. He tasted the second and didn't like that either. But when he tried the third, he ate it all up. Then he went upstairs to the bedrooms. He went into the first one, but found the bed too hard. Then he went into the second one, and found the bed too soft. He went into the third one and the bed was just right. So he climbed in and went to sleep. The three old maids came home after their walk. The first said, "Someone has been tasting my porridge." And the second said, "Someone has been tasting my porridge." And the third one said, "Someone has eaten mine all up." Then they went upstairs, and the first old maid said, "Aha, someone has been sleeping in my bed!" And the second one said, "Aha, someone has been sleeping in my bed!" And the third one looked into her room and said, "Aha, goodnight, sisters!" [*See under* College *in* part one.]

The Three Sisters

Once upon a time there were three sisters; their dad was a farmer and they lived in a little country village. The girls were named Faith, Hope, and Charity. Things were awfully slow in the village, so Faith left for the big city, where she very soon got a job in a Ziegfeld show. It wasn't long before she was wearing very expensive jewelry, riding around in a Rolls Royce, and living in a lavishly furnished apartment on Riverside Drive. She told Hope how she was doing in the big city, so Hope came to join her sister. Faith went down to the station to meet her. Very soon, Hope was decked out like her sister in the latest fashions, running around town in a Rolls Royce, wearing expensive diamonds, and enjoying a swell apartment on Riverside Drive. One day they got a letter from Charity, who said she wanted to come to the big city to pay the sisters a visit. So they both went down to the depot in their Rolls Royce cars to meet Charity. When the train came in, Charity got off dripping in furs and jewels and wearing a Parisian dress. Although she announced that she was planning to stay just a week, she had four maids with her, sixteen hand grips, and fifteen trunks. The moral of this story is, Charity began at home.

PROVERBS ILLUSTRATED

(Done with Mr. Alton and Miss Lewis)
(A woman walks across the stage and meets a man. She mimes a vamp routine, salaciously looking over the man. The man does a double take, grabs for a pair of glasses, puts them on, and stares at the girl. Blackout.)
MC: Four eyes see more than two.

(A boy is showing a girl in a short skirt how to do cartwheels and roll-overs.)
He: That's the way. It's easy. Now show me what you've learned.
She: Oh, I can't in this dress.
He: That's all right. I don't care. Do some turns for me.
(The girl turns and the boy watches, getting an eyeful. Blackout.)
MC: One good turn deserves another.

(A woman is seated on a sofa reading. A man enters.)
He: Good evening, Mrs. Katz. Is Mr. Katz in?
She: No, Mr. Katz is away.
He: Sweetheart!
She: Darling! *(They embrace.)*
(Blackout)
MC: When the cat's away the mice will play.

(A man is holding a telephone and calling for a number.)
He: Hello, give me Jefferson five thousand. Jefferson five thousand. No, no, I did not say Evergreen. Jefferson, Jefferson! Hello? Hello, who is this? What? The morgue? For heaven's sake. Operator, operator, give me Jefferson five thousand. No, Jefferson, you dumbbell! . . . I did not say go to hell. I want Jefferson, J as in joke, E as in egg, F as in fool, F as in fiddle. Five like five fingers. Oh, oh, oh. Hello, hello, hello? What's that? There's something wrong with my number? What the devil do I have to ring it again for? I want Jefferson five thousand. Jefferson five thousand! Hello, hello? Who is this? What? This IS Jefferson five thousand! My God! *(Dies.)*
(Blackout)
MC: If at first you don't succeed, try, try, again.

ROUTINES OF JOKES STRUNG TOGETHER

(Done with Catherine Wright)
He: You thought I wouldn't recognize you. You're little Elsie Schultzenheim! Don't you remember when we used to go to school together?
She: Remember? I should think I do. Do you remember those little hats I used to wear?
He: Uh, huh.
She: And those little sailor blouses?
He: Uh, huh.
She: And remember those funny little shoes I used to wear?
He: Uh, huh.
She: And those little red panties, do you remember?
He: So you really are little Elsie Schultzenheim!

He: You're just the kind of girl I'd like for my wife.
She: Well, tell your wife she can't have me.

He: I'm not married. I mean . . . you're the kind I'd like to marry.
She: You don't want to marry me. I'm a vampire.
He: You're a what?
She: A vampire.
He *(hugging her):* That's all right, you go to your church and I'll go to mine.
She: No, I am a vampire, a woman who ruins men's souls.
He: So what? My dad's a shoemaker.
She: But are you in a position to get married?
He: No, but I can get into a position. *(He bends over.)*
She: Oh, Eddie.
He: Come on, marry me. I won't be home much.

(Done with Grace Johnson, March 15, 1929)
He: You know, Grace, you're a very distinctive tripe—sorry, I mean type. Don't think I'm being personal, but what nationality are you?
She: Well, Ed, I'll tell you. My mother was Spanish and my dad was Irish; and I was born in New Orleans.
He: Good heavens, how did you all get together?
She: Oh, but Ed, I'm so hungry. Boy, I'm so hungry I could eat a doorknob.
He: Well, Grace, if I had a doorknob I'd give it to you.
She: Oh, but Ed, I'm really hungry. Take me out someplace to eat.
He: No, sirree. I should feed 'em and fatten 'em for someone else to take? No, I'm finished with all that. Feed 'em and some one takes 'em away from you. Keep 'em thin and they stick to you.
She: But Ed, you couldn't be an Airedale.
He: Come on, let's stop talking about food. Let's get silly. Let's play post office.
She: Post office? Why, that's a kid's game.
He: Not the way I play it.

(Done with Marie Welsh)
He: Say, that's a nice dress you have on *(he feels the material)*—a very pretty dress.
She: Oh, this is just a cheap little thing I picked up. It cost only five hundred dollars.
He: Lord and Taylor have mercy, and glory be to Famous and Barr.
She: That's a very nice suit you have on.
He: You really like it? Oh, it's just an old bit of tweed. It only cost a thousand dollars.
She: Well, it's very good for the money. Say, Ed, don't you think clothes give one confidence?
He: I certainly do. I go lots of places with them on that I wouldn't go with them off.
She: How do you like these stockings? I got them in Paris. They

only cost two dollars over there, and here you couldn't touch them for less than fifteen dollars.

He: Say, how did you know what I was thinking? (*Or:* how did you know what was on my mind?)

(Done with Grace Johnson, March 9, 1929)
He: If you have lonely nights it's your own fault. Why is it you are never at home when I phone you?

She: Just born lucky, I spose.

He *(embraces her):* Grace, there is something I want to ask you.

She: What is it?

He: Is it proper for a girl to hold her sweetheart's hand in the parlor with the lights turned down low? *(Repeats the question.)* Well, it's not only proper, but sometimes it's necessary. *(She slaps the man's face.)* Say, are you from Chicago?

She: And what if I am? Does it make any difference where I am from?

He: It certainly does. In Chicago, the girls make boom and faw down. But in St. Louis, they faw down and make boom. *(Or vice versa)*

She: I'm going to sing a song: "I'd Rather Be Blue Over You."

He: Than black and blue over somebody else.

She: Do you know the difference between a good-looking girl and a horse?

He *(puzzled):* No, what is the difference?

She: I bet you have some great dates.

Ed: Now we have a little girl here by the name of Sugar. She is sweet—and refined. I hear you're from the South. Guess you feel the cold up here.

Sugar: You're right.

Ed: Have you ever been ice skating?

Sugar: No.

Ed: Well, you don't know what you've been missing. Right after the show we'll go skating. I'll go right out and buy you three skates.

Sugar: But Ed, I've only two feet. What do you mean, three skates?

Ed: Well, you won't be on your feet all the time.

(The girl stands on Ed's foot.)

Ed: I know something you don't know.

Sugar: Oh, tell me what it is.

Ed *(shouts):* You're standing on my foot. *(He pushes her away.)* Here's a little something I have for you. *(He gives her a lollipop.)*

Sugar: Oh, thanks. *(She proceeds to eat it with the paper on.)*

Ed: No, you have to take the paper off and eat it.

(She takes off the paper, throws away the lollipop, and eats the paper.)

(Done with Madeline McKenzie)
(Song Lead-in)
He: How old are you?
She: Sixteen.
He: I beg your pardon?
She: Sixteen, sixteen! I said twice . . . sixteen!
He: Twice sixteen, that's better. Whatever made you take up singing?
She: I just did it to keep the wolf from the door.
He: Well, you could sure keep a whole pack away now.
She: I'd have you know that I played in opera. I was Carmen the Flower of Spain.
He: That's nothing. When I was in opera, I was Gold Medal the Flour of Minneapolis.
She: I studied opera in Europe. Have you been to Europe?
He: Yes, I was over there. I was in Venice. Did you ever go to Venice?
She: Yes, but when I was there the darn place was flooded.
He: Say, that's a nice pair of stockings you have on.
She: I'd like to be your mother, young man.
He: All right, I'll speak to the old man about it.

(Done with Lillian Dawson, in Philadelphia)
She: Eddie, I had a wonderful dream last night, I dreamt about you. I dreamt that you and I were married.
He: Were you happy?
She: Yes, when I woke up.
He: Say, you shouldn't talk like that. Do you remember when we were both in that show together? When we used to take those long moonlit walks? I guess I used to propose to you at least four or five times a week. Remember? And do you remember how you used to refuse me?
She: Yes.
He: Those were the happiest moments of my life.
She: Oh, but Eddie, I'm really in love now. I'm in love with the sweetest boy. He's really good looking.
He: Hey, I don't like the way you said that. You've seen worse looking fellows than me, haven't you? *(No answer)* Say, I'm talking to you. You've seen lots worse looking guys than me?
She: Don't rush me. I'm trying to think.
He: One time you'll talk to me like that and they'll be dragging the river for my body. But they won't find me.
She: Why?
He: 'Cause I'll be home in bed.

(Done with Peggy Bernier)
He: I like that outfit. You look sweet enough to eat.
She: I do eat.

He: I mean, I like that dress.

She: I'm glad you like it. My dad bought it for my eighteenth birthday.

He: Gee, it certainly wears well. Now keep still while I tell the folks about our next act. *(Peggy tries to interrupt.)* Will you go away or else keep still? *(Again she tries to interrupt.)* Please stop that! Go and tell your mother you're a pest.

She: She knows it.

He: Look here, if you don't keep still I'm going to put you over my knee and spank you.

She: Don't be silly. Don't you know it doesn't do any good to spank a girl after she's sixteen?

He: It may not do any good, but it's lots of fun. Say, you're getting older now; you ought to be thinking of your future.

She: I am thinking of my future. I'm going to marry a man with a lot of money.

He: What? Would you marry any fool if he had money?

She: Well, I don't know, Eddie. How much money have you?

(Variation)

(As Ed starts to introduce the show, Peggy runs on and interrupts.)

She: I just couldn't wait.

He: Why did you never reply to any of my letters?

She: I never got any letters from you. And what's more, I didn't like some of the things you said in those letters.

He: Well, as long as you're out here, I've something for you. *(Gives her an apple. She takes a bite out of it. He tries to embrace her. She pushes him away.)* Hey, what's the matter? Don't you like me any more?

She: I never did like you.

He *(snatches apple away)*: Give me that! I'm not going to sling my money around. I should never have given it to you in the first place. You know what trouble an apple caused in the Garden of Eden.

She: It wasn't an apple caused all that trouble, it was a green pear. *(Exits. Then she enters again for another interruption. She is choking a cat and shouting at it.)* Give it to me now! I want it! give it to me!

He: Hey, what are you doing with that cat?

She: Well, I just heard the stagehands playing cards and they said there's eight dollars in the kitty. *(To cat)* And I want it. Give it to me! *(Exits shaking the cat.)*

Autograph

Girl: Oh, Mr. Lowry, will you give me your autograph?

Ed: Say, you don't want my autograph. You ought to go after

some big man, some famous person. That's the kind of auto-
graph you ought to have.
Girl: I know that, but things are so tough these days you've got
to take what you can get.
Ed: All right, give me the book. Say, what's your name?
Girl: Bobbie, but people call me Bob for short.
Ed: Okay, Bob. How do you spell that, with two o's? Say, I'll bet
you'd like to be on stage, wouldn't you? (*Or:* I'll bet you'd like to
be an actor, wouldn't you?)
Girl: Yes; so would you, I guess.
Ed: Do you go to school?
Girl: Yes, I'm in the seventh grade. I've been in the seventh grade
four years now.
Ed: What? You've been in seventh grade four years? How old
are you?
Girl: Nineteen.
Ed: Nineteen and in the seventh grade? Don't you want to go up
to the eighth grade?
Girl: Well, I do, but you see my dad's in the eighth, and I
wouldn't want to move up and embarrass him.

(Done with Belle Baker)
She: I'm coming up to your house tonight.
He: I wasn't expecting you.
She: All right, it'll be a surprise. I don't know why I'm so crazy
about you. Maybe it's because you're so handsome—so sweet.
He: I wish I could say the same about you.
She: You could, if you lied as I do. Say, Eddie, are you married?
He: That's my business.
She: How's business? No fooling, Eddie, are you really married?
He: Yes, I'm the proud father of two children.
She: How many rooms have you?
He: A two-room flat.
She: How do you raise them?
He: In the elevator. Say, are you married?
She: Yes, I've been married nine years.
He: Have you any children?
She: I have ten rooms.
He: I said: have you any children?
She: No, no children.
He: What's the matter?
She: The elevator broke.

(Done with Myrtle Gordon, January 1928)
He: Myrtle, I've sure missed you. We haven't been together in
four years.
She: Yes; I was wondering if you still remembered me. Remem-

ber the last time we saw each other, and the gift my dad gave you? Didn't he give you a pair of socks?

He: Yes, one in each eye (or: ear). Well, Myrtle, I'm sure glad to see you back in the (name the theatre).

She: Yes, but that isn't why I came here, just to play _____ Theatre. You know, Ed, when I was playing Scranton, Pa., I went in the stage door to get my mail and left my little boy outside. While I was inside, some gypsies stole him. I heard that he was here in (name the local city), and that's why I'm here.

He: What? Some gypsies stole your boy, and he's here in _____?

She: That's right, Eddie.

He: Is he dark?

She: Yes.

He: Has he got wavy hair?

She: Yes!

He: Does he like music?

She: Yes!

He: Has he a mole on his left shoulder?

She: Yes!

He: Mother! (He embraces her.)

(Done with Ted Leary, at the Academy-NYC and Fox)

(Ed runs on and cuddles with a woman. Ted enters and is clearly upset by what he sees.)

Ted: Pardon me, I hope I'm not interrupting!

Ed: It's all right. Go ahead, you're not bothering us.

Ted: Now look here, Eddie, you've got to admit that since I joined this show a week ago, I've been a pretty regular fellow. You know, I introduced you to my sister, a very sweet girl. Immediately, you went for her hook, line, and sinker. Took her out riding every afternoon on that bike of yours. Took her out slumming to the Warwick Hotel. I didn't bother you, did I?

Ed: Nay, nay, nary a once.

Ted: Hey, what is this, a horse act? And then I introduced you to my cousin.

Ed: Hah, cousina.

Ted: Not cousina. Her name is Rifkila. And you immediately started giving her the rush act: tea dances and bridge parties. One night a policeman looked under the bridge, and there you were, finessing. And then I introduce you to my sweetheart, and what do you do? Never mind, I'll leave that out. Now, I find you making love to my wife. (The woman strikes a pose.) Alas, the same thing happens—the same thing! (He dramatically turns on his heels and starts to exit.)

Ed: So what? I made love to your sister, to your cousina, to your sweetheart, and now to your wife. So what? Don't I appeal to you?

(Done with Grace Johnson)
Ed: You know, Grace, you're a very distinctive tripe, er . . . type. I really looked forward to you coming here, Grace. I just can't wait till we get the show over so's I can run you home in my new car.
Grace: That's sweet of you, Ed, but I live only two blocks down the street.
Ed: All right, we'll go by way of Hackensack. If there's one thing I enjoy, it's driving experienced girls home.
Grace: But Ed, I'm not experienced.
Ed: You're not home yet.
Grace: Well, if you're going to take me home, I may as well tell you that I had a little surprise planned.
Ed: What's that?
Grace: I arranged to have a nice home-cooked supper all ready for you.
Ed: Gee, that's sweet of you, Grace. I just can't wait.
Grace: But remember, Eddie, I'm a nice girl.
Ed: Sure you're a nice girl.
Grace: I repeat, Eddie, I'm a nice girl. Now I guess you won't want to come.
Ed: I never knew you could cook, Grace. What have you pre-pared for supper, a can of salmon?
Grace: Now listen, Eddie, I can cook. In fact, I'd rather be a cook than anything else.
Ed: I'll bet you can't boil water without burning it.
Grace: One thing I can make is toast.
Ed: Any nitwit can make toast; even I can.

(The MC enters with a saxophone and announces that he will accom-pany the woman instrumentalist during the next number.)
He: I'm going to put you over. I'm going to play the song
with you.
She: What is that thing?
He: What do you mean, that thing? What do you think it is, a lavaliere?
She: Are you going to play it?
He: Play it? Of course I'm going to play it. Say, when I play people cheer and scream and applaud vociferously. Women throw children from the balcony. I move people. Now, are you ready? Boys, watch the maestro for the down beat. *(He beats with his foot, starts to play, and repeatedly blows wrong notes on the wrong beat. She plays artistically but is misled by his bad playing. She there-fore keeps shooting him killing looks.)*
He: You're flat. *(She grabs his hand.)* Say, don't do that. It gives a tremolo effect. You take care of the song, and I'll take care of the obbligato. I'm playing for my own amazement.

She *(tries to play again but fails. She gets terribly annoyed):* Say, what
are you playing?
He: I'm blowing in "You Didn't Have to Tell Me" and I'm press-
ing the right keys. What comes out I can't help.
She *(angry):* You've spoiled the song and ruined my appearance
before this audience. I hate you, and I'm through with you, Mr.
Lowry, professionally, socially, and every other way. Goodbye,
Mr. Lowry.
*(As she goes off, the band goes into a vamp of the sax; and as she exits,
the man blows a note after her.)*

(Done with Harriet Hilliard)
She: Say, Ed, I don't know what to do, though I think I ought to
tell you. One of the boys in your band tried to kiss me just now.
He: That's terrible. We must get to the bottom of this. Tell me,
did he succeed in kissing you?
She: No.
He: Then it couldn't have been one of my boys. Say, I like that
ring you have there.
She: Yes, that's an antique. It goes back to my great-great-
grandmother.
He: That's nothing. See this suit? It goes back to my uncle at
the end of the show. What have you got there? *(Points to a bag
of peanuts.)*
She: Oh, these, I'm going to the zoo to feed them to the mon-
keys. Have one.
He: Now, what's the song you're going to sing?
She: _____.
He: I think I should tell the folks what this song is about.
She: Go right ahead.
He: Well, in this song, the scene is a prison. The time is exactly
twelve noon.
She *(coming up behind him):* No, Ed, one o'clock.
He: I said twelve noon.
She *(a little louder):* No, one o'clock!
He: I said, twelve o'clock noon.
She *(shouts):* One!
He: All right, all right! The time is twelve-thirty noon.
She *(screams):* No, ONE!
He: All right, all right! The scene is a prison. The time is one
o'clock. *(He looks at the woman and then says to the audience.)* Day-
light saving time!

(Done with Ilomay Bailey, January 23, 1929)
She: Well, Ed, what sort of a Christmas did you have?
He: It was rather shocking. You might say it was an electric
Christmas. Little brother got an electric train. Sister got electric

curling tongs. Mom got an electric washing machine. And dad got the electric chair. What sort of a Christmas did you have?

She: I was given this for Christmas. *(Displays a ring.)* Isn't that some rock?

He: Rock? I should say that's a monument. Is that an engagement ring?

She: Yes.

He: So, you went away and forgot to remember, eh? Funny thing what time will do, isn't it? Remember when we were kids of fourteen together? You said you'd always love me. Let me see, that's sixteen years ago. Yes, funny thing, now I'm thirty and you're twenty-one.

She: Oh, but Ed, you should see him. He is good looking.

He: You say that funny. Aren't I good looking? You've seen worse looking fellows than me, haven't you? I say, you've seen worse looking fellows than me, haven't you?

She: Don't rush me. I'm trying to think.

He: I don't know why you have to be like that. You know I'm a fellow trying to get ahead.

She: Yes, you need one. But Ed, tell me, have you dated any new girls lately?

He: Yes, I dated one girl I was crazy about, but she gave me the air.

She: Well, d'you let that trouble you?

He: No, I'm just sorry for her. I don't worry about girls. As far as I'm concerned girls are like street cars—there's another one along every minute.

She: Yes, Ed, but you work rather late, and at the hour you leave the theatre, the cars don't run so often.

He: That may be so, but those that run, run much faster.

(Done with Ted Leary at the Academy-NYC and Fox)

Ted: Hey, there, Eddie, I just heard you talking about your brother Lillie.

Ed: No, no, not Lillie, Willie.

Ted: Say, don't tell me. I know him.

Ed: Listen, who are you?

Ted: I'm Leary.

Ed: You're Leary; I'm nervous.

Ted: No, no, that's my name. I'm part of this show.

Ed: Oh, you're Ted Leary! There's such a similarity in the names Leary and Lowry. A fellow stopped me at the stage door just now and told me we looked like brothers. He said I looked like you.

Ted: Somebody said I looked like you? Where is that mug?

Ed: Don't bother. I just killed him.

Ted: Many thanks. Say, was it in Johnstown you got that suit?

Ed: Yeah, thirty-five dollars. How d'ya like it?

Ted: You paid thirty-five dollars for that suit? You could have got a new one for that much money.

Ed: Well, my dog likes it. I don't care whether you do or not. I'm a dog fancier.

Ted: You don't look it.

Ed: Yeah, I have a pip of a pointer.

Ted: Me, I have a wonderful dog. It's this long. *(He holds out his arms.)*

Ed: Oh, it's a dachshund.

Ted: No, Eddie, it's two dogs long and half a dog high.

Ed: Yeah, I know. It's a dachshund.

Ted: I know what kind of a dog it is. It's my dog. I eat with it and sleep with it. It's my dog!

Ed: Tell me, Ted, has your dog got a pedigree?

Ted: Eddie, it isn't that kind of a dog.

Ed: You don't understand. I mean: has your dog a family tree?

Ted: Oh, a family tree? No-o-o, any old kind of a tree'll do.

(Done with Peggy Bernier)

He: That was a nice song, Peggy.

She: I enjoyed singing it, but I don't like dancing to those jazz tunes. It's nothing but hugging set to music.

He: Well, what don't you like about it?

She: The music. You know, I'd like to dance with you.

He: I'm married. You know what bigamy means?

She: Sure, having two wives at one time.

He: That's right. Now can you tell me what word means having one wife?

She: Yeah, monotony.

He: Oh, you're smart.

She: Sure I'm smart.

He: Well, come here, I'm going to see how smart you are. Tell me an important date in history.

She: Sure, the one Anthony had with Cleopatra.

He: You know too much for your age. How old are you?

She: I stopped growing when I was ten years old and I've been the same size six years.

He: That makes you sixteen, doesn't it?

She: Aha, and today I asked the bandleader *(give his name)* how old he is.

He: Yeah? How old is he?

She: He's just eighteen.

He: Let me get this right: you're sixteen, and _____ is eighteen?

She: Yeah, how old are you?

He: I'll be three next Wednesday. It kills me. Remember when we were both kids together? We were both eight years old. Now I'm twenty-six and you're sixteen.

She: Well, you grew up so fast and so big.

He: Yes, I weigh a hundred and seventy-six pounds; and just think, when my father was born he weighed only three pounds.

She: Gee, did he live?

(Done with Phyllis Hoover)

Ed: I was just telling the folks, Phyllis, about us knowing each other.

Phyllis: Yes, that's right. You know I had a dream about you last night, Eddie.

Ed: You did?

Phyllis: Yes, I dreamt you gave me a lovely fur coat.

Ed: You did? Well, you can keep it. Remember when we used to be in that show together?

Phyllis: Yes.

Ed: Remember those long walks we used to take in the moonlight? I guess I proposed to you five times a week. Remember?

Phyllis: Yeah, I remember.

Ed: Aha, I used to ask you to marry me. Remember? And you used to turn me down.

Phyllis: Ah, yes.

Ed: Yes, those were the happiest moments of my life.

Phyllis: Oh, but Eddie, I'm really in love now. I'm in love with the sweetest boy . . . and he's so good looking.

Ed: Hey, I don't like the way you said that. Certainly you've seen funnier looking fellows than me, haven't you? *(Pause)* Hey, I'm talking to you! You've seen funnier looking fellows than me, haven't you?

Phyllis: Don't rush me. I'm trying to think.

Ed: Oh, what I could do to you!

Phyllis: Just what do you mean?

Ed: Aw, I don't mean what you think I mean.

Phyllis: Well, what do you think I think you mean?

Ed: I don't think you think what I think you think you mean.

Phyllis: Oh, what I could say to you.

Ed: Do you know, if I had the nerve, I'd lean right over and give you a kiss.

Phyllis: You mean like this? *(Phyllis kisses Ed.)*

Ed: No-o-o-o-o . . . I mean like this! *(He throws his arms around her.)* Come on, let's slobber!

(Done with Maureen Marseilles)

He: Well, Maureen, I think you're a great girl.

She: Why do you kid me, Ed, talking about me being a nice girl when you had all those bathing beauties here last week. Haven't you any memory?

He: You can't have any fun with a memory.

She: But, Ed, don't you like bathing beauties?

He: I don't know. I didn't bathe any of 'em.

She: But don't tell me you didn't go out with any of 'em. I saw you out with one little peach myself. Didn't I see you in that cafe up in _____ Avenue?

He: Oh, you mean that one where they have music on the window?

She: Yes; well, who was that little peach?

He: That was no peach, that was a grapefruit. Every time I squeezed her, she hit me in the eye. Talking about bathing beauties, I'm going swimming next Sunday. Do you know anything about how to give lessons? I have to give a girl lessons how to swim.

She: Ed, where have you been all your life? You mean to tell me you don't know how to give a girl lessons how to swim?

He: No; I can teach most every other thing, but not swimming.

She: Well, you first go out to the place where you're going to swim.

He: I don't need any lessons what to do on the way out.

She: Then when you get there, you gently take her hand and lead her to the water. When she gets near the water, she will say, "Oh, it's wet!" or something like that.

He: But don't I wear a costume or something? I don't want to wear one of those Uncle Ezra things. *(Mimics bowlegs.)*

She: Yes, you have a costume. And then when you get into the water a little way, you take her hand and say, "Come on, it ain't cold," brave like.

He: Yes, I know. *(Shivers.)* Come on in, it ain't cold.

She: Then you go a little further out.

He: But when do I know I've gone far enough?

She: She'll tell you that.

He: Yeah, but this is my sister I'm taking to swim.

She *(beat):* Oh, just shove her in.

(Done with Evelyn Wilson, February 5, 1932)

(The band plays "Come On, Slowpoke." Ed and Evelyn enter.)

Ed: Evelyn and I started out in this business together. I don't mean monkey business; I mean show business. We were in a show together. We were just kids at the time, weren't we?

Ev: Yes, that's a long time since.

Ed: That must be about ten years since. Remember you were sixteen and I was seventeen.

Ev: Yes.

Ed: Funny, isn't it? Ten years since, and now you're twenty-one and I'm thirty-two. Remember the long walks we used to take together?

Ev: Yes.

Ed: I guess I'm the only guy who ever set out walking.

Ev: Yes.

Ed: And do you remember how I used to propose to you every ten minutes?

Ev: Yes, and I used to turn you down.

Ed: Yes, those were the happiest moments of my life. *(He pretends to run away.)* Oh, what I could do to you.

Ev: Just what do you mean?

Ed: Aw, I don't mean what you think I mean.

Ev: Well, what do you think I think you mean?

Ed: I don't think you think what I think you think you mean.

Ev: Oh, what I could say to you.

Ed: Do you know, if I had the nerve I could lean right over and give you a kiss?

Ev: You mean like this?

(She kisses him.)

Ed: Nooo, I mean like this! Come on, let's slobber.

Ev: Oh, Eddie, I shouldn't do that. You know, I'm engaged to be married to the most wonderful boy . . . and is he good looking.

Ed: I don't like the way you said that. Say, what's the matter with me? You've seen worse looking guys than me, haven't you?

(She pauses, and he repeats the question.)

Ev: Oh, be quiet. I'm trying to think. But Eddie, I'm engaged now to the most wonderful boy in the world.

Ed: Come on, tell me something about this Adonis.

Ev: There's just one thing wrong with him. He's deaf and dumb. He has to make love with his hands.

Ed: Say, he may be deaf, but he's certainly not dumb.

(Done with Myrtle Gordon)

He: Say, where were you this morning? I was looking for you all over the place.

She: Oh, I was hiding myself this morning.

He: Behind what building? Now, _____, I've been thinking it over and I don't think I've been really fair to you this week. When I invited you to my hotel room, there were five other guys sleeping there.

She: No, I don't think you've been fair. You've neglected me something terrible.

He: Well, now I'm going to make up for all that. You've seen that new car of mine, haven't you?

She: That brand new Cadillac? Yes, seven seater, isn't it?

He: Seven seater? I had fourteen in it this morning.

She: Fourteen? Impossible! How did you manage it?

He: Took two trips. But listen, I've had all the springs reinforced, and it will seat five comfortably, so you'll be able to ride okay.

I'm going to take you out riding after the show. We're going to ride and ride and ride, and forget everything.

She: Stop!

He: Don't stop me till we get in the car.

She: Ed, I think it's very nice of you to want to take me out riding. But remember, I don't drink, I don't smoke, AND I don't neck. Now do you want to take me out?

He: I think I'd rather crochet.

She: Anyway, I'm not too eager to go out. Besides, I have another engagement. I'm booked to go to a charity ball.

He: A charity ball? What are you going to do at a charity ball?

She: I'm going to sell kisses.

He: Oh, charity, what sins are committed in thy name! But tell me, what are you going to charge for your kisses?

She: I was thinking about charging a dollar. Do you think it's too much?

He: Oh, I don't know. At those affairs, they expect to be cheated. Well, anyway, here I am. I'll start you off. Give me a kiss and I'll give you a dollar.

She: No, give me the dollar first. I've played these charity affairs before.

He: Aw, come on, you'll get the money. Come on, slobber and I'll give you two dollars.

She: Give me the money first.

He: Come on, don't be a miser. Here's the money. *(He hands her a dollar.)* Now where's the kiss?

She *(she gives him a chocolate Hershey kiss):* There's your kiss.

(He immediately announces her act and walks off disgusted.)

(Song Lead-in. After the first introduction, the MC leads the singer aside. The boys play "Rhapsody in Blue." The MC interrupts.)

MC: Boys, boys, stop that music. "Rhapsody in Blue" . . . I wonder why it is every time two fellows get together with two pianos, they play "Rhapsody in Blue?"

Girl: Well, you see, one of the boys has a friend who has a cousin who has an uncle who has a sister who has a boyfriend who has a nephew who knows George Gershwin.

MC: But "Rhapsody in Blue" . . . that isn't for you. I imagine you singing something romantic. Let me see. I remember you in a picture—"Don Juan"—with John Barrymore.

Girl: Ah, John Barrymore, what an actor!

MC: Yeah, he's good, too. Come on, do one of those romantic scenes with me. Go ahead, emote for me, will you?

Girl: What? So soon?

MC: Yeah, I can't wait.

Girl: I warn you, you'd better not get me started. I'm a vampire.

MC: You're a what?

Girl: A vampire.

MC: All right. You go to your church and I'll go to mine.

(The band plays "Here Comes the Bride." After the wedding number, the MC thanks everyone for attending the wedding.)

MC *(to girl):* Don't you feel funny when you get married? I do.

Girl: You always do. Me, I could find my way to the altar in the dark.

MC: Yes, I remember your last wedding. I was the best man.

Girl: Yeah, I found that out.

MC: You might think you were married a lot in the past, but do you realize this week you're going to be married four times a day? We may as well do it for real. What do you say? Let's get married next Saturday.

Girl: Why next Saturday?

MC: I've got a half day off and I don't know what to do with myself.

Girl: Go away! Don't be silly.

MC: Please, marry me, will ya? Will ya? I won't be home much.

Girl: But are you in a position to get married?

MC: Am I what?

Girl: Are you in a position to get married?

MC: No, but I can get in one. How's this? *(He lies on the floor.)*

Girl: You don't understand. I ruin men's souls.

MC: I should worry—my old man's a shoemaker. Say, listen, if you won't do a love scene with me, will you sing a love song?

Girl: Ah, now you're talking. What would you like to hear?

MC: I wrote a song myself—by Irving Berlin—"How Deep Is the Ocean?" *(To the audience)* Would you like to hear that?

(Cue: she sings.)

(Done with Ilomay Bailey)

He: You and I have to come to some kind of understanding. Is it Buddy or is it me?

She: Why, don't you know, Ed?

He: No.

She: You should. It's Irving.

He: You know you haven't treated me right since you've been here. The last time you were here I gave you a beautiful diamond ring. Where is it?

She: I don't wear it any more.

He: Why not?

She: Because there was a big flaw in it.

He: Well, that proves one thing to me.

She: What's that?

He: I always thought love was blind.

She: Maybe so, but not stone blind.

He: Well, you might at least return it to me. I know someone I could give it to who would appreciate it.

She: Yes, I saw you out with her last night.

He *(to the audience):* Say, didn't she say that dirty? Kitty, kitty, kitty, kitty. If there were three women in the world, two of them would be talking about the other one.

She: Yes, and if there were only three men in the world, do you know what they would be doing?

He: No.

She: Running after those three women.

He: Surely, you do care for me a little, don't you? Say, do you care for olives, all kinds of olives, even those with the little tail lights on them?

She: Yes.

He: Did you always like them?

She: No.

He: Well, then, won't you give me an even break with an olive? Have you ever kissed anyone else? I mean fellows.

She: No.

He: Well, they didn't miss much.

She: Do you think that's nice—to stand out here and talk about me that way? Haven't I always said nice things about you? I tell everyone how nice you are, what a wonderful man you are, how hard you've worked to get where you are. *(To audience)* Really, Ed has worked very hard to get where he is. *(She points a finger at him.)* Now, there is the result of unskilled labor! Did you hear the news today? We have a brand new baby at our house.

He: You mean to say you pulled up the shade and in came the SUN. Who brought him?

She: Dr. Brown.

He: Gee, that's funny, we take from him, too.

(Radio Routine Done with Estelle Taylor)

Estelle: Good evening, ladies and gentlemen. I want you all to know we're having a perfectly wonderful time at the Oriental Theatre this week. I never knew it was possible to have so much fun and get paid for it. I'm rather shy of a microphone, but I do wish our many friends would come down to the theatre and say hello.

Ed: Estelle, I wish your many friends could see you as I see you now. That dress is adorable. You look like a million dollars.

Estelle: Yes, and I'm just as hard to make.

Ed: You're telling me! Four times a day at the Oriental Theatre I'm asking you to marry me . . . five shows yesterday.

Estelle: You ought to have asked me last night. After the last show, I had no resistance.

Ed: Tell me something about Hollywood and the pictures you've appeared in.

Estelle: Well, I was in *Cimarron*.

Ed: Oh, yes, *Cinnamon*. I remember. Wasn't that the one when you went riding with Richard Dix in his covered wagon, and you had to walk back?

Estelle: I made Richard Dix get out and walk. I was also in *Street Scene*; do you remember?

Ed: Sure, that's where your husband came home unexpectedly and your milkman sweetheart jumped out of the window.

Estelle: That was because he had more milk to deliver. He hadn't covered his whole route.

Ed: Don't I know it. I was the milkman.

Estelle: Eddie, I want to tell you some secrets about Hollywood.

Ed: Secrets! Aha, just like a woman. A great place you pick out to start telling secrets—in front of a microphone. Why don't you wait till we get on a national hookup. Well, what are they?

Estelle: Here's one. You know George Arliss? Well, it's all off between him and Mitzi Green. She's suing him for breach of promise. And Marie Dressler is suing Jackie Cooper.

Ed: Is that a breach too?

Estelle: Aha.

Ed: I suppose now you're going to say that's a pair of breaches.

Estelle: No, two suits.

Ed: I'll bet I have some news on Garbo that you don't know.

Estelle: Oh, Greta; what is she doing now?

Ed: She's got a contract with the Swedish government—stamping out forest fires. Tell me, Estelle, what was your greatest thrill since you began in pictures?

Estelle: Well, Eddie, I'll never forget when John Barrymore made love to me in *Don Juan*. I'll never experience anything as wonderful as that as long as I live.

Ed: Oh, I wouldn't say that. You've still got five days to go at the Oriental.

(Done with Peggy Bernier in Philadelphia)

She: I've got something I want to tell you. It's about the boys in your band. One of them tried to kiss me.

He: He tried to kiss you?

She: Yes, he tried to kiss me, but he didn't.

He: Oh, that couldn't have been one of my boys. They don't miss. You know, you're cute. You're sweet enough to eat.

She: I do eat.

He: No, No. I was admiring your dress. It's very pretty.

She: Like it? My dad gave it to me for my fifteenth birthday.

He: It certainly wears well. *(She is acting slinky.)* Say, don't act like that. You're growing up. Why, it's almost time you were thinking of marriage. Would you marry a stupid goof if he had hardly any money?

She: I don't know. How much money have you?

He *(trying to embrace her):* What's that? Don't you like a hug?

She: No.

He: Do you pet?

She: No.

He: Do you kiss?

She: No.

He: Do you smoke?

She: No.

He: Do you burn the candle. . . . No, I mean don't you neck at all?

She: No, but I'll tell you what I do do.

He: What?

She: I tell a lot of lies.

He: Come here, now. I'm not going to ask any more questions. I'm going to tell you something. Did you know that while you were away, I became a psychic? I can tell fortunes. Let me look at your hand. Say, there's something here. There it is. There's a line that says you will be married before you're nineteen.

She: Oh, but I'm over that now.

He: Are you? Well, you should have that line fixed. I know something you don't know.

She: What is it?

He *(pushing her):* You're standing on my foot.

She: Oh, you think you can tell fortunes. I can tell them better than you. I can tell you all about yourself by just looking at your face.

He: Hey, wait a minute! You can tell me just what I'm thinking? All right, then. *(He makes different faces.)*

She: Yes, I can tell you exactly what you're thinking. Shall I tell the people?

He: I'll dare you, I'll double dare you to tell me just what I'm thinking now, right this second.

She: You dare me, eh? Shall I tell the people?

He: Ladies and gentlemen, if she tells you what I'm thinking, this theatre will be empty in two minutes.

She: I'm going to tell them, anyway. You're thinking how nice it would be after the show for you and me to take a ride out into the country in your car, have dinner, and then—

He: Say, I wasn't thinking that, but it sounds to me like a damn good idea.

She: Eddie, I've lost my wedding ring. Help me find it, please.

He: Gee, you lost your wedding ring out here? That's too bad.

She: I should say it is. And I had such a hard time getting it!

He: Was there anything in it you could identify it by?

She: Yes, my finger was in it.

He: No, I mean any inscription. Wasn't there some kind of a message in it?

She: Oh, sure. It said, "To my own sweetheart." *(Then ad-lib on and on and on.)*

He: Hey, wait a minute. You didn't lose a ring. You lost your diary.

She: Eddie, to show you that I appreciate the humor of that remark, tonight after the last show, I want you to come over to my house and have a midnight dinner.

He: That's fine. I'll get the car out.

She: But, Eddie, I don't live so far away.

He: All right, we'll go home by way of McKeesport, and we'll ride and stop and ride and stop . . .

She: Stop!

He: Don't stop me till we get in the car.

She: Eddie, I live on Highland Avenue, and I want you to come out after your last show.

He: What's the number, Myrtle?

She: Oh, you can't miss it. It's a right on Highland Avenue. We'll have midnight supper and . . .

He: Yes, but what's the number? Where do you live?

She: Haven't I just told you? On Highland Avenue.

He: Yes, but what number?

She: Oh, the number you want!

He: Yes, yes, the number.

She: Oh, I don't remember, but you can't miss it. It's right over the door.

(Done with Fay Brady at the Academy-NYC)

She: Pardon me, I have something for you.

He: What is it? *(She gives him flowers.)* Oh, this is lovely. I never thought I'd get flowers and be able to smell 'em. But I don't want you to go around spending money on me like that.

She: Oh, I didn't pay for them.

He: Where did you get them?

She: They were hanging on a door knob.

(He throws the flowers at the musicians; they throw them around among themselves.)

He: What do you want?

She: Can I have your autograph?

He: You want my autograph? What are you, an autograph collector?

She: Yes, Mr. Dunn.

He: Mr. Dunn?

She: Aren't you Dunn?

He: No, I'm not even half Dunn . . . my name is Ed Lowry.

She: Oh, are you Mr. Lowry? I'm so glad to meet you. You know, you're just the kind of boy my mother always told me about.

He: Repeat that so the boys can hear you—and burn.
She: You're just the kind of boy my mother always told me about.
He: Hear that, boys? *(To woman)* What else did your mom say?
She: She told me to be careful.
He: I think you're fresh. I really shouldn't give you my auto-
graph. And anyway, people go around seeking the autographs
of famous people, people who mean something.
She: Oh, well, the way things are now, I'll take anything.
He: Look, there's no boom on for me either. I'll give you my
initials. *(He signs.)* You know I'm only giving you this because I
think you're a nice girl.
She: I like you too.
He: We ought to get together, you know.
She: Oh, I know all about you. You're married.
He: I remember . . . I know that, too. I've had lots of experience
remembering. You just ask me to go out somewhere, and see how
quickly I arrange it.
She: That's great. We're going to have a party at our house
tonight. Wanna come over?
He: No, I don't like parties. Last week, I was asked to go out to a
place. A friend of mine was throwing a party. I was the party—
and landed on my head.
(*Or:* A friend of mine called me up and said come on over to the
house we're throwing a party. I was the party—and landed on
my head.)
She: Aw, you couldn't get away anyway.
He: You think not? I'm the boss in my house. I'll show you how
I arrange my domestic affairs. Where's that phone? *(He picks up
a phone and calls.)* Hello, sweetheart! *(In an aside, he says to the
woman.)* I'll just give her a little oil. *(To wife)* I'm going to be tied
up . . . *(From off stage, we can hear the wife loudly complaining about
his late nights. He says to his wife)* I must have the wrong number. I
can't get through. Hey, it's my nickel. *(He hangs up.)* You heard
me shout at her. She can't get away with this. That woman was
vaccinated with a Victrola needle. Well, you saw me hang up on
her, didn't you?
She: You're certainly the boss at your house.
He: Wait a minute, she can't get away with that. She didn't give
me a chance to get in. Now, listen: this time, I'm going to call her
back and tell her some stuff and things. Oh, Webster, give me
words. *(He picks up the phone and his wife is still talking.)* Now I will
go to your party. I need consolation. If you have any consolation
at your house, I'll be right over. Where do you live?
She: Oh, right around the corner from Hillside Avenue.
He: Yes, but where? Where is the house, the place?
She: Oh, you must come over, 'cause we're going to have a swell
time.
He: But wait a minute. Where is this going to be?

She: There's going to be a crowd of people and all.

He: But where is this going to be? Houses have numbers. What's the number of your house?

She: Oh, I can't remember the number, but you'll see it. It's right over the door.

He: Oh, are you dumb.

She: Are you telling me or asking me?

He: I'm telling you: you're dumb. D-U-M-B, dumb!

She: You think I'm dumb, you should see my sister. She's dumber than me.

He: Don't say that. Say, "She's dumber than I."

She: All right, she's dumber than the both of us.

He: Now come on, get off! This is a stage where people act.

She: But I want to work in the show, too.

He: Well, what can you do?

She *(opens a hanky that holds an imaginary flea)*: Look what I've got.

He: What have you got there?

She: That's Alexander, my trained flea.

He: Hey, what is this? Don't be bringing fleas around here. We have enough troubles. What can he do?

She: Isn't he cute? Don't you love him?

He: Oh, he's got a little gold band around his neck—and he's bowlegged. Can he do anything?

She: Sure he can do things. He can do somersaults, nip-ups, and—

He: Let me see him do a somersault.

She: Come on, Alexander, do a somersault. *(Drumroll)*

He: Say, that's great. Let me see him do a nip-up. *(Drumroll)* Now let me see him walk on his hind legs. *(She puts the flea on the man's coat.)* Hey, come and get him off me. *(Picks it off.)* Try to make him do another trick now.

She: Alexander, do push-ups. *(Beat)* Something seems to be the matter. Alexander, do a cartwheel. *(Beat)* Something IS the matter. *(She shouts)* Alexander! *(She throws the flea on the man and cries)* That's not Alexander!

ROUTINES ON A SINGLE THEME

Audiences

—There's no chance of getting anything on this crowd, chief.

MC: What? You can't find the criminal?

—No sir, this is the toughest bunch I ever had to deal with. They even pinched my watch and a diamond ring and . . . *(Someone snatches his pants as he talks.)*

Auditions

—Have you had any stage experience?

—No.

—I suppose you're the talk of your town.

—Oh, no.
—But you expect to be a star some day?
—Of course not.
—Can you sing?
—Very little.
—Can you dance?
—Not a lot.
—Good heavens, woman, you're hired—for a curiosity.

Automobiles

(Done with Bert Wheeler)
Bert: Eddie, I want you to help me tell a gag. Will you do that?
Eddie: Sure.
Bert: See, I say to you I was run over by a car this morning and you work it up for me and then I tell the answer. Get it? Now, come on. Say, Eddie, I was run over by an auto this morning and wasn't even hurt.
Eddie: What kind of car was it?
Bert: Oh, Ed, please help me with it. Give the gag some enthusiasm. Put it over. Now, come on. We'll start again. Say, Ed, I was run over . . . and I wasn't hurt.
Eddie: That's too bad.
Bert *(engages in more explanations and finally arrives at the answer)*: I was standing under a bridge.

Borrowing and Lending

Friend: Say, Ed. I just came from the bank. I need five thousand dollars. Now don't get me wrong. I don't want to borrow the money. The manager of the bank asked me if I knew Ed Lowry, and I told him I did. So he gave me this slip of paper and said, "Go get HIM to sign this and we'll give you the five thousand." So just sign your name right here.
Ed: Ted, I'm surprised at you. I thought we were pals. When you need money, why do you go running to the bank? Just come to me, and I'll give you the money. Look, I'll tell you what. You take this paper back to the bank manager and have him sign it. Then I'll give you the five thousand.

Charlie Chan Takes the Stand

—As the foremost detective in modern fiction and the motion pictures, you have attracted widespread notice, and the American public would like to hear a few words from you on the subject of criminal investigation, as well as some facts about yourself.
—Noisy cat make poor mouse catcher.
—Maybe so, but you can at least tell us some things. Now why do you attach so little importance to fingerprints?
—Does smart fox bite initials in hen?

—No-o, but sometimes foxes aren't so smart.
—Stupid fox soon live in zoo.
—I get you. Well, when there aren't any fingerprints, where do you look for clues?
—Human heart show up well in X-ray.
—I see—the motive's the thing, eh? But suppose there is none?
—Man without motive same thing as dog without fleas.
—No such thing, you mean? But what do you do when the murderer has an unshakable alibi?
—Ostrich with head in sand appear to have perfect alibi 'till shot in tail feathers.
—This is getting too complicated for me. Only natural historian with copy *Aesop Fables* should interview sleuth.
—Not even whitewashed crow can coo like real pigeon.
—Even thick-skinned rhinoceros react to sharp barb. Goodbye, Mr. Chan.

Dating and the Go-Between

(After a couple have finished their act, the man goes to one side, the woman, the other. The MC sidles up to the man and says)
MC: Gee, she's cute. Does she ever go out stepping?
Man: Why, surely, she goes out.
MC: Do you think she would go out with me?
Man: I don't see why you should be an exception.
(The man calls the girl over and introduces her to the MC, who kisses her hand.)
Girl: Oh, you sweet thing.
MC: I was just telling your partner how much I admired you— your grace . . . your beauty. Would you like to go out with me?
Girl: I'd love to, but you see I'm married.
MC: That's nothing, so am I.
Girl: Yeah, but my husband—
MC: Who is your husband?
Girl *(points to her partner)*: Him! *(She laughs and walks off.)*
Man: Well, I did all I could for you.

Hats

—Hey wait a minute! Where do you think you are? Don't throw my hat around like that. It's a new hat.
—Well, you threw my old hat on the floor.
—Yeah, but mine's a new one.
—Well, mine's an old one. So pick up my old hat.
—You pick up my new hat.
—First, you pick up my old hat.
—Why should I pick up your old hat?
—Now listen, if you were walking along Broadway, and you saw a taxicab hit a young girl and knock her down and the same taxi-

cab hit an old lady and knocked her down, which would you pick
up first?

—Well, naturally, I'd pick up the old lady.

—Then pick up my old hat.

Health and an Icy Shower

First He-Man: Boy, there's nothing like an icy shower in the
morning to fill you full of pep.

Second He-Man: You said it. It beats all the medicine in the
world.

First: Why, the mere thought of bounding out of bed and into
that bracing water just makes me tingle with vigor.

Second: And how that snappy rubdown afterward will make the
blood pound in your veins! A cold shower is a rejuvenator, that's
what it is.

First: Yeah, it'll take the years off your shoulders and put on live
muscle. And will it chase away the fat! Say, there's nothing like
cold showers to give you a figure like an Apollo.

Second: These people who can't stand a little cold water don't
have my sympathy. If they knew what a tonic it was, they'd all
jump under a shower every morning, winter and summer alike.

First: Yeah, these weaklings get on your nerves. You can't get anywhere on the road to health and vigor if you're afraid of a little
cold water.

Second: That's the truth. How long have you been taking cold
showers?

First: I'm going to start tomorrow morning.

Second: That's a coincidence. So am I.

Homecoming

He: Well, _____, I'm glad you're back.

She: I'm glad to be back.

He: I'm glad you're glad to be back.

She: I'm glad you're glad I'm glad to be back.

He: I'm glad you're glad I'm glad you're glad to be back.

She: Well, you're glad, that's settled.

He: But there's one thing I'd like to tell you.

She: And what's that?

He: I'm glad you're back.

She: But I didn't see you in the parade when I got in.

He: Oh, I couldn't bother. I saw you come into the theatre.

She: Yes, and stopped eight other people from having a look. But
I'm disappointed at you not being down at the train station. It
wouldn't have cost you anything to come down.

He: Oh, I just didn't want to. Why were you so anxious?

She: Well, we had a fine procession—cars and everything—but
we didn't have one elephant.

He: Are you implying . . . ?

Imagination

—Imagination is something that isn't and couldn't be. But if you think it can, it is. I'll bet I can do something to you and you won't know it. You'll just imagine it.

—Nonsense!

(They bet. "A" slaps "B" on the face.)

—Hey, why did you slap me?

—I didn't slap you. That was imagination.

—You said yourself, "Imagination is something that isn't and couldn't be. But if you think it can, it is." You slapped me. It actually happened. You lose. So hand over the money.

—Ha, ha, I never had any money. That's your imagination.

Interruptions

(A man and a woman routine; the woman keeps interrupting.)

> Dogs roll on their backs,
> And the little duck quacks
> And the crickets crick over the hill.
> *Interruption:*
> The piggies are happy,
> They look so sweet.
> They eat and eat and eat and eat.
>
> You can tell by these signs
> And the quivering pines
> Spring is about to come.
> *Interruption:*
> They just sleep around
> And grow fat and big.
> Don't you wish you were a pig?
>
> The autumn leaves are falling
> And how the winds do hum.
> 'Tis plain to see, 'twixt you and me
> Spring is about to come.
> *Interruption:*
> The falling leaves,
> And the poor bare twigs
> Serve to remind of the dear little pigs.

Names

—Hello, who's speaking?

—WHAT's my name.

—I'm asking what your name is.

—I told you. WHAT is my name.

—What's what?

—That's my name.

—What's your name?
—WHAT! JOHN WHAT!
—John what?
—Yes.
—What's your last name?
—That's my last name.
—JOHN THAT?
—No. JOHN WHAT.
—I get it now. JOHN WHAT.
—Yes. Now tell me your name.
—WILL KNOTT.
—Why not?
—KNOTT's my name.
—That's not your name?
—My name is KNOTT.
—Not what?
—KNOTT! WILL KNOTT!
—Oh, Hello, Mr. RUMPLEMEYER.

Parties

(Two men, on opposite sides of the stage, are talking to each other on the telephone.)
—I want you to come on up to the house.
—Thanks loads.
—We'll have cocktails . . . by the way . . . I'm out of gin.
—Okay, I'll bring some up with me.
—Say, at the same time, as long as you're in the market, would you mind getting me a dozen oranges?
—Sure.
—Incidentally, I'm all out of ice. I wish you'd bring some along.
—Listen, you come over to my place. I don't have to go out for anything.
—No, no, this drink is on me.

Restaurants

—What's yours?
—A ham sandwich and coffee, please.
—What?
—Ham sandwich and coffee.
—Ham sandwich isn't on the menu, but I can give you a sandwich with ham in it . . . like a Sunset Special.
—What's that?
—A triple decker with ham, cheese, tongue, baloney, tomato, lettuce, onion, pickle, and mayonnaise on raisin bread, toasted with coleslaw on the side.
—Look, have you any ham?

—Yes, sir.
—White bread?
—Yes, sir.
—Could you place a piece of ham between two slices of white bread and serve same to me on a plate?
—Why, sure. Oh George! One Sunset Special. Make it on one deck. Hold the cheese, tongue, baloney, tomato, lettuce, onion, pickle, mayonnaise, and coleslaw and make the raisin bread white, untoasted. Right?

Robbery and the Watch Theft

She: Say, I'm very angry with you. You've done a terrible thing: a terrible, terrible thing.
He: What have I done now?
She: You've stolen my watch, and I want it back.
He: Go on, get off it. What do you want to say things like that for? Are you trying to show off! Get away from here.
She: But I want my watch back. You stole it. The stage door man saw you coming out of my room. Give me back my watch.
He: Say, what are you talking about? Are you trying to call me a thief?
She: You are a thief. I want my watch back.
He: Haven't I known you since you were a pup? I used to help your mother push your baby carriage, even before I could reach up to the handles. And when you were fourteen years old and a fresh little kid, who was it used to protect you from the fellows? And then when you were sixteen and wanted to be an actress and you went out on the road and got stranded, who was it sent you money to get home? And then when you had appendicitis and you wanted an operation, who did you write for money?
She: You.
He: You're darn right. If it hadn't been for me, you might still have your appendix. And then you accuse me of stealing your old watch! Oh, it's too much! *(He starts to cry, followed by the band members.)*
She: Oh, _____, I forgive you.
He: What?
She: Oh, _____, please forgive me; please forgive me.
He: I might forgive you, but I can't forget.
She: Oh, _____, I guess I was wrong.
He: You guess you were wrong!
She: I know I was wrong.
He: All right, then, say you're sorry in front of all these people.
She: I'm sorry in front of all these people.
He: Okay, it's over. We'll forget it.
She: Yes, it's all over. So now can I have my watch back?

SKITS

Arguments

The MC (or boss) and two girls are fighting. He says that both girls are fired. One of them makes up and begs the MC to keep the other in the show. The MC goes into a long speech about how he knows the two girls have always worked together and are as close as sisters; and how it would be a shame for them to split up just because of him. The girl who has apologized builds on what the MC has said and urges him to reconsider. The MC finally reconsiders—and tells her that she's fired, too.

Auditions

(The number has just ended.)

He: Gee, you must be thrilled to hear such applause. It's great. You're a big hit in the theatre. I heard you over the radio and I think you're swell. Gee, there's only one thing for you to look forward to now . . .

She: What's that?

He: An opportunity to get in the movies. Tell me, would you like to get in the pictures?

She: Oh, gosh, would'I!

He: Young lady, I can do a whole lot for you. I know all the movie maggots—er, er, magnates. I know the Warner Brothers. I know Mr. Fox. I know Mr. Paramount. Mr. RKO. Tell me, do you think you could follow in Greta Garbo's footsteps?

She *(looks at her feet):* Well, I don't know.

He: I'll tell you what. I wrote a scenario, and I'll explain the idea to you. Then we'll just see if you can do it. In the opening scene it shows you and me getting married . . .

She: Already?

He: Yeah, I couldn't wait. Now look, just as they join us in the holy bonds of matrimony, I hear "Ta tatatatata" *(bugle),* and I rush off to war in my homeland, China *(ad-lib).* I'm gone for seven long months, and during my absence you have been sitting and pining, pining and sitting, waiting for the return of your Bertram. Now, get it clear: you are sitting on the steps of your bungalow and I suddenly return. *(Girl squats.)* As I turn the corner, you see me. I rush to you, and we embrace. Now, by the way you greet me, I'll know whether or not you are any good for the movies. *(He walks downstage rubbing his hands. Upstage, the girl is squatting.)* All right, let's go. I enter and you're sitting in front of the bungalow. "Sweetheart, it's me, your husband, remember?" *(He rushes over to the girl, who hugs him listlessly.)* Pee-ew! Honey, you've got to act. Do you realize that we're married, and that as soon as the ceremony was performed I was called away to war? You can't wait. We didn't even have a honeymoon. I went straight to the front. Now, here we go. *(As he's reciting the motiva-tion, he's showing her how to hug him. Again he rushes over to hug the girl, but this time they miss one another. The man looks disgusted.)* Say, maybe it's me. Maybe you don't go for me. Do you think if I were somebody else . . . ? Is it me? Tell me, if I were Clark Gable would it be better?

She: Definitely.

He: All right then, I'll be Clark Gable. *(He resumes his position.)* Remember now, I've been gone for seven months and we haven't even been together. You've been lonesome. You've really been lonesome. We've got one of those new style bungalows, with a Frigidaire and everything. You haven't seen anybody. Here I come! Sweetheart, my loved one, come to me. *(This time the girl really hugs. When the man lets go of her he's out of breath.)* Whew! Now you're acting. I'll give you some more tips. Come here! In the movies, you do everything by counts. When you hug and kiss, you don't go like this. *(He gives her a peck on the cheek.)* Not one of those quick things. There's a guy down there with a cam-era he has to grind. Now, for instance, when you kiss, you hold it while the director counts one, two, three; you don't let go till he says "Break." And boy, I know the director. *(Walking away)* Are you ready? *(Rushes to her.)* Sweetheart! Loved one! Honey! *(As he is kissing her, he signals for the spotlight to be turned off.)* *(Blackout)*

(Variation, done with Sylvia Froos)

Ed: Now that you've been such a big success on the stage wouldn't you like to go into pictures? Haven't you ever thought you'd like to emote on the screen?

Sylvia: Oh, I'd love to go into pictures, Eddie.

Ed: Yeah, well I think I could do a lot for you. Do you think, though, you could act for pictures? Do you think you could fol-low in Garbo's footsteps?

Syl *(looks at her feet):* Well, I don't know, Eddie.

Ed: Well, do you have any dramatic ability? If you have, I could help you a whole lot. You see, I know Mr. Lasky and Mr. Zukor and Mr. Universal and Mr. Paramount and Warner Brothers. Let me see you emote. *(Sylvia pants.)* She's got the heebie-jeebies, all right. Now here's the scene. We are getting married, and just as we enter the holy bonds of matrimony I hear the bugle call *(a bugle sounds)* and I rush off to war in China. I'm gone for seven months, and when I return you are sitting on the steps of the bungalow, pining and waiting for me. All right, have you got it? Remember, I've been away seven months. We're married. I'll know if you have any dramatic ability by the way you greet me. Now, here I come, Sylvia. *(They embrace.)* Pee-ew! That was ter-rible. You're supposed to be glad to see me. I've been away for seven months. You know, we were married and we didn't even get to—. I had to go away right after the ceremony. Come on, let's try it over again. Put some life into it. You know, put some zest into it. *(Musical action on zest)* Now, get it in your mind, you're sitting on the steps of the bungalow. I've been away seven months. Get ready. Here I come. *(They embrace.)* Blah! Is that the way you make love? Now listen, get this: we got married. You've been living in one of those new style bungalows with all the latest improvements. You've been alone. You have a Kelvinator and everything. Listen, would it help if I was somebody else? I'll try to be Gable *(biz with ears)*. I'll give you a quick résumé of the scenario. *(Aside:* "Get that, you mugs, *résumé.")* Come on, get in the nude . . . I mean the mood. *(They embrace.)* Now you're acting! Let me give you a tip. In the picture, you don't go just like this. *(Short kiss)* You see, when you kiss, there's a director and a cameraman. You don't go just like this. *(Short kiss)* It has to grind, because they do everything by counts. When we kiss, we hold it and the director counts one, two, three, and so on. We don't let go until he says "break." And I know the director. All right now, remember everything I told you. Here I come. *(They embrace, and Ed waves his hand to tell the lighting man to black out the spot while he is kissing the girl.)*

Candy

A fellow went to see a girl and brought a box of candy. Every time he handed her a candy, he whispered in her ear. The fourth time he whispered, she made a face and put the candy back in the box.

(Variation)
A man gives a girl a box of candy. While she eats, the man is making nice to her. Finally, he whispers to her and she takes the candy out of her mouth, puts it into the box, and hands the candy back.

(Variation)
A man gives a girl a lollipop. He remarks, "I remembered your favorite flavor." She takes it and starts licking it. The man tries to embrace her. She pushes him away. He tries again. She shoves him and says, "I never did like you." This time he yanks the lollipop from her and says, "I'm not throwing my nickels around."

Clothing

(A man enters. He is surrounded by three men who beat him. A cop enters and asks the cause of the melee.)
Man 1: Just look at my hands!
Man 2: And mine!
Man 3: Ruined!

Cop: They do look pretty bad. *(Turning to the man who has been beaten)* Who are you?

Man 1: He's the guy who puts pins in new shirts!

Cowardice and Toughness

Two men are bragging about not being scared of anything. They talk about how tough they are, and eventually mention a third tough guy, who is expected at the theatre. Both men agree that they are unafraid, and brag about what they will do if they come upon the third guy. One man says to the other, "If you see him, just blow this whistle." As he leaves, the tough guy enters, scares the man on stage, steals his money, and, before leaving, makes him take his pants off. Sans pants, the man blows the whistle. The other man comes running on without pants.

A lot of fellows are acting tough, swaggering about the stage and brandishing knives and pistols. They talk about a fellow who has to be PLUGGED: rubbed out. The men turn to one of their own and indicate that since he's the toughest of them, the most ruthless killer of all, he should be the one to do the job. Then the victim enters and begs for his life. Just as the killer is about to shoot him, there's a commotion off stage. A woman enters. The killer says, "Honey!" One of the toughs in an aside indicates that she's the killer's wife. The little woman goes up to her husband and slaps him around, as the victim runs off. Then she says, "I told you to buy skimmed milk, not regular."

Dancing

(A dancing skit on saying "Essence of Peppermint and Poopoopa Doop") A mother sends her little girl to the store for peppermint and impresses on her the importance of not forgetting what she is going for. She tells her to remember the name by dancing and by singing "Essence of Peppermint, tra la la la la" *(repeat)*, on her way to the store. The little girl goes into the store with her little dance and asks for "Essence of Peppermint tra la la la la," and the man behind the counter says, "We don't have Essence of Peppermint tra la la la la," but we have some "Feenamint Poopoopa Doop."

Deaf and Dumb

A man and a woman on a golf course. They are both hard of hearing.

He *(calling loudly to the lady)*: Fore! Pardon me, are you looking for the pro? *(Repeat.)*

She: No, I don't think it is going to snow. Are you going to tee?

He: I just did. *(He stoops to pick up a glove.)* Pardon me, is this yours?

She: Thank you. Do you know, it is the second time I lost it, and each time I get it back A-gain *(long "A")*.

He: Yes, it did rain. Let's you and me play the round. It's a nice course.

She: Course? Say, did you call me a horse? I wouldn't say that to you. You seem like a nice fellow. Where are you going when you get through playing?

He: Yes? Will you and I go and get something to eat?

She: Yes, I have to get something to eat.

He: I haven't a thing to do from Saturday till Tuesday. Do you have a cold? What do you think I ought to do with my weekend?

She: Put a mustard plaster on it.

He: Yes, I will go there.

She: It's old-fashioned but it's the best cure.

He: Look at that! My watch stopped. Is it that late? I am always having trouble with my watch.

She: Why don't you go to a good dentist. Maybe it's your teeth.

He: It's a fake!

She: Then you'll have to take ether. Are you married?

He: No.

She: Any children?

He: Three.

She: What are they?

He: Airedales. Dogs. *(He points at his feet.)*

She: Oh, you have new shoes!

He: I raised them from pups.

She: So am I.

He *(looks at her closely)*: Ain't you from Altoona?

She: You'll have to talk louder.

He: I say, ain't you from Altoona?

She: I used to live over there.

He: I remember you. My, how that place has grown. I remember you when you were a little girl and I spanked you.

She: Yes, you wouldn't know the old place now.

He *(takes her by the hand)*: Let's go get something to eat.

She: But I can't, I'm too hungry.

He: Won't you eat with me?

She: All right, if you insist.

He: Goodbye.

Divorce

A husband and wife are arguing. "I want a divorce," she says. He replies, "Let me. You needn't incur the trouble and expense. I'll do everything." A policeman enters with a man in handcuffs. The husband remarks, "Why, it's Jack Simon. He's been arrested. Say, Jack, what have you been doing? What are you going up for, kid?" Jack replies, "Two weeks, I murdered my wife." The husband says, "Only two weeks for murdering your wife!" Jack says, "Yeah—" The husband immediately shoots his wife, as Jack finishes his sentence: "And then the electric chair."

Drunks

A man is sitting at a bar talking to the bartender about money. The bartender says that one has to be careful these days because there are thieves everywhere. The man takes a roll out of his pocket and asks the bartender to put it away in the safe, which is beside the bar. The bartender says he needs something to tie up the wad. A drunk enters. The bartender notices that the drunk's trousers are fastened with a string. He asks the drunk for it. The drunk says that the string is all he has to hold up his trousers. The bartender offers him a free drink in return for the string. The drunk takes off the string, and his pants fall to the ground. He pulls them up, and they fall down. *(Repeat several times.)* The bartender ties up the wad, goes to the safe, and dials the combination. The drunk observes the combination. The barman invites the drunk to have another drink and asks the man at the bar to join him downstairs, to meet some friends who are hosting a private party. The two men exit. The drunk, still struggling to keep up his pants, looks around, dials the combination, opens the safe, takes out the roll of money, unties the string, fastens his pants, puts the money back, and exits.

Editing

A man is reading a letter and indicating where the quotations occur. A second man, who has never read the letter, keeps correcting the quotation mistakes.

Exaggeration and Hyperbole

(Ed and Bob meet as they walk across the stage in front of the closed curtain.)
Bob: Hello, Eddie.
Ed: Well, Bob, what's the matter? You're not looking good.
Bob: Oh, I feel terrible, Eddie.
Ed: What's the matter? You look as if you're in love.
Bob: That's just it. I'm in love with a girl, and I want to marry her.
Ed: I thought so. You've got a pained expression. Why do you want to get married?
Bob: Well, I'm just crazy about this girl, Carol Wylie.
Ed: You're crazy, all right. What's the matter? Why don't you just marry her?
Bob: To tell you the truth, Ed, I'm afraid of her father.
Ed: Well, I've heard of suitors being afraid of the girl's mother, but not the father.

Bob: Just the same, Eddie, I'm afraid of her father.

Ed: What's the matter?

Bob: Well, he's a very wealthy influential man, and I'm only a poor actor.

Ed: Poor actor? You're not a poor actor; you're a good actor! Never admit you're a poor actor. Make people believe you're not what they think. Talk success and you'll be a success.

Bob: Well, in that case, Eddie, I'd love for you to go along with me and put me over with the old man. Tell him I'm great—a real success.

Ed: Will I help you? Sure I will!

Bob: They live right down the street here.

(The curtain opens on the girlfriend's living room. The father is sitting on a sofa reading a newspaper.)

Bob: Hello, Mr. Wylie, I want you to meet my friend Ed Lowry.

Father *(shaking hands with Ed)*: Glad to meet you, Mr. Lowry. Please sit down.

Ed: Glad to meet you, Mr. Wylie. It's a pleasure—for you. I'll stand for a minute. I've been playing polo all morning.

(Bob sits on the sofa. Ed stands for a minute and then sits on a chair.)

Bob: Mr. Wylie, I've come to see you on a very important matter. I want your daughter for my wife.

Father: But Bob, this is rather sudden. Do you realize what a great responsibility you're undertaking?

Ed: Undertaking! That's a great word for marriage.

Father: You know, Bob, my daughter is used to luxury and everything that money can buy. Now, what have you to offer her?

Bob: Well, I have a little home in the city.

Ed: A little home in the city! Pardon me, would you mind moving over and letting me talk to the governor. Now, Mr. Wylie, you just heard my modest young friend say that he had a home in the city. Mr. Wylie, he has a mansion, the most palatial home you ever saw: three hundred and fourteen rooms, with elevators on every floor.

(Bob, trying to stop Ed from boasting too much, motions and pulls at his coat.)

Father: Well, Bob, I'm very glad to hear that, but there're other things. For example, my daughter is very fond of motoring. What have you to offer in the line of automobiles?

Bob: Well, I have a little runabout.

Ed: A little runabout! Hell, he has two Packards, three Cadillacs, four Buicks, and an Austin. He straps the Austin on the side of the car to amuse the children. In addition, he has two Rollses and employs fifteen chauffeurs. Six of them run in front to keep the traffic out of the way.

Father: Why, that's fine, Bob. I'm glad to hear you're doing so well, but you know, Bob, my daughter is very fond of sports, especially yachting. What have you to offer in that line?

Bob: Well, I have a little tug boat.

Ed: Mr. Wylie, did you hear my modest young friend? A tug boat! Hell, he has a boat that accommodates a crew of two hundred and five passengers. It's often been mistaken for a battleship. You have no doubt heard of Vincent Astor's yacht. Well, he has one like that which he uses for a lifeboat strapped on the side of his boat.

Father: Well, that's wonderful, Bob. I'm certainly glad to hear that.

Ed *(aside to Bob)*: Am I helping you, old boy?

Bob *(aside to Ed)*: You may want to tone it down a little.

Father: There's just one other little thing I would like to ask you, Bob. You know in this hot weather, my daughter likes to have some little place in the country where she can go to avoid the heat of the city.

Bob: Actually, I have a little place in the country.

Ed: Did you hear him? He has a little place in the country! Hell, Mr. Wylie *(he throws his legs over Mr. Wylie's knees),* he has an estate. Have you ever seen Rockefeller's house? Well, that's a bungalow compared to Bob's place. He has one of the most gorgeous homes in America, with two hundred rooms and fifty baths. He has a swimming pool with seawater that he pumps from the Atlantic and Pacific, and a lake fourteen miles across.

(During Ed's exaggerations, Bob has been anxiously trying to get his eye and starts to cough to attract his attention.)

Father *(noticing Bob's coughing)*: Bob, you ought to take care of that cold. You have a terrible cough.

Bob: It's just a little cough. It's nothing.

Father: Oh, just a little cold?

Ed: Just a little cold! Did you hear that? Little cold! Mr. Wylie, Bob's just being modest again. Cold, hell, he's got consumption!

Food

(The scene is a restaurant, with tables and settings.)

He: Gee, I'm hungry, aren't you, dear?

She: I'm starved.

He: It's so good to be dining out. You have no idea how I feel about you.

She: You're so sweet!

He: Would you like some oysters, dear?

She: Oh, I just love oysters.

He: Same with me. I go crazy over oysters . . . stark, raving mad. Let's call the waiter.

Waiter: Did you ring the bell?

He: Yes. *(To girl)* What will you have, dear?
She: I'll have half a dozen oysters on the shell.
He: And I'll have half a dozen oysters on the half shell.
Waiter: Sorry, sir, we have only one order of oysters.
He: What? Only one order of oysters?
(He shoots girl.)

French

A man and a woman friend meet. The man says that he's been learning French since the last time he saw her. She asks him to tell her about the lessons. He says he won't tell her, he'll show her. He says three short phrases, all of which are endearing terms that she understands. She replies in French. Each time he says something, they embrace. She enthusiastically encourages him. After his last phrase, they hug and kiss. He then walks off to one side, ponders for a moment, and says to the audience, "Hell, if I only knew some more French."

(Variation)
A man enters wearing a straw hat and reading a French phrase book. A girl enters. She speaks some French, which she mixes with English words. The man turns a couple of pages in the book and says a phrase: "Promenade avec moi, mam'selle." She says, "Oui, oui," and kisses him. He says, "What a language! What a language! Don't go 'way." He looks up something in the book and again speaks French to her. And again, she kisses him. He turns the pages and says, "Hey, here's something that really looks promising. 'Mam'selle, voulez-vous coucher avec moi?'" The girl slaps him. The man tears out the page and says, "Wrong page, wrong page." The girl indignantly walks off.

Funeral Service

(A funeral parlor. The stage is set with two chairs: the kind used in moving picture houses. A white spot discovers a couple entering.)
Mr. Clark: Usher . . . say, it's dark in here.
Usher: Mastbaum service. Your names, please?
Mr. Clark: The Clarks. Will you please show us down the aisle?
Usher: Yes, sir. This way.
(The white spot illuminates the seats.)
Mr. Clark *(tripping)*: Hey, why don't you pull in those suit cases? *(Sits.)* I understand this is a great picture. It's lovely here, isn't it? Cool and comfortable.
Mrs. Clark: It may be cool but it's certainly not comfortable.
Mr. Clark: Listen, sour apple, I came here to enjoy the picture, so stop beefing.
Mrs. Clark: Aw, these darn seats are hard. I wish I had a cushion.
Usher *(brings a cushion and whispers)*: Mastbaum service.

Mrs. Clark: Thanks.

Mr. Clark: Fine, now shall I have the band play "April Showers"? *(Beat)* Will you please stop chewing that gum!

Mrs. Clark: Well, I've got to do something. And anyhow, if you're such a big shot, why didn't you buy me some candy?

Mr. Clark: Before I'd buy you candy, I'd buy you poison.

Mrs. Clark: Before we were married you used to buy me candy.

Mr. Clark: Sure, but who ever heard of running after a streetcar after you've caught it?

Mrs. Clark: Well, I wish I had some candy.

Usher *(enters with candy and whispers):* Mastbaum Service.

Mrs. Clark: Starting to eat some of it. Say, this is good.

Mr. Clark: Let me have a taste. After all, I bought these tickets. *(Fumbling with the wrapper)* This can't be much good or they wouldn't wrap it up. *(He picks out soft ones, bites, and puts several in his mouth.)* Now, put about six pieces in your mouth and let's watch the picture.

Mrs. Clark: Oh, who wants to see this silly old picture. I know just how it ends. See, that fellow marries.

Mr. Clark *(interrupting):* All right, all right. If you're so good, why aren't you in Hollywood writing 'em?

Mrs. Clark: I wish I was in Hollywood.

Mr. Clark: I wish you were. Go to Hollywood. See if I care. Go to Hollywood.

Mrs. Clark: Do you know what would go good with this candy?

Mr. Clark: Yes, a muzzle.

Mrs. Clark: No, an apple. I wish I had an apple.

Usher *(enters with an apple and whispers):* Mastbaum Service.

Mr. Clark: You're not going to sit here and chew on an apple.

Mrs. Clark: Oh, shut up! I wish I'd stayed home with mother.

Mr. Clark: I wish you'd go home to your mother.

Mrs. Clark: I will go home to my mother.

Mr. Clark: That's better than bringing her here.

Mrs. Clark: Well, I don't like this picture. I thought we came to see Clara Bow. I never heard of Mastbaum's Service. It's dead. Nothing happens.

Mr. Clark: Will you please be quiet.

Mrs. Clark: Let's leave.

Mr. Clark: Just keep your eye on those suitcases. Mastbaum is probably an escapologist, like Houdini.

Mrs. Clark: Why don't you ever listen to me? You make me sick.

Mr. Clark: You're no health resort.

Mrs. Clark: Oh, I wish I were dead.

(A shot)

Usher *(enters):* Shhh, please. Mastbaum's—and Mrs. Clark's service.

(Blackout)

Golf

The MC announces that he's going to show the audience just
a few trick shots at golf, but that he needs a man from the
audience—one with the physique of a Douglas Fairbanks, with
the courage of Napoleon, and above all with what Elinor Glyn
calls IT. "Let such a man come up on stage." A scrawny guy
volunteers. He stands there to get laughs. Then the MC walks
over to him, looks him over, and says:

MC: You just heard me make the announcement, didn't you?
What are you doing up here? I said I wanted someone with IT.

Man: I thought you said IF.

MC: Who are you? What's your name? You DO have a name?

Man (trying to think): I can't think of it.

MC: You've forgotten your name? What letter does it begin with:
A, B, C, D, E, Z?

Man: That's it—Z!

MC: Oh, Z. Zenobia? Zola? Zambuk? Zimo?

Man: No, no, no. I mean Z. (With his arms, he makes the shape of
a C.) That's a C.

MC: Did you ever play golf?

Man: Yes and no.

MC: Well, did you ever play with knickers?

Man: No, white folks.

MC: You're my protege and I'm going to take you to this wonderful club. (Name some Jewish-sounding club.) What's your name?

Man: McCarthy.

MC: Well, that'll be a novelty at this club. How much money have
you got?

Man: Six hundred.

MC: Six hundred dollars?

Man: No, no, six hundred cents.

MC: All right, now we're at the golf club. All the members are on
the porch waiting for you.

Man: Eh?

MC: All on the stoop. (The man stoops.) Now we're going out
to play this wonderful game. The members of the four hundred to the left of you, the members of the four hundred to the
right of you, and the members of the four hundred at the back
of you.

Man: And into the valley of death rode my six hundred—

MC: Come over here, I want to show you how you should have
played. Get that golf stick. Now put your head on the floor. (The
man throws down the golf club and puts his head on the floor.) No,
no, no, the head of the golf stick. Take the stick in your left hand,
and put your right hand in front of it. (He demonstrates.) Now
raise your head up. (He demonstrates. The man follows these instruc-

tions and throws his head back.) Higher, higher, higher! Now keep your eye on the ball.

Man *(gets disgusted and throws the club down):* Oh, I can't do that.

MC: Well, take the stick again in your hand and I'll show you. Now swing back like this. *(The MC takes a swing.)*

Man: I'll try. *(He takes a swing with a trick club, which bends.)*

MC: Now look what you've done! What are you going to do with that club now?

Man: Eh? Shoot around corners.

MC: Stand over here. Next to me. I want to examine your form.

Man: My form?

MC: Yes.

Man: Next to you?

MC: I'll just stand behind you and put my arms around yours . . .

Man: You don't know me well enough yet.

MC: How else are you going to learn?

Man: I heard about guys like you! *(He walks off.)*

Hard Times and the Depression

(Done with Irvin, Charlie Schmatt, Joe Winters, Alistaire Wylie)
The MC announces this skit as a street scene during hard times. Two men are walking in opposite directions. They meet center stage. They know each other. Dan tells Moe that he is broke, that he lost everything in the stock market.

Dan: I wonder could you let me have a loan of ten dollars or even five or maybe one? I'll even settle for a quarter.

Moe: Sorry, I can't let you have it. I'm married, and I need every quarter I can get. But I have an idea.

Dan: Sew a button on it. What is it?

Moe: Well, when I was broke, I let the city look after me. If you get put in jail, you get a good bed, four square meals a day, and you don't have to worry about a thing.

Dan: Say, that's not a bad idea. If all I have to do is get locked up, I'll do that. Thanks, pal.

Moe: I wish you luck. *(He exits.)*

Dan: What can I do to get locked up? I know what I'll do: I'll rob someone. Here comes a pigeon now.

(A man enters. Dan pulls out a gun.)

Dan: Stick 'em up! Come on now, stick 'em up.

Man: Dan, it's me, Herman! You don't have to hold me up. I apologize. Here's the ten bucks I owe you.

Dan: I don't want your money. All I want is to get locked up.

(Enter a cop)

Cop: Hey, what's this, a holdup? Hey!

Dan: Yes, it's a holdup. I'm after this guy's money. Go on and arrest me.

Cop *(looking at Herman):* Oh, I know you: Slick Herman. Come with me! *(He grabs Herman and marches him off, leaving Dan holding the gun and looking disgusted.)*

Dan: I know what I'll do. I'll insult someone, then I'll get arrested. *(A girl enters.)* Hello, tootsie!

She: Hello!

Dan *(touching her face)*: I'm gonna kiss you.

She: Thanks! *(Dan looks bewildered.)*

(The cop enters again.)

Cop: Hey, what's this about? *(He walks past the man and addresses the girl.)* Haven't I told you to keep away from this beat? I have my orders to clean up around here. Now come on! *(He takes the girl off, leaving Dan looking puzzled.)*

Dan *(crying)*: Oh, I want to be arrested! What can I do to get arrested? I know, I'll steal something. *(A fellow enters carrying an umbrella. Dan snatches the umbrella.)*

Man *(cringes and starts to run off)*: I'm sorry, mister, I didn't know it was your umbrella. Don't call a cop, mister! *(He exits as Dan throws the umbrella down in disgust.)*

Dan: What must a guy do to get locked up around here? I know, I'll start a fight.

(Two boys enter doing a nance routine. Dan goes up to them and begins to fight with them.)

Dan: Come on there and fight! *(Yells.)* A fight!

(Another cop enters. He, too, is a nance and carries a club with a piece of pink ribbon attached. He politely extricates the two boys and walks them off.)

Dan: I know what I can do. There's a fire box. I'll ring the alarm and then they'll have to arrest me.

(He goes over to the box and pulls the lever. A bell rings off stage. Two firemen enter wearing helmets; they are carrying a fire hose and hatchets. After they rush across the stage, an old man in a nightgown and night cap enters. The firemen ask him if he sounded the alarm.)

Dan: No, I sounded the alarm. Now have me arrested!

Man: You saved my life! There's a fire in my house. Here's a hundred dollars. *(He gives Dan the money.)*

Dan *(counting the money)*: And to think that I wanted to get arrested. What a fool I was! A hundred smackers: I'm rich!

(He is still counting the money when the first cop enters, looks at him and the money, pulls out a gun, and says)

Cop: You'd better let me see that. *(He takes the money and starts to walk off, saying)* And you thought I was a cop, sucker. *(Then he turns and shoots Dan.)*

(An alternative ending)

(As Dan is counting the money, the cop enters and says, "Let me see that!" *He takes the money, looks it over, manacles Dan, and drags him off with:* "So you're the guy who is passing all this counterfeit money. Come with me!")

Infidelity

A husband has to leave on a trip. His suitcase is packed. He has second thoughts and starts to unpack. All the while, his wife is telling him that she wishes he didn't have to leave, that she'd love for him to remain home with her. But as he unpacks and throws his clothes on a chair, she immediately folds and repacks them.

A husband tells a friend that he doesn't know the color of his own wife's eyes. The curtains part, and the husband finds his wife in the arms of a lover. The husband dashes in, looks his wife right in the face, and says, "I knew it, brown." The lover replies with some surprise, "How do you know my name?"

(Lights low) A woman is on the phone presumably sending a wire. The wire concerns the absence of her husband and the good care she is receiving from her husband's best friend, Charlie. After each short phrase, she says, "Stop!" Finally, she ends the message with a very loud, "Stop! Will you please stop, Charlie!" *(Charlie is discovered under the bedclothes.)*

A spot illuminates a husband on one side of the stage. He is sending a telegram and repeats out loud its contents: "Will arrive home tomorrow night, Love, Harry." The spot follows him as he walks to the other side of the stage, where he discovers his wife in the arms of a man. The man says, "Darling, I love you. When will your husband be back?" She answers, "Oh, not for a week at least, I'm sure." The husband looks amazed and says, "Why dear, didn't you get my wire?"

A husband comes home late and finds his wife on the settee with another man. He says, "What's going—", when she interrupts. She asks him where he has been; but before he can reply, she says, "Don't give me your usual lies. I KNOW all about your late nights!" He tries to stop her, but she continues in this vein. At last, he manages to get a word in. "Wait a minute! Who's this guy? What is he doing here?" She replies, "Don't change the subject."

(Variation)
A man staggers in drunk and finds his wife loving another fellow. She beats him to the punch by bawling the hell out of him first. When he finally gets a word in, asking, "Shay, who is that guy?" she says, "Don't change the subject."

(Stage center) Lou asks Ben where he can go for a drink and a good time. "Some place out of the way," Lou says. Ben tells him to go to 57th Street, and Ben leaves. Lou runs into an old girlfriend, now married, and they walk off together. The curtain opens to find them in her house, sitting together, drinking, mak-

ing eyes at one another. There's a knock on the door. Lou gets under the table or hides in a closet. The husband enters, bawls the hell out of the wife, and as he is leaving goes to Lou's hiding place and shouts, "I thought I told you to go to 57th Street!"

A couple, sitting on a settee, are hugging and kissing. The woman says that she never loved her husband and that she should never have married him when all along she was in love with the man she is fondly embracing. "You are the only man in my life," she says; "you have always been the only one." She goes on to declare her belief that a girl should be true to only one man. Her husband calls out. He has returned. The woman tells her lover to hide in the closet. The lover looks around, sees the wardrobe closet, dashes over to open the door, and finds three other fellows in there already.

(Stage setting: two chairs and a table with a telephone)
The husband sits down to the telephone, asks the operator for Jefferson 5000 *(he plants the number by repeating it several times)*, and speaks to his wife. He tells her that he will be home for dinner immediately. As soon as he is through calling, a friend comes in and they talk about going out. The husband calls up his wife again and tells her that his boss has come back into town and he has to go to a meeting. When he hangs up, he and the friend discuss blondes and brunettes. The friend says he knows a suitable one, sits down at the telephone, and says, "Give me Jefferson 5000."

A man enters and catches his sweetheart in the arms of the MC The man threatens to kill the MC. The MC tells him not to shoot, explaining that he and the woman are sweethearts. The woman exits. The man and the MC argue as to whose sweetheart the girl really is and come to an understanding that they will fire two shots in the air and then pretend that they are both dead. The man she makes the biggest fuss over is the one she truly loves. They fire two shots in the air and lie down. A third man comes in and looks at them. The woman comes rushing in and says they killed themselves over her, turns to the third man, and says, "Sweetheart!"

A woman and her lover are hugging and kissing. The woman's little boy is present. She tells him that her husband has gone on a trip. They are interrupted by a knock on the door. Confusion. She tells the man to hide in the boy's room. He hides and the husband enters, saying that he has missed his train and won't be able to leave till tomorrow. The little boy keeps looking at his father and then at the door through which the lover has exited. Finally, the father notices and asks his son what's the matter. The kid says, "Bogeyman." The wife tells the little boy not to be silly.

There is no bogeyman. She says it two or three times. The husband, now suspicious, goes to the door and throws it open, discovering the man. He bawls the fellow out: "Say, don't you feel ashamed of yourself, frightening a poor kid?"

A husband comes home drunk, staggers into the bedroom, and puts on the light. A fellow is in bed with his wife. She tells her husband to be quiet. The husband hasn't noticed anything. She watches him as he takes off his clothes: jacket, pants, shoes, and socks. He climbs into bed wearing his underwear and a hat. He gets into bed on the free side of his wife and pulls up the blanket, revealing three sets of feet. He looks at them and counts on his fingers. Then he says, "Shay, how many people are there in this bed?" She says, "Two." He says, "I count three." She replies, "Don't be silly, you're seeing double; there's just the two of us." The husband goes through the business of counting again and says, "I count six feet." After he figures a third time, she tells him to get out of bed and count them. He does and counts four feet. Then he says, "Thash right, there's just the two of us."

(The stage is set with a table and chairs. A wife is helping her husband pack for a trip.)
Wife: Take a minute to have a cup of coffee before you leave.
Husband: No time.
(She kisses him goodbye, and he exits. As soon as he's gone, she picks up the phone, calls her lover, and tells him to join her. The lover enters. The two hug and kiss. There's the sound of a key in the door. From offstage, the husband calls to his wife that he has left something. The lover crawls under the table.)
Husband: I have a few moments to spare, so I'll just take a cup of coffee now.
(He sits. She pours the coffee. Then she takes the sugar.)
Wife: Two?
Husband: Two for me—and one for the guy under the table.

In a dim light, a man rushes across the stage and is stopped by a gypsy fortune teller. He tells her that he is in a hurry to get home, that he is going to be a father. The fortune teller says she sees trouble in store for him. The man is very concerned and asks, "What is it?" "I see by the stars," says the fortune teller, "that if the child is a girl, the mother will die. If the child is a boy, the father will drop dead." *(Open curtain on a hospital setting.)* The father explains to a nurse what the fortune teller has told him. As he talks, the iceman enters. The nurse exits. Both men pace back and forth and show signs of anxiety. The father tells the iceman this is a terrible time to think about ice, and keeps repeating what the gypsy said. The nurse brings a little bundle to the door. The father asks in a scared voice, "Tell me, nurse, is it a boy or a girl?" The nurse replies, "It's a boy." At that moment, the iceman drops dead.

(The curtain parts discovering a couple sitting on a sofa. The lights are low.)
Wife: Sweetheart, I want to thank you for the wonderful time we had last night. It was certainly wonderful to be with you again.
Lover: The pleasure was all mine. I'm glad you enjoyed the evening. Tomorrow evening, I am going to take you out to another theatre, and the night after that to a swell cabaret, and the third night I'm going to give you the surprise of your life.
Wife: Darling!
Lover: Sweetheart!
(In a dim light, a man and a woman embrace. The husband enters upstage and stands behind the couch. Immediately the lovers slide to opposite ends.)
Husband: So that's the kind of guy you are. You steal the love of a respectable married lady. You entice her away from her husband, her home, and her family with a lot of hot air. I know your kind, and you are going to get what you deserve. In fact, I'm going to kill the pair of you. *(He shoots both. The lover rolls off the couch, and the wife throws her head back as if she were dead. The husband switches on the lights and looks into the face of the woman and screams)* My God, I'm in the wrong apartment!

(Variation)
MC: We hear so much these days about triangle tragedies, one man falling for another man's wife. It's becoming very popular. Just to give you an idea of what things are coming to . . .
(In a dim light, we discover a couple on the couch; they are hugging and kissing, sighing and kissing, sighing and moaning. A man pops up from behind the couch.) "That's the sort of guy you are, eh, making love to another man's wife? You rat, take this!" *(A shot. The man looks at the woman.)* "My God, I'm in the wrong apartment."

After a woman has finished her act, the MC brings her back, woos her, and tells her that he would like to take her out that night. But first he must ring his wife. The woman asks the MC if his wife will agree. He replies, "Sure. I'm the boss at my house." He then goes to the phone, asks for the number, is connected, and begins to make excuses to his wife: "I won't be home . . . I'm having late rehearsals . . . I'll eat out." The wife's voice (off-stage) starts bawling him out. As he tries to placate the woman on stage, his wife's voice goes on talking. The MC gets all confused and tries to put the telephone receiver in his pocket. He finally succeeds, but the voice continues. Then he removes it and says, "Okay, dear, I'll be home. Goodbye!" The wife's voice, however, continues to be heard. The MC keeps trying to "bury" the receiver in order to stop the voice. Finally, he hangs it up and takes the woman's arm and the two of them walk to one side of the stage. The MC pauses, leaves the woman's side, walks back to the telephone, and lifts the receiver again. The voice is still coming through. The MC repeats this whole business. The woman exits with the remark, "Oh, boy, you SURE are the boss in your house!" Then the MC walks away from the telephone and says, "Well, I really didn't want to go out anyway."

(Setting: a kitchen where there is a leaking faucet. [A washbasin with taps is needed.] The lady of the house paces. She has been waiting a long while for the plumber. Knocking. The lady rushes to the door and admits the plumber.)

Lady: So, you're here at last.

(The plumber enters with a bag of tools.)

Plumber: I came as soon as I could. *(He looks in his bag and removes a wrench.)*

Lady *(pointing)*: Well, there's the faucet.

Plumber *(he goes to the faucet and turns it)*: No hot water.

Lady: What are you going to do about it?

Plumber: I've got just what it takes.

Lady: I've waited so long.

Plumber: I'll fix you up all right.

Lady *(stopping him)*: Not now, my husband may come home any moment.

Plumber: Shall I come back later when he's gone?

Lady: Yes, come back when he's gone.

Plumber: All right, later then. *(He puts the wrench away and picks up his bag.)*

Lady: Wait a second. Take this with you. When you return, it may come in handy. *(She hands him a gun.)*

Plumber: That's not how I plug leaks.

(The lady of the house has been waiting some time for the doctor. She has a thermometer and keeps taking her temperature. There's a knock at the door and she admits the doctor.)

Wife: So, you're here at last.

(The doctor is carrying a little black bag.)

Doctor: I came as soon as I could. *(He looks in his bag and removes a stethoscope.)*

Wife: It's my chest.

Doctor *(as he listens to her chest, she moves his hand to her cheek)*: Why, it's cold!

Wife: What are you going to do about it?

Doctor: I'll fix you up. I've got something for you.

Wife: Not now, my husband may come home at any time.

Doctor: I don't see a problem.

Wife: You don't?

Doctor: Not at all.

Wife: Well, you're a daring one.

Doctor: Shall I come back later when he's gone?

Wife: Yes, come back when he's gone.

Doctor: All right, later then. *(He picks up his bag.)*

Wife: Wait a moment, take this with you. *(She hands him a key.)*

Doctor: What's wrong with a knock?

Wife: Nothing, that's just what I want!

(Two men are seated in a restaurant.)

Len: You look terrible, Joe. Why do you look so sad?

Joe: I feel terrible. I'm all broken up.

Len: 'Smatter?

Joe: My girl went back on me, Len. I had a beautiful girl, and we were going to be married tomorrow. But last night I went to a cabaret, and there she was, sitting at a table with my best friend. He was making love to her.

Len: Don't tell me you just sat there and didn't do or say anything!

Joe: I went over to their table and . . .

Len: Yeah, what happened?

Joe: What happened? *(He assaults Len, leaves him on the stage, and exits, saying)* Then you asked me why I looked so sad.

(Sam enters. Len is lying on the stage moaning from his injuries.)

Sam: Say, what's the matter? Why do you look so sad?

Len: What?

Sam: Why do you look so sad?

Len: Well, Sam, I'll tell you. I went into a restaurant last night, and there was my girl with another fellow.

Sam: Yeah, go on!

Len: Ask me what happened.

Sam: Was she blonde?

Len: Yeah, but ask me what happened!

Sam *(interrupting):* Where did she live: 320 North Grand on the third floor?

Len: Yeah, but you're killing it. Ask me what happened!

Sam: Was her name Mary?

Len: Yeah. *(Disgusted)* Ask me what happened!

Sam: Why you dirty dog, that's my wife! *(Beats him up.)*

(A husband and wife are seated on a couch. The man is reading from a newspaper.)

Husband: It says here, honey, that the terror has surfaced again, and that he breaks into homes and makes love to neglected wives. This is terrible, dear. Now listen, if that terror breaks into our house, I want you to protect yourself. Take this gun and if that terror appears, shoot—and shoot to kill! Now, I have some

work to do in the drawing room. Don't forget: if that terror
shows up, shoot—and shoot to kill!
*(The husband exits. Pause. A masked man jumps through an opening in
the backdrop.)*
Man: Sh, Sh, Sh. I'm not going to hurt you.
Wife: Oh, I know you. You're that bad man. You're the terror.
Man: I'm not going to hurt you. They call me the terror, but I'm
not a bad man. I'm a good man. *(He caresses the woman and kisses
her on the forehead.)* Now that didn't hurt, did it?
Wife: No it didn't, but I was warned to avoid you.
Man: Why? I just go around taking care of neglected housewives.
I'm the ladies' home companion! It's only the husbands who call
me the terror. *(He kisses her again, this time on the lips.)* See, that
wasn't so bad, was it?
Wife *(coyly)*: No, but my husband would object if he knew.
Man: There's no need to tell him. *(He ad-libs affectionate phrases,
and with each one the wife gives in more.)*
(The husband enters.)
Husband: Honey! That's the terror. Shoot!
*(The wife looks at the terror and then at her husband. A brief pause.
Then she shoots her husband.)*

The stage is set with a big clothes closet, a chair, a sofa, and a
small table with a telephone. The scene opens with a woman in a
dressing gown rushing around helping her husband pack his suitcase, which rests on the chair. He is talking all the while about
missing the train if he doesn't hurry. The woman grabs his coat
and hat from the closet. He tells her not to worry; he won't be
away long. She says it's awful that he has to run off on business
when they're on their honeymoon. He tells her not to cry over
his absence; he won't be gone long. He kisses her and starts to
leave. But half way to the door, he turns back and embraces and
kisses her. He repeats this routine three or four times. Finally, he
exits. The woman listens to make sure that he's gone. Then she
locks the door, walks over to the phone, asks for a number, and
says, "Is this Sam? Yes, honey, he's gone. He'll be away two days.
Yes, come right up. Yes, I'm alone. You'll be right up, okay." She
sits down on the sofa. There's a knock at the door. She goes
over, admits another man, and locks the door. They embrace
and exchange loving phrases. Just as they get seated on the sofa,
there's a knock at the door. The husband's voice is heard shouting, "Open the door, sweetheart, open up!" The couple inside
become frantic. She says, "It's my husband!" The man says, "My
God, where can I hide?" She looks around, sees the wardrobe
closet, and hurries him inside it. Then she straightens her hair
and opens the door. The husband dashes in and says, "Honey, I
left my bag." He goes over and takes his bag off the chair, saying

he'll miss his train if he doesn't hurry. She showers him with affectionate phrases. As he dashes to leave with the bag, they repeat the business of repeatedly hugging and kissing. After the last kiss, he goes to the wardrobe closet, stops for a second, knocks loudly on the door, and shouts, "Goodbye, Sam!"
(Note: On the repeated goodbyes, she keeps saying, "Goodbye, honey," and he, "Goodbye, sweetheart." The actors should keep on repeating "goodbye" to plant the last line for the husband's "Goodbye, Sam.")

MC *(to audience):* Impresarios from other countries have come to America to learn these skits. Then they take them over to their respective countries and perform them. If people will call out what country they would like to hear this skit represent, we'll do it as done in that country, any country at all. Russia! A gentleman down here says Russia.
(Musical introduction: "The Volga Boatmen." Three men and one woman enter, dressed in exaggerated Russian costumes. The first and second man are not so bad, but the third is fully dressed in trousers, beard, and hat. As the third enters, he loses his pants. Then the woman and the last two men exit. The first man remains standing in front of the curtain. As the curtain opens, the woman enters.)
Lover: Aha! Toot-ski!
Wife: Darling-ski.
Lover: Where is your husband-ski? Is he away-ski?
Wife: In Poughkeepskie.
Lover: Goodski! How about a little drink-ski?
Wife: Yeah, whiskey.
Lover *(clapping his hands):* Service-ski.
(A girl enters with a tray of drinks and exits as the couple serve each other.)
Lover: That's good-ski. Come to me-ski.
Wife: My lover-ski!
(The "Volga Boatmen" song is played as the husband enters.)
Husband: Ha-Ha-ski. My wife-ski.
Wife: My husband-ski.
Lover: My God-ski. My hat-ski.
Husband: So-ho-ski. I come home to find my wife-ski in the arms of my friend-ski. Minoshski, go-ski to your room-ski! *(She exits.)* Now for you-ski!
Lover: I love your wife-ski.
Husband: My wife-ski loves me-ski.
Lover: No-ski! Your wife-ski loves me-ski.
Husband: We will prove it-ski. We will both take a gun-ski and pretend-ski to shoot-ski the other.
Lover: Yes-ski, and when she comes running-ski, she will run to the one she loves-ski best-ski.
(Both men take out guns, discharge them, and lie down. The wife comes running on stage.)

Wife: My God-ski, they have shot themselves over me-ski. *(She waves to someone off stage. The third man, the one with the outlandish costume, comes running on.)* Aha, darling-ski! (They embrace, and blackout.)

(Variation)
(The MC asks the audience which country they would like to see represented in a skit.)
MC: Spain! Some lady shouted Spain. Okay, Spain.
Boy: Aha, my Señorita!
Girl: My Señor.
Boy: My Cascaretta, your husband, he is go away, no?
Girl: No, my husband he is go away, yes.
Boy: Tis good for me, but bad for your husband.
Girl: You like a little vino, no?
Boy: Ah, no vino, yes. ·
(The girl dances on and off with drinks. Both drink to each other in ad libbed toasts.)
Boy *(embracing the girl):* Aha, Señorita, my Cascaretta.
(A man enters on their embrace. Toreador song)
Man: Aha-ski! My wife in the armski of my pal-ski.
Boy: Hey, hey, what country are you in? This is Spain! Get back into character.
(The man goes off and makes another entrance.)
Man: Señor, you hug my wife. I keel you like a peeg.
Boy: Get a load of that. He's supposed to be a bullfighter and he's going to keel me like a peeg.
Man: Cascaretta, you leeve here. I will settle with this lover.
(The girl tries to leave but each man grabs an arm.)
Man: Let her go!
Boy: I won't!
Man: If she's got to go, she's got to go!
Boy *(to man):* Say, aren't you Mickey the Rat from Chicago?
Man: Yeah! I thought I knew you. You're Lefty the Louse from the South Side.
Boy: Well, what are we waiting for?
(Tense for a moment, then one does a nance.)
Man: Say, I'd like to spend some time with yooou!
(Both men embrace for blackout.)

(A man, the lover, and another man's wife are passionately embracing. She is wearing a negligee. He is in shirt sleeves and is wearing house slippers.)
Wife: Darling! This is so heavenly.
Lover: Wonderful. *(They kiss. He breaks free of the embrace.)* Are you sure it's all right?
Wife: You have absolutely nothing to worry about. George is a very modern husband. We never interfere with each other.

Lover: Never interfere with each other? *(She nods.)* I'm sure glad to hear that. *(He passionately embraces her.)* Darling!
(Offstage noise. He tries to break off the embrace. She restrains him reassuringly. The husband enters carrying a lunch box.)
Husband *(cheerfully):* Good evening, dear.
Wife: Hello, George, you're early tonight.
Husband: Dinner ready?
Wife: I didn't have time. You'll find the can opener on the sink.
Husband: I see. *(Crosses to center.)* By the way, have my shirts come back from the laundry?
Wife: Oh, I forgot to send them out.
Husband: Oh, that's all right. I can wear this shirt for another two weeks. *(He crosses to left of stage.)* Have you seen my slippers anywhere?
Wife *(pointing to lover's feet):* He's wearing them. Do you mind?
Husband *(muttering as he exits):* It's quite all right. I have to find the can opener.
Lover: He is modern, isn't he?
Wife *(as they embrace):* You see, I told you we had nothing to worry about.
(As the lovemaking becomes intense, the husband reenters, carrying a jacket over his arm.)
Husband *(tapping lover on shoulder):* Pardon me! *(The lover looks up.)* Is this your jacket?
Lover *(looking at jacket):* Yes, it is.
(The husband pulls out a gun and shoots the lover. The wife screams.)
Husband *(holding up jacket to audience):* No union label.

(There are two spots, one on each side of the stage. A woman sits on a couch. A man phones her from the side of the stage.)
He: Sorry, hon, I can't get home till very late. I'll probably be tied up at least until three o'clock. I've got a big deal going.
She: Is she around again?
He: Now, honey, you have no need to be suspicious. Just go to bed and get a good night's sleep.
She: No, I'm going to wait up for you.
He: Darling, I insist you tuck your little footsies under the cover and go to bed.
She: I won't go to bed!
He: Go to bed!
She: I won't be told what to do!
He: Now, sweetheart, you know you're all worn out.
She: Nonsense! I'm fit as a fiddle.
He: Okay, I'll see you around three. But if you decide to turn in, don't worry about me.
(They hang up the phones. She sits and pouts for a minute; then she goes to the right, picks up the phone, and calls some fellow.)
She: No, God, no, don't come here! I'll come to your place. *(She*

exits. Blackout. A clock tolls three times, and the orchestra plays "Three O'clock in the Morning." Lights up as the woman returns to her place, out of breath and nervous. She calls) Eddie! *(When no one answers, she shows great relief. A key is heard in the door. The man enters dressed in a large overcoat with a muffler and hat. They embrace.)*

He: Sorry to be so late.

She: You poor dear, having to work such terrible hours.

He: Thanks for waiting up.

She: Don't even mention it. Here, let me help you out of your things.

(He flops into a chair.)

He: No need, really.

She: Oh, do let me help you.

(She takes off his hat and starts to remove his muffler.)

He: Gee, honey, I wish you wouldn't make such a fuss. Just because I've worked late, you make me feel like a big sap fussing over me this way.

(She keeps helping him, all the while using endearing terms. Finally, she takes off his muffler and then his coat, revealing that he is wearing only his underpants.)

She: Eddie, where are your clothes?

He: My God, I've been robbed!

(Scene: A table and three chairs. A woman is excitedly straightening the room.)

Wife: Jack said he would be here. I do hope he gets here before my husband gets home.

(Two men enter.)

Husband: Hello, dear, I came home early and met Jack in the hall on his way up.

Wife: Hello, dear. Hello, Jack.

Jack: Hello, Mary, delighted to see you. *(To Husband)* Nice place you have here. Nice and bright.

Husband: Oh yes, we're way up on the thousandth floor. There are a few floors higher, but they have to be taken in at night to let the moon pass.

(Jack and Mary secretly motion to each other and act very nervous.)

Jack: Shall we do something?

Wife: Yes, for heavens sake, let's do something.

Husband: Like a game of cards?

Jack: That's fine. What shall we play, pinochle?

(Everyone agrees, and they sit at the table. The husband deals.)

Jack: What's trumps?

Husband: Hearts.

(They start to play. The husband makes the first trick, saying, "Ah, that's mine!" He is much pleased with himself. On the next trick, he is ready to pick it up again when Jack uses a trump.)

Jack: That's mine.

Husband *(horrified):* What, no clubs? *(He moans through the next three or four hands, holding his head and making a fuss.)*

Jack: Don't you think now is the time, dear, to tell Oswald everything? We ought to make a clean breast of it. Now listen, Oswald!

Husband: My goodness . . . he has no clubs!

Jack: Oswald, your wife and I are very much in love. We have loved each other honorably for some time now, haven't we, Mary?

Wife: Yes, dear. Jack and I are very much in love. We want to get married, and we feel that you should be deceived no longer.

(All through these speeches, the husband constantly repeats, "My God, he has no clubs." The lovers continue.)

Jack: We are crazy about each other.

Wife: We adore each other.

Husband: But you have no clubs.

Wife: Oh, come on, lets play another hand.

(They play, and Jack again uses a trump. In a frenzy, the husband jumps up, draws a gun, and shoots Jack.)

Wife: Oh, my manly husband! You killed him because he wanted to steal me away from you. My hero! You really do love me!

Husband: No, no, no! He had no clubs!

(During the above blackout, the scene is changed to a domestic one: a table, with a cloth, is set for dinner. There are two chairs. It is a year later. Instead of murdering his wife's lover, the husband has shot himself. She has married her lover. After a song is played, we see the newly-weds. The wife is standing beside the table. The husband enters.)

Husband: Good evening, dear. *(He goes to embrace her.)*

Wife *(coldly):* You're late for dinner again.

Husband: I couldn't help it, dear, I was detained at the office. *(Sits.)* A big proposition.

Wife: That big proposition, is "she" in again?

Husband: Is dinner ready? *(He picks up the newspaper.)*

Wife: No, it isn't ready.

Husband: Then what are you chewing about? *(Reads.)* You make me sick.

Wife: Well, you're no health resort to me. *(Grabs at paper.)* Put that paper down.

Husband: What do you want me to do?

Wife: I want you to talk to me.

Husband: What's the use, you don't understand English.

Wife: I thought I did when you promised me clothes, jewels, and a beautiful home.

Husband: Oh, be glad with what you've got.

Wife: What have I got? You get me out here in the country, eight miles from a trolley and put me in a wrapper. If it wasn't for the iceman I don't know what I'd do.

Husband: Oh the iceman, eh? Well, I'll soon alter that. Tomorrow we get a Frigidaire. Anyhow, you took me for better or worse.

Wife: Yes, and I got the worst of it.

Husband: Aw, shut up.

Wife: I won't shut up. You can't make me either.

Husband (crosses to her): Shut up, or I'll give you a bust on the nose.

Wife (screams): That's right, you brute, go and strike me.

Husband: Did I attempt to strike you?

Wife: No, but you wanted to. I'm going home to mother. (Weeps.)

Husband: That's right, go, go, go to your mother. But you can't go home to your mother.

Wife: Why not?

Husband: Your mother went home to her mother.

Wife: Oh, when I think how you fooled me. (Weeps.)

Husband: Oh, yes, you were just a little innocent. I fooled you! You were married before I ever saw you.

Wife: Yes, I was a widow.

Husband: A widow: what's a widow?

Wife: A widow is a woman who knows all about a man. And the man who knows all about her is dead.

Husband: Yes, that's right: dead and happy!

Wife: But sweetheart, I want to make you happy. (She caresses him.)

Husband (breaking away from her): Well, why don't you?

Wife (pulling out a revolver): I will! (She shoots him.)

(The curtain opens, and a girl is discovered sitting on a sofa. There's a knock at the door, and a man enters.)

Lover: Hello, sweetheart. (They embrace.) Oh boy, is it good to see you.

Girl: And I'm so glad to see you. You look fine.

Lover: Where is he—your hubby?

Girl: Oh, he's away. He left this morning for Pittsburgh.

Lover: Too bad for him. Sweetheart, you look wonderful. I can't imagine why you wanted to marry an old fossil like him. His eyes are as dull as the seat of my dad's old serge pants. Don't you ever feel the call of youth? Oh, sweetheart! (They embrace.)

(Noise off: shouting and knocking. The husband enters.)

Wife: My husband!

Lover: My God!

Husband: Just as I thought. I knew I would catch you. I guessed this was going on. (To his wife) Go to your room. I'll see you later. (The man starts to leave with her, but the husband pulls out a gun.)

Husband: Come back, you! We need to talk. Then I'm going to kill you.

Lover: Don't do that; I haven't paid my last club dues.

Husband (menacingly): Yes, I'm going to kill you. But I will try a

better way to kill you than just doing it in cold blood. I'll make you kill yourself. I'll make you say "fire" and when you say the word, I'll shoot to kill.
Lover: You'll never get me to do it. Do you think I'm so silly as to say "fi . . . " Oh, oh, oh, I nearly said it.
Husband: What do you keep in your kitchen stove?
Lover: Gin.
Husband: What kinds of insurance are sold in this country?
Lover *(nervous):* Ther-ther-there's auto, theft, collision and—
Husband *(urging):* Yes, yes, go on!
Lover: And there's auto and fi-fi-fi-
Husband *(preparing to shoot):* Yes, yes!
Lover: Oh, if I could only think. *(The husband is disappointed.)*
Husband: If you do this with your cigar lighter, what do you get?
Lover: A sore thumb.
Husband: Now tell me, what do you cook your bacon with?
(Pause)
Lover: I don't eat it.
Husband: If you had a clothing store that caught fire, what would you shout as you ran to the door?
Lover: Whoopee!
Husband: If you put a light to a cask of gasoline, what would happen?
Lover: The cask would go boom and I would go up and then down.
Husband: I give up. You're too dumb to kill.
Lover: Oh yeah! You think I'm too dumb, eh? *(To the audience)* What a boob! He thought I was fool enough to say FIRE.
(The husband shoots him.)

(Scene: Doctor's office. Dim light. The doctor is out. The phone rings. An assistant answers.)
Asst: A bad back and lameness in one leg. Yes, sir, the doctor can see you right away. Who referred you? I see. Come right over. Is he rough? Well, he is a chiropractor and will need to crack your bones. But he is very good.
(The assistant exits. The doctor enters and is illuminated by a white spot. On the other side of the stage, a white spot illuminates lovers embracing. The man, while in the arms of the woman, reaches for the phone and asks the operator for the number of the doctor's office. The phone in the office rings, and the doctor answers it.)
Lover: Is this Doctor Farthington?
Doctor: Yes.
Lover: I want you to know I'm in love with your wife—and she's in love with me. In fact, at this very moment we are embracing.
Doctor *(furious):* If you were a man, you'd tell me in person. And then I'd have the pleasure of tearing you limb from limb.

Lover: Well, it just so happens that I'm across the street in my apartment and I'll be right over.

(The doctor bites the phone, punches it, hangs up, and exits. The assistant enters leading a man who walks as if he has one leg in the grave.)

Asst: Are you sure you want to see a chiropractor? Wouldn't an undertaker be more appropriate?

Patient: I told you on the phone, I was in awful shape.

Asst: Well, just make yourself comfy. The doctor will be here in a second.

Patient: You said the doctor was rough.

Asst: Yes, but he'll help you.

(The assistant exits. The doctor enters, sees the man, glares at him, and says)

Doctor: Oh, so you came up!

Patient: Did you get my message?

Doctor *(threateningly):* Yes, I got your message. *(He goes up to the patient, slaps his face, and bangs him around.)* Now, how did you like that?

Patient: If that's the way you do it, I guess it's all right. I just hope it works. *(The doctor knocks him around again and shouts)*

Doctor: Why don't you fight back? *(The doctor pushes him around some more.)* Hit me!

(The patient picks up a club and hits the doctor on the head. The doctor falls down. A second later, the lover enters from the opposite side of the stage and swaggers up to the patient.)

Lover: Oh, so you're the guy! *(He throws the patient to the floor and starts beating him.)* Why don't you fight back?

(The patient gets up, takes the club, and knocks the man to the ground, where he remains. The woman enters from the opposite side of the stage and screams. The doctor, lying on the floor, looks up and says)

Doctor: My wife!

(The other man, lying on the floor, looks up and says)

Lover: My sweetheart!

Patient *(throws open his arms as if to cry, "Take me!" and says):* My back is cured!

Wife: My hero!

(They embrace.)

Doctor: My God!

Lover: My loss!

(Blackout)

(Offstage noise)

Wife: Sounds like my husband.

Lover: I thought you said it was safe?

Wife: It's my husband! Quick hide!

Lover: Where can I hide?

Wife: In the closet.

Lover: Do I have to go in that closet again? *(Aside)* I wish some-one would write a skit without a closet.

Wife: Hurry, get in there quick! *(Leaving hat on the table)*

Husband *(enters in long fur coat and hat):* Hello, sweetheart. Oh, I'm so tired. My feet are all jumping terribly. Where are my slippers?

Wife: They're in the other room. I'll get them for you.

Husband: No, dear, they're in the closet.

Wife: No, sweetheart, they're in the other room.

Husband: They're in the closet, I tell you. *(He holds his hand out. The lover puts the slippers in his hand.)*

Wife: There, what did I tell you; they were in the closet.

Husband *(He sees the hat.):* Whose hat is this?

Wife: It's your hat, darling.

Husband: That's not my hat. I wouldn't wear a thing like that. *(He starts twisting the hat.)* I never had a hat like this.

Lover *(looking out of the closet):* Hey, what the hell are you doing with my hat?

Husband *(surprised):* Aha! There's a man in this house.

Wife: There's no man in this house.

Lover: Hey! I'm here. I don't know about him.

Husband: There's a man in that closet, and by God, I'm going to kill him.

Wife: There's no one in that closet.

Lover *(coming out of the closet):* You're right, there's someone in that closet and it's me. Look here, why don't you take a turn in that closet. I'm always in that darn thing.

Husband: Frankly, I like it better out here. What's more, I'm the husband.

Lover: Oh yeah! Well, I've been around a bit, too. Come on, get in there.

(Comedy of taking the fur coat off. The lover falls down under the weight of it.)

Husband: Aha, you're going to make a swell husband. *(He enters the closet.)*

Lover *(in the role of the husband, he sees the hat):* Whose hat is that?

Wife: That's your hat, darling.

Lover *(to husband in the closet):* Hey, what the hell have you been doing with my hat?

Husband: I'm dying of the heat in this closet, and you're telling jokes. Get on with it!

Lover: There's a man in this house, and by God, I'm going to kill him!

Wife: There's no man in this house.

Husband: You're right, there's a man in this house. It's too hot in that closet. I can't stand it.

Lover: Well, someone's got to be in the closet or else there is no skit.

Husband: Well, it's not going to be me.

Lover: I have it! *(To girl)* Hey, come on—in there. *(He tries to put her in the closet. She objects, and he kicks her in the pants. She enters the closet. Both men pull up chairs and sit.)*

Husband: It was much too hot for me in there.

Lover: Same for me.

(A third man emerges from the closet and says)

Man: It's too hot for me, too!

(Blackout)

(Scene: an apartment. At left, a small table, with writing materials, a chair, and a cabinet, on top of which stands a large doll. At right, a lady's writing desk, with writing pad, pens, and ink stand. At rise of curtain, the husband and the scientist are discovered.)

Scien: You seem worried this evening, my friend, what is it?

Husband: Well, to tell the truth, I am worried—about my wife.

Scien: She isn't ill?

Husband: No, it isn't that. It's about her habits. I hate to say so, but I suspect that my wife simply cannot tell the truth.

Scien: That's an unfortunate state of mind to be in.

Husband: And the trouble is I can't very well accuse her of it, because I am never absolutely sure.

Scien: Well, my dear fellow, would you like to have your mind put at ease?

Husband: I should say I would.

Scien: Well, I believe I have the means, right here.

Husband: Why, what do you mean?

Scien: My latest invention is an infallible test of whether someone is telling the truth or a lie.

Husband: Why, professor, you interest me greatly. I never dreamed that science had made such remarkable strides.

Scien: Oh, my dear fellow, in the matter of thought transference, progress has been extraordinary. You think the radio is wonderful. Well, I have given the greater part of my life to the study of thought waves and have achieved results that will surprise the world.

Husband: I surely would like you to demonstrate for me.

Scien: Nothing easier. Here is my latest invention. I call it the truth doll.

Husband: The truth doll? How does it work?

Scien: It is so delicately attuned to the waves of human thought that it can instantly detect a lie.

Husband: You mean that this doll can tell a lie from the truth? How?

Scien: Absolutely.

Husband: How?

Scien: The lie thought in the mind immediately imparts itself to the delicate mechanism of the doll and it starts to dance.

Husband: Remarkable!

Scien: And the greater the lie, the wilder its dance becomes. It is my masterpiece. No family should be without one.

Husband: That is the very thing I want. Are you sure it will work?

Scien: When a lie is really told, the doll will surely dance. *(Wife enters.)*

Wife: Hello, dear. Oh, how are you, Professor?

Scien: Good evening. *(To husband)* Well, I must be going. Good-bye and good luck.

Wife: What did he mean, good luck?

Husband: Oh, nothing. *(He goes over to the left.)* Where have you been, my dear?

Wife: Shopping in town. Oh, I saw some of the most gorgeous things. Would you believe it? I didn't buy a single thing.

Husband *(looks at the doll. It does not move.):* Strange.

Wife: What's strange?

Husband: Why, strange that you didn't buy anything. Didn't you have any money?

Wife: It wasn't that. When I thought of all the poor people who have so little, I couldn't bring myself to waste money on luxuries.

Husband *(looks at the doll. It does not move):* I knew it wouldn't work. Meet anyone you knew?

Wife: Yes.

Husband: Man or woman?

Wife: Alice Brewster.

Husband: Did you lunch anywhere?

Wife: Yes, at the club.

(The doll dances a little.)

Husband: Alone?

Wife: Yes.

(The doll dances a little more.)

Husband: That's funny. I phoned the club, and they told me you had not been there.

Wife: Why, that is absurd. The doorman saw me and said it was a nice day for ducks. How stupid these hired help are!

(The doll dances rapidly.)

Husband: Why should he say, "a nice day for ducks"? It isn't raining.

Wife: I don't know. I distinctly remember him saying, "It's a nice day for ducks."

(The doll dances a little.)

Husband: It's no use. I know you were not at the club. Now where were you?

Wife: Well, if you're going to be so peevish . . . I was at the Coronado.

Husband: Alone?

Wife: No, with Alice Brewster.

(The doll speeds up.)

Husband: I know you're lying. I ran into Alice, and she said she hadn't seen you for three or four days.

Wife: Look here, why should you cross-examine me in this way?

Husband: Because I know you're lying. Now, I want the truth. Who were you with?

Wife: Well, if you must know: with Harry.

Husband: At the Coronado?

Wife: Yes.

(The doll dances rapidly.)

Husband: No, you were not!

Wife: Well, I didn't think there was any harm in it. We went to his apartment.

Husband: His apartment? That's fine. What were you doing there?

Wife: Nothing.

(The doll dances violently.)

Husband: Nothing? You mean to stand there and tell me that you were at Harry's apartment, alone, and you were doing nothing?

Wife: I didn't think anything of it. Don't be so silly. You know he's harmless.

(The doll dances violently.)

Husband: So that's the way you act. I work my fingers off for you, and you go to men's apartments and do nothing. You expect me to believe that? Well, let me tell you something: I know that every word you've uttered is a lie. The professor left me his latest invention, the truth doll, and every time you told me a lie, the doll danced.

Wife: I think that's a mean, lowdown trick to play on anyone. Anyway, my lies are only little white ones. How about you? I suppose you always tell the truth?

Husband: I never told you a lie in my entire life.

(The doll blows up with a loud explosion.)

Insurance

(A man is lying on stage with a tire round his leg, his hat to one side, and his face covered with dirt. A stranger enters.)

Stranger: Have an accident?

Man: Yes, I just hit that tree over there. *(He moans.)* Has the insurance man arrived yet?

Stranger: No.

(A noise offstage)

Man: I think I hear him coming now.

Stranger *(lying down):* Move over and make room for me.

Interruptions

The MC tells a gag about being out with a girl last night. He is standing next to a young woman. Each time he comes to the line, "And the girl said to me," the woman interrupts him. She pulls him by the pants and he shouts in continuance of the line, "And the girl said to me—'let go of my pants!'"

(Done with Joe Penner)
—I want to tell some gags with you, but you must let me get in the answer. For instance, when I ask you what general in the American army wears the biggest hat, you have to say, "I don't know," and then I'll give the answer. Ready? Okay, let's go.
—Fire away.
—What general in the American army wears the biggest hat?
—The one with the biggest head.
—No, no, no! I give the answer. You mustn't do that. Now, let's try again, and this time I'll say the punchline. I ask you, what's the best way to raise corned beef and cabbage? and you have to say, I don't know, and then I answer. Come on, let's try again.
(They walk away and then meet each other center stage.)
—Say, _____, can you tell me what's the best way to raise corned beef and cabbage?
—Sure, with a knife and fork.
—No, no, no! You mustn't do that. That's wrong. I give the answer. You have to say, I don't know. Now, come on, let's try again and this time, I'll give the answer.
(Same stage business)
—Hello, _____, say can you tell me, what kind of a chicken lays the long . . . *(Trying to prevent being robbed of the punchline, he fails to complete the joke and shouts the answer himself.)* a dead one! Aha, I got that in!

(Variation)
—I want you to help me tell a gag. Will you do that? See, I say to you I was run over by a car this morning, and you work it up for me and then I give the answer. Get it? Now, come on. Say, _____, I was run over by an auto this morning and I wasn't even hurt.
—What kind of a car was it?
—Oh, _____, give it some enthusiasm. Help me put it over. Now, come on. We'll start it all over again. Say, _____, I was run over by a car this morning and I wasn't even hurt.
—The speed limit is out of hand.
—*(same complaints; repeat)*: I was run over . . . *(etc.)*
—They ought to post cops on every corner.
—*(same complaints)*
—Where did the guy get his license?
—*(same complaints)*
—That reminds me, I gotta renew my license.
—*(Throws up his hands in disgust and walks off.)*
—I was just getting to the punch line.

Kissing

(Done with Bert Lahr)
A man is wooing another man's wife, but she resists. He says,
"All I want is one little kiss. Think about it. Just one little kiss. I'll
give you a thousand dollars!" She ponders the idea for a moment
and agrees. The man says he'll be right back with the money. He
exits and the woman phones her mother to ask her opinion.
From the phone conversation, we can tell that the mother agrees.
The man returns and gives her the money. She throws herself
into his arms, and they madly kiss. *(The lights go up and down to
indicate passion.)* After the last kiss, the man jumps up, skips
around, and exits. The girl lovingly gazes at the money and ad
libs that it's enough to more than pay off the family debts. The
husband comes running in and asks, "Has Eddie been here?
My pal, Ed, has he been here?" He sees the money in her hand.
"There it is! I knew he could be trusted. Ed was just down to the
office to borrow a thousand bucks. He said he needed it for just
a few hours and he'd have it here for me when I came home. I
knew he wouldn't go back on his word. He's a true friend. A real
pal!"

Laundry

*(Two men: one on stage; the other enters later. The first man is looking
over the laundry. Every shirt but one is torn. He is getting ready to put it
on when a man enters.)*
Two: Did you get some laundry just now?
One: Yes.
Two *(looks over laundry and grabs the one untorn shirt.):* We forgot
to tear this one.
(Blackout)
MC: From he who hath not shall be taken away even that which
he hath.

Life's Lessons

A blind man stands center stage wearing glasses and a sign, and
holding a tin cup. First, a drunk comes by, reels against the blind
man, looks at him, pours a drink into the cup, drinks it himself,
wipes the blind man's mouth, and reels off. Second, the drunk
returns, tosses up an imaginary coin, juggles with the imaginary
coin, kicking it with his heel into the cup. *(Have a coin in the cup to
make noise as though the coin had really been tossed and kicked from
heel to cup.)* Third, a girl walks by, sees the blind man, and says,
"My mother always told me it was lucky to be kind to a blind
man, so here is the money she told me to put in the bank." She
lifts up her dress and removes a wad of bills from her stocking
top. The blind man looks when she lifts up her dress. The girl

puts the wad of bills into his cup. The blind man pulls out a gun and shoots her, remarking, "She's too good to live."

Marriage

Mrs. Harris is advising Mrs. Walker how she should treat Mr. Walker. "Don't bully him, don't complain when he's late, be understanding and forgiving." Mrs. Harris exits. Mrs. Walker waits for her husband: pacing, looking at the clock, and mumbling about her husband being late. Mr. Walker enters drunk. Mrs. Walker pets him. He looks surprised. She helps him off with his coat and repeatedly hugs and comforts him. "Now sit down, honey, and I'll give you a nice big kiss before I take your shoes off for you." Mr. Walker looks round and says, "I might as well, since I'll catch hell when I go home."

(A husband and wife enter a fancy restaurant to celebrate their first wedding anniversary.)
Man: I'm not very hungry. Why don't you go ahead and order.
Woman *(summons the waiter):* I'll have oysters and mussels, lemon soup, the salad with French dressing, steak and lobster with two baked potatoes, asparagus, and a bottle of your best red wine. I'll give you my dessert order later.
Waiter: You're sure that's enough?
Man: She eats like a bird—a vulture.
Wife: I resent that!
Man *(to waiter):* Cancel her order and bring us two hot dogs.
Wife: I've never been so insulted in my life! You're a beast. What kind of anniversary dinner is this! *(Hysterical)* Unless you let me have what I ordered, I am going to leave here and shoot myself. *(The husband is silent. The wife leaves. A shot is heard offstage. The husband summons the waiter.)*
Man: Cancel one of those hot dogs.

(Scene: a table, three chairs, a crystal ball, and a cabinet. Dressed in a robe, a female medium greets a husband and wife, who sit at the table.)
She: I want information about my late husband.
He *(to medium):* The old battle-axe, she just won't let him rest.
She: What did you call me?
He: A shrew.
(The wife and husband quarrel, eventually calming down.)
She *(to medium):* Are you sure that, if I enter that cabinet, I can see and speak to my dead husband?
Med: Absolutely.
She: What do you charge?
Med: Five dollars.
She *(to husband):* Oh, please give her the money and let me speak with my first husband! Please!
He: Why can't you just let him rest in peace? Leave him alone.

She: But I want to see him.

He: All right. *(To medium)* Here's the money. Now materialize her first husband, since she insists on seeing him.

(The medium directs the woman to enter the cabinet. After she does, the medium passes a wand over it and mumbles some words.)

Med: She has now entered the land of the unknown. *(The medium opens the cabinet, and it is empty.)* Only one person in the world can return her to this world: me! *(To the husband)* Just say the words "Bring her back" and I will do so.

He: Are you sure there is only one person who can bring her back: you?

Med: No other person on earth can bring her back—only me. She is now in the land of the unknown, among the spirits.

He: Are you sure that no one else can bring her back?

Med: No one!

(The husband pulls out a gun and shoots the medium.)

Two lovers are seated on a park bench. The man is proposing to the girl and tells her that he has bought her a beautiful ring. He gives her flowers, remarking that he found them outside a house, hanging on the door. He takes out the ring and points to the hole, saying that if he were a rich man that's where the stone would be mounted. The man talks about the future: she'll be at the door to meet him and greet him after his hard day's work. He says, "I can just see you and me doing our shopping together, buying the little things for our home and you whispering sweet nothings in my ear." This is the cue for a couple to enter and walk across the stage without stopping. The man is loaded down with parcels and staggering under their weight, while the woman is bawling him out for being a lazy good-for-nothing. The lovers watch in silence. Then the man tries to slip the ring back in his pocket. As the couple walking across the stage exit, the man goes on proposing and trying to avoid any mention of the ring. The woman asks him to let her see it. He says, "If you agree not to shop and have everything sent." The man talks about the lovely things they'll have for dinner when he comes home from work. They exchange talk about what each other likes. In the midst of this talk, another couple enters, quarreling about food. The man has a can in his hand and is saying, "Beans, beans, beans! All I get is canned stuff. I've put up with it long enough! I should have married a can opener." She tells him if he's not careful he'll get the beans and she won't trouble to open the can for him. They exit shouting at each other. The lovers on the bench intently watch them exit. The man seems very nervous. The woman tries to coax him to talk about the ring. He nervously says, "Maybe we ought to wait a while. I think it's better not to rush things." Another couple enters with a baby carriage that holds three babies. The husband is just a little guy and the wife an Amazon. She is bawling him out for sitting all day at the office doing nothing. As they leave, the man on the bench intently watches them. Then he moves to the other end of the bench, away from the girl. As soon as the couple with the baby carriage exit, the man looks at the girl, draws a gun, and shoots her.

Medicine: Hospitals

(Scene: A nurse is comforting a patient in the hospital.)
A doctor enters, asks the nurse how he is, and tells the nurse that the patient can see visitors, if he wants. The phone rings three times, and the nurse tells each caller that the patient can have visitors. Three men, one after the other (but not together), come in and talk about friends sewn up with sponges and scissors inside of them, owing to their surgeons' incompetence. The patient groans more deeply with each succeeding story. Just as the last visitor is through telling the patient about a syringe left behind in his friend, the doctor pops his head into the room and asks, "Anyone here seen my umbrella?"

(Scene: A hospital. A patient is lying under the covers, and a very nervous man is sitting at the end of the bed. A nurse is in attendance.)
Man: Please do something! Hurry! It's critical! Get help!
Nurse: The doctor will be here in a moment. Please contain yourself, won't you?
Man: Oh, I can't wait. Why doesn't the doctor come?
(The doctor enters.)
Doctor: What's the matter here? What's the problem?
Nurse: It seems that the patient has swallowed a golf ball.
Doctor: Good heavens! Swallowed a golf ball! That's very strange. *(To the nervous man)* Does your friend have an appetite for such things as golf balls?
Man: We were playing golf. He stepped on the fairway, yawned, and a golf ball landed in his mouth. Instead of spitting it out, he swallowed. It was a good thing he wasn't playing football.
Nurse: He seems to have difficulty with his breathing, doctor.
Doctor: Oh, I'll soon put a stop to that.
Man: Please, doctor, do something! The man has swallowed a golf ball. Operate! Get it somehow! It's there inside. Cut him, make a hole in him, do something!
Doctor: Will you please keep quiet. Anyone would think you were the patient. Who are you?
Man: I'm not the patient, I'm the IMpatient.
Doctor *(removing instruments from bag)*: It looks like we'll have to operate. Now, what's this here?
Man: Oh, that's only his Adam's apple.

Doctor *(threatening):* Will you please be quiet? *(To nurse)* How did this man get in here anyway?

Nurse: He came in with the patient.

Doctor: It seems as though we'll have to operate on his diaphragm.

Man: It's no use operating on his frying pan. You'll have to rip him open, or blast, or reach down his throat with some tongs.

Doctor: Now, you listen here! Will you keep quiet? Anyone would think that you were the surgeon. Do you know anything about an operation?

Man: No, I know nothing about an operation, nor do I know anything about laying an egg. But I know more about an omelet than a hen does.

Doctor: Say, who the dickens are you? Are you a friend of his?

Man: No.

Doctor: Are you his brother?

Man: No.

Doctor: Are you his cousin?

Man: No.

Doctor: Are you related at all to the patient?

Man: No, no, no!

Doc *(shouting):* Then who the devil are you?

Man: It's MY golf ball!

Medicine: Illness

(Scene: a hospital)

Hello, Bill! How's the cold? Thought I'd drop in and cheer you up. Y'know, Bill, the worst thing about being sick is that it's so easy to sit around and worry about things. And usually a fella isn't one-tenth as bad off as he thinks. Sure! Grin a little! That's the stuff! Nothing like keeping the ol' morale up, Bill! How's the throat? Still sore? That's bad. Bill, remember Eddie McFoozle? He had a little sore throat last week . . . started just like yours . . . and in two days. . . . Oh, don't look alarmed, Bill! Huh? Oh, that cough of yours isn't anything, Bill. But I'd watch it. You never can tell about a cough. The wife had a cousin who developed a cough last July. He's just about . . . what? No, I didn't go to the party last night. No, I haven't heard that one. But let's not be telling jokes, Bill. I was just watching how your hands shook when you reached for that medicine. Bill, if I was you I'd go see a specialist right away. You're all right, Bill, understand? But there's something funny about your eyes. Remember Tom O'Tizzy who used to work with us? His eyes got a funny look like that and . . . say, weren't you surprised so many people turned out at his funeral? Well, you know how double pneumonia is, Bill. Sneaks right up behind you and . . . hey! . . . eight-thirty already!

Well, I'll be running along. What? Oh, that's all right, Bill. Glad I came around. Just wanted to cheer you up, see? And get your mind off yourself for a few minutes. Well, so long, Bill. Say, just one thing more: Is everything all right at the office—just in case! I ask because, well, you know, Bill, it's always good to be prepared.

Medicine: Maternity Ward

MC: If I seem nervous, there's a reason. Just a year ago I got married, and any moment now I'm expecting word that the stork has paid a visit to my home. Inasmuch as my professional duties require my presence at this "mike" (or: in this theatre), the boys at the studio have volunteered to communicate news of the happy event the moment it occurs. One shot will mean it's a boy, and two shots, it's a girl. (One shot is heard. The MC is joyful.) It's a boy! (Another shot is heard. His response this time is not quite so jubilant.) No, it's a girl. (Another shot is heard.) It's twins. (Another shot is heard. He groans.) That means triplets. (A succession of shots is heard.) Jiminy Crickets . . . the birth of a nation!

(Variation)
(Done with Hal Sherman at Loew's State Theatre)
(Setting: a maternity ward. A man is pacing in the waiting room and sighing, "Oy, oy, oy!")
Doctor (enters): Quiet, please! The maternity ward is just next door.
Man: I'm so nervous.
Doctor: We've never lost a father yet.
Man: I can't tell you, doctor, how much I want a boy. That's why I'm so nervous. You must tell me the minute you know.
Doctor: If you'll be quiet and settle down, I'll signal you the moment I know. One toot on my whistle will mean it's a girl. Two toots, a boy. And three, twins.
(The doctor exits. Again the man starts to pace. Offstage, a whistle toots once.)
Man: Well, it's a girl. (Then the whistle toots a second time.) Hooray, it's a boy! (Then the whistle toots a third time.) My God, twins! (Then the whistle toots four or five times, and a man dressed in white enters selling fish.)

(Setting: a maternity ward. A man is pacing back and forth, chewing his nails and pulling his hair.)
Ed: Oh, this suspense is driving me mad! What did I ever do to suffer this way? Nurse, nurse! (Nurse enters.)
Nurse: My dear man, you will have to be quiet. There are other patients here. When I have news, I'll bring it. (Nurse exits.)
Ed: Oh God, I'll go daffy. I'll go mad. Every minute seems like a

year. Such agony! I'll never be able to go through with it. *(Nurse enters.)*

Nurse: Mr. Lowry, I told you, you will have to be quiet, you have nothing to worry about. We just delivered a lovely eight-pound baby to the woman across the hall from your wife.

Ed: My baby?

Nurse: No, no. Now please be still. I'm sure I'll have news for you any minute. *(Nurse exits.)*

Ed: She says I should be still. How can she know the pain I'm experiencing? Some people are heartless! *(Do business of having paper under fingernails, biting them, and spitting them out. The nurse enters.)*

Nurse: Mr. Lowry, Mr. Lowry, news, news! It's a beautiful baby girl.

Ed *(joyful):* Oh, a girl! Thank heaven! Good fortune has smiled on me! What luck!

Nurse: Mr. Lowry, you seem elated. Men usually prefer a boy.

Ed: What, I should bring a boy into this world to suffer as I just did? God forbid!

(Variation)

Ed: Oh, I just can't stand this much longer. I tell ya, I'm going out of my mind. Every second seems like a minute, every minute seems like an hour, and every hour seems like a year. I tell ya, I'll go crazy. Oh, nurse. Nurse!

Nurse: Please, please, Mr. Lowry. I'll have to ask you to be a little more quiet. We can't have that noise around here. Remember, there are other people in this hospital besides your wife. *(The nurse exits.)*

Ed: See that! See how mercenary they are. They don't care what happens. I tell you, I just can't go on like this. I've got pains in the back of my head and black spots in front of my eyes. *(Biting his fingernails)* Oh, I'll never go through this again.

Nurse: Please, Mr. Lowry, you must be quiet! There's nothing to get so excited about. Why, a lovely baby was just delivered to Mrs. Brown.

Ed: What, my baby?

Nurse: No, no. This baby was delivered by Dr. Raye.

Ed *(pushing the nurse out the door):* Oh, hurry back in there. He's our doctor also. Hospitals get babies mixed up. Oh, if I don't hear something soon, I'll go out of my mind. Oh, what did I do to suffer this way?

Nurse *(returns):* Mr. Lowry, I have news for you.

Ed: Quick, what is it?

Nurse: You're the father of a lovely seven-pound baby girl.

Ed: Oh, gagalaggals. A baby girl. *(Kisses nurse.)*

Nurse: But I don't understand you, Mr. Lowry. Men usually pray for a boy.

Ed: What? I should bring a boy into the world to suffer like I just did? Heaven forbid!

Men's Room

(Dim lighting: only enough to reveal the form of a man who sneaks on, looks over his shoulder this way and that, and acts mysteriously. Muttering to himself, he approaches a door and knocks. When it doesn't open right away, he begins to shout and rave.)

—You must let me in, I tell you. You must open this door. Immediately!

(He keeps shouting until the door is suddenly opened, disclosing a brilliant light and a sign inside the room reading: Men's Room.)

Newspapers

On stage, a newspaper editor is pacing back and forth. He is ranting about the lack of hot news. "No one," he says, "knows how to go about getting news any more. Make news if no one else will. Go out and let me have things to print." A reporter rushes in with an idea for a story. The editor bawls him out and tells him that's been printed in three editions today already. "Go out and don't come back if you haven't got a front page story." Another reporter comes rushing in and says, "A man down the street just committed suicide by taking poison. It happened not a block away from this building." The editor dismisses the reporter with the comment that he saw it himself and that it's on the streets already. Tearing his hair and asking about his star reporter, the editor says, "If only that guy would show up, he'll have something for the evening edition." There's a noise off stage and the star reporter bursts in. "Get on to the teletype right away . . . man murdered in broad daylight . . . name and address to follow." The editor storms, "Where is it? When is it? What is it?" The star reporter replies, "It will be on the streets in five minutes. Just listen!" The reporter pulls out his watch. "Four o'clock." Shots are heard off stage. The reporter says, "That's the guy!" The editor exclaims, "Now, that's news!"

Paternity

The stage is set with a baby's crib and a chair at the head of the crib. A woman (or a man dressed as a woman) is seated in the chair. There's a knock at the door. The woman calls, "Eddie!" He enters and asks how she knew it was he. They talk about the minister who married them. Eddie saw him in the subway just now and learned he was a fake. The man admitted he was broke and just wanted the eight dollars. He wasn't a minister at all.

Eddie says, "I feel terrible." The wife says, "You feel terrible? How about me?" *(Both repeat the line.)* Then the baby pops up out of the crib and says, "How about me?!"

Paul Revere

A man enters, riding a dummy horse. He knocks on the first door and shouts, "The British are coming!" An old fellow comes to the door with a butterfly net and field glasses, and says, "I'm going after 'em." At the second door, an ugly old maid bays, "Goody, Goody!" At a third door, a beautiful girl says, "Gee, I'll be so lonesome all alone in the house." Revere says, "To hell with it," and goes in, waving the horse off.

Police

While walking in the park, a fellow is accosted by one nance after another. Finally, he stops a tough-looking cop and asks, "What sort of park is this?" The cop does a nance routine, wiggling his shoulders and lisping, "Say, I wonder."

Two men are walking in opposite directions across the stage. One pulls a gun and acts real tough. The other man starts handing stuff over: wallet, watch, ring, cuff links. As he does so, a cop walks across the stage swinging his club. The cop exchanges hearty greetings with the holdup man.

(Done with Bert Lahr)
Two policemen are talking, center stage. One is dressed shabbily, the other smartly.
Cop 1: On my beat, I regularly have to deal with Evil Moe. But once I showed him who was boss, he acted like a sissy.
Cop 2: You know Lefty Louie? Once I got hold of him, I gave him the old one-two. Well, he knits now.
(A couple walk across the stage, arm in arm. When they reach the other side, a woman dashes on stage, pushes the cops aside, brandishes a gun, stops the couple, and cries)
Woman 1: At last I've caught you together. Well, let me tell you: you can't have him! He's mine!
Woman 2: You can't take him away from me!
Woman 1: All right, then, I'll take you away from him. *(She shoots woman 2.)*
Man: How could you? This is terrible!
Woman 1 *(shoots him, too, then hysterically yells)*: What have I done! *(She staggers off. Shots are heard after her exit.)*
(During the murders and suicide, the cops have been quaking, one looking over the other's shoulder. After the suicide, they turn to each other and resume their conversation where they left off.)
Cop 1: What was it you said about your district?

Cop 2: The toughest in the city. There's nothing I can't handle.
Cop 1: Me, too.
(They saunter off, swinging their clubs.)

Prison

Two men meet for the first time as they're exercising in the
prison yard. Initially, they exchange names. The second time,
they ask each other how long they're in for. The third time, one
of the men says, "Thirty years." The fourth time, the second man
asks, "When you get out, will you mail this letter for me?" The
fifth time, they are holding shovels and complaining about working on the rock pile. A guard comes over to talk to them. The
first man steals his key. After the guard leaves, the prisoner opens
his manacles and those of his friend, and points toward the gate
and freedom, handing the second fellow the key. The second prisoner goes off stage. A shot is heard. The first man picks up his
shovel and says, "That's what I wanted to know."

The Rehearsal

(Done with Benny Feldt, Ken, and Dominic.)
*(Setting: a dressing room with a piano, table, and couch. On the table is
a jar of candy and a telephone. Irv is playing the piano; Ben is lying on
the couch; and Ed is pacing back and forth.)*
Ed: I've got to go on in just a few minutes and I don't know the
song. Play it again.
Irv *(plays a few bars, stops, and picks up a newspaper):* Listen to
this. Some guy suggests equipping all cars with bikes so you can
ride to where you park.
Ben: Ed, here's a gag that'll lay 'em out in the aisles.
Ed: I'll kill 'em . . . that's fine . . . now will you leave me alone so
I can learn this song?
*(Benny takes a piece of candy and resigns himself to looking at the ceil-
ing. The song plugger enters.)*
Plugger: Oh, Ed, I just got this song. It's brand new. You'll wow
'em with it. I'll sing it for you and then—
Ed: Will you go out and lose yourself for a while? Can't you see
I'm trying to learn a song? And don't slam the door on the way
out. *(Turns to piano player.)* Let's try it again.
Plugger: All right, Eddie boy. You don't mind if I wait, do you?
(He sits down.)
*(After a few more bars of the song, Benny dashes to the piano and stops
everything, saying)*
Ben: Say, Ed, wait a minute. Have I got an idea! Oh, boy!
Ed: If you have an idea, sew a button on it. Not now!
Ben: Now, don't get funny. Listen! If you'll do this song like
this, you'll have 'em lined up the boulevard waiting to get in
the theatre. *(He plays a few bars on his violin.)*

Ed *(interrupting):* Benny, you're marvelous. Irving Berlin is a bum. Now will you go over there—and die!

Ben: All right, be that way. But if you flop, don't blame me. *(He walks away and takes another piece of candy. The plugger does the same thing.)*

Ed: Have a piece of candy, boys. *(Disgustedly)* Help yourself! *(A telephone rings. Ed looks around at Benny.)* Will you answer that, Benny? *(Benny looks annoyed.)* It's the least you can do if you're going to eat all my candy.

(Benny goes to the phone; the piano player and Ed continue to try to rehearse the song.)

Ben *(picks up the receiver):* Hello! *(To pianist)* Knock it off, will you? How do you think I can talk with all that row? Hello, yes, this is Ed Lowry's dressing room. Yes, dear, I take care of all that for Mr. Lowry. Yes, dear, surely not. Just come around to the stage door and ask for Ben. Sure, I'll look after you. Goodbye, dear. *(Hangs up.)* It was for you, Ed.

(Ed looks disgusted and goes into the song again. The plugger comes up behind him and starts to hum over the song. Ed breaks off the song he's been learning and starts to sing the one being hummed. Then Ed turns round and kicks the song plugger in the pants. The plugger takes a piece of candy and retires up stage. The telephone rings again. Ed answers it.)

Ed: Hello, yes, dear, this is Eddie. Yes, I took the tonic. Yes, I'm looking after myself. Yes, yes, yes. I'm very busy, dear, very busy. Yes, I'm well. I'm well. I said well. Goodbye. *(He hangs up and finds the piano player opening his mail.)* Please, Irv, I have to learn this song. Read your mail at home. *(The telephone rings again. Ed answers it.)* No, dear, I did not say, "Go to hell." I said, I'm well. Yes, goodbye. *(He hangs up the phone.)*

Ben: Who's that, Ed?

Ed: The wife.

(The phone rings again, just as Ed is ready to sing. Irv jumps up from the piano, grabs the phone, and starts nattering on with his girlfriend.)

Ed *(interrupting):* Please, Irv, will you tell her to call some other time? *(Irv continues to talk, taking no notice of Ed, who begins to rave. Finally, Ed shouts)* Irv, enough! Come on back to the piano!

Irv: Yes, dear, I'll be there. Now I'll have to ring off. He's getting kind of crabby. Goodbye, dear.

(He returns to the piano and they rehearse again.)

Plugger: Ed, I got another idea for a song.

Ed: Lie down somewhere and expire, will you?

(The song plugger and Ben are exhausting the supply of candy, and Irv, every chance he gets, is reading his mail. A fourth man enters, Don.)

Don: Oh, Ed, are you busy? I want to try this record on your victrola.

Ed: Will you please leave me alone? I have to sing this song in half an hour and I don't know a word of it. Go away!

Don: Oh, but Ed, this has the most wonderful cello cadenza. Look at this title. (*He mentions the very song that Ed is trying to learn.*)
Ed: What? You have a record of _____? My dear Don! (*He kisses him.*) I can't tell you what a godsend this is. Oh, boy! Now will you leave with Benny and Irv and the other imbecile, and don't bang the door on the way out. I can learn this song on the victrola before the show.
(*There's a call from off stage that the overture has started. The boys dash off. Ed puts on the record and walks around listening and singing with it. He has his back turned to the victrola when a man, all muffled up, enters, looks around, sees the victrola, shuts it off, and picks it up.*)
Ed: Hey, where are you going with that machine?
Man: You know where I'm going. Pay your bills!
(*Blackout*)
(*After the curtain closes, Ed comes forward and announces*)
Ed: You have just seen how I learn a song.
(*He launches into the song, messes up the lyrics, smiles weakly, goes into a dance, and exits.*)

The Retirement Party

Setting: a banquet table. Seated at the table are men in white uniforms. A sign indicates that this is the street cleaners' union and displays an insignia of a shovel and broom. One of the union members makes a speech in praise of the presentation gift: a silver shovel. The retiring member then gives an acceptance speech.

Robbers and Robbery

One man pulls a gun on another and asks for his money. The victim gives the holdup man a hard luck story. Midway through the story, the holdup man stops him and says, "You think things are bad with you! Why, I can't even afford bullets for this gun."

A holdup man robs a messenger. The latter says that the robbery will look like a phony if he just goes back to the office without a scratch. He therefore asks the robber to shoot some holes in his coat and through his hat so that his employers will think he put up a fight. The holdup man obliges and empties his gun by shooting holes in the messenger's coat and hat. Then, once the gun is empty, the messenger slugs him.

Sales and Selling

Woman: If you'll pretend to be a housewife, I'll show you how to drum up business and sell radios, and thus make a lot of money. (*The man sits down in a rocking chair. The woman wipes her feet on an imaginary doormat and pretends to ring a doorbell. The man doesn't move.*)

Woman: I'm ringing.

Man: I can't hear you 'cause my twenty children are making too much noise.

Woman: Twenty children!

Man: It's an old country custom.

(The woman starts her selling spiel, and the man interrupts.)

Man: I do, I do, I do!

Woman: You do what?

Man: I do not want a radio.

Secretaries

(A scene in an office)

Merchant: Miss Remington.

Stenographer: Yes, Mr. Cooper.

Merchant: I'm going into my private office for an important conference, so do not let anyone disturb me.

Stenographer: Very well, sir.

Merchant: If anybody says they must see me, just reply, "That's what they all say."

Stenographer *(repeating):* That's what they all say.

Merchant *(repeating):* That's what they all say.

Stenographer: I'll remember, sir.

(The door slams to indicate that the merchant has gone into his private office. A stern woman enters.)

Stern Woman: I want to see Mr. Cooper.

Stenographer: Sorry, he's in conference in his private office.

Stern Woman: But I'm his wife.

Stenographer: That's what they all say.

Stern Woman: Oh, they do, do they.

(In succession, we hear the following sounds: a door slamming to indicate that Mrs. Cooper has entered her husband's private office, slaps, and glass breaking.)

Stern Woman: Look out below!

(Repeat: sound of breaking glass)

Sex

A man removes a piece of white bread from a loaf. A girl enters. They commence a hot love scene. The man pushes the bread into his pocket. After the torrid scene, he pulls a piece of toast out of his pocket.

Two men are sitting next to a sign that reads: "Mind Readers." A girl walks across the stage. The two men bark. The girl looks at them; they both show plenty of interest. She walks past, stops, and comes back to them. Then she slaps them both and exits.

On stage: a ticker machine. Three men in a row enter (one after the other), read the tape, and shoot themselves. All three are laid out on stage. A girl enters, reads the tape machine, sees the men, and screams, "Wall Street! It's crashed!" She holds up her skirts as she steps over the bodies to exit. Each man in turn takes a peek. Once she has stepped over the men, all of them leap up, lasciviously look at the audience, and follow her out.

(A man is dressed in a Mexican outfit. He swaggers about on the stage. Another man enters and says)

Man: Chief, we have kidnapped a rich girl, as you ordered, and will now ask her husband for the ransom.

Chief: Bring her in! *(The chief woos her.)* You have mucho beautifool eyes and hair. Mucho lovely piquito nose and mouth. Do you know, I am the best damn cavalier in all Mehico? And do you know that if de ransom, he not arrive by six o'clock, I am going to keel you! You are held for ten thousand dollars. Let me see your pretty face! Yes, if the ransom he not arrive, I keel you with love and kisses. *(He embraces her.)*

(The man enters and announces)

Man: The ransom, it has arrived!

Woman *(to the chief):* Don't take it. Tell my husband to keep it!

(Man on stage. Five girls enter and surround him. The girls are agitated and talk at once.)

Girls: Oh, Mr. Lowry, Mr. Lowry, you've got to help us. You must help! Please! We need you!

Man: Hello, girls! What is this, a convention?

Girl 1: Please, Mr. Lowry, we need your help. Will you do us a favor?

Man: Will I do you a favor? At once! What do you want?

Girl 2: It's this way, Mr. Lowry, our night watchman is sick.

Man: I see. You want me to be the night watchman.

Girl 3: Oh, Mr. Lowry, we're so nervous. There isn't a man in the building. We're all alone. Suppose a burglar breaks in—in the middle of the night—we'd be helpless.

Man: Wait a minute now. What do you want me to do?

Girl 4: This is the passkey to the building. Tonight, you can sleep in the basement. We want you to protect us.

Man: This is the passkey to the building? Not another man in the house? Will I protect you? Give me the key!

(Four girls exit, saying "Isn't he nice?" "Such a great guy!" "I knew he'd do it!" "A real pal!")

Girl 5: Oh, Eddie, there isn't another man in the building. You mustn't expose yourself to such danger. Give them back the key. Suppose a burglar breaks in during the night, finds you in the basement, and shoots you? Just think, Eddie, a burglar could catch you in the basement and shoot you!

Man: Sweetheart, if a burglar breaks in and catches me in the basement, I deserve to be shot.

Smoking

Two men are seated. One is smoking a clay pipe; the other takes a cigar out of his pocket. The man with the cigar asks, "May I have a light?" The pipe smoker hands over his pipe, from which the cigar smoker lights up. The cigar smoker sniffs the pipe, throws it off stage, and hands the man a cigar from his pocket. The pipe smoker sniffs the cigar, throws it off stage, and hands the cigar smoker a pipe from his pocket. This routine can be repeated several times.

Ed *(smoking a cigarette)*: It's called the wisdom cigarette. Imported from China. One puff and you get wonderful ideas. Immediately you become brilliant.
Man: Give me a puff.
Ed: Go away! These things cost ten dollars a box, and there's only one in a box. I'm not tossing my money around.
Man: I'll give you five bucks for the rest of the cigarette.
Ed: All right, but wait a sec. *(He takes a couple more puffs and hands over the cigarette.)* Here, there's about seven dollars worth left.
Man *(takes a couple of puffs)*: Wait a minute. What do you mean, wisdom cigarette? This is an ordinary Lucky!
Ed *(smiling at him)*: Ah, you're getting wise already.

Special Effects

The MC announces that since the actors didn't appear for the next routine and the lights are all set, the show will continue without them, just using the lights. Work up some well-known operatic number, preferably a quartet. The MC explains the action and says the lights will substitute for the actors. Then the lights produce the effect of people (1) walking or running toward each other, (2) fighting, (3) walking or running away from each other. (The girl is represented by the blue spot, the villain, the red, and the hero, the white spot)

Stinginess

In a dark corner of the stage, a girl is crying that she lost five bucks. The MC consoles her, reaches into his pocket, and builds up to the idea of giving her money. Then he pulls out matches and tells her, "I don't want to see you out five bucks. Here're some matches. Go look for it."

Suicide

A businessman is sitting at his desk filing his nails with a huge nail file. The secretary enters and breathlessly announces that such and such stock has dropped another fifty points. The businessman dramatically replies, "I'll kill myself." He opens a drawer and pulls out a revolver, points it at his head, pulls the trigger, throws it down, and curses the prop man for forgetting to put bullets in the gun. He then picks up a letter opener and takes a stab at himself, but the knife bends. Again he directs a mock curse at the prop man. He looks around for poison. "No poison! What's wrong with that prop man?" Finally, the business-man clutches his throat and drops dead. The secretary comes in, looks at the body, and tries to find the cause of death: gun, rub-ber knife, poison. At last, she says, "My God, he swallowed the file."

Women

(Lots of shouting off stage. A man on stage shouts)
Father: My daughter! Who will save her? *(Pause)* There! The life guard has got her. She's in his arms. He's swimming in with her. She's saved!
Guard *(enters with the girl in a weak condition, hanging on his arm):* Here, sir, I've resuscitated your daughter.
Father: What's that?
Guard: I've resuscitated your daughter.
Father: Then by God, sir, you'll have to marry her!

STUTTERING

My friend Joe Frisco came around to see me at the hotel where I stop *(name a large local one)*. He didn't find me so he came to the hotel where I live *(name a small one)*. I hadn't seen him in years, and he stutters terribly. I said, "Joe, where have you been the last few years?" He said, "Oh, I've been to S-s-s-s-s." I said, "I know, Cincinnati." He said, "N-n-no, I've been to S-s-s-s-s." I said, "I have it, St. Louis." He said, "N-n-no, S-s-s-s-s." I said, "Oh, San Francisco." "N-n-n-o, I've been to S-s-s-s-s P-p-pitts-b-b-burgh."

Joe was supposed to leave for Pittsburgh at six this evening, so I went down to the station to see him off. There were about fifteen men all standing in line at the ticket office. He rushed right up in front of these fifteen men and said, "P-p-please, l-l-let me have a ticket for S-s-s-s-s P-p-pitts-b-b-burgh." The ticket agent asked, "Did you say Pittsburgh? Joe said, "L-l-let m-m-m." The agent repeated, "Pittsburgh, right?" Joe said, "Yup," and threw down two dollars. The ticket man said, "You can't go to Pittsburgh for two dollars," and Joe said, "Oh, G-g-gosh, w-w-where can I go?" And the fifteen men told him.

Anyway he got his ticket and as he rushed into the gate to catch his train, a fellow came running out. They evidently were friends and he stuttered just as badly as Joe. Joe said, "Hell-hell-hello." The other chap said, "Hi! W-w-where you going, Joe?" Joe said, "S-s-s-s-s P-p-pitts-b-b-burgh. I'll have to catch the s-s-six o'clock train." The fellow remarked, "You b-b-better hurry, I j-j-just missed it."

They both waited and left together at eight o'clock. On the train, Joe asked, "W-w-what are you going to S-s-s-s P-p-pitts-b-b-burgh for?" The other guy replied, "I'm g-g-going to see Dr. Kronkheit. He's g-g-going to c-c-cure me of my s-s-stuttering." Joe said, "He's v-v-very g-g-good; he c-c-cured me."

Although he says his prayers only once a year, Joe's a smart boy. Every New Year's night he says his prayers, and from then on each night he just says, "D-d-ditto."

I wish you could see Joe make love. He has his own ideas. He likes to take a girl out on a lonely road in a horse and buggy. One day he had his girl away out in the country and the horse slipped, fell down, and died. The girl became hysterical. Joe said, "Honey, c-c-calm yourself, we'll j-j-just sit here till help comes." It was a beautiful moonlit night, and Joe started getting romantic. He slipped his arm around her waist, and she liked it; and then he kissed her on the forehead, and she looked at him like a dying duck. Then he gave her one of those long lingering kisses. She said, "Oh Joe, what's that?" "That's a s-s-soul kiss," he replied. "A s-s-soul kiss inspires one, it in-v-v-vigorates one, it g-g-gives one life." And she said, "Oh yeah, well, kiss the horse and let's go home."

They finally got married. I was the best man. I found that out later. Just as soon as the ceremony was performed, Joe deliberately leaned over and slapped the girl across the face. She said, "Joe, what's that for?" He said, "That's f-f-for nothing. Now b-b-be c-c-careful!"

TRICKS

Put an egg or golf ball in a glass and make the ball rise and fall in the glass. The object is fastened to a piece of thread hooked on to your vest. This trick always gets a good laugh.

How to turn water into ink, and back again into water. Use a glass of water and a piece of black tin cut to the size of the glass. Turn away from the audience and slip the tin into the water; then reverse the process.

APPENDIX
GLOSSARY OF NAMES
INDEX

APPENDIX: ED LOWRY LAFFTER

In 1929, Ed Lowry privately published a chapbook of jokes entitled *Ed Lowry Laffter*. The book, now a collector's item, has been included here as part of Ed's enduring legacy.

I, MYSELF, AND ME

It seems to be quite the vogue for an author to preface his book by writing something about himself. I can't think of anything that would give greater pleasure.

I, myself, and me were born in New York City. I couldn't help it; my folks happened to be living there at the time.

Both Ma and Pa were very fond of children, which accounts for my still being among those present.

I have two brothers living—and another is in Mexico.

In the same family there are two sisters, both of whom are married, except Tillie—her husband is a traveling salesman.

We all lived home happily with our parents, until I took up the saxophone.

My only claim to fame is that a restaurant in St. Louis named a sandwich after me. This may not seem so flattering, but look what a great guy Bismarck was and they named a herring after him.

RILED BY THE DIAL

I know a lot about the nervous system, but I didn't know how much I really knew about the nervous system till the first time I tried the telephone dial system.

I worked on a Jefferson number for about half an hour before I discovered that Jefferson doesn't start with a "G."

After getting seven wrong exchanges, I shouted, "I want Jefferson," and someone on a crossed line yelled, "Pipe down, he's been dead for years!"

Yesterday I asked my secretary to get a number for me, and it took two stagehands and a surgeon to release his little finger from the dial.

After all, learning to dial a number is just as easy as playing a flute, only a flute has fewer holes.

I really do think the dial system will be an improvement on sending a post card, but we will miss the operator when we get the "wrong number." We'll have no one to shout at.

COLLEGIATE

At Northwestern University, you can be a Phi Pi or a Pi Phi, but when you become Pi I'd, it's Bye, Bye, Bye!

After a rum quiz, the heads of the board found that at the frat houses, liquor was flowing like glue, so they Delta Blowa to the Kegga Beera.

The frat song now is:

> Sigma Chi, Sigma Sig—
> Stay away from the Old Blind Pig!

The heads of the Phi Pi and the Phi Mu Delta were expelled. It seems they were studying to be bartenders and no such course is included in the curriculum.

In the future the boys will have to Eta Bitta Piea or Drinka Bowla Soupa but no more Sippa Pinta Ginna.

All the students at N.U. aren't just whoopee makers. Many already have their L.L.D.'s, their L.L.B.'s, and their B.V.D.'s.

IS THERE A MAN IN THE MOON?

Mary Garden suggests bathing in the nude by moonlight as a sure way for women to reduce. It will also add to their health and, might I add, good will.

Mary said she did it in Europe and lost thirty pounds. If she does it here she'll lose her reputation.

Policemen should be careful about "pinching" these aesthetic creatures—they bruise very easily.

Think I'll look for a job as a beachcomber.

What a great break for the man in the moon.

Even the prohibitionist will now pray for moonshine.

OVER THE BOUNDING MANE

This is being written standing up. Today marks my first experience as a horseman, and I have decided that Paul Revere was not only a hero but a martyr.

The only thing I'm proud about is that I'm one up on the Prince of Wales. I didn't "Faw Down."

He gets sore about falling off and I got sore sticking on.

There were two real horsemen in my party, and every time they started to gallop their horses, my horse decided it was a race. I won each time and I wasn't even playing.

The three horses and the other two fellows enjoyed it, but I was sore—in fact, I'm still sore.

I thought I knew something about rhythm, but this horse had no ear for music. While I was trying to swing graciously to and fro in waltz time, he insisted on the Black Bottom.

BETTING ON HIS OWN HOOK

There was one man who did penance for his faith in Al Smith during the recent presidential election. He had to push a peanut eleven miles with his nose.

This is the first intimation we have had of Al losing by a nose.

The stunt attracted the attention of thousands of people along the road, and there were many arguments as to which was the nut.

Guiding a nut over eleven miles of road is no easy task, nor do you have to be a fool to do it—but it helps.

Regardless of what odds were given this fellow, it still comes under the heading of "A Shell Game."

During the payoff, he was hit by a Ford and the nut was run over. I mean the peanut.

The fellow said it wasn't at all hard. He's always been getting his nose into trouble.

WHEN DO WE EAT?

A statistician selected a group of three hundred Broadway chorus girls to ascertain their mode of living. It would be more logical to have three hundred statisticians to figure out one chorus girl.

Only ninety-seven of the three hundred smoked. He didn't say how many burned.

Forty-eight of them were mothers, but the statistician lost his nerve and was afraid to inquire if any of them were mother's mothers.

Two hundred and ninety-nine of them admitted they were hungry—and the other one said she was on a diet.

Only nine of them maintain limousines. The others motor A La Carte!

Only eighty-nine of them admitted they drank anything. I guess the others drink everything.

I DIDN'T WEAR A MONOCLE

During 1927, I spent eleven months in England. On my return, I wore spats and carried a cane. When my folks saw me with the walking stick they wanted to know if I'd hurt my foot.

Mother was with me when I unpacked my trunk and when she saw a high hat, she immediately asked me if I was studying magic.

In America, high hats are used only to make rabbits come out of.

Every theatre in London has a public bar. If the audience doesn't like an act, they go into the bar and have a drink. Whenever I played in London, business was tremendous—at the bar!

In London, the people often see the same show six or seven times. Over here, if we don't get it the first time, we give it up.

English audiences laugh louder and longer. Maybe it's because they get it later.

DIGESTING A WIFE

A famous specialist says marriage is good for digestion. That's fine, professor, but does the stomach know that?

Personally I can get the same results from Spearmint gum—and it's cheaper.

He claims married folks eat slower because they talk throughout the meal—and how!

I can't eat corn on the cob at home. My wife talks my ear off.

You couldn't exactly refer to King Solomon as a bachelor and he suffered with indigestion. It was nervous indigestion. Do you wonder?

Seems to me if men are going to have to decide between a wife and a bottle of bicarbonate, the drugstores will be doing a land office business.

COLLEGE BREAD

Two college girls walked all the way from Louisville to Atlantic City. Yes, sir, they hiked all the way. Rah! Rah! But they got into an automobile accident. Raw! Raw! Raw!

They left Louisville, Kentucky, with twelve dollars and two loaves of bread. Each carried a loaf to show she was bred in Ole Kentucky.

They admitted they were given seventeen lifts and were insulted only once. That's a discouraging average, I'd say.

Everyone they met on the trip treated 'em great. They must have been treated wonderfully—and often—as they still had ten dollars when they arrived in Atlantic City.

They are going to hike back. Though they have no bread left, they certainly retain their crust.

They started the hike back on Labor Day. That's a good day for it.

EDISON TELLS A PHONY

Thomas Edison says happiness is a myth. Pleath excuth my ego when I thay Edithon made a Mythtake.

It seems a very broad statement to say that nobody is happy. Gee—not everyone is married!

He says he never met anyone who is happy. He never met me. At least, I think I'm happy. But maybe I'm just sappy.

Anyway, how can Edison expect to be happy driving around in that 1913 Ford?

But Edison doesn't even give himself credit. Didn't he give us many electrical inventions that lead toward happiness: electric lights, electric irons, electric washing machines, and the electric chair?

He says there is no formula for happiness. But how about the fellow who eats, sleeps, drinks, and doesn't work?

FOOD FOR THOUGHT

A Mr. Kelly went to Ireland and was surprised to find no Irish stew. Another traveler went to Hungary and asked for goulash. He got it—like Kelly did!

Kelly might be surprised to hear that cauliflower ears do not come from cauliflowers, nor do alligator pears come from alligators.

In China they won't know what you're talking about if you ask for chop suey. In fact, they won't know what you're talking about regardless of what you ask for.

Spanish omelets were invented by a cook whose only claim on anything Spanish was that he once had influenza.

You can find as many horseflies around a mule as you do Jersey cows in Texas.

Chile is made on a hot stove?

OUR FAMILY

By trade my dad was a contractor, and I always had the idea I was one of the things he didn't contract for.

Dad hated to work, and all we kids took after him. We took after him at the dinner table, too.

Pop seldom worried about himself. His interest was all in us. Why, when we started to work, for fear we would squander our salary he took it—and squandered it for us.

Mother was always kind, loving, and trusting. Pop had her trusting at every store in the neighborhood.

Mom didn't like to see Pop drink. So he used to go outside and do it.

We were seven kids in our family. I was the seventh and it must have been a sort of dice game 'cause when the seven came, it was all over.

TRICKY RICKY

Oh, Gordon! What gins are committed in thy name! When you pull the cork out of some of those bottles a blue flame leaps out!

Some of these bootleggers are certainly putting the liquor business on a "pain" basis.

They should give out coupons with every bottle and a whisk broom to brush yourself off with, when you get up.

For twelve coupons you get a free quart. If twelve bottles don't kill you, the thirteenth will.

If you still survive, you receive a beautiful engraving of the Eighteenth Amendment. Play this on your Victrola, no needles required. It's "needled" plenty.

LOOKING THROUGH HENRY'S WINDSHIELD

Have you read Henry Ford's psychology of life? Honk! Honk! Jump on, take a rattling good ride with the man who made a lady out of Lizzie!

Henry does not approve of, or like, Charity; and he didn't bother giving his views on Faith and Hope.

Prosperity, he says, is a state of mind. But I'm from Missouri and prefer to have my pocketbook in the same state.

He says, "Prohibition is a huge success," so evidently the thousands who cross from Detroit to Canada every day go just for the ride.

Incidentally, Ford says Edison is the happiest man he knows. Several days previous Edison said: "There is no happiness in the world." Now who's lying?

Ford says a good wife assures success, and the only real argument I ever had with my wife was because I bought a Ford.

OH, PROFESSOR! THAT'S SILLILLY

Professor Emile Coue taught us to say, "Every day and in every way, I'm getting better and better." The words of the song disappeared, but the malady lingers on.

Coue's successor, Professor Passat, says: "Look in the mirror and say to yourself, 'I am perfect.' That will give you self-confidence," says he, "and possibly a punch in the nose," says I!

He says colors will cure ills. Paint your room blue if you have rheumatism. Now wouldn't that get your gout?

Pink, he says, cultivates love and gentleness. I guess he's right; imagine a great big holdup guy catching you in your pink pajamas! He'd most likely kiss you.

The color of red eliminates fear. Any guy who will wear a red necktie knows no fear.

MEN'S BARBERSHOP OR LADIES' LOUNGE?

I have a great idea. Why doesn't someone open a barbershop for men?

Now instead of subscribing to the *Police Gazette* the shops are using the *Ladies' Home Journal.*

It's getting disgusting. I'd like to let my hair grow. Only I can't play a fiddle.

And what great traveling salesmen stories we used to bring back with us from the barbershop! But now, while we wait our turn, we are expected to knit or crochet.

The only thing that remains the same is the "talk." There's always plenty of that. It reminds me of tuning in on a radio and getting four stations at once. But you can always turn a radio off.

I tried a new system on my barber today. I sat in the chair and said: "It's a lovely day; business is great; I don't follow baseball; I hate stories; I know my hair falls out but it grows fast so just give me a trim and a shampoo—and send the manicurist over to me."

NOT SO NICE IN NICE

In Nice, France, they have discovered a hypnotist who gets control of his victims and makes them give him money. That's Nice!

That may happen in France, but instead of hypnotize he'd have to paralyze if it were in Glasgow.

He made one fellow turn over his whole salary. My wife makes me turn over my salary every week—and she's no hypnotist.

One victim said he was just powerless and had to remain silent. I'd like to see him work on my mother-in-law.

He made one fellow go to the bank to cash a check. It was honored by the teller, but when he tried to tell his wife, he had to get the teller to tell 'er.

To hypnotize means to put in a trance. When the police closed in on this fellow he fooled them by putting himself through a trance-om.

ETTIKET

Volumes have been written on etiquette, and in the finest places one still sees terrible breaches. (I said breaches, not breeches.)

When escorting a young lady to a theatre always allow her to enter first. Of course, if the usher says: "One seat down front," it's every man for himself.

When you take a lady to dinner, it is permissible to allow her to carry her own tray.

If a gentleman is seated on a streetcar and a lady is standing in front of him, he should pretend he's sleeping. Never sit and deliberately flirt with her.

While seeing a moving picture it is excusable for a girl to hold her beau's hand; in fact, it's not only excusable, it's sometimes necessary.

MEET THE HUSBAND—BUT DON'T LAUGH

In a society column, I read an account of a wedding. It mentioned the maiden name of the bride, the bride's maids, the flower girl, the best man, but nary a word about the poor guy who supplied the name and the ring.

We still don't know who the groom is; but this is leap year, and when the article went to press maybe the bride didn't know on whom she intended to leap.

I've heard many a crack about giving the bride away, but in this instance, maybe they didn't want to give the groom away.

Maybe he's one of those guys who puts everything in his wife's name.

On the honeymoon the register will probably read, "Miss . . . and her husband."

Anyhow, he took her for better or for worse, and it looks like he's getting the worst of it already.

Looks like the best man was the best man after all.

ROSENSWEIG GOT HIT ON HIS LOUDSPEAKER

A thief in Chicago stole a portable radio and slipped it under his overcoat. It's not unusual these days to see a coat leaking, but his coat was speaking.

As he dashed out of the store his overcoat started to play: "You know you belong to somebody else so why don't you leave me alone."

Charlie Rosensweig, the proprietor, started to chase the thief down the street and the jolting turned the dial to "Clap Hands, Here Comes Charlie."

The thief turned and hit Rosensweig with a blackjack, right on his loud speaker.

As Rosensweig hit the floor some radio announcer cut in with "V. E. X. signing off."

At this point the police joined in the chase to the accompaniment of "The Prisoners' Song."

However, they may have tuned in but they got no reception; and now instead of playing a radio, Rosensweig is playing a Victrola and his favorite tune is "Goodbye Forever."

ATLANTIC CITY

Seems to me the main sport in Atlantic City is to first walk up the boardwalk, then down the boardwalk, then on the boardwalk, and finally along the boardwalk.

There's many a Spanish shawl on the boardwalk one week that's back on a piano the next.

The hotels in Atlantic City charge two dollars extra if you have a dog. Mine was a police dog; so just for spite I wouldn't let him help the house detective.

To have a baby with you costs three dollars extra. So evidently rugs are cheaper than linen.

Most men go hatless. That makes you tip-less on the boardwalk and also in the restaurant.

I figured up and found I had bought my hat back three times in two weeks.

CAPITAL PUNISHMENT

Capital punishment has been abolished in many states, but the Federal Reserve System is sure giving the stock market speculators a real taste of "capital" punishment.

Talk about the directors of the Federal Reserve taking an interest in their work! When it comes to interest, they make Shylock seem like a spendthrift.

Shylock asked a pound of flesh for his interest. Now with the interest rate occasionally hitting twenty percent, I know many fellows who have lost pounds and pounds.

However, the speculators can rest easy now, as things are rather normal again, and there is little danger of losing more than everything.

The main intent of the Federal Reserve is to stop gambling. They feel that money used for speculation is "tainted" and they are right. By the time they are through, tain't yours and tain't mine; it's theirs.

Of course they are fighting for a principle, but meanwhile they are taking all the interest.

WHAT PRICE GLORY?

Who will be the first mother to fly across the Atlantic—and why?

We've tried to interest Mom, but she's too interested in flagpole sitting.

Pop refuses to go in for flying, but he says it's all right with him if Mom wants to try it.

Brother is driving us crazy practicing juggling. He wants to be the first one to fly the Atlantic juggling four balls with one hand, waving a handkerchief with the other, and whistling "Yankee Doodle" while guiding his plane.

Have you heard that the Hilton sisters are planning on being the first Siamese twins to fly the Atlantic?

Their destination is not certain, but it's positive that they are both planning on alighting at the same place.

GET A LOAD OF THIS

Mussolini changed the legal marrying age to fourteen for girls and sixteen for boys. They'll be celebrating their wooden wedding anniversary before they're old enough to vote.

They'll be getting married with a lollipop in one hand and a skipping rope in the other.

The latest excuse to the teacher will be: "I can't come to school tomorrow, I'm getting married in the morning."

It's a peculiar state of affairs. The first thing you know, Baby Peggy will be suing Jackie Coogan for breach of promise.

Instead of using the Justice of the Peace over in Italy, marriages will be performed by the Children's Aid Society.

Can you imagine what some of those family albums will look like twenty years from now? The Breath of a Nation!

DO BLONDES PREFER GENTLEMEN?

A famous Maitre D'Hotel will only hire blonde waitresses. Maybe he thinks all businessmen are gentlemen. He's evidently never been a waiter.

He can't kid me. The reason he prefers blondes is, the customers can't see the hair in the butter.

At that he is taking an awful chance. Hotels say that the guest is always right, and he might strike some unreasonable customer who is not a gentleman and demands a brunette.

However, peroxide, like charity, can cover a multitude of sins, so:

> Cheer up little waitress, don't you sob,
> Bleach your hair and you'll get a job.

He also claims businessmen prefer their waitress about a hundred pounds. I've never seen a hungry man stop to have his waitress weighed.

This man says he has had twenty years' experience picking girls, and he knows the type men like—the type they don't like don't live!

SILENT CAL

Publishers of the Encyclopedia Americana offered ex-President Coolidge a dollar a word for his writings. We hope for his sake that he will write more than he talks.

The following conversation was said to have been heard at the home of the famous "Word Miser."
Mrs. Coolidge: "Where have you been, Cal?"
Cal: "Church."
Mrs. Coolidge: "Who preached?"
Cal: "Minister."
Mrs. Coolidge: "What was his subject?"

Cal: "Sin."

Mrs. Coolidge: "What did he say about it?"

Cal: "Wrong."

Mrs. Coolidge: "What kinds of sin, Cal?"

Cal: "Several." *(Business of picking up hat and walking toward door.)*

Mrs. Coolidge: "Where are you going, Cal?"

Cal: "Out."

Curtain

N.B. (No Business) At this rate, Cal would make six dollars.

TINKLE TINKLE

To protect the birds, a town in Illinois has revived an ancient law providing that cats must wear a bell. It's going to be some serenade now on the back fence.

It may be a good idea to put bells on cats, but at least give them an even break and put earmuffs on the mice.

It used to be awfully tough to hit one when you fired something out of the window at 'em, but now with the bells to help, it's a good thing cats have nine lives.

Possibly they won't be so noisy now at night. When Tom wants to make a date with Maria, he'll simply have to give her a ring.

On Christmas Eve, the poor kiddies won't be able to sleep at all. Every time they hear the tinkle of a bell, they'll think it's Santa Claus.

PASSING THE TIME

"Time flies" for some people. I know a fellow who is suing his wife for divorce because she socked him with an alarm clock.

When the alarm rang he wouldn't get up, so she knocked him down.

Instead of using it to awaken him, she darn near put him to sleep with it.

Among other things in the divorce papers, he complains of the way she passed the time.

One consolation for him was that it was a Little and not a Big Ben.

There's a time and a place for everything, but she found the wrong place for the time.

He'd often kidded her about someone having a face that would stop a clock, only to find that he did pretty well at it himself.

The Moral is: Never get up early in the morning to go to work. Stop in on your way home.

PAGE MR. VOLSTEAD!

A man has invented "cocktail tubes." Carry 'em in your pocket, drop one in a glass of water, and what'll you have, boys?

Volstead will probably try to prohibit the use of pockets. The Scotsmen won't mind. They seldom use theirs anyhow.

They can't keep us from getting water; we can always get some out of our milk.

Now the bootleggers will be carrying samples in a snuff box.

Instead of shipping truckloads of liquor now, we might have our shipment sent by carrier pigeon.

Even the carrier pigeon will have to watch out for the stool pigeon.

Had a girl to dinner and asked her if she cared for an oyster cocktail. She said: "No, thanks, I never drink."

MAMMY OF MUMMY?

News! News! News! We now learn that mammy songs originated in Egypt. Who are the mammy song tracers and why?

Possibly they are a little mixed up with this Egyptian business and instead of mammy mean mummy.

Al Jolson did his bit for mammy songs, and if they were handed down to him from his ancestors, it certainly wasn't from Egypt.

Mammy songs got many a man's goat; but after all, had it not been for a goat, we probably never would have thought of writing songs about "Ma-ha-ha-ha-ammy."

Hundreds of years from now, those fellows who do all the tracing will probably be telling their children that Berlin's songs came from Germany.

It's impossible to trace the origin of popular songs. The best Southern songs were written on the East Side of New York. All we are sure about is "Sleep-tight" was written by a Scotsman.

THE SAP OF THE FAMILY TREE

I have three brothers. One is a baker, one is a loafer, and the other one doesn't work either.

They should all be bakers. They're always needing dough.

Brother Bill was rightfully named, only his middle name should be Due. There's so much due around Bill, he's all wet.

At home we call him Willie. He loves to hang around the house, but Willie work? No!

My one sister married an heir, and believe me, he got plenty of it when he hung around our house.

His father left him a lot of money, but he's never located the lot.

FORE!

Aerial golf is the latest fad. So many golfers blow up in the air on a course, maybe it will be easier to play from an airplane.

You sort of fly around the golf course and try to drop balls in a hole, so if you ever get hit on the head with a golf ball, you'll know some crazy golfer is practicing his putting.

The players, instead of going around the course in knickers, will go around in airplanes, while the caddie will fly around under the airplane on the back of a carrier pigeon.

I understand twenty-eight will be par for nine holes, not counting the holes that are made in other peoples' heads.

If one of the players takes a spill, it will prove he was off his driving.

Lindbergh watched a game, but that doesn't prove it's good. Many people go to an insane asylum out of curiosity.

SOUND INVESTMENTS?

Talk about stock fluctuations, Chinese wives have dropped in value from four hundred dollars to one hundred and fifty, and you can do business in the Chinese market on a ten point margin. Whoopee!

They are such a drug on the market that in some instances a guaranteed dividend goes with them.

Sounds to me like a good investment. In time it's bound to draw interest.

I'm thinking of doing a little investing myself, and putting it aside to see if it develops.

I don't know much about the Chinese market, but a fellow with a couple of thousand dollars can be an awful bear.

Understand they don't have much of a Stock Exchange over there. All the business is done on the curb.

FARM RELIEF

We hear much about Farm Relief. Texas Guinan and her gang can give the farmers more relief than Hoover.

Ford could also do some relieving by trading the farmers Lincolns for Fords. As a matter of fact, what the farmers need most is a Lincoln.

Some farmers have found that instead of talking loudly about their crops, it is more profitable to keep a little "Still."

I know one farmer who got his relief by keeping a "Blind Pig."

The biggest profit being made on corn is on the corn that's sold by the bottle.

COO KOO! COO KOO!

At the state asylum in Pittsburgh, they have installed a beauty parlor for the insane. This is not the first time a cause has been used as a cure.

Permanent waves are barred. One of the patients had a permanent wave, and then tried to drown herself.

They gave one inmate a "mudpack" and when she looked in the mirror she thought she was Al Jolson and started to sing "Mammy."

A brunette had gone crazy believing that gentlemen really preferred blondes. A bottle of peroxide fixed her up. She was released.

Eventually she came back in worse shape than ever. She had found out that her boyfriend was no gentleman.

One inmate wanted wrinkles put in her face. She thought she was an accordion.

RAPID MULTIPLICATION

Another endurance record broken! Frau Voellner became the mother of eighteen children in nine years. She has been the cause of a small town, called Demmin, Germany, hiring two more census takers.

She raised two baseball teams in nine years and she's still only twenty-eight. In another ten years she's liable to own a whole league.

The birth of a baby is usually considered a "Smile from Heaven," but this isn't a smile, it's loud laughter!

Four sets of quadruplets in six years! And the first set is singing harmony already.

The last child born was named Alice. Pop christened it when he said "Momma, dass ist alles."

They buy everything wholesale in dozen and half-dozen lots, but dad never actually buys till he calls up home to make sure there aren't any more.

MY COUNTRY TEARS OF THEE

A learned judge says that divorce will benefit America. If he is right, the country is certainly full of patriots.

Soon we will have the slogan: "Don't join the Marines. Get a divorce and benefit America!"

The judge says man is more generous and more anxious to make the best of a bad job. He has to be, 'cause anyone who says, "It's the woman who pays," is crazy.

One man seeking to benefit America stated his wife continually played the horses. He charged her with nagging.

He found tickets in her pocketbook, with numbers on them—all dealing with horses. But it seems one of the horses called up.

In Chicago, a woman seeks a divorce because her husband, in one year, bought her only one dress and a pocketbook. Wonder what the pocketbook was for?

SCHOOLHOUSE TO WHITE HOUSE

Hoover's former school teacher tells us that "Herbert, as a boy, always kept his mouth shut, except when he wanted to say something." Those school teachers are so enlightening.

That statement is to let the world know that Hoover is not a ventriloquist, even if he does have a few dummies around him.

The fact that he has been married to the same wife for thirty years proves he can keep his mouth shut.

The teacher says he never fought as a kid, he always turned the other cheek. Gosh, as president he'll soon run out of cheeks.

He was the only boy in the class she never caught fighting or boxing, but she wants to make it clear that he wasn't one of those kids who was afraid of his own shadow. I guess he was a shadow boxer.

Herbert always had a very dry sense of humor. Don't know anything about his sense of humor, but he's still dry!

A SAXOPHONE AS A LAVALIERE

Why do people mock saxophone players and saxophones? There's plenty of good music in a sax, only it's darn hard to get out!

The saxophone was invented by a Belgian named Sax. For hundreds of years it has been called a saxophone in the musical world, but the outside world has called it lots of things.

Most saxophone players hook the instrument around their neck, so it hangs like a lavaliere. Not me, if I have to run, I don't want anything dangling in front of me.

Musicians continually talk of their art, but most of them play for money. I play for spite!

I like to use the upper notes so I can play with one hand, then I have the other free to defend myself.

Some terrible sounds emanate from saxophones. But have you ever heard a Scotsman tune up his bagpipes?

NO QUARANTINE FOR MEASLES

Henry Measles was arrested at Hot Springs, Arkansas, for theft. After being in jail several days, Measles broke out.

The search is on. This is probably the first time a posse, loaded with guns, went looking for measles.

The jail keepers were entirely unprepared, as usual. Measles don't break out until winter.

Orders are out that if anyone catches Measles they should vaccinate him with lead.

The description of the escaped prisoner reads, "A face full of freckles." So if you see a man with freckles, it might be Measles.

If they catch Measles, they'll make him look like he has the mumps.

DIGGING THE GREEN

I once read of some thieves who stole three hundred yards of green from a golf course and sold it to a cemetery. Guess that was their idea of celebrating Decoration Day.

Stealing on a golf course isn't original. There are plenty of strokes taken the same way.

But I think the fellow who would steal the turf off a golf course must be so mean and petty that he could easily hide behind a blade of grass on a putting green.

It's a wonder they didn't try to steal the holes and sell them to some doughnut maker.

I wonder why they didn't do someone a favor and walk away with a ditch or a couple of water holes.

Or, why not reverse, and steal a grave or two to sell on the golf course? Many a golfer would like to bury his clubs.

NIGHTIE NIGHTIE

What's all the excitement about men wearing pajamas in the streets? Chinamen have been wearing them for years.

Men in pajamas! Gosh, it seems hideous but still it beats the old-fashioned nightie.

Gee, now you won't be able to tell a somnambulist from a Democrat.

At last a fellow will get a chance to use those pajamas he got for Christmas.

Personally I think I'll stick to the good old-fashioned flannels. I never did go in for evening clothes.

Can you imagine getting caught in the rain? Wow! "You can rain on me, and I'll shrink up on you!"

REGISTERING EMOTION

In New York, they held a blindfold kissing contest to test a hypersensitive stethoscope. Under the heading of science, they get away with murder.

A showgirl won the contest. The kiss lasted ten seconds, and the fellow, as he took off his blindfold, smacked his lips and said, "Old Gold!"

The girl insists she could have registered a dozen more heart-beats privately, but the public demonstration cramped her style.

She further stated that if she had had Buddy Rogers as her part-ner, the doctor would have had to buy a new stethoscope.

They knew they would have plenty of men volunteers but ex-pected to have to pay the ladies for the experiment. However, there were so many applicants, it looked like the bargain base-ment of a department store.

One old maid pushed her way through the crowd and insisted she should be used as a subject. She said: "I don't want pay—science is science!"

OFFICER, QUICK, CALL A COP!

With the molds and the necessary implements of a counterfeit-ing plant, two convicts were turning the Missouri Penitentiary into a mint.

These convicts certainly should be arrested.

Passing lead half-dollars has led many a fellow to jail, but making lead half-dollars in jail is original.

I don't see why they wanted money. They didn't have any place to go.

Their alibi was that they wanted to help put the Missouri Penitentiary on a paying basis.

The other convicts are disgusted. They complain that things are getting so bad, a fellow can't even feel safe in jail.

PRAY FOR STATIC

It is claimed by radio experts that every sound ever uttered in this world can, and will, someday be picked up by radio. Ouch! What a blow!

Even the words of Moses, he says, are still floating around. Does he mean Senator Moses?

Imagine sitting at the radio with your wife when suddenly something you once said to some other femme pops right through the loudspeaker. Oh, Mamma! Spank your boy, he's been naughty!

The old saying that you can never be shot for thinking may be true, but lots of us may be hanged for talking.

When we hear the things that have been said at some of those bridge parties, many an aerial will immediately be taken down.

Profanity has always been prohibited on the radio, but the censor will have a terrible task now.

ALL ABOARD FOR HEAVEN

A conscience stricken man handed a Chicago Northwestern Railroad agent thirty dollars and said: "This pays for the rides I've stolen. Now I'll go to heaven."

Can you imagine going to heaven on the Chicago Northwestern? He must have his places mixed up.

Nothing like easing your conscience. This man is so happy and optimistic about going to heaven that he is taking harp lessons.

Now if he doesn't go to heaven, will the company make a refund?

The man probably figured that when St. Peter learns of his stealing a train ride, he'll square matters by sending him below to shovel coal.

One consolation, if he gets to heaven he'll have wings, so he won't have to steal any more rides.

ONCE UPON A TIME

Hi diddle diddle, the cat and the fiddle, the cow jumped over the moon.

Sir Oliver Lodge says the moon and the earth at one time were one. He evidently has been reading the nursery rhymes.

Perhaps there is some logic in what Lodge says. The moon must have been close or how could the cow have jumped over it?

He says the moon will some day come back to earth. It will return I suppose, just like the prodigal sun.

Lodge further states that the earth is the moon's parent body. Well, we know we're not Mars, so I guess we're Pa's.

When the moon does return it will crash right into this earth. I hope all that talk of green cheese being in the moon is a myth. Ugh, how I hate cheese!

AIN'T LOVE GRAND

Love is a wonderful thing, but personally I like spinach.

Every season, business seems to increase in the marriage license bureau. But the month of June seems to be set aside as the record-breaking period for people to go crazy.

They hear a tune about a wedding in June, and they believe it. They should wait until December; the opposition isn't so great, and the presents will come bigger and better.

The funniest thing about a marriage license is that first you must get permission from the City Hall. Then you can go crazy.

You are buying a passport to a foreign country called Matrimony. If you don't care for it, you can pass on to Alimony, only it's more expensive.

Saturday is the rush day at the bureau. A lot of fellows get a half day off and don't know what to do with themselves.

HEY! PULL OVER THERE

Due to traffic congestion in the air, there is talk of installing traffic laws. Now if you're five thousand feet in the air and another plane crashes into you on the wrong side, you can sue the aviator.

It'll take a high-class artist to paint the white lines up there.

The big airships complain that the smaller planes create the jam and keep getting in their way. The pilots of the big airships should be provided with flyswatters.

Instead of "Stop and Go," the signals will be "Drop and Go."

The main thought is to eliminate the drops, because after all when an airplane takes a drop, it's no bargain.

They say that hereafter traffic cops will have wings. If there is a hereafter, I can picture traffic cops with horns but not wings.

Can you forgive me if I say an airplane taking a fall in a jam may be preserved?

DO YOU REVERSE

In England, the newest style is a reversible coat for men. An Englishman claims the patent, and a Scotsman claims the idea.

My brother and I have been wearing reversible suits for years. Whoever gets up last has to reverse.

Reversible clothes are also made for women, and one coat that was on exhibit had a raccoon collar on one side and skunk on the other. Gee, they're likely to start snapping at one another!

I don't know how practical this reversible idea is, but it certainly gives a wife more pockets to go through.

Men's coats are being made with tweed on one side and water-proof fabric on the other. The inventor evidently planned for a rainy day—and that's every day in England.

As soon as suits that are bulletproof on one side can be made, tailors in a certain city in Illinois will do a turnaway business.

LAUGH, CLOWN, LAUGH

Grouches are a menace to business—and they are certainly no help socially.

There are different kinds of grouches that you meet in different walks of life, each being a committee of one, appointed by themselves to make others miserable.

For the grouch on the road who drives everybody else's car but his own, I would suggest a diet of green apples and water.

The restaurant grouch who insists on spoiling everyone else's meal because his eggs are a little too soft—I'd make him eat twenty-two pickles and two quarts of ice cream.

I'd rather spend a day with a half-wit than a grouch, because a grouch isn't even half-witted.

MONKEY BIZNIZ

When Dr. Cadle returned from Africa recently he claimed to have found the monkey men who prove that our ancestors used to play baseball with coconuts.

The doctor reports that they go about nude and represent the only true democracy in the world. Durn it, this country just went Republican.

When one of these youths intends to marry, he must first chase a gazelle for at least twelve hours. So even monkey women give their intended husbands a run for their money.

A gazelle is a form of an antelope. In other words he must catch an antelope or he "Cantelope."

Once he has caught his antelope, he doesn't ask her to be his wife; he just takes her. We take 'em too, but take it from me, they'll take it from you after you take 'em.

If they catch two gazelles, they take two wives, and so on. That probably explains their relationship to humans. Some of them never get through hunting.

I THOUGHT I'D DIE

Feeling blue, a woman decided to die. She turned on the gas and ten minutes later changed her mind, calling the police; they rushed her to the hospital and she was saved.

It's every woman's privilege to change her mind.

And anyway, she said the gas smelled horrible, and she was nervous about being in the dark alone.

Next time instead of using gas, the sweet thing should try an atomizer full of Coty's Rose Perfume.

She's as bad as the fellow who tried to hang himself. They found him with the rope tied around his waist. When asked why he didn't put the rope around his neck, he said he had but it nearly choked him.

While we're on the subject of suicides, we can't overlook the Scotsman who went next door to turn on the gas.

TABLE MANNERS

If the roast beef falls in your lap, be nonchalant, light a Murad!

Never leave your spoon standing straight up in your cup. Bend it over.

If you insist on leaning on the table, at least take your elbow out of the butter.

It is considered poor taste to tell the host which part of the chicken you wish. You can always pretend you're not hungry.

When peas are served, it is advisable to mash 'em in with your potatoes. They stay on the knife better.

Yes, it is permissible to pick up asparagus with your fingers, but you don't have to go after it like a sea lion reaching for a fish.

FOOL AROUND WITH THIS

Added to the eternal triangle, we now have the infernal triangle. Can you imagine a woman divorcing her husband so that her daughter can marry him?

Yes, sir! She says that her daughter loves him, and she hates him, so let her daughter have him. She evidently couldn't hate him enough as a wife, so she decided to become his mother-in-law.

Cleared up, it means the present wife will become her husband's mother-in-law, and the stepfather will become the husband of his stepdaughter. And I suppose the children will be stepladders.

Madam "Ex" was prosecuted by her son. Here's a daughter making her mother an "Ex."

The ex-wife says the ex-husband was excessive, so the ex-step-daughter ex-pressed an ex-ceptional desire to ex-change places. Someone tried to tell her of a man who was going to marry his widow's niece, but that can't be because if his wife is a widow, he is either dead or lives in Philadelphia.

THE SPRINGS FALL

John and Kitty Spring, fifty-five years old, are suing Dr. G. A. Raw because they say they got a "Raw" deal.

With the help of a couple of goat glands he was going to make them both twenty years younger. Isn't that gland?

He promised them that the glands from the goats would make them feel like a couple of kids.

The doctor was supposed to supply the goats, but the way it turned out, in the end, he got the couple's goat.

He told the Springs that he would turn the clock back twenty Summers and how they did Fall.

He was only kidding, but the doctor found that experimenting with goat glands was butting into trouble.

Turning the clock back was always said to be bad for the Springs. I don't know whether it broke these Springs, but according to report it cost them $3000; so if it didn't break them, it certainly bent them up a bit.

IS THIS A STEADY JOB?

September 6th, 1929, marks three thousand performances for yours truly in the City of St. Louis. Three thousand performances and the show, just like the old red flannels, must be changed every week.

During the 3000 shows I've told so many bad jokes, that if these were olden days, and I a court jester, I'd have been beheaded 3000 times.

After the first thousand shows I had to give up singing mammy songs—the knees wouldn't hold out.

Like most actors I have one little superstition. Every week, I put a little notch in my trunk. Last week I had to buy a new trunk.

On returning to the city from a vacation, I was greeted by the Mayor. This was a new experience. I've been greeted by the Chief of Police before but never the Mayor.

MUST IT BE SCOTCH?

My uncle is so thrifty that, as a gold digger, he makes those old fellows you read about back in 1848 seem like tourists on an excursion.

He has a roadhouse, and when business is slow, he breaks milk bottles on the road so people will drop in while their tires are being repaired.

However, he isn't entirely heartless. Every Sunday morning he jumps into his Rolls-Royce and drives to the poorhouse to see his mother.

When he goes out with his wife he spends hours embarrassing her so that she'll blush and won't have to buy rouge.

The maid was once caught rinsing out his shaving brush, and he shot her.

He cuts all his liquor with water and he's broken-hearted because he hasn't found anything to cut water with.

PIPE DOWN, OLD BEAN

Cigarette smoking is on the wane in jolly Ole England. The Prince smokes a pipe, so it's a pipe pipes will be popular.

Cigarettes are now considered effeminate. Every time you reach for a sweet she reaches for your Luckies.

One Englishman asked another what to smoke in his pipe. "Velvet," was suggested, and the darn fool went home and cut up his wife's dress. It's a good thing he wasn't told "Barking Dog."

Most people who come back from London will now be smoking pipes. Let's hope they stay away from Norway; they're smoking herring there.

The bigger the pipe, the more stylish you are considered. At last a lot of those old saxophones will be put to use. People would rather smoke 'em than hear 'em anyhow.

I prefer clay pipes because if you drop one, you don't have to pick it up.

THANKS, MARTYRS

If the contents of this book did not hand you a laugh, upon request, I'll forward you my photograph.

Getting funny is a serious business. If I didn't get funny it's because I didn't get serious, and I hate to get serious 'cause I like fun.

If you've seen some of these jokes before, don't be too censorious. Remember, you're apt to see a homing pigeon away from its loft.

Bugs Baer, the famous humorist, once contracted to go into vaudeville. Asked if he had an act prepared, he said: "No, I'm just going to steal back a lot of my old jokes."

If a joke could write its autobiography, we would learn that many a joke we thought was just created, did service for Aristophanes, Aesop, Halitosis, Childs and a lot of other ancient Greek restaurant owners.

They say a good joke lives forever, but I've had many a good one die on me.

Merrily,
Ed Lowry

GLOSSARY OF NAMES

Alton, Frank [Frank De Azazio] (1890–1970): dancer; appeared for many years with the Dorsey brothers orchestra; performed for the USO (United Services Organization) during World War II.

Antony, Mark (c. 82–30 B.C.E.): Roman triumvir; general for Julius Caesar; took Cleopatra for his mistress and then his wife while still married to Octavia; died fighting with the Egyptians against the Romans in a battle near Actium.

Arliss, George Augustus Andrews (1868–1946): English actor and author; appeared in many Broadway productions and films; established a reputation for his stage portrayals of historical figures; won an Academy Award (1929–30) for the sound version of *Disraeli*.

Astor, Vincent (1891–1959): businessman, reformer, and publisher; son of John Jacob Astor (1864–1912), who died on the *Titanic;* managed his vast inherited real estate holdings in New York City; broke with the family's conservative politics and promoted social reforms; headed from 1937 the corporation that published *Newsweek* magazine.

Bacon, Sir Francis (1561–1626): English statesman, scientist, author; served in Parliament and the courts; wrote about philosophy, religion, literature, and science; propounded the inductive method.

Bailey, Ilomay: no information.

Baker, Belle (?): singer; noted for the crying quality of her voice; loved to toy with audiences.

Barnum, P[hineas] T[aylor] (1810–91): showman and lecturer; revolutionized the amusement business through skillful advertising; exhibited freaks and oddities; in 1841, opened Barnum's American Museum, a major entertainment center, in New York City; in 1881, teamed with circus owner James Anthony Bailey (1847–1906) to create "The Barnum and Bailey Greatest Show on Earth"; in 1882, their purchase of Jumbo the elephant from the London zoo (Bailey's idea) made the circus famous and rich.

Barrymore, John (1882–1942): famous stage and screen actor, as were his sister, Ethel, and his brother, Lionel; a matinee idol, called the "great profile"; enjoyed his greatest success as a romantic idol during the 1920s.

Beck, Martin (1867–1940): impresario and entrepreneur; known for his ruthless business dealings; developed and directed the

Orpheum vaudeville circuit, making it into a major theatre force; built the Beck legitimate theatre and, in 1913, the Palace Theatre.

Berlin, Irving (1888–1989): one of America's most popular songwriters; built the Music Box Theatre; wrote music for Broadway hits *Annie Get Your Gun* (1946) and *Call Me Madam* (1950); composed music for films, notably *Top Hat* (1935), *Follow the Fleet* (1936), and *Carefree* (1938); his single biggest song hit was "White Christmas" (1942).

Bernie, Ben "The Old Maestro" (1891–1943): master of ceremonies, violinist, and orchestra leader; performed as a classical musician, a vaudevillian, a bandleader, and a radio host; remembered for his signature greeting: "Yow-sah."

Bernier, Peggy (?): singer; a hellion on and off the stage; known as "Wacky Peggy" for her frenetic, often irrational behavior; other entertainers imitated her vocal style, which was "to tear apart a popular song, put it together again, and then rip it wide open" (Ed Lowry).

Boasberg, Al (1892–1947): journalist, director, and prolific gag writer; introduced the first commentator or gossip stage act that humorously treated Hollywood affairs; wrote for Jack Benny, Burns and Allen, Eddie Cantor, Bob Hope, and the Marx brothers and for variety shows, radio, and movies.

Bow, Clara (1905–65): silent film actress, famous for her performance in the film *It*, which led to her 1920s sobriquet, the "It" girl; married to the cowboy actor Rex Bell; institutionalized at the end of her life for mental problems, probably rooted in a difficult childhood.

Bowes, (Major) Edward L. (1875–1946): originated radio's weekly *Amateur Hour*, initially booking the winners into local theatres but subsequently employing them profitably in his own vaudeville groups; gave many young performers their start, including Robert Merrill and Frank Sinatra.

Brady, Fay: no information.

Brown, Joe E[vans] (1892–1973): acrobat, comedian, actor; popular for his elastic face and wide expressive mouth, which enriched his broad slapstick style of humor; made numerous low-budget farces; retired in 1943 but later returned in occasional cameo roles.

Browning, Robert (1812–89): English poet; known for the great variety of his verse forms; perfected the dramatic monologue, a poetic form not unlike a soliloquy; secretly wedded the poet Elizabeth Barrett, whom he lived with in Florence until her death.

Burbank, Luther (1849–1926): American plant breeder; applied the techniques of hybridization and selection to develop more than eight hundred new varieties of flowers, foliage plants, fruits, grains, grasses, and vegetables; one of the first to see that individual plants were rooted in heredity and environment.

Burns, Robert (1759–96): Scottish poet; had an ear for dialects and colloquialisms; wrote numerous poems in Scottish dialect and thereby revived an interest in that language.

Caesar, Julius (100–44 B.C.E.): general, dictator, man of letters; wrote *The Gallic War*, which is still read today; stabbed to death by Brutus and Cassius on the ides of March; changed the Roman calendar to the Julian, the basis of our current calendar.

Calloway, Cabell "Cab" (1907–94): Scat-singing bandleader, dancer, songwriter; immortalized as the "Hi-De-Ho" man; performed on Broadway, in movies, and in jazz clubs, including the Cotton Club; had an immense influence on the music world; trademark song, "Minnie the Moocher."

Cantor, Eddie (1892–1964): pop-eyed singer-comedian; began on vaudeville and became famous on Broadway as a blackface comedian; during the Depression, moved to radio, with a listening audience of sixty million; appeared in films and on television; was a major force in show business for fifty years.

Capone, Alphonse "Scarface" (1899–1947): Chicago crime boss and bootlegger suspected of masterminding numerous murders but never convicted of homicide; imprisoned for tax evasion (October 24, 1931); served eight years in federal prisons and was eventually paroled for good behavior and bad health.

Carroll, Earl (1893–1948): lyricist turned producer; became famous with his risqué *Vanities* variety show of 1923 and later editions; built two theatres, both of which he named for himself.

Caruso, Enrico (1873–1921): Italian operatic tenor; during his day considered the greatest tenor in the world; in some cities where he performed, people adoringly carried him through the streets; appeared in a few silent films.

Chan, Charlie: Chinese detective created by Earl Derr Biggers; based on a real detective, Chang Apana of Hawaii; noted for his wrongheaded sons, Number One and Number Two (of ten), and his aphorisms; always unmasked the criminal after assembling all the suspects in one room.

Chevalier, Maurice (1888–1972): French entertainer, singer, actor; sang in Paris cafés, variety halls, and the Folies Bergère; had a limited voice but enriched his act with comedy and charm;

was popular in Hollywood films; known for his trademark boule-vardier outfit.

Cimarron (U.S. film, 1930): an early talkie, set in Oklahoma, about a western family homesteading from 1890 to 1915.

Cleopatra (69–30 B.C.E.): Macedonian queen of ancient Egypt, who ruled in Alexandria as the last of the Ptolemaic line; known for her seductive charms; was Caesar's mistress and then Mark Antony's mistress and wife.

Congressional Record: reports the debates and proceedings in both houses of Congress; issued daily when Congress is in session; also publishes the annual Presidential message to Congress, inaugural addresses, petitions and memorials, correspondence, and other matter.

Cooper, Jackie (1921–): child actor; known as the "Little Tough Guy"; appeared in dozens of films but found it difficult to obtain roles as an adult; became a major television executive.

Crosby, Bing (1901–77): pop singer, actor; career encompassed virtually every type of entertainment except legitimate theatre—presentation houses, nightclubs, radio, recordings, film, and television; Oscar winner (1944); called "The Groaner" and "Der Bingle."

Dale, Charles [Joseph Sultzer] (1881–1971): comedian; started Avon Comedy Four with Joe Smith; appeared with Smith in "Dr. Kronkhite" skit, which always made the "ten best" list of vaudeville dream bills; cared about welfare of other actors, working on their behalf as board member of the American Guild of Variety Actors. *See* Smith, Joe

Darwin, Charles Robert (1809–82): British naturalist; transformed the science of biology by showing that evolution occurs over time through natural selection, which affects all forms of life; revolutionized scientific thinking, which had previously embraced the idea of a static world.

Dawson, Lillian: no information.

Dix, Richard (1894–1949): actor; started his career on Broadway, then moved to the screen, enjoying great success in the 1920s playing strong, silent types.

Don Juan (U.S. film, 1926): an immensely popular movie in its day; treats the adventures of the famous lover at Lucretia Borgia's court; starred John Barrymore; first feature-length sound film (effects and music, but not dialogue, prerecorded and synchronized) made in the United States (Warner Bros).

Dressler, Marie (1869–1934): actress and singer; started in vaude-ville and by twenty was a veteran in light opera and on the legiti-mate stage; became a popular star in movie comedies, winning an Academy Award (1931); in the 1930s was the number-one box office draw.

Ederle, Gertrude (1906–   ): swimmer; in 1926, became the first woman to swim the English channel, breaking the men's record by two hours; in the 1924 Olympics, won three medals and helped the American Olympic women's swimming team win a gold medal in the four-hundred-meter relay.

Edison, Thomas Alva (1847–1931): inventor and pioneer industri-alist; was granted more than a thousand patents, including those for the phonograph, a practical incandescent light and electric system, and a moving picture camera.

Einstein, Albert (1879–1955): German-American scientist famous for his theories on relativity; made contributions also to the ki-netic theory of matter and to the theory of specific heats; helped pioneer quantum theory.

Fairbanks, Douglas (1883–1939): actor; performed on Broadway and in 1915 moved to Hollywood; married Mary Pickford in 1920; they teamed with Charlie Chaplin and D. W. Griffith to form United Artists, which distributed their productions.

Feldt, Benny: no information.

Feldt, Dominic: no information.

Feldt, Ken: no information.

Ford, Henry (1863–1947): automobile manufacturer, anti-Semite, philanthropist; revolutionized car production and transportation with his assembly-line methods and low-cost Model T; railed against Jews; regarded scholarly history as "bunk" and yet en-dowed the Ford Foundation, which funds scholarly endeavors of all kinds.

Foster Girls: sixteen dancers who performed their dance rou-tines in midair.

Friml, Rudolf (1879–1972): American composer of Czech birth; helped to establish an American school of Viennese-style oper-etta; had two great successes, *Rose Marie* (1924) and *The Vagabond King* (1925).

Frisco, Joe (1890?–1958): jazz dancer and comic; said to have originated eccentric jazz dancing; immortalized by F. Scott Fitzgerald's mention of him in *The Great Gatsby*; noted for his stuttering, horseplaying, and rapier comic retorts; appeared in vaudeville, nightclubs, supper clubs, and movies.

Froos, Sylvia: no information.

Gable, Clark (1901–60): actor; became MGM's leading man; won an Academy Award (1934); known in Hollywood as "The King"; had a reputation for being a man's man and a woman's dreamboat; played Rhett Butler in *Gone with the Wind;* married to Carole Lombard, who died in a plane crash (1942).

Gandhi, Mohandas (1869–1948): Indian politician and spiritual leader; called the "Mahatma," or Great Soul; spearheaded the Indian movement for independence from England through the practice of nonviolent action; led an ascetic, vegetarian life, which left him emaciated.

Garbo, Greta (1905–90): Swedish actress; came to America in 1924; appeared in a number of films in the role of an aloof, enigmatic figure of loveliness; became known as the Mysterious Stranger and the Swedish Sphinx owing to her coldness with reporters; twice named best actress by the New York film critics.

Gershwin, George (1898–1937): began as a song plugger; moved on to become a rehearsal and vaudeville pianist; composer best known for *Strike Up the Band* (1927), *Girl Crazy* (1930), *A Rhapsody in Blue* (1924), *An American in Paris* (1928), and *Porgy and Bess* (1935).

Glyn, Elinor (1865–1943): English novelist and essayist; wrote the novel *It,* which was made into a successful movie starring Clara Bow, who became the "It" girl, that is, a glamorous, sexy woman.

Goldwyn, Samuel (1882–1974): movie producer; started S. Goldwyn Productions and turned out hundreds of films, among them *The Best Years of Our Lives, The Secret Life of Walter Mitty,* and *Wuthering Heights;* known for his philanthropy and hilarious malapropisms.

Gordon, Myrtle (?): blues singer; called a young Sophie Tucker; comedienne.

Gould, John Jay (1836–92): American financial speculator; one of the most important railroad leaders and stock traders of his day; controlled more railway mileage than anyone in America; known for his unscrupulous business practices, particularly the bribing of high officials.

Green, Mitzi (1920–69): actress; became a child star in early talkies, playing Becky in *Tom Sawyer* and the title role in *Little Orphan*

Annie; retired at age fourteen; returned as a supporting actress in two films in the 1950s.

Guinan, Texas (1884–1933): rodeo driver, singer, film actress, and nightclub owner-hostess at the El Fay, Club Moritz, and the Three Hundred Club; arrested and acquitted (1927) for selling alcohol during Prohibition; famous for her greeting, "Hello, Sucker!"; first singer to present her songs from a swing suspended over the stage.

Henie, Sonja (1910–69): skater, actress; won skating gold medals in three winter Olympics; turned professional and had a successful film career in Hollywood; in later years, produced and starred in the Hollywood Ice Reviews and spectacles at Madison Square Garden.

Henry, O. [pseudonym of William Sydney Porter] (1862–1910): writer; wrote a short story weekly for the *New York World* newspaper; his fiction became famous for its unexpected endings; *O. Henry* was also the name of a candy bar.

Henry, Patrick (1736–99): American revolutionary leader famous for his oratorical skills; rallied the patriots with his legendary words, "Give me liberty or give me death!"

Hilliard, Harriet [Harriet Nelson] (1909?–94): vocalist with Ozzie Nelson's band and actress; married Ozzie in 1935; in the 1940s appeared in various film roles; her family life was adapted into a long-running radio and television series, *The Adventures of Ozzie and Harriet.*

Hilton, Violet and Daisy (1908–69): Siamese twins joined at the base of the spine; born in England; started in show business at four; came to the United States in 1916; worked on the major vaude circuits with a song and dance act; later they added instruments to their routine.

Hitler, Adolf (1889–1945): leader of the German fascist party; author of *Mein Kampf;* precipitated World War II; notorious anti-Semite; caused millions to die in death camps.

Hoover, Herbert Clark (1874–1964): thirty-first president of the United States (1929–33); spent thirty years in public service but had the misfortune of being president during the Depression, which led to scathing criticism of his policies.

Hoover, Phyllis: no information.

Irvin: no information.

Ivanhoe (published 1819): novel by Sir Walter Scott that depicts the glories of chivalric twelfth-century England through the story of how Wilfred of Ivanhoe wins the Saxon princess Rowena and champions the Jewess Rebecca.

Joan of Arc (1412–31): French patriot, soldier, martyr; claimed a divine vision told her to raise the siege of Orléans, to have the dauphin Charles crowned king at Rheims, and to drive the English out of France; fought in a dozen military actions; condemned as a heretic and burned at the stake (May 30, 1431); canonized in 1920.

Johnson, Grace: no information.

Johnson, Hiram (1866–1945): politician; twice governor of California; five times U.S. Senator; in 1912, cofounded with Theodore Roosevelt the Progressive Party and stood for vice-president on T.R.'s ticket; an isolationist who opposed "all foreign entanglements."

Jolson, Al (1886–1950): singer, actor, entertainer; as a child, sang in synagogues, a circus, cafes, and vaudeville; rose to stardom on the New York stage as a blackface comedian and singer; appeared in films, starring in the world's first talkie feature, *The Jazz Singer* (1927).

Joyce, Mae: no information.

Joyce, Peggy Hopkins (1894–1957): showgirl, actress, and socialite; appeared in the Ziegfeld *Follies* and Earl Carroll's *Vanities,* in stage plays, and in movies; famous for her association with the gangster Arnold Rothstein and for her numerous marriages.

Ladies' Home Journal (1883 to present): popular women's magazine featuring articles on courting, marriage, beauty, fashion, foods, recipes, menu planning, nutrition, and consumer information of interest to women; publishes fiction of a romantic nature.

Lahr, Bert (1895–1967): comedian; appeared in vaudeville, burlesque, serious plays, and films; famous for his role as the Cowardly Lion in *The Wizard of Oz* (1939); notable for the plasticity of his face, which enabled him to enrich a joke with his facial expressions.

Lasky, Jesse (1880–1958): film producer and movie pioneer; in 1914, he formed a production company that had a great success with *The Squaw Man;* gained control of Famous Players movie company and then Paramount; subsequently produced films for Fox, Warner, and RKO.

Lauder, Harry (1870–1950): Scottish songwriter and comic; mixed Scottish wisdom with songs and old-fashioned jokes to create a routine beloved by thousands of theatregoers.

League of Nations: an international organization formed after World War I to "promote international cooperation and to achieve peace and security"; headquartered in Geneva, it functioned from 1920 to 1946; the United States never became a member owing to conservative opposition.

Lee, Gypsy Rose (1914–70): stripteaser, actress, writer; started in vaudeville; became the burlesque queen of the 1920s; wrote two mystery novels, a play, and her autobiography, *Gypsy*, which was turned into a successful Broadway musical and film.

Lewis, Fay: no information.

Lindbergh, Charles (1902–74): test pilot, aviator, conservationist; first man to fly the Atlantic Ocean solo and, simultaneously, to fly from New York to Paris in a heavier-than-air craft (May 20–21, 1927); the first of his six children was kidnapped and murdered (1932), leading to the conviction and execution of Bruno Richard Hauptmann.

Long, Huey Pierce (1893–1935): populist politician; attacked big business and proposed a "progressive" domestic program, for example, free books for all schoolchildren; built a powerful political base in Louisiana; dreamed of being president of the United States; was assassinated.

Louis XIV (1638–1715): king of France; autocratic, industrious, patient; created a personal system of government, presiding over the council and many of its committees; reigned longer than any king in European history; had numerous mistresses, the most famous being Madame de Maintenon.

Louis XV (1710–74): king of France; anointed at age five; took little interest in affairs of state; lived a debauched life; a man who "opened his mouth, said little, and thought not at all"; had numerous mistresses, the most famous of whom were Madame de Pompadour and Madame du Barry.

Luther, Martin (1483–1546): German-Augustinian friar, professor, author; attacked the Catholic Church's practice of indulgences and thereby launched the Protestant movement; wrote political commentaries, catechisms, sermons, tracts, and hymns set to his own music.

Marseilles, Maureen: no information.

McIntyre, O[scar] O[dd] (1885–1938): wrote America's most widely read newspaper column, "New York Day by Day"—syndicated in more than 500 papers—and also wrote for *Cosmopolitan;* had a penchant for fancy shirts and ties; known for his sartorial splendor.

McKenzie, Madeline: no information.

Mellon, Andrew (1855–1938): industrialist, financier, banker, public official, and philanthropist; secretary of the treasury (1921–32); made a fortune as a venture capitalist; gave his extensive and valuable art collection to the federal government, as well as the funds to build a National Gallery of Art in Washington, D.C.

Mix, Tom (1871–1940): cowboy actor; appeared in more than four hundred low-budget Westerns; performed in his own circus, as well as rodeos and Western shows; received a fabulous salary for his film work; did his own stunts and was often hurt; rode a famous horse, Tony; wrote occasionally for *Variety*.

Moore, Grace (1901–47): singer (lyric soprano), actress; performed in Broadway musicals, at the Metropolitan Opera, and in two MGM films in the early 1930s; at Columbia, starred in several successful movies that helped popularize opera on the screen; killed in a plane crash during a European concert tour.

Moses: regarded by Jews as the founder of the Hebrew nation, its greatest prophet, and the central figure in Judaism; brought the Children of Israel out of Egypt; received from God on Mount Sinai the Ten Commandments and other laws; led the people in their forty years of desert wanderings; mediated between God and the Children of Israel.

Murray, Mae (1885–1965): dancer and actress; danced on Broadway as Vernon Castle's partner; starred in several editions of the Ziegfeld *Follies*, also in a number of silent films.

Nana (U.S. film, 1934): intended as a star vehicle for Anna Sten; the story, set in the 1890s, treats the high living and subsequent degradation of a Parisian prostitute (demimondaine).

Napoléon Bonaparte (1769–1821): emperor of the French and a brilliant military commander; exiled to Corsica for his political misrule; married to Josephine de Beauharnais (1763–1814), a beautiful aristocrat and libertine who was empress of France until 1809, when her failure to bear an imperial heir induced Napoléon to divorce her.

Nelson, Lord Horatio (1758–1805): one of the greatest naval leaders and tacticians in history; lost his right eye at the siege of Calvi and his right arm at Tenerife; though married, he lived with Emma Hamilton, whose husband, Sir William, accepted the arrangement.

Nero (37–68 c.e.): Roman emperor; brought architectural improvements to Rome but is remembered for his extravagance and sexual excesses; blamed the great fire of 64 c.e. on the Christians, condemning them to the lions or burning them alive; eventually committed suicide.

Novarro, Ramon (1899–1968): actor; appeared in silent films in the 1920s, becoming a romantic idol; studio publicity billed him as a "Latin Lover"; starred in *Ben Hur*, his most famous part.

Paderewski, Ignacy [Jan] (1860–1941): Polish pianist, composer, nationalist, politician; famous for his successful European and American piano tours; wrote a well-received piano concerto (1888), a symphony (1903–7), and the opera *Manru* (1901); served for ten months as prime minister of Poland (1919).

Pearl, Jack (1894–1982): comedian; appeared in a number of Broadway shows; enjoyed his greatest success on radio, as Baron Munchausen, who responded to any challenge of his veracity with the now-famous line: "Vas you dere, Sharlie?"

Penner, Joe (1905–41): comedian; appeared in burlesque, in vaudeville, and on radio, which made his name; a terrible worrier; every new script and performance put him into a frantic state, causing him to periodically check into a hospital for a few days; his catch phrase was "Wanna Buy a Duck?"

Pilgrim's Progress (published 1678): allegorical book written by John Bunyan that details a journey—namely, Bunyan's religious life—from the City of Destruction to the Celestial City.

Pinkham, Lydia (1819–83): feminist and manufacturer of a patent medicine, Lydia E. Pinkham's Vegetable Compound, which consisted mainly of unicorn root, pleurisy root, and alcohol; it was popular with women who were reluctant to consult male doctors about female problems.

Police Gazette (1845–1977): magazine; professed to expose criminals but catered to lurid interests, for example, lynchings and the so-called "yellow peril"; breathlessly described female misbehavior; known as "the barber-shop Bible"; its line drawings often depicted women in a state of partial undress.

Revere, Paul (1735–1818): silversmith and patriot; famous for his craftsmanship (Revere ware) and for his midnight ride (April 18, 1775) to warn the countryside that British troops would be advancing the next morning on Lexington and Concord.

Rockefeller, John D[avison] (1839–1937): industrialist and philanthropist; created the modern petroleum industry; pioneered large-scale philanthropy, giving millions to education and medical sciences; often called the richest man in the world—and a robber baron.

Schmatt, Charles: no information.

Scott, Sir Walter (1771–1832): Scottish poet, novelist, and collector of ballads; developed the genre of the historical novel. *See Ivanhoe*

Sherman, Hal (?): performed a comedy dance routine.

Shoot the Works (U.S. film, 1934): based on Ben Hecht and Gene Fowler's book *The Great Magoo;* originated as a stage review (1931), featuring two acts and thirty-four scenes of singing, dancing, and cracking jokes.

Siamese Twins: *See* Hilton, Violet and Daisy

Smith, Al[fred] (1873–1944): politician; one of America's great political reformers, even though he never finished the eighth grade; reorganized New York state government; preserved and expanded individual, legal, and political rights; passed welfare legislation; known for his gravel voice, poor grammar, and colorful language.

Smith, Joe [Charles Marks] (1884–1981): comedian; teamed with Charles Dale in "Dr. Kronkhite" skit, a comedy routine famous for its wit and timing; appeared in films with Dale (for example, *The Heart of New York*); the two men provided the model for Neil Simon's *The Sunshine Boys. See* Dale, Charles

Smith, Kate (1909–86): singer; famous for her booming voice, robust physique, and enthusiasm, especially in her immensely popular rendition of *God Bless America;* recorded about three hundred popular songs and introduced more than a thousand others.

Sten, Anna [Anjuschka Stenski Sujakevitch] (1908–93): Russian actress born in Kiev and brought to Hollywood in 1933 by Goldwyn, who hoped to make her the equal of Garbo and Dietrich; audiences didn't take to her; was called "Goldwyn's folly"; subsequently devoted herself to painting.

Street Scene (U.S. film, 1931): a husband shoots his adulterous wife in a slum street on a hot summer night; early attempt at slice-of-life realism.

Sultan of Turkey, Mehmed VI (1861–1926): last sultan of Turkey; abdicated in 1922; the word *sultan* applies to any ruler of the Ottomans; the title originated in the eleventh century and means "to dominate" or "to master."

Sunday, William Ashley "Billy" (1862–1935): baseball player and Presbyterian revivalist; held mass meetings in cities and towns across the country; preached a colorful type of evangelical fundamentalism; railed against alcohol and evolution; noted for his leaping about in the pulpit; said to have made a million converts.

Swanson, Gloria (1897–1983): film star; one of the reigning queens of silent films; rose to fame at Paramount in suggestive bedroom farces; produced her own films—bankrolled by Joseph P. Kennedy, her reputed lover—but lost money; retired and then made a memorable return to the screen in *Sunset Boulevard* (1950).

Tannen, Julius (1881–1965): monologist, columnist, character actor; started in vaudeville, moved on to Broadway, films, and television; a cerebral comic, breaking off a joke just before the climax, leaving the punch line to the audience; credited with pioneering the stand-up comedian style.

Tarzan: a character found in the tales of William Rice Burroughs; the man who spoke to apes became the central figure in a series of MGM films, originally acted by Johnny Weissmuller as the king of the jungle.

Taylor, Estelle (1899–1958): stage and film star (silents and talkies), singer in vaudeville and nightclubs; noted for her beauty and glamour; once married to Jack Dempsey, then heavyweight champ; active in the movement to protect animals.

Tell, William: legendary fourteenth-century hero of the Swiss struggle for freedom from Austria; refused to pay homage to an Austrian cap hung in a square; consequently commanded to shoot an arrow through an apple on the head of his son (the shot was true).

Tunney, Gene (1897–1978): boxer; reigned as heavyweight champion from 1926 to 1928; lost only one professional fight; beat Jack Dempsey twice, the second time as a result of the "long count."

Vanderbilt, "Commodore" Cornelius (1794–1877): shipping and railroad tycoon; established his own steamship line (1829) and owned numerous railroads; donated a million dollars to what became Vanderbilt University.

Walker, Jimmy (1881–1946): politician; served as mayor of New York City from 1925 to 1932; personified the Roaring Twenties with his dapper dress, sophistication, financial speculations, and freewheeling politics; forced to resign from office because of graft and maladministration.

Weissmuller, Johnny (1904–84): swimmer and actor; in the 1924 and 1928 Olympics won five gold medals for swimming; the best-known Tarzan of the movie series, though he insisted, "I'm an athlete, not an actor"; spent four years as host and greeter at Caesar's Palace, Las Vegas.

Wells, H[erbert] G[eorge] (1866–1946): English novelist and teacher; voracious reader; detested Victorian social values;

wanted an integrated global civilization; wrote *The Outline of History* (1920), as well as other books on the subject, because he believed that the future would be a "race between education and catastrophe."

Welsh, Marie: no information.

West, Mae (1892–1980): buxom stage and screen sex symbol; famous for her enjoyment of sex and frankness about it; driven from the screen by moralists; subsequently wrote her own material for such shows as *Sex* (1926), which was closed for obscenity, *The Drag* (1927), and *Diamond Lil* (1928), a huge success.

Western Union (telegraph company): established in 1851; completed the first transcontinental telegraph line; by 1900 had a million miles of lines and two international cables; synonymous with telegram service.

Wheeler, Bert (1895–1968): comedian; started as a child performer; in his early twenties became a vaudeville comedy headliner; played in Ziegfeld *Follies;* kept audiences laughing with simple jokes and zany behavior, like wiping his eyes with a sandwich and eating his handkerchief.

White, George: no information.

Whiteman, Paul "Pops" (1890–1968): bandleader, author; reputed to have "made a lady out of jazz" in his historic Lincoln's Birthday concert in New York's Aeolian Hall (1924); called King of Jazz for his symphonic syncopations; theme song was "Rhapsody in Blue"; made numerous recordings; appeared in films; rode horses; raced cars.

Wilson, Evelyn: no information.

Winchell, Walter (1897–1972): columnist, newscaster; chronicled the affairs of the famous and infamous; syndicated in some one thousand papers; the undisputed "Boswell" of New York nightclubs; catapulted people and places into fame and fortune with his plugs.

Winters, Joe: no information.

Wright, Catherine: no information.

Wylie, Alistaire: no information.

Wylie, Carol: no information.

Wynn, Ed (1886–1966): comedian; called the Perfect Fool (from 1921 musical); went from vaudeville to radio to films to television; never uttered an off-color joke; made films playing fey old gentlemen (1950s); had his own television show (1958); idolized by other comedians.

Ziegfeld, Florenz "Flo" (1867–1932): Broadway showman and impresario; probably the most publicized theatrical manager in American stage history; created the Ziegfeld *Follies,* patterned after the *Folies Bergère;* launched innumerable performers on famous careers; had three films named after him.

Zukor, Adolph (1873–1976): Hungarian-born film pioneer and producer; started as a film salesman and penny-arcade owner; served as treasurer of Loew's movie theatres; formed his own production company, Famous Players, which he merged with Jesse Lasky to subsequently create Paramount, where he served as president.

INDEX

accidents, 13; automobile, 38–39; hit-and-run drivers, 40; pedestrians and, 210; riddle about, 224
acknowledgments (of sponsors), 295
acting and actors, 13–14; comedians, 14
advertisements and advertising, 14–15
Africa and Africans, 15
African Americans, 15–17; fright, 17
age and aging, 17–19
air-conditioning and heating, 19
airplanes, 19–20
alcohol. *See* drinks, drinking, drunks, and drunkenness
alimony: marriage, divorce, and, 171–84; separation, divorce, and, 183–84
Americans, 20
ancient Rome, 20
animals, insects, and wildlife: ants, 20; birds, 20; boll weevils, 20; camels, 20; cats, 20–21; chickens and roosters, 21–22; cows, 22, 225; dogcatchers, 24; dogs, 22–24, 225; elephants, 24; fish, 24, 225; fleas, 25; frogs, 225; hogs and pigs, 25; horses, 25–26, 226; insects, 226; lions, 26; mice, 26; monkeys, 26–27; mosquitoes, 27; moths, 27; mules, 27; parrots, 27; rabbits, 226; rats, 27; sheep, 27; skunks, 28; snakes, 227; storks, 28; whales, 28; wild animals, 28
answers, fractured, 287
anticipation, 28
ants, 20
appearance, 28–35; beards and mustaches, 29; bowlegs, 30; cosmetics, 30; cross-eyes, 30; dandruff, 30; ears, 30; eyes, 30–31; feet, 31; figure, 31; hair, 31–32; haircuts, 32–33; height, 33; noses, 33; obesity, 33–34; sex appeal, 34; teeth, 34; ugliness, 34; weight, 35
Arabs, 35
arguments, 35; skit about, 362
army, 35
assurance, 35–36
astrological signs, 36
audiences, 295–96; routine about, 355
auditions; routine about, 355–56; skits about, 362–64
autograph routine, 338–39
automobiles, 36–38; accidents, 138–39, 224; buying, on time, 39; cost of, 39–40; hit-and-run drivers, 40; hitchhiking and, 40; parking, 40; pedestrians and, 210; riddle about, 224; routine about, 356; rumble seats in, 40; speeding, 40; streamlined, 40–41;

types of, 41–42; women backseat drivers, 42; women drivers, 42

babies, 51–52
bachelors, 193
band biz, 296–308
banks and bankers, 42–43
"Barfly's Dictionary, A," 98–99
Barnum and Bailey, 117
baseball, 251–52
bathing suits, 65
beards and mustaches, 29
beds, 43
begging, 43–44
bets, 128. *See also* gambling
biblical references, 44
birds, 20
blackmail, 45
blondes, 281
boardinghouses, 134–36
boll weevils, 20
bonds, 257–58
boomerang, 225
borrowing and lending, 45–46; routine about, 356
bowlegs, 30
boxing, 252–53
Broadway, 46
Brutus, 117
Burbank, Luther, 117
buses, 46
business, 46–48; Jews, money, and, 159–61
buying on time, 39

Caesar, Julius, 117
California, 48–49
camels, 20
"Candle, The" (monologue), 326–27
candy, 364
cards, gambling, 126–27
cars, streamlined, 40–41
Caruso, Enrico, 117
cats, 20–21
caught speeding, 212
censors, 49
chair, electric, 108
charity, 50
"Charlie Chan Takes the Stand" (routine), 356–57
chat-up lines and flirting, 86–88, 317–19
Chevalier, Maurice, 117
Chicago, 50
chickens and roosters, 21–22
children, 51–63; babies, 51–52; discipline of, 52; fathers and young sons, 52–53; innocence of, 53–54; mothers and, 55; parents and, 56; prayers

Paul M. Levitt, a professor of English at the University of Colorado at Boulder, teaches modern drama and theatre history. He has written *A Structural Approach to the Analysis of Drama, J. M. Synge: A Bibliography of Published Criticism,* articles about theatre, radio plays for the BBC, trade books about medicine, tales for children, and a novel, *Chin Music.* He also edited *Joe Frisco: Comic, Jazz Dancer, and Railbird* by Ed Lowry with Charlie Foy.